Reading diagnosis and instruction

an integrated approach

Reading diagnosis and instruction

an integrated approach

Melvin Howards
Director, Reading Clinic
Northeastern University

Reston Publishing Company, Inc.
A Prentice-Hall Company
Reston, Virginia

Library of Congress Cataloging in Publication Data

Howards, Melvin.
  Reading diagnosis and instruction.

  Includes bibliographies and index.
  1. Reading—Remedial teaching. I. Title.
LB1050.5.H68   428'.4'3   79-26503
ISBN 0-8359-6443-4

428.43
H837 r

© 1980 by
Reston Publishing Company, Inc.
A Prentice-Hall Company
Reston, Virginia

10   9   8   7   6   5   4   3   2   1

Printed in the United States of America

To my parents and sister, who live with courage and dignity
To my children and yours
and to Marcia for the allness of every

Would that I had unknown speeches, erudite phrases in new language which has not yet been used, free from the usual repetitions, not the phrases of past speech which (our) forefathers spoke. I shall drain myself for something in it giving free rein to all I shall say. For indeed whatever has been said has been repeated, while what has been said has been said.

R. O. Faulkner, W. K. Simpson, E. F. Wente, trans., "The Lamentations of Khakheperre-Sonbe", in *The Literature of Ancient Egypt: An Anthology of Stories, Instructions, and Poetry*, ed. by W. K. Simpson, (New Haven and London: Yale University Press, 1973), p. 231.

Contents

Preface

Like the ancient Egyptian scribe, I too have wondered whether there is anything new or restructured that would be helpful to teachers, students, and specialists in diagnosing and correcting reading and related language problems. The skills to be taught in word recognition, meanings, study skills, vocabulary, and writing are widely known; I have invented no new ones; the diagnostic and testing instruments are also widely known; I have modified one type. What then distinguishes this work from others? Essentially the emphasis on *interpreting* the results of diagnostic work differently from most writers today, and the emphasis on *integrative contexts* for all diagnosis and correction. These two emphases are closely interrelated and produce a *qualitatively* different approach to diagnosing and teaching reading and related language skills to persons of all ages and backgrounds.

This book does have a clearly defined point of view which combines the Pragmatist philosophy of education and Gestalt psychology of learning. Many current texts present the Behaviorist approach to diagnosing and teaching reading and most other skills and subjects. The essence of the differences between these two is the emphasis placed on part-whole relationships, the nature-nurture controversy, and the reliance on qualitative or quantitative data.

Behaviorists generally believe that learning is characterized by stimulus-response behavior abetted by a system of rewards and punishments that condition the desired responses. They believe that what is learned is derived from the environment, so that manipulating the environment at home, in school, and on the streets will produce the appropriate behavior. They divide any task into small, overlapped parts, with drill, repetition, and rote memory producing the learning. They believe that human behavior is measurable and predictable.

The Gestaltists disagree with these interpretations of human learning, rather emphasizing the interrelationships of cognitive and affective responses. They take man whole and they take learning, perceiving, and responding to be organismic, a blending of nature and nurture. They see the whole of any behavior or skill to be greater than the sum of its parts. Therefore, they do *not* suggest drill activities, repetition of isolated letters, sounds, and words. For the Gestaltists, *meaning* is central to understanding human growth, development, and learning, which emphasizes relationships among parts in a particular context, whole. My interpretation of learning, of growth, and of language is that *the whole integrates related parts infusing each with its essence*. Meaning and form are altered by the fact that any given part is in a particular whole. A detailed discussion of the differences between these two views of learning and behavior appears in Chapter 1.

These then are my educational genes: Pragmatist and Gestaltist, and these principles guide my concepts and practices in the diagnosis and correction of reading and related language problems.

The book is divided into two parts: Part 1 includes Chapters 1-5, which discuss and illustrate what we need to know about language, the learner, and the reading process; diagnosis and misdiagnosis, testing and tests; causes of reading and related language problems; planning correction within integrated contexts.

Part 2 is even more practical in Chapters 6-10, offering many specific suggestions for teaching word recognition, meanings, vocabulary, writing, and study skills, in these integrated contexts or core concept plans. Throughout the book you will find numerous suggestions concerning diagnosis and correction for classroom or clinical work. New ways of diagnosing and interpreting diagnostic assessments are presented in detail, as are ways to incorporate skills and informational needs of students (of all ages and backgrounds) into integrated instructional lessons.

Some other distinctive features of the book include a detailed discussion with illustrations of good questioning techniques; case studies with critiques; comparisons and contrasts of standardized, criterion-referenced and Individual Diagnostic testing; sample core concept plans and lessons at several levels; an extensive presentation of interpretation skills (Chapters 8 and 9). It is my hope that this book will help you as a student, teacher, reading specialist, learning disabilities specialist, or clinician to choose alternative modes of diagnosing and correcting reading and related language problems wherever you may find them.

Much of what I offer here for the improvement of diagnosis, planning, and teaching of reading and language skills is taken from the Northeastern University Clinic which I founded in 1970 and which I have directed since that time.

More than 2500 persons of all ages and backgrounds have come to the clinic for help in that time. Some students come for one quarter (about

9 weeks of teaching) while others come for two or more quarters of assistance depending on their needs. The *average* gain in reading skills for all of these students has been 6-7 months as indicated both on Individual Diagnostic Analyses and standardized tests.

These are good gains when one considers that most of the tutors are undergraduate students and the rest are graduate students at the master's degree level. They all take two clinical courses under the careful supervision of the faculty person teaching the course and by experienced practitioners in the field. Tutoring is done predominantly on a one to one basis, but some small group instruction has occurred.

This alternative approach to diagnosis and correction of reading and related language problems cannot claim to solve all of the problems you will face or are facing in the classroom or clinic, but it will provide you with *a new perspective* on the learner, the language, and the processes of reading. You will have an alternative and so will your students. Three decades of experience and study convince me that this integrated approach is successful and stimulating to teachers and students. We can achieve our common goal of improving the mastery of reading and language skills and understandings of students if we have the courage to make a change. If we do, the lament of our Egyptian friend will be less mournful. Students who do not achieve the mastery needed in these language skills, and they are legion, become aliens. *Competent literacy is the cultural passport.*

Melvin Howards
Northeastern University

ACKNOWLEDGMENTS

I gratefully acknowledge permission to reprint material which is copyright from the following publishers and individuals:

Liveright Publishing Corporation for: "somewhere i have never travelled, gladly beyond . . . ", reprinted from VIVA, Poems by E. E. Cummings, with the permission of Liveright Publishing Corporation. Copyright 1931 and renewed in 1959 by E. E. Cummings.

The Poems of Dylan Thomas. Copyright 1939 by New Directions Publishing Corporation. Reprinted by permission of New Directions.

From Collected Poems 1930-1976 by Richard Eberhart. Copyright 1960, 1976 by Richard Eberhart. Reprinted by permission of Oxford University Press, Inc.

Reprinted with the permission of Charles Scribner's Sons from *Look Homeward, Angel* by Thomas Wolfe. Copyright 1929 Charles Scribner's Sons; renewal copyright 1957 Edward C. Aswell as Administrator, C.T.A. of the Estate of Thomas Wolfe and/or Fred W. Wolfe.

The Complete Poems and Stories of Edgar Allan Poe, with Selections from His Writings, Volumes I and II, edited by Arthur Hobson Quinn. "Bells" reprinted with permission of Alfred A. Knopf, Inc. publishers.

From *The Teaching of Reading,* Fifth Edition by Martha Dallman, Roger L. Rousch, Lynetter Y. C. Char, and John DeBoer. Copyright 1978 by Holt, Rinehart and Winston. Copyright 1960, 1964, 1970 by Holt, Rinehart and Winston, Inc. Reprinted with the permission of Holt, Rinehart and Winston.

One very special acknowledgement is due my friend, student, and colleague Dr. William Costello of San Francisco State University. His careful and caring criticism has made this book a better work than it was when he read its first flamboyant draft. I thank him and salute his professionalism, intelligence, and patience.

Part one
Foundations

Chapter one

LANGUAGE

Introduction and Overview

For at least two hundred years scholars and researchers have been studying language from many viewpoints: historical, philosophical, psychological, sociological, anthropological, and linguistic. Several of these approaches overlap; in fact, if some of these scholars would share their insights, viewpoints, and conclusions we would know much more about language acquisition, language structure and function, meaning, and translation. They rarely do, however, and that leaves us with enormous quantities of information from these varied viewpoints, making it difficult to synthesize the most relevant data for diagnosing and correcting reading and related language problems. I shall attempt to synthesize some of the most pertinent data we have about language, particularly English, so that we can establish a common base for what follows.

What is language?

According to *Webster's Seventh New Collegiate Dictionary* (1971, p. 474), language is "the words, their pronunciation, and the methods of combining them used and understood by a considerable community . . . a systematic means of communicating ideas or feelings by the use of conventionalized signs, gestures, marks, or esp. articulate vocal sound . . . ." This definition emphasizes the *phonology* or sound system, the *syntax* or methods of combining words in phrases and sentences, and alludes to the semantics of language when it speaks of the words being used and understood by a "considerable community." Also included in this

Language, learning, and the reading processes

lean definition is the word communicating, which the dictionary defines as "making common." This is closely related to the public, social nature of language. Words like "systematic" and "conventionalized" highlight the fact that we are dealing with a standardized code comprised of signs, gestures, and vocal sounds. Thus language is described as a symbolic code of standardized verbal and nonverbal gestures and marks which we use to "make common" to others in our culture our thoughts, feelings, and information.

Wherever man exists there is and has been language that fits the definition just cited. For millions of years man has been speaking some kind of language, and whether a language uses clucking sounds, whistles, grunts, or articulate forms more like our own, it is considered as complex as any other language form spoken by anyone, anywhere. Written language as best we can tell dates back to the Sumerians, who used cuneiform symbols as early as 5000 B.C. The Egyptians followed shortly thereafter with their hieroglyphics, and the Chinese with their ideograms. We are certain of these facts of written language but we are uncertain of how language began; there are many theories, but none has captured widespread agreement among language scholars.

In addition to these facts, we do know that there are about five thousand different languages spoken or written on the planet now. Some of these languages are spoken by fewer than fifty people, while others are spoken by hundreds of millions. They will share the general characteristics mentioned above, whether they are written or not, and if they are written, whether they are *alphabetic* like English, Spanish, French, or German, for example, or *ideographic* like Egyptian hieroglyphs or Chinese ideograms.

All languages share not only these *common features of structure* and *general purpose*, but they share common *functions*. All languages are generated in a particular cultural environment and since culture does modify and shape personality we can readily see that the interrelationships among language, culture, and personality are crucial to any understanding of man. Without language there would be no culture as we know it and the personalities of the creatures living in such a state would be something other than human, for man and language are one and inseparable. *Language is the ultimate human technology which organizes man's thoughts, feelings, and perceptions*. It makes it possible for him to communicate and it directs how and what he will communicate, to whom, and in what circumstances. The language he uses thus directs his learning, and his learning alters his behavior on many levels and in many ways. Hence, we as teachers, specialists, and clinicians must become unusually sensitive and alert to the learner's use of language. If all humans can speak and understand the language of their culture, why do so many have such difficulty learning how to read and write that language? What are the *changes* in the written language as compared with the spoken or heard forms? How do they affect the learner? These and many other questions will be answered specifically and concretely as we move through this book.

Common Linguistic Principles

Following are some areas of agreement among linguists concerning the nature of language and language learning:

1. *Spoken language preceded written forms*. Research shows that man did not develop what we can call written language until about 7000 years ago, in Sumer, although traces of what may be writing appear earlier in cave paintings some 30,000 years ago. For millions of years man did develop social groups, did cooperate in thousands of ways as evidenced by his tools, weapons, fire making, and traces of ritual celebrations including burial of the dead and sacrifices. To do these things that created cultures, spoken language had to exist.

2. Most linguists also agree that there are some *universal principles* applicable to all languages. Lenneberg (1964, pp. 65-68), summarizes this very well: "Although language families are so different, one from the other, that we cannot find any historical connection between them, every language, without exception, is based on the same *universal principles* of semantics, syntax and phonology. All languages have words for relations, objects, feelings, and qualities... It is an axiom in linguistics that any human being can learn any language in the world. Thus, even though there are differences in physical structure, the basic skills for the acquisition of language are as universal as bipedal gait."

3. *Language is a symbolic code*, an abstract and arbitrary system of signs standardized among a group of speakers in a particular cultural context.

4. More and more linguists agree with Whorf and his followers on the power of any language to influence the total behavior of its users. Whorf (1956, p. 252) says, "And every language is a vast pattern-system, different from others, in which are culturally ordained the forms and categories by which the personality not only communicates, but also analyzes nature, notices or neglects types of relationships and phenomena, channels his reasoning, and builds the house of his consciousness."

5. This concept of language's impact on our total behavior is related to another area of agreement among many linguists: *languages have both surface and deep structures*. Chomsky (1966, p. 33) says, " . . . we can distinguish the "deep structure" of a sentence from its "surface structure." The former is the underlying abstract structure that determines its semantic interpretation; the latter, the superficial organization of units which determines the phonetic interpretation and which relates to the physical form of the actual utterance, to its perceived or intended form."

Simply put, surface structures allow phonic and structural analyses, and deep structures are imbedded in yourself, your culture—in your experiences and the concepts you develop from them.

6. Clearly, one of the basic functions of language is *naming*. Naming includes how we learn to identify people, objects, and feelings with some kind of verbal label, and it also includes how we group or classify our experiences according to attributes which make them fit together nicely or which separate them clearly from each other. Naming is not only essential to language development and usage, but it satisfies the universal need for order which produces the illusion of control over our world. See Brown's (1958) excellent article on naming.

7. More and more researchers in language and perception agree that *in reading we perceive wholes first and then the parts*, and the whole is greater than the sum of its parts. (Gestalt research supports this theory.) M.D. Vernon (1971, pp. 101, 102) says, "In pursuance of the idea that children perceive "wholes" rather than parts or details, the teaching of reading is often begun by presenting whole words rather than isolated letters for recognition. This method also has the advantage that the words can be spoken, and those spoken words have meanings which are immediately familiar to the child; whereas letters by themselves are meaningless to him. Indeed, it has been shown in experiments in which letters and words are presented tachistoscopically that letters can be perceived more rapidly than meaningless figures. Again, words can be read more rapidly than isolated letters in jumbled order, because we have become extremely familiar with the words of our native language and the kind of structure they possess. The probability of such structures occurring is high, and therefore once we have seen one or two letters, we expect the remainder."

Yet, how many reading or LD programs of correction are laden with activities, games emphasizing isolated letters, sounds, or words? How often in certain linguistic readers do we find nonsense words and syllables as part of the reading instruction? In fact, how much emphasis is there in many primary level reading programs on meaning, on life and language experience, as opposed to drill and rote activity to master phonics skills?

From Lenneberg (1967, pp. 276-277) we learn

> "The linguistic development of utterances does not seem to begin by a composition of individual, independently movable items but as a whole tonal pattern. . . .Perceptually, the child reacts to whole patterns rather than to small segments, and so the intonation pattern of a sentence is the more immediate input rather than individual phonemes. . .The first things that are learned are principles—not items; principles of categorization and pattern perception. The first words refer to classes, not unique objects or events. The sounds of language and the configuration of words are at once perceived and reproduced according to principles; they are patterns in time, and they never function as randomly strung up items. . . ."

In both cases, Lenneberg is emphasizing the wholeness of language and the language acquisition process which must guide us in diagnosis and planning. Lessons cannot be collections of skill and content fragments, for that violates these precepts of how people acquire language and how they perceive their world. From the neurologist R. Brain (1968, pp. 318-319), who did a great deal of work with aphasics* and alexics,** comes this:

> "This leads naturally to the fact that a word is perceived as a whole which is something different from the mere sum of its parts. This, of course, has long been familiar in all forms of language. It is illustrated by the general principle that in a given time a much larger number of units of speech, whether they be heard phonemes or printed letters, can be recognized if they are presented as words than as nonsense syllables, or as sentences than as isolated words. . . a patient with alexia may be able to read an individual word, though he cannot read the letters of

---

* *Aphasia:* A serious speech and language disorder caused by an anatomical lesion or damage to the brain which alters the physiology of speech and affects the psychological factors in language production and reception. Four common characteristics are defective word formation, defective syntax, defective naming, and defective comprehension of words and phrases as a whole.

** *Alexia:* A serious reading disorder caused by an anatomical lesion or damage to the brain. The loss may be partial or total. Such an individual might be able to read an individual word although he cannot read the letters of which it is composed.

which it is composed. All these observations point to the fact that physiologically a word is an organization of a higher order than the units of which it is constructed, and the organization of these units which follow one another in time actually modifies the perception of the units themselves—an idea closely related to the Gestalt approach of Conrad."

8. An area of increasing agreement among linguists is that *language is biological*. We already know that Lenneberg (1967) strongly supports that conclusion on the basis of his extensive research. He makes a very convincing case for the view that language learning and usage is as biological as reproduction, respiration, excretion, and growth itself. Imitation as the mode of learning and using language seems to have fallen into general disrepute among linguists, except for some hard-core behaviorists. To say language is biological does *not* preclude the importance of learning in an environment. No one is saying that language is there fully formed in infants and that it merely unfolds year by year with more proper pronunciation and better syntax. Like intelligence, language is to a large degree genetically shaped, but it is very much influenced by environment. Later we shall see how the behaviorists and Gestaltists view this; for now we can accept this interdependence and interrelatedness of nature and nurture.

9. The existence of *linguistic universals* also has many supporters in the field. In essence, they are saying that all children on the planet acquire their language and develop it in the same stages. The research and observations currently available indicate that preschool children all over the world babble before they make sentences and they all babble at about the same time in their development. They make one and two word sentences in another phase of their language usage, and they all do it at about the same time in their growth. The phonological, syntactic, and semantic dimensions of language occur in much the same way and in the same developmental stages for all language users. Clearly, this body of research supports the view that language is biological in nature.

These notions fit very well into Piaget's genetic theory of knowledge, which is rooted in the nature of all biological organisms. His six stages of learning and intellectual development emphasize *adaptation, accommodation,* and *assimilation* of experience in the context of each person's internal and external environments. Biology tells us that all organisms have characteristic needs and that they develop in stages in relatively predictable ways. So whether one is an ethologist, anthropologist, psychologist, linguist, or teacher, one must study the organism, whole and integrated, in the context of other natural processes and events.

Pulaski (1971) and Furth (1970) have presented good summaries of many of Piaget's views, but I would strongly recommend some of the original sources listed in the bibliography at the end of this chapter.

Summary of linguistic universals

These certainly do not encompass all of the agreements on language principles, but they do identify some of the most universal and those which are most pertinent to diagnosticians and teachers. Language is both verbal and nonverbal; it is limited in its spoken and written forms; all languages have phonological, syntactic, statistical, and semantic dimensions; all children on the planet learn to speak their native language in much the same stages; all speakers generate an almost infinite number of utterances, many of which they have never heard before; language learning and perception are organismic acts, emphasizing context and meaning—wholes not parts, patterns not individual acts. Language is written on the cells of each speaker. Language, culture, and personality are inseparable and all three must be understood before any one can be. The key implication for us as teachers and specialists is that, in dealing with language in any of its dimensions and forms, it must be treated as whole and integrated just as the learner should be.

Now we will look at English with its irregularities, borrowings, variants, and statistical and symbolic qualities in order to prepare ourselves for diagnosing and teaching reading and language skills in a much more comprehensive manner.

The English Language

What can you do with a language that has suited Shakespeare, e.e.cummings, the Beatles, graffiti, military men, adolescent gangs, modern movies, you and me? A language that allows *ough* in rough, though, through, cough, hiccough; or that allows seven spoken equivalents for the vowel *a*; that permits words like *bank* to mean almost anything it chooses, e.g., place to deposit money, side of the river, group of lights, pool shot, turning an airplane, dependence on another; a language that permits FAA, CCC, CAB, and acronyms, puns, deleted expletives, cocktail palaver, colloquialisms and slang like *pressed vines, rap, laid back, snowman*? There is nothing for us to do but to love it, respect it, enjoy it, and get irritated with it. It is the language spoken by more than 220 million Americans, and by a large percentage of the 4½ billion people on the planet. In spite of its many perversities and irregularities, it is very flexible.

Irregularities of the English language

The English language contains about one million words which are produced by 26 letters (graphemes) so that many words are composed of the same letters and combinations. This causes many learners great difficulty aurally and visually since so many combinations look or sound alike. These 26 letters or *graphemes* are equivalent to 44 *phonemes*, or distinctive speech sounds, so that we do *not* get the one-to-one correspondence in English between what we say and what we write. There is a mismatch as in the examples above of *ough* and the vowel *a*, both of which have six or seven spoken equivalents. Our logic wants us to be able to spell words the way they sound. We want our language to have the phonetic qualities of such languages as Spanish, Rumanian, Finnish, Hebrew and others which do match the spoken forms with the written forms.

For example, look at the vowels in Spanish:

a is a (as in ah)
e is a (as in day)
i is e (as in be)
o is o (as in go)
u is oo (as in do)

That's it! Almost no exceptions. Wherever you see *a* you say *ah*, and when you say *ah* you write *a*, and so on. Most of the consonants in Spanish are equally regular.

No wonder that poor readers and poor spellers often believe that English is some kind of planned disorder and chaos. Variable yes, chaotic no! After all, about 80% of the children in public and private schools do learn how to read and write English acceptably. The 20% of children and adolescents who do not learn how to read and write acceptably fail for many reasons including the irregularities of the language itself, and for educational, psychological, and physical reasons as well. Even those languages that are much more regular than ours report reading and related language difficulties among their students.

Therefore, it is not fair to say that most of the reading and writing problems of any language are largely attributable to its morphology (form). Granted it does not help either to have a language which is not entirely regular, but apparently we and our ancestors have built in ambiguity, variability, even novelty, since that suited us best. After all, not everyone makes computers, prosthetic devices, cars, cigarettes, dirty movies, too many clothes, appliances, waste, etc. But we do; that is our culture, the expression of our collective needs, values, desires and goals.

Nevertheless we're stuck with our 26 letter alphabet (graphemes) with 44 phonemes (distinct spoken sounds) producing a million words strung together in accord with less than perfect rules of phonology, syntax, and grammar, but rules nonetheless. I'd rather struggle with English and its idiosyncracies than with Japanese, which would require learning hundreds of symbols in order to communicate effectively. Each language has its own forms, shapes, rules, and idiosyncracies—just as the cultures and the personalities that produce it.

What is it about the English language that has contributed to the reading and language difficulties of some 10 million school children and some 20 million adults classified as functional or total illiterates? What is it, in fact, that makes English irregular? Several major factors need to be explored including borrowing, variants and dialects, the statistical properties of our language, and its symbolic qualities. Perhaps if we can begin to understand some of the forces operating in our language, or any language, we can devise better diagnostic and corrective programs.

Factors contributing to reading and language difficulties

Borrowing. In many ways English is really not English at all, at least not in the way Latin is Latin, or Greek is Greek, or French is French. The major difference between English and many other languages is the amount and type of borrowing we have done to make and change our language. We have borrowed thousands of our words from Latin, Greek, German, French, and Anglo-Saxon, not to mention Spanish, American Indian, and other sources, so that to skim through our dictionary is to take a world tour. Borrowing is not good or bad, but it does complicate the language by contributing to the amount of difficulty many people experience when trying to learn to read, particularly when they try to match spoken with written forms. This massive borrowing has brought words into our language in their original form, that is, spelled as they were in their native language, for example, *lieutenant* and *handkerchief*: we then pronounce those words in our own way, which is different from the pronunciation of the speakers of the language from whom we borrowed the word. Immediately we have a discrepancy between what we say and how we write it. Lieutenant was borrowed from the French, and is pronounced by most of us as *loo ten unt*, but is spelled *lieu ten ant*, since that is how it was spelled by the French. Since there are several thousand words that have gone through this borrowing and changing of pronunciation it is not too difficult to see why many of us have some problem with spelling.

Regional differences. These massive borrowings from other languages and the accompanying change in pronunciation are only one part of the problem of our language. If we look further into pronunciation we find that Americans speak in different ways reflecting regional differences.

Context and function. Another part of the problem is that in English, pronunciation and meaning are often derived only from the context of other words and phrases. How many words do you know in English which have only one meaning? Not very many, since most words can be altered by syntactic arrangement, i.e., where they are in the sentence, which can affect pronunciation, e.g., *lead and lead*. What part of speech is the word *feature*? Noun as in "you have beautiful *features*"; verb, as in "the movie *features* John Wayne"; adjective as in a "*feature* movie." So one word is used as three different parts of speech—same pronunciation but with variant meanings. The meanings of *feature* are only minimally variant because at the root of it is something distinctive; but what about words like *race* (and thousands of words like it) that drastically change meaning as well as function? For example: I won the *race* (noun); *racing* car (adjective); he belongs to the Caucasian *race* (noun—but changed meaning).

The point is now clear enough: language is whole in its phonology, syntax, and grammar; only context provides clues to pronunciation and function (part of speech) and most importantly, meaning. Meaning is not in a letter, word, or isolated phrase, but in connected text, related to a topic, in short, to the deep structures.

Language is not a collection of letters, specific sounds, and sound combinations, words, phrases, sentences, rules and principles—it is all of that and more. It is feeling, thought, concept, culture, personality, and all the possible interactions among all of these elements which produce the whole, which is indeed more than the sum of its individual parts— just as you and I, animals, plants, oceans, clouds, and stars are organic, integrated wholes who are more than the cells, drives, needs, growing and dying, which are integral parts of us. *Of all human behavior none is more integrated and integrating than language, nor is anything more confounding and divisive.*

Variants. In addition to borrowings as a cause of difficulty for many readers and writers of English, we must include the effect of variants and nonstandard usage as a source of great difficulty for many students, particularly those with minority ethnic backgrounds, i.e., Spanish speaking students, Chinese speaking students, Greek speakers, and Black students who frequently speak and write what is considered to be nonstandard English. There are many kinds of variations and not all foreign language speakers have difficulty learning to deal with English and its irregularities, but enough do to make it a significant problem. Nonstandard forms such as Black English similarly cause problems that are not entirely different from those who speak a foreign language or whose regional dialect is different from the so-called standard American English.

The major problem with nonstandard and other variant forms of language is that *they violate our expectations of what is being said* or *is about to be said, or written*, and that *reduces our ability to anticipate and to predict the message and its intent.* Since language is a code of conventionalized symbols and sounds conforming to specific rules, and since both phonology and syntax directly affect meaning or the semantic dimension of language, any breaking of the rules can cause a breakdown in communication. How do you react when someone speaks unclearly, with a heavy accent, or ungrammatically? And what if a person uses words in ways you are not accustomed to? That communication becomes "noise" to you; what is being said and how it is being said does not make the facts, ideas, or feelings common to you; in fact, they make them uncommon, unfamiliar, and hence a bit disorienting or even irritating. That is not the purpose or value of language and anyone who speaks or writes in a variant or nonstandard form closes doors and separates people from each other.

Two things are operating here: (1) The variation produces dissonance rather than harmony, and meanings which are unfamiliar. (2) The variation often leads to negative judgments about the speaker or writer since he or she seems to be deliberately violating our expectations. The probabilities of language represent our internalized knowledge, deep structures, of the phonology, syntax, and semantics of the language. Variations disturb us because they fall outside of the borders we have marked for acceptable language usage. *The variations and nonstandard usages* are more than just incorrect, inappropriate, or even annoying—they *attack our sense of what goes with what, of the expected* This rarely mentioned aspect of language—probabilities and statistical properties—is so pervasive and subtle that we tend to overlook its effects. The speaker or writer who disregards or is ignorant of the acceptable patterns of language risks being ostracized. Private languages or idiolects are acceptable for small, homogeneous groups who use such a language form for specific purposes on particular occasions, i.e., in their own limited context. But when they use the same colloquial, slang, or nonstandard forms in general communication they disturb our sense of order.

Language acquisition involves learning the generally accepted pronunciation, sentence structure, and vocabulary usage. These patterns constitute our expectations, as do the other components of the communication context, i.e., who is speaking to whom, for what purpose, drawing on or referring to some common knowledge and experience. Any variant, whether it be a regional dialect, or street talk, will alter our perception of the message and the transmitter. Labov (1972, p. 276) makes the point well: "Some teachers are reluctant to believe that there are systematic principles in nonstandard English which differ from those of Standard English. They look upon every deviation from schoolroom English as inherently evil, and they attribute these mistakes to laziness, sloppiness, or the child's natural disposition to be wrong."

Black English.   Labov (1972, p. 276) goes on to describe specific types of language problems Black children have in grammar and phonology. He offers several suggestions for reading and language teachers based on his research, which include: "learning to distinguish between mistakes in reading and mistakes in pronunciation which are part of the nonstandard language; spending more time on the grammatical function of certain inflections, especially suffixes, in the early stages of teaching reading and spelling."

Most researchers in the field of nonstandard English, especially Black English, seem to agree that the nonstandard forms do have their own rules, principles, and structures; that these variants *are* language and *not gibberish*. They agree to a large extent that we can identify many specific linguistic differences which can be treated in the classroom or clinic. None of the leading authors on this topic (Goodman, Labov, Baratz and Shuy, Dillard) recommend forcing every Black child, or any child who speaks a variant or dialect, to speak standard English. They encourage teachers to work toward that end, but to do so slowly and with sensitivity. Since language is so much a part of everyone of us, so deeply embedded in our cells and our total personalities, we cannot change everything at once. They report many specifics relative to the way the variants are used and how they compare and contrast with the standard forms.

Labov's excellent article in *Teaching Black Children to Read*, edited by John C. Baratz and Roger W. Shuy (1969, pp. 29-67) summarizes many of the major phonologic, syntactic, and semantic variations of Black English:

1. *r* lessness: god for guard
    nor for gnaw
    sore for saw
    par for pa
    fort for fought
    court for caught

2. *l* lessness: Cal for Carol
    Pass for Paris
    test for terrace
    toe for toll
    hep for help
    too for tool

3. short i for short e: pin for pen
    win for when
    tin for ten

4. changes in clusters st, ft, nt, nd, ld, zd, md: pass for past
    riff for rift
    men for meant
    men for mend
    hole for hold

    other cluster changes /-s/-or/-z/: sick for six
    bock for box
    mack for max
    mick for mix

5. weakneening final consonants: boo for boot
    row for road
    feet for feed
    poor = poke = pope

    other variations include: cents for since
    bear for beer
    chair for cheer
    ball for boil
    deaf for death
    shore for sure

Labov, and others, also point out the *misuse or absence of possessives*, how the loss of the *l* affects future tense, dropping copula or using be for is, e.g., He be working. Use these as a guide to the major areas of difficulty, but do not get caught in the trap of rigidly forcing a particular sequence on the student. Accept divergence in culture and the language it uses, and allow individuals their time to grow and develop. Clearly we *do* want children to speak, read, and write English in a standard fashion since that is the only way we can assure communication.

We can bridge the gap between nonstandard and standard language usage if we know more about the patterns of those forms and how they compare and contrast with the standard forms. We must respect the students' language as we do their selfhood, and share with them our patterns not as better or right, but as more commonly used. If students see that we know something about their language usage and do not reject it and condemn it, we have a much better chance to teach them the standard forms. The students benefit from having an alternate form of language to use where it fits best. They can then participate in both worlds most effectively.

Acquisition.   Normal language acquisition is a process that clearly reflects the statistical properties of language and learning. Children revise their speech and later their reading and writing in accord with the probabilities of the language. They learn to pronounce words so that others will respond with understanding by constantly comparing and contrasting what they say and how it sounds with what others say and how they react. They learn to form good sentences and attach commonly known meanings to the words they use. If they do not revise and alter their usage and pronunciation it soon becomes clear that they are not being understood so that their essential need to communicate is frustrated. Few of us can bear that kind of isolation and rejection. So children continually shape and alter their phonology, syntax, and semantics in accord with what others expect of language. These expectations of what can be said, how and in what context, is governed by the statistical properties of the language and the culture which it expresses in and through us. In time we learn when we can use certain forms of speech, e.g., colloquial, formal, slang, and obscenities, and when we cannot. We learn to alter our speech and writing patterns for particular purposes. We have several vocabularies, or at least alternate vocabularies, sentence structures, accent, and idiolects. We know that certain words and expressions are impossible, e.g., one cannot write *frldxm* and expect any one to understand it; one cannot say or write *I tomorrow house go*, even though the idea is almost clear. If the rules of language or any other human behavior are broken or ignored, order is jeopardized, and when that happens communication, cooperation, and social interaction are impaired. For more information about variants and nonstandard forms, refer to the bibliography at the end of this chapter which contains selected sources on Black English and on other variant and nonstandard forms.

Now let's look at some of the other statistical properties of language so that we will be able to incorporate them into our diagnostic and corrective work.

Probabilities. The point of this explanation of nonstandard English is that it illustrates another aspect of the probabilities of a language system. These forms obviously violate expectations in standard communication. The nonstandard forms do have their own rules, patterns, and structure, and they do have their own probabilities and expectations. A street kid who said to his friends, "My, what elegant garb," or, "I must comment upon your sartorial splendor this evening," or even "super," "neato", would be violating the rules and patterns of his nonstandard form. He would be alienated from his friends in that circumstance.

Imagine what it would be like to read literature with totally unusual, esoteric words, presenting images and symbols which are rare in our experience and knowledge. It would be painful and slow. We try to avoid such material since we can not anticipate or predict any of it with certainty. That subtracts from the impact of the material; it clouds meaning by raising the dust of ambiguity.

For example, many people did not care for plays like *Waiting for Godot, Who's Afraid of Virginia Woolf, A Streetcar Named Desire,* and *The Subject was Roses,* because of the shocking and unexpected use of language, symbols, and topics. It took some time for the majority of people to familiarize themselves with the techniques and language of these avantgarde works. The same was true in movies like *Blow-Up* and *A Clockwork Orange* of the 1960s; in the 1970s films like these were almost commonplace, familiar, much more predictable, so they enjoyed greater success. The novelties had almost become clichés.

When the established probabilities of any language usage are violaged by any communicator, the receivers are thrown off their guard; they are uncomfortable and often shy away from such persons or art works. Communication breaks down; the language and symbols make the experience uncommon.

The obscene outburst of 2-, 3-, and 4-year-old children shock us out of our comfortable, predictable mind sets. Psychotics distress us for many reasons, perhaps the most prominent of which is that they display such disorder in their thinking, behavior, and language usage. They speak of people, places, and events not present or verifiable by us. They hear and see things which we cannot see or hear, and when they put that into language and perseverate, it causes imbalance in us as language receivers. It is threatening. Like all sickness it seems contagious to us. We fight off the disorder of the language usage by adhering to the statistical properties of the language. We need order and the predictability it engenders; we need it in people's behavior, thought, and language.

Perhaps a few more examples will clarify this discussion of statistical properties of English and how they do affect reading and writing diagnosis and correction. For example, Mandlebrodt (1965) described a formula that reflects our language processing. Here is how the formula is applied: If I were to start a message or utterance with the word *I*, the number of words which could follow it are manifold—thousands of words could follow and make sense in English. We can state just how many that would be because English is a finite system of letters and words. If I add another word to my message to make *I am*, for example, the number of words that could follow in proper English would still be very large, but considerably reduced. In fact, the number of words possible now would be reduced logarithmically. If I were to add a third word to the message to create: *I am eighteen*, the number of possible correct words to follow it would again be reduced logarithmically, so that the number of choices is much smaller. The same principle applies in all messages: as you add another word to the message you tend to reduce the number of possible choices available, so that predicting what will come next becomes increasingly easy. After all, the language does stay within its established patterns.

Applications.   In teaching speed reading in the past I have often placed this message on the board:

Lv Chi 9 PM Arr JFK 12 Meet

The students are asked to figure out what is meant by this telegraphic message. With few exceptions and rather quickly, students can translate this string of fragments to read: "I am leaving Chicago at 9 pm and shall arrive at JFK (Kennedy) airport in New York at 12 (midnight). Please meet me." Low level readers would have great difficulty with such a message, but this technique was used for speed reading which should be taught only to developmental readers who are masters of underlying word recognition, meanings, and study skills. But how do we do such a translation? Obviously, our knowledge of the patterns of language and our experience with its usage in many contexts gives us enough information to complete the word fragments and the sentence fragments. We know that we cannot say "Leave Chicago 9 pm;" our language requires subject-verb-object, and qualifiers and connectors. We know what makes a sentence and what does not; we know that LV suggests leave, but we cannot be sure until we see either form in some larger context. *The context then eliminates most possibilities and leaves the most likely, the most probable.* This process of sorting, sifting, and eliminating appropriate choices in a context is crucial to all reading acts for people as well as for computers. The statistical properties of the language we have acquired through our lifetime guide us in our usage.

Another application of this statistical knowledge useful in speed reading instruction involves teaching students that fast readers are more *selective* of what they read and what they do not read—or at least do not attend to as much. Once readers can see that the meaning of reading is not embedded in any one word or phrase, but in the total context, and that they can fill in some blanks with very few clues based on this overall knowledge, they note that in most nonfictional writing, nouns and verbs tend to bear most of the meaning. Readers are then lead to notice that many words in each sentence are there for grammatical and syntactical reasons and do not significantly alter the meaning of the sentence or paragraph. An activity students enjoy is to go through a newspaper or magazine article and to black out what they consider the least meaningful words, leaving just a skeleton of significant words, mainly nouns and verbs. They could read this almost telegraphic message and discover they could answer many comprehension and interpretation questions easily. This helps them to see why they could read faster using this knowledge of the statistical properties of our language. Obviously, this is no way to read literature or artistic work because such material often depends on ambiguity—multiple meanings, allusions. It transmits several messages and meanings simultaneously. In most nonliterary writing, clarity and directness are the goals. The limitations on what is said and how it is said are more clearly defined, hence more predictable.

The statistical properties of language are integral to understanding and use of the language. The effects are multiple on both the transmitter and the receiver of the message. One of the elements of all language that makes it usable among many people is its general predictability. My spelling, syntax, and grammar will follow the established rules and, consequently, my meanings will be understood.

You do not know everything I will say here, but you have probably read the preface and the table of contents and skimmed the chapters, bibliography, and index so that you will indeed be prepared for this journey. Because you can predict some of what is here you can call up your previous knowledge of the topics and participate in reading.

Poor readers and language users have serious problems with this statistical dimension because they do not always know what to expect in a book or reading exercise. We can help them through our diagnosis and corrective work to become much more aware and sensitive to the nature of the language they are using and how it works. They need the assurance that English is not a random collection of letters, sounds, words, and phrases. They need to be shown and to experience how it does work and they need to know that their aural-oral knowledge and usage is a good place to begin. They must not be made to feel that they are dealing with a totally unpredictable code known only to the initiated and chosen, but that they already know a great deal about their own language even with their problems. I have often presented some of this material to poor readers when they have given up hope of ever being able to figure out how to read or write acceptably. I have simplified this presentation so that they could see and feel that there is some order, some predictability; they could learn it, just as they learned to speak and understand as much as they do.

Another pervasive aspect of all language is its symbolic qualities, which relates closely to some of the facts we have just discussed in this heading on statistical properties.

Symbolic dimensions

All languages are symbolic codes which have been standardized within a group of speakers sharing the same or similar culture. Words are symbolic to the extent that they are not actually the things or persons named, e.g., *house, John, car, window*, etc., but rather they are pointers to these things or persons, referring the receiver of the message to a cluster of facts, feelings, and impressions about them. In linguistic terminology, the words are the surface structures which are understandable only when they help us probe our deep structures—our concepts, our total experience, and knowledge.

Symbols are abbreviations of related cognitive and affective data; they conjure up in us a host of impressions colored by our personalities operating within a particular context. If we look at some common symbols it may clarify what I am trying to say: flag is a word referring to an object usually made of cloth and decorated with stars, stripes, a hammer and sickle, an animal, person, etc. The choice of colors in the American flag for example, is thought to represent the white of purity and honesty, the red of blood lost in wars fought for freedom, and the blue of the seemingly infinite sky. You may have a different set of associations with the colors of the flag, its stars and stripes, than I do, but we all generally agree that the flag cues our feelings of loyalty, freedom, and individuality.

The thoughts and feelings ignited by any symbol are derived from the deep structures of our being, so that it is extremely difficult to define any symbol so specifically as to make its boundaries conspicuous. Many symbols are so closely interrelated within any culture that one flows into another, meshing subtly with other symbols and all of our reactions to them. Like feelings, symbols overlap, occur simultaneously, and cause many reactions cognitively and affectively.

Chapter 8 will delve into certain practical approaches to teaching symbols and other interpretational skills, so I will reserve this discussion for a more general consideration of the topic. The key point is that all language transmits several messages at the same time to any of its listeners and readers. Information is usually presented with gestures, both physical and oral, which alter the message's meanings. If I say the word *oh* to you, I can say it in one of several ways, for example: "*oh?*" or "*oh!*" The first implies doubt, perhaps even suspicion; the second anger, or perhaps surprise. "Oh" could also be said in a pugnacious way, as when you are feeling aggressive. There are many other ways it can be said, modified by your inflection and intonation, and your facial expression and movement of arms, fists, and shoulders. The message, like all messages in all languages, is easily altered by both the form of your verbal gesture (speech and its inflections and choice of words) and by your other gestures, smiles, grimaces, stares, etc. In essence, we all modify our messages, spoken and written, the way adjectives modify nouns and pronouns in typical English sentences. There are symbolic overtones to these facets of communication, just as there are overtones and echoes evoked by the flag (the word or object) by words like liberty, love, war, equal rights, busing.

In literature, examples abound of entire poems, plays, novels, and short stories which are in part or whole symbolic. Remember *Alice in Wonderland* and *Through The Looking Glass; Gulliver's Travels*; Dante's *Inferno*; Cervantes' *Don Quixote*; Frost's *Two Roads in a Wood*; Milton's *Paradise Lost*; the Greek Tragedies? All of these works are filled with symbols and symbolic usage. *Alice* is both a children's story and a mature interpretation and criticism of the British government and its often ridiculous political, social, and economic behavior at the time. Swift did similar things with Gulliver, while Frost represented choices in life in "two roads in a yellow wood"; and Cervantes poignantly illustrated man's struggle for values, beliefs, and ideals in the face of change. The Greek Tragedies are filled with heroic deeds and human flaws; choices of war and peace, love and hate, life and death.

My point is not to interpret these works here, but to illustrate that language in its many forms is symbolic: bearing messages, meanings, and feelings beyond the stated. Any message in any language exists on several levels at the same time. As reading and language teachers, or specialists, we must pay special attention to these qualities of language. The effects of symbolic behavior are evident in both our diagnostic and corrective work. We test children and adults with many instruments and interpret them both literally and figuratively or symbolically. We must not allow the symbols to become our reality, when in fact they are a suggestion of it. Chapters 2 and 3 delve into this in greater detail.

McLuhan

A most interesting and provocative discussion of the symbolic nature of language comes from Marshall McLuhan. His concepts of how language, or any medium of communication, affects the user is related to some of the ideas we encountered in the quotation from Whorf (1956) earlier in this section.

Language is a technology

McLuhan's basic concept is that language is a medium and a technology and as such it shapes, molds, and alters the message which it carries in its written and spoken forms. He said the medium (in this case language, but it could include radio, TV, etc.) is the message. By this he meant that the way you transmit a message—the nature of the language and its form alters the meaning of the message in a variety of ways. McLuhan (1964, pp. 86-87) says,

> The phonetic alphabet is a unique technology. There have been many kinds of writing, pictographic and syllabic, but there is only one phonetic alphabet in which semantically meaningless letters are used to correspond to semantically meaningless sounds. . . .The phonetically written word sacrifices worlds of meaning and perception that were secured by forms like the hieroglyph and the Chinese ideogram. . . . Only the phonetic alphabet makes such a sharp division in experience, giving to its user an eye for an ear, and freeing him from the tribal trance of resonating word magic and the web of kinship. . . .
>
> As an intensification and extension of the visual function, the phonetic alphabet diminishes the role of the other senses of sound and touch and taste in any literate society. The fact that this does not happen in cultures such as the Chinese, which use nonphonetic scripts, enables them to retain a rich store of inclusive perception in depth of experience that tends to become eroded in civilized cultures of the phonetic alphabet. For the ideogram is an inclusive *gestalt*, not an analytic dissociation of senses and functions like phonetic writing."

I have chosen this particular quote because it summarizes McLuhan's key concepts of the relationship between any technology and the people who use it, and who are in fact, used, altered and affected by it personally, socially, economically, religiously, and politically.

When McLuhan speaks about the phonetic alphabet as a technology he means that it is a tool, and like any tool it can be used to make other tools, to increase our efficiency and productivity of cars, radios, TVs, cultural ideas, and behaviors. The phonetic alphabet is *the* tool, the technology man uses to control himself, others, and the environment. He calls the phonetic alphabet "unique" because it is composed of individual letters and sounds which must be seen one at a time in a linear (one after another) order. It forces us to think and organize the world in fragments, piece by piece, sequentially. McLuhan contrasts the phonetic alphabet with ideographic languages like Chinese or Japanese, in which each symbol or ideogram represents a word or an idea rather than a spoken equivalent which is meaningless. Comparing the letters of our alphabet with an ideogram is comparing parts with a whole.

The result of this technology of the phonetic alphabet is that our perceptions and our other technologies reflect this piece-by-piece, linear approach. Therefore he finds it very logical that our culture has invented conveyor belts, mass production of parts of cars, TVs, etc. He also thinks the effect of phonetic alphabets on their users has directly affected all realms of their thought and action including their political systems, economic systems, religious beliefs, and artistic productions.

McLuhan elaborates on the phonetic alphabet by pointing out that *only* in such an alphabet as ours do we find meaningless letters corresponding to meaningless sounds. He means that *b* does not mean anything, nor does it conjure up a scene or people or feelings, anymore than saying the letter *b* does. The alphabet has arbitrary forms and relationships; we could have used other letters (forms) and attached whatever sounds we wanted to them. In individual letters and even in combinations such as blends and digraphs there is no intrinsic meaning, any more than there is meaning in the fact that we use 44 phonemes (speech sounds). But, and this is the important *but*, since we have settled on the 26 letters and 44 phonemes, and the grammer and syntax we now know, English is a technology of fragments put together in the way we put a space shuttle, car, train, or toaster together. According to McLuhan and phonetic alphabet reduces meaning because it uses meaningless letters and other word parts, and does not evoke the same kind of *total response* that ideographic languages do. Let me elaborate this point because it is essential to understanding McLuhan, as well as the media.

What is the difference in your reactions when you look at a picture and when you look at a word? Most of us have several kinds of reactions as we look at any picture. Generally, we get a whole impression of the picture, not necessarily seeing every person, tree, house, and line, but an impression that it is a scene of a quaint street somewhere. We may feel a kind of softness depending on the painter's use of colors and how he uses line and perspective. But we have a general impression of a street and some emotional reaction of warmth, coldness, or softness. Much of this is not in words, just a feeling, a sense. As we continue to look at the picture, we notice more of the detail—the people, their clothing, their sizes, their manner of moving, store fronts, signs, doorways, windows; we think fat, pretty, ugly, poor, rich, many, few. As we pick up these impressions, very rapidly we are filtering these through our own experiences with similar situations and scenes, and unconsciously adding our feelings to that scene. Thus much of us is involved in seeing and perceiving that picture as it is related to particular times, places, and feelings in our own lives. All of this, and more, is occurring whenever we view a picture. Our response to the medium of a picture is total, including our own past and present, our own hopes, fears, joy, and other feelings depending on what we are as we look at that picture, hieroglyph, or ideogram.

Contrarily, when we look at printed words like these, we must first see and respond to these word by word in linear order—one after the other. You cannot read this work of our alphabet and language if you jump from the top of the page to the bottom, to the side, to the middle and around as you might do in viewing a painting, a movie, or a TV show. In responding to this you must at first respond word by word, sometimes letter by letter or structural element (prefix or root or suffix) in the sequence in which it is printed. After you have figured out words you catch the sense of a phrase, clause, and sentence. Then it begins to make sense, including the variant meanings of certain words; for example, if I write "Act your age, please," you read *act* and cannot be sure what it means or what part of speech it is since it could be a noun, verb, or adjective. It could mean *act as in a play, act as in perform*, etc. So in linear, alphabetic languages we are forced to deal with parts (letters, roots, prefixes) one after another in a predetermined order (grammar and syntax) so that meaning accumulates slowly and piecemeal, like pieces of a puzzle. This kind of piece-by-piece, letter-by-letter, word-by-word, phrase-by-phrase, clause-by-clause, sentence-by-sentence reading guided by definite rules of what letters can go together in what order and what words can go together, forces us to respond in that way, or we will not understand what is written. Emotion does not affect our responses until we have accumulated several words or phrases in the context—whereas *in a picture or musical piece we react all at once on several levels* (intellectual and emotional), not in linear fashion.

Pictures, music, dance, ideographic writing, and language systems all call up more total, wholistic responses from us than does alphabetic writing. McLuhan's point is that the medium, the language, does affect how we see what we see, how we interpret it, and how and what we feel. His analogy is simply that in alphabetic cultures the development of technology that produces millions of cars, refrigerators, shoes, bottles, corn flakes, eye glasses, etc., is directly related to the way we think in parts and fragments. We do our linear (assembly line) thing in our thinking, our manufacturing, and industry because we make machines following the principles of our alphabetic culture—letter by letter, word by word, in a line, sequenced one after another in a prescribed order in time and space. Cars and sentences are made piece by piece.

Oriental cultures and languages, which are ideographic (Chinese, Japanese, Korean for example), look at the world very differently. They did not invent and initiate the kind of mass production, assembly-line technology we did because they do not perceive the world that way.

McLuhan would relate this behavior to family life one finds in alphabetic cultures as compared with those in ideographic cultures. Ours is fragmented, everyone for himself; theirs is together and close-knit, even including ancestor worship in most Oriental cultures. For them the family is the picture, the whole; for us the family is made up of movable pieces, like type in a printing press. Briefly, this is what McLuhan means by the medium is the message on one level.

I am attempting to translate his remarks by simplification and amplification and by probing some of the contexts to which he is referring. His contexts include science and technology, history, anthropology, sociology, psychology, and literature, among others. A problem for all of us in our communication and teaching of reading and writing concerns contexts. If we do not know what contexts or referents authors are using, we can miss a great deal of what they say, and most of what they mean. An important sidelight here is that McLuhan's writing is quite metaphoric and figurative, not literal or factual. Also, he dictated *Understanding Media* to a secretary, and speaking is very different from sitting behind a typewriter, alone, typing one word at a time. One is social and the other is private.

McLuhan goes on to say that our phonetic alphabet makes a sharp division in experience and because of it we use our eyes more than our ears, whereas nonphonetic cultures depend almost exclusively on the spoken word for information. When that is true the people who use only spoken language for a medium get a different message from the one we do, when we read silently and alone from a book or paper. In the former instance, tribal peoples have historically transmitted their beliefs, religions, technologies, and customs to the next generation orally from elder to younger in some kind of dramatic, emotional ritual. Reading a book does not give that additional feeling, drama, and human contact. When you listen to others, especially those believed to be important, magical, or authoritative, they watch you as you listen and that affects what you hear and how you treat what is being spoken. Reading and writing take much of that feeling, drama, and human interaction out of the situation. In reading and writing you are usually alone, talking to yourself, translating others' ideas, and creating your own emotion and drama. No other humans are physically present to speak, gesture, and react to their own speech and to your reaction to it at a given moment and in a specific place. McLuhan is saying that we lose that magic and we lose what tribal people without phonetic alphabets have—the "web of kinship." We lose the family, the extended family, and all those human, emotional relations they have with others, because we don't need them with our private, personal technology of the phonetic alphabet. When you listen in the presence of important others (those who feed you, clothe you, shelter you, and love you) you react quite differently from when you read words about love and family in a book. The experiences are qualitatively different.

McLuhan's theory and teaching language

Understanding McLuhan's theory about the symbolic uses of language will assist us in teaching language in its several forms—written, spoken, and heard. It will sensitize us to the effects language has on learners, and it may help us gain greater mastery over it. We should be able to use our phonetic alphabet effectively to transmit our thoughts, feelings, and ideas to others and to escape from some of its technological bondage. Our teaching and planning can be more wholistic, ideographic than it has been.

We can escape the behaviorist linearity and their almost complete submission to what McLuhan says about phonetic alphabets. The Gestalt view is an attempt to get the best of both worlds—that is, to use carefully the technical skills we have mastered in the production of goods and their distribution, and in the control of some aspects of nature, but to plan learning activities for humans much more wholistically. Both can occur at the same time in the same world; we do not have to choose one way or another and students should learn this early.

Just as your heart and lungs reflect to a large degree how you have lived and what you inherited in the genes, the language we make reflects us as persons in a culture. In addition to the linearity of the alphabetic languages there exists one of the great beauties of alphabetic languages; we can transmit information, feelings, and ideas flexibly, and we can conceal as much as or more than we transmit. Individual words can have several denotations (dictionary definitions) and many connotations (emotional and interpretive elements), and the context in which they are used alters them in several ways to create other meanings and other contexts. Steiner says that we may need a theory of misinformation more than we need a theory of information, referring to our need to learn more about what people hide and obscure from themselves and others in communication. The relationship between a language and its users—what they do to each other and how they change and direct each other—is illustrated by a quotation from Steiner (1975, p. 87): "The linguistic world-view of a given community shapes and gives life to the entire landscape of psychological and communal behavior. It is language which decides how different conceptual groupings and contours are to be 'read' and related within the whole." Steiner agrees with aspects of McLuhan and Whorf on the medium's pervasive effects on the message it transmits and on the receiver of that form of the message.

We have come a long way from the more common discussions of language and reading. We cannot accept the notion of language as a system of symbols and sounds separate from the user of that language, to be diagnosed and corrected blend by blend, digraph by digraph, phoneme by phoneme. Our perspective has been expanded by these authors and others. Now our view of language in the reading process must include statistical properties and symbolic qualities much more than in the past; in short, our view may now become much more organismic and wholistic. Our job as teachers and specialists is not to start the conveyor belt of language skills and to place students somewhere along that line. Neither the student nor the language can be understood in isolated fragments, pieces of behavior.

Summary of Language

We have looked at language in terms of differing linguistic views and in terms of commonly accepted principles of language development, language acquisition, and language structure. In discussing the English language we have noted that several forces have contributed to the irregularities that plague so many students. Among these forces are the effects of massive borrowing from other languages, variants including regional differences and Black English. Some general principles of language acquisition were presented.

Mention was made of the four dimensions of language: the phonological, the syntactic, the semantic, and the statistical. In addition, a discussion of some of the symbolic qualities and aspects of language was offered using McLuhan's concepts as the foundation. Hence we have had an overview of the nature, functioning, and structure of language emphasizing its wholeness.

LEARNING

Now let's look at two dominant theories of learning—one behaviorist in nature, the other Gestaltist— and how they will affect our diagnosis and correction of reading and language problems.

If there is any topic more comprehensive than language, it is how people learn. Theorists and practitioners disagree with each other and among themselves; behaviorists do not all agree with each other, nor do the Gestaltists. For each of these two major groups of learning theories (behaviorists and Gestaltists) there are shades of emphasis, some subtle and very technical, others more apparent. I cannot begin to delve into all of these shadings, nor would it be appropriate here, since our major concern with the behaviorists' and the Gestaltists' learning theories is to understand the essential conclusions of both groups and try to see how they relate to choosing an approach to diagnosing and teaching reading and related language skills. It would be impossible to be a pure behaviorist or a pure Gestaltist, because there is a core of common knowledge and because none of us seems able to be all of anything; we accept some blending of elements from both theoretical sources. Teachers, clinicians, or specialists without a solid grounding in either learning theory would lack a critical guide to thinking about how to diagnose and correct reading and learning problems. We must have a philosophy of education and a psychology of learning which are compatible and consistent so that all of our work with students attains meaning. When you integrate a philosophy of life and a psychology of learning, it serves you in all aspects of the teaching act and you become more effective with students, because you know what you are doing and why you are doing it. Students perceive this consistency.

Key Factors of the Two Major Learning Theories

What are the major components of the two major learning theories? Hilgard and Bower (1975, pp. 7–8) offers us a summary of the key factors in learning which any theory must address:

1. *The limits of learning* including capacity and individual differences. Who can learn what?

2. *The role of practice in learning* including the effect and value of repetition: how much and under what conditions? Can repetition be harmful as well as helpful to the learner?

3. *The importance of drives and incentives, rewards and punishments* including the interest factor and whether consequence of rewards and punishments are equal and opposite; differences between intrinsic and extrinsic motives as they effect learning.

4. *What is the place of understanding and insight?*

5. *Does learning one thing help you learn something else?* This relates to transfer of training, how it happens, with what, and in what circumstances.

6. *What happens when we remember and when we forget?*

What is learning?

Let's start with a definition of learning which attempts to be inclusive enough to incorporate most of the areas of agreement on facts from both behaviorist and Gestaltist viewpoints. Here is Hilgard's definition (Hilgard and Bower, 1975, p. 3): "Learning is the process by which an activity originates or is changed through reacting to an encountered situation, provided that the characteristics of the change in activity cannot be explained on the basis of native response tendencies, maturation, or temporary states of the organism (e.g., fatigue, drugs, etc.)."

He is downgrading pure stimulus-response behavior here which is emphasized by many behaviorists and he is emphasizing that learning is changing behavior by more than mechanical or reflexive means. That leaves room for understanding and insight which the Gestaltists consider essential to all learning. My own view is clearly on the side of the Gestaltists although I cannot deny that some human behavior and learning show traces of the stimulus-response pattern. The whole issue of which group of learning theorists is correct is impossible to solve; one is left always with the need to interpret the facts and research of both groups, and then to organize diagnostic and corrective measures in keeping with those conclusions.

What is clear in all learning theory is that learning is changing behavior overtly and covertly so that information collected by the senses can be organized, compared, and contrasted, sorted into logical groupings called concepts, and then applied to new situations.

Behaviorists and Gestaltists

The behaviorists have dominated much of education since the turn of the century and men like Pavlov, Watson, Thorndike, Skinner, and Guthrie laid the foundation for much of what has occurred in curriculum development, testing, diagnosing, and correcting reading and related language problems. The Gestaltists have made an impact on learning and teaching but it is in no way comparable. Among Gestaltists were men like Wertheimer, Kohler, and Koffka. Lewin is included in the group although his "field theory" stresses life space and the effects of interaction upon learning and is not totally congruent with the other Gestaltists.

But they all recognize the power of the whole, the field, to organize the parts within it and thus to give them meaning and feeling. The behaviorists are much less concerned with meaning and feeling. On the one hand the Gestaltists' research has focused largely on perception—itself a wholistic and organismic set of behaviors, while the behaviorists have tended to focus on reflexive behaviors, traces in the nervous system, habit, repetition, and drill for learning. The Gestaltists have generally placed relationship in the foreground of perception and learning, and the behaviorists have placed relationship in the background. Perception and learning are inseparable to most Gestaltists; they are separate to most behaviorists. Some of these differences are well summarized by Hilgard and Bower, (1975, pp. 9–10): "The stimulus-response theorist tends to believe that some sort of chained muscular responses, linked perhaps by fractional anticipatory goal responses, serve to keep a rat running to a distant food box. The cognitive theorist, on the other hand, more freely infers central brain processes, such as memories or expectations, as integrators of goal-seeking behavior."

Clearly, the behaviorists hold to the view that only observable and measurable behavior is relevant in studying human behavior and learning. Therefore they look to physical acts and to the physical causes of these acts to explain learning; the Gestaltists include some of this but place more emphasis on thinking and seeing relationships, comprehending wholes of words, ideas, senses, and situations as the way we integrate our knowledge, experience, and feelings. The behaviorists tend to explain learning in terms of the organism receiving a stimulus to which it responds habitually because of past traces or connections in the brain and nervous system. Understanding or seeing relationships is for them the result of putting pieces of experience and responses together; the Gestaltists work the other way, from the whole to its parts and then back again. Behaviorists see great value in repetition of tasks, drill and practice, while the Gestaltists see some value in it but recognize that repetition and drill can be harmful and distracting. The Gestaltists emphasize meaning, and that meaning in any situation is derived from a context in which persons, ideas, concepts, words, and sounds are related. The context, the whole, then interacts with and guides the relationships among the parts.

The behaviorists' classic statement, paraphrased here, that if you gave a behaviorist a child he could make it a doctor, lawyer, teacher, or thief, illustrates their emphasis on the environment. Believing that, many behaviorists encourage teachers and others to manipulate the learning environment so that the proper *responses* are elicited. That is why they have devised programmed instructional materials and mechanical devices for learning, and why they have constructed games, flash card activities, and a host of similar exercises designed to alter responses. They emphasize parts of any learning act; they emphasize altering or manipulating responses, what they refer to as conditioned responses. The whole learning process by their description takes on a mechanical quality.

The Gestaltists on the other hand emphasize *organization* in the brain and nervous system; sensory impressions are not taken in and comprehended one by one, but are rather sorted in our minds according to groups of relations: large, small, smaller; near, far, distant; smooth and coarse. The organization of sensory and other impressions and information is rooted in our total personalities—our life and language experiences grouped into relationships. The Gestaltists agree that *the whole is greater than the sum of its parts*. A word has full meaning when you can see how it relates to the whole sentence or even the whole paragraph, not by itself. A person cannot be described as an isolated creature apart from his family, friends, social groups, his country and his culture. The meanings he takes on and emits from himself are the result of the interactions of his whole life. He is a democrat or republican, a Buddhist or Catholic, he speaks English or Greek, he wears a turban or a derby depending upon his culture and the language it develops to express itself.

A major problem with the typical behaviorist study of human behavior and learning is its overemphasis on the scientific validity of their conclusions. Why is it a problem? All scientific study necessitates identifying a problem, delimiting it, isolating the variables which may affect the outcome, then testing the hypothesis and verifying it. The age-old difficulty with all social science research has been the inability of the researcher, behaviorist or Gestaltist, to identify all the variables and to control them for study.

We do not always know all of the possible variables that might affect a particular person's behavior on a certain day, in a certain place, and under certain circumstances. We can control the space and time people inhabit to some extent, but not totally. Since we cannot identify all the possible variables that might affect any human behavior, that means we have to use and work with those variables we *can identify* and measure. But who is to say that the variables *not identified*, or those which have been identified but *not currently measurable* with our knowledge of statistics, are not as significant as those we have identified and measured? Is a variable of behavior important only if we can measure it? Do events occur only if we observe them?

This problem is not exclusively the problem of the behaviorists. Anyone engaged in research with humans has to deal with it. Having said that, I don't want to leave the impression that there is no point in setting up research studies which attempt to gather scientific data about human behavior; what I am warning against is believing that research is somehow magical and omnipotent; like all human activities it is subject to omitting some variables, mismeasuring some, and doing our best with limited knowledge. That is human, and any researcher of humans who believes that his statistics or technology can somehow account for all possible human behavior, and that the results will be generalizable to other humans, needs a lesson in both science and humility.

The behaviorists leave out feeling and emotion except in the isolated instance of the learner's pleasure with success rewarded on a specific task or skill. They seem to ignore the powerful and distorting effects of one's attitudes, needs, and urges on what is learned and remembered. Somehow they seem to think that we are all limited to thinking, doing, and feeling one thing at a time. Unfortunately for them, we tend to be involved in numerous feelings, thoughts, and actions simultaneously. How do you separate your past from the fleeting moments we call present? And how then do you draw the line between such fleeting moments and events in the expected future? *In a sense all time occurs at once in most of us*. The same holds true for feelings—they simply do not sit still as one about to be photographed. Our feelings and thoughts are very complex, occurring on many levels simultaneously.

In leaving out feeling and emotion, the behaviorists mislead us into believing that perception, that all-encompassing behavior, is also measurable and divisible. Perception in human beings is *not* divisible. Perception means the ways in which we filter all our experiences, feelings, and knowledge through each other and through our total personality. Perception is not a reflex, like a knee jerking when hit by a rubber mallet. How we perceive, and what we perceive, are all part of us as whole human beings. Perceiving is not seeing, or hearing or feeling—it is that plus all the thought and feeling we have organized into concepts throughout our lives. We perceive in terms of what we are, cognitively and affectively.

Another oversight by many behaviorists is that *human beings are the only creatures who can and do deny rewards and accept or even choose punishments*, or in serious cases can fail to respond at all. This is critical to a major thrust of behaviorist notions of how and why people learn. They still hold to concepts of stimulus-response with a system of rewards and punishments as a means of establishing certain desired behavior—the conditioned response. Behavior modification, a fairly recent offspring of behaviorist learning and teaching theory, essentially offers several external rewards like m & m's for good work and some more human means like praise of certain types at certain times. The gist of this is that we can and should control and manipulate human behavior by conditioning the responses we want, and to a large extent that is achieved by a system of rewards and punishments given at the right moment.

This is probably a little harsh on behaviorists, but it is not grossly wrong or unfair. As in the cultures of phonetic alphabets, behaviorists merely support and nurture a fragmented approach to all aspects of life and learning; it leaves us efficient, fast, and uniform, but alone and uncreative. We reproduce but do not re-create.

Another major difference between the behaviorists and the Gestaltists is in their emphasis on the *quantitative* and *qualitative* measures of all human behavior. Behaviorists obviously are strong for the *quantitative measures*—standard tests, statistical treatments of observed behaviors, and attempts to make as scientific as they can their conclusions about what has happened and why it has happened. The *Gestaltists* measure behavior too, but they place major emphasis on *qualitative data* when they deal with the variable creature called man. They know how difficult, if not impossible, it is to identify, control, and then measure such human behavior as emotions, or how some emotions in some people at some times and in certain situations affect any kind of learning or other behavior. Feelings, thoughts, attitudes, needs, your own life history are very difficult to separate from each other and from other conditions.

How shall we pick out which feeling, emotion, need, urge, concept, or fact is operating in any given moment? How shall we measure it? If you get seven right and three wrong on your test, can we conclude that you are mediocre? That is one measure in one specific human context and looks at one piece of your behavior which is measurable and leaves out everything else.

Think how such emotional currents run through your every day existence. Have you not been in class, with your friends, and found yourself several seconds into a heavy conversation thinking of other times, places, people, so much so that you do not even hear the human voice right next to you? Have your ears failed, or your eyes? No. You have emotionally masked a present stimulation with the tidal and undulating past and images of the future. You have literally removed yourself from the present context and began, for the moment anyway, to live in another time and place — a different context. We all do these things and they affect how we learn, what we learn, and what we retain for later processing. But most of it cannot be and is not measured by behaviorists or anyone.

The Gestalt views emotional tides and currents as a normal part of the whole human being in his context. They do not abstract one or two characteristics, traits, and pieces of behavior and measure them in a totally separate and unreal context. Such measurement distorts the information gathered since it does leave out so many important and influential forces. The gist of all Gestalt psychological thinking is that *the whole is greater than the sum of its parts*; that no behavior can be understood out of the context of the *whole* organism in its *whole* environment, and that the internal environment is as important as the external, measurable, "real" environment.

How does this Gestalt approach relate specifically to learning anything? And how does it affect behavior? How does the idea of *the whole being greater that the sum of its parts* relate to diagnosing and teaching reading?

The whole is the *field* of experience at any time past and present, cognitive and affective. The whole may be affected by the imagined future. Let's look at perception first, since it is the broadest area of the subject.

When you look at a painting, sculpture, or any graphic representation what do you see? Do you see the little dots in a painting by Seurat (the Pointilist) or do you see people, scenery, grass, trees, boats, umbrellas, dresses, shoes, sky, clouds, or sun? On first glance you see the whole scene. You get an impression of a summer scene with people near water on a clear day in another era of time. Then as you look more closely and carefully, you begin to notice some figures or other items in the canvas. You will see, very soon, that Seurat used thousands of little separate colored dots to create the impression of people, trees, and water. He did not use regular brush strokes. His choice of the dots, his soft colors, his perspective all contribute to your overall, whole impression of the painting.

The same holds true for a musical piece. When you first heard Beethoven's *Ninth Symphony*, "Ode to Joy" movement, it is most likely that you picked up the major melody and tempo, the pace and melodiousness. You probably did not hear specific notes or even chords, like c sharp, b natural, or c seventh, etc. Upon further contact with this piece you did begin to hear contrapuntal themes, specific chord arrangements, and detail in the composition. This is another example of the principle that the whole (painting, sculpture, musical piece, new person) is perceived first and then the analysis into what the parts are follows. The parts then become more meaningful when they are seen in their natural relationships with the other parts of the field. The melody or theme cannot be detected one note at a time.

The whole, the gestalt, the field, represents related experiences, events, and objects and must be understood as a dynamic environment. To understand any of it, you must first grasp its wholeness, its form, shape, color, concept, sound. According to leading Gestaltists, perception is organized in humans and it operates in this wholistic relational manner, rather than in a piecemeal object-by-object, piece-by-piece fashion which so attracts behaviorists.

Approaches to reading: code emphasis and meanings emphasis

How are these two basic learning theories applied in the field of reading? Where are the behaviorist emphases most obvious, and where the Gestaltist? Two authors have presented the major approaches to teaching reading and language skills: Ralph Aukerman (1971) and Jeanne Chall (1967) categorized the numerous approaches to teaching reading as "code emphasis" and "meanings emphasis." The code-emphasis approaches stress the process of decoding the language through phonic and structural analysis, while the meanings-emphasis programs tend to place meaning first, in the foreground and word analyses in a less prominent position, background. Both types of reading approaches do teach phonic skills and structural analyses skills, but the background for one approach is the foreground for the other. For example, code-emphasis programs like *Phonetic Keys to Beginning Reading, The Royal Road Readers* (Diack), *Open Court Basic Readers, Reading with Phonics* (Hay-Wingo), and closely related linguistic approaches to teaching reading including Bloomfield's *Let's Read*, Walcutt's *Lippincott Basic Reading Program, Merrill Linguistic Readers* all share the behaviorist concepts of learning as we have discussed them. Gestaltist reading programs fall into the meanings emphasis category and they include the language-experience approach, which I shall elaborate upon in Chapter 5. Reading programs reflecting the Gestaltist view of learning include Lee and Allen (1963), *Learning to Read through Experience, The Chandler Reading Program*; Warner (1963), *Teacher*; Stauffer (1970), *The Language Experience Approach to the Teaching of Reading*. The key differences between the code-emphasis and meanings-emphasis approaches to teaching reading reside in the psychology of learning which undergirds them. In the code-emphasis programs we find behaviorist influences and in the meanings-emphasis programs we find the Gestaltist influences. Children learn to read by any number of approaches, methods and materials, classroom settings, and organization, so no one type of approach can claim it is the only way and the right way, but meanings-emphasis programs are more in keeping with normal human development.

The research reported and analyzed by Chall (1967) and the national study of reading in the mid-sixties can be summed up in this fashion: no one method, approach, set of materials, or methods was significantly superior to any other in the study. The single most significant influence on whether children learned to read or not was *the quality of the teaching*. Just as we must interpret the research of behaviorists and Gestaltists since some of the data are the same, so must we decide for ourselves as teachers and specialists, which type of approach is most suitable to us as persons and to our students. Poor teachers obviously can ruin what appears to be good material, and good teachers can make poor material work with her students. Chall concluded in *Learning to Read* that a code emphasis approach to teaching reading would be most effective, while Aukerman (1971) seems neutral with perhaps an edge toward meaning emphasis programs.

Confusion exists concerning the definitions of what is meant by both types of approaches, since variations exist in both camps. There is no pure code-emphasis approach, but some come very close to purity, and there is no pure meaning-emphasis program. This is not to say that any kind of eclecticism is acceptable. I firmly believe that as a teacher you should adopt an approach that fits snugly into your philosophy of education and your psychology of learning. Consistency and coherence do matter in teaching and learning, just as they matter so much in child rearing and discipline.

The subsequent chapters will spell out in practical detail how I apply Gestalt learning theory to all aspects of diagnosis and correction of reading and language problems. Chapters 2 and 3 describe the diagnostic process from this viewpoint and Chapter 5 details how to plan an integrated, wholistic instructional program which I call *core concept* planning. All of the diagnostic and corrective principles and practices are rooted in Gestalt psychology of learning and in the philosophy of education called Pragmatism.

Very briefly, Pragmatism has influenced American education since the turn of the century, peaking in the 1920s and 1930s. Its chief spokesman was John Dewey and included Royce, Kilpatric, and Bruner. Dewey (1938, pp. 19-20) concisely summarized the philosophy: "To imposition from above is opposed expression and cultivation of individuality; to external discipline is opposed free activity; to learning from texts and teachers, learning through experience; to acquisition of isolated skills and techniques by drill, is opposed acquisition of them as means of attaining ends which make direct vital appeal; to preparation for a more or less remote future is opposed making the most of the opportunities of present life; to static aims and materials is opposed acquaintance with a changing world."

You should also read Jerome Bruner's *The Process of Education* for an updated application of Pragmatism as well as Piaget's concepts of growth and development.

Summary of Learning

What are the major differences in interpretation of human behavior and learning as presented by behaviorists and Gestaltists? To the behaviorists, behavior is learned in the stimulus-response, conditioned-response fashion nurtured by a system of rewards and punishments. Their view emphasizes man's physical nature, and they seek their explanations of man's behavior in measurable, observable data. They emphasize responses, specific responses to specific stimuli accumulating one by one. They emphasize the parts of a task. In reading instruction they tend to follow the code emphasis programs, which are basically analytic in nature.

Behaviorists emphasize extrinsic motivation and encourage such isolated activities as rote drills, workbook exercises, flash cards, games, machines. There are all *parts* of the reading process and because they are presented in isolation often fail to produce long-term success and transfer of learning. Some students do experience success with some of these isolated activities and then transfer the skills and learnings to other skills and learnings, but many do not. Many of these contrived and temporary successes are soon understood by the failing student for what they are. Clearly, extrinsic motivational forces are not enough to insure learning; intrinisic motives are more effective and more enduring, but they need some extrinsic support. There must be a *balance*.

The Gestaltists on the other hand believe that human perception and learning are inseparable and are an integral part of the body's organization. This organization produces understanding and insight so that behavior can be, and often is, novel, creative and unpredictable. These emphases place *meaning* in the center of all behavior highlighting relationships of many types, not just those of the stimulus-response variety. Emotions are embedded in thought and thought is infused with feelings. Gestaltists hold that the whole is greater than the sum of its parts and that the whole, the pattern or organization of the field, gives meaning to the parts. In reading instruction they favor the meanings-emphasis approaches so that from the earliest days of reading instruction, relationships among parts within a context are foremost.

In looking at persons, behaviorists see a collection of well meshed parts, while the Gestaltists see a whole organism. In reading instruction behaviorist theorists take a path strewn with pieces of a puzzle, which they proceed to put together hoping it will make sense, while the Gestaltists take the path that begins with an image of the whole puzzle and then fit the pieces in where they make the most sense. In McLuhan's terms we might associate the behaviorist view with that of the phonetic alphabet, while the Gestaltist view would be more analogous to the ideographic languages.

Today we see much more the wholistic approach to such universal problems as ecology, ethology, medicine; and psychotherapy, for instance has moved a distance from doing only one to one counseling to involving the family and the community; corrections has moved from trying to rehabilitate each prisoner alone, to family and community involvement. In all of these instances we see that some of the behaviorial and natural sciences have become much more wholistic in their thinking than they have been. Before you write a poem, novel, or textbook, or paint a picture or build a bookshelf, you must have a concept, an image of the finished product before you begin. The whole conception of such works then gives sense, meaning and proportion to the particular steps in the process.

At the end of this chapter are sources offering more detailed discussions of learning theories and approaches to teaching reading.

THE PROCESSES OF READING

Reading is commonly referred to as *a process*, but when you study what happens when people learn to read you quickly discover that reading involves many *processes* simultaneously. Among the most relevant processes involved in learning how to read are psychological, physical, intellectual, cultural, linguistic, and educational. Obviously, there is much overlap among these processes since intellectual capacity directly relates to affective and cognitive learning behavior; cultural influences are so pervasive and powerful as to affect not only attitudes and values, beliefs, and customs, but the language spoken and the way we perceive ourselves and the world. The linguistic processes have been mentioned and we have seen how any language affects the perception, thinking, and personalities of its users. If we look at the skills dimension of learning to read we find we can get our hands on something tangible and concrete, which produces relatively immediate results. The child who has learned how to recognize some sight words and who then can generalize and begin to recognize similar phonic and structural elements in other words has begun to read. If the same child can syllabicate parts of words, or fuse and blend letters into recognizable spoken words, he has begun to read. But he must do so much more in the process of learning to read. He must not only make the match between written forms with spoken forms, he must understand grammar and syntax so that phrases and sentences make sense and carry meaning. The child must be able to follow a development of thought and information, to draw conclusions, to recall the information presented, to assess its validity, its aesthetic qualities, and more. Clearly, this is why many authors do not even venture a definition of reading, but rather talk about some of its components, ways to discover problems, ways to assist in learning basic skills.

Growth Areas

Keeping in mind that learning to read includes psychological, physical, intellectual, cultural, linguistic, and educational dimensions, we can describe what learning to read any language will require in the way of basic skills. Very simply, reading requires knowledge of the interrelated and interdependent skills in *word recognition, meanings,* and *study skills*. It also requires the planning of learning experiences to build concepts to which language will be attached much more meaningfully. Reading and life must not be separated; experience in applying skills in the basic growth areas must be supplemented by first-hand, live experiences with people, places, objects, sights, sounds, smells, and textures.

In the following outline of these growth areas you will find some of the most important and commonly taught reading skills. All of the skills in each area can be taught in such a way as to enhance the others. The sequencing of the skills in each area is to be taken as a general guide; it is *not* always necessary to follow it or any scope and sequence chart in a linear, rigid fashion. In Part two you will find a chapter devoted to each of these growth areas detailing many ways to plan and teach them in context in an integrated fashion. One of the key problems with children experiencing difficulty learning to read is that too often they are taught from books, series, or activities which isolate the skills as well as the elements within each skill or skill area. Before we get into how to teach these skills, let's look at what they are:

The Growth Areas in Reading

I. Word Recognition
   A. Readiness Skills
   1. sight words
   2. auditory and visual discrimination
   3. picture and other context clues
   B. Phonic Analysis
      1. Single consonants in the initial, final and medial positions
      2. single vowels (short then long sounds) in the initial, final and medial positions
      3. blends (two letters, two sounds)
      a. consonant: st, br, gr, dr, tr, bl, cl, gl, sl, etc.
      b. vowel: oi, ai, ou, ew, au, etc.
      4. digraphs (two letters, one sound or a new sound)
      a. consonant: sh, wh, ch, th, ph, ng, etc.
      b. vowel: ee, ie, ei, ea, ae, oo, etc.
      5. vowels followed by l, r and w producing neither a long nor short sound.
   C. Structural Analysis
      1. compound words: break fast, some thing, base ball, no where, etc.
      2. syllabication: hop/ing, de/light/ful, hap/py, etc.
      3. affixes
      a. prefixes: in, un, de, pre, im, a, anti, etc.
      b. suffixes: ly, ic, ate, ed, ion, etc.
      4. root words path, ced, mort, anim, port, path, cred, etc.
      5. hyphenated words
      6. contractions
   D. Using the dictionary as an aid in learning
   1. syllabication
   2. etymology
   3. accent
   4. pronunciation
   5. common meanings
   6. synonyms and antonyms
II. Meanings
   A. Comprehension
      1. literal recall: who, what, where, when, how many
         a. facts, names, places, etc.
   B. Interpretation and Critical Reading
   1. drawing conclusions

    2. making inferences
    3. making generalizations
    4. detecting propaganda techniques
      a. glad names
      b. bad names
      c. testimonial
      d. transfer
      e. plain folks
      f. card stacking
      g. bandwagon
    5. interpreting imagery and figures of speech: simile, metaphor,
        symbols
    6. interpreting satire, allegory, etc.
III. Study Skills
    A. Previewing
    B. Finding main ideas and details
    C. Outlining and summarizing
    D. Classification
    E. Using guide words
    F. Patterns
      1. question-answer
      2. cause and effect
      3. sequence
      4. fact-opinion
    G. Following directions

Vocabulary development occurs in *word recognition* under structural analysis for, as you will see in Chapter 4, one major technique is to work with affixes and roots. Vocabulary is also taught as part of *interpretation*, and in fact, whenever it comes up. Those two places are the most logical most of the time. Since we should not teach words and their meanings in isolation off vocabulary lists, they will be taught contextually. There are no "vocabulary words" as such.

Many published reading programs and texts contain scope and sequence charts that some people find helpful, and since my outline of the growth areas is not technically such a chart, I recommend Harris and Sipay (1975) for an incredibly detailed one. Do not feel compelled to follow each step in the sequence exactly as presented since it is, at best, a general guide. Your student is a good guide, as is your own diagnostic data. In all cases, be flexible and take your cues as much as possible from the learner.

Word recognition

Readiness skills. In teaching readiness skills and activities, we assist the nonreader to hear, see, and connect auditory and visual symbols—the first step in discovering the spoken language in another form (a kind of picture of one's speech). Auditory and visual discrimination emphasize the similarities and differences in both the visual forms and the auditory forms. Children and beginning readers of all ages need to develop skill in noting that *b* and *d* are not alike, that *p* and *q* are not alike, and that both are different in that they are reversals of each other (d is b backwards, visually). They also need to listen more carefully to spoken language to be able to hear that *line* in not *lime*. The abilities needed for auditory and visual discrimination are not the only requirements for reading skill, but they do reduce the amount of potential confusion.

Auditory and visual discrimination activities will occur in your teaching at low levels (nonreader through third or fourth grade level). Even though these discriminations represent a rather low level of skill in the total reading process, they are essential. But don't teach them in isolation using word or letter lists or flash cards; use words in a context of interest to the learner. (More on this will appear in Chapter 6.)

In the readiness stage, sight words are learned for the five-year-old, ten-year-old, forty-year-old, and anyone functioning at this low level. Sight words are merely words memorized by the learner so that they are recognized on sight, at once, without the benefit of any phonic analysis or structural analysis—just rote memory and familiarity. For young children one of the ways a sight vocabulary is developed is through the picture filled preprimers introducing approximately ten words per book, each word repeated ten times, and also using pictures as clues to the few printed words. With older students we recommend other ways of building up a sight vocabulary, e.g., using names of family members, street addresses, survival signs (Exit, Stop, Men), and common everyday language one can pick up in buses, trains, store windows, and advertisements. *Wherever the words come from they will be memorized by the learner through frequent repetition in some real, meaningful context.*

With a group of sight words, and auditory and visual discrimination sharpened, we have the basic ingredients of teaching reading from scratch.

Phonic analysis.   After the readiness activities and skills, the reader then moves into the heart of word recognition: phonic and structural analysis. In phonic analysis most reading programs teach the student how to develop principles or generalizations regarding how letters and combinations of letters represent spoken sounds in print. In phonic analysis, as you note from the detailed outline of the growth areas, the student learns how to identify single consonant sounds in the initial, final, and medial positions; he learns to identify some short or long vowels depending on the particular reading program he is in; he learns to identify the consonant blends and digraphs, vowel blends and digraphs; silent letters; the effects r, l, and w have on vowels, e.g., the *a* in *all* does not sound long or short, nor does *i* in *fir* sound long or short any more than the *o* in *cow* sounds long or short. These are some of the components presented and practiced by students in the growth area of word recognition in phonic analysis.

The presentation of these skills follows the readiness work, because we try to use the sight words and the heightened awareness of auditory and visual likenesses and differences as the base from which to generalize about letters and their sounds. For example, the person who knows such sight words as stop, go, look, see, man, and who knows their meanings, can be taken to the next relatively small step by noting that the word stop has two combinations, *st*, and *op*, and that the learner has in his listening and speaking vocabulary many words containing these elements. Ask the students how many words they know that sound like *stop* in the beginning. If no answer, say, Listen: stay, stick, house. Which words sound alike in the beginning? We get stay and stick going with stop (the sight word). We write these words while talking about them so that the learner uses his visual as well as his auditory discrimination, to see and hear that the sight word *stop* begins with the two letters *st* which are written the same way in other words, and sound as they do in the word *stop*.

Hence, in this phonic analysis activity we tie together auditory and visual discrimination and generalize from a known sight word a particular phonic element (*st* blend). Much of what happens in phonic analysis, especially at the outset, is of this nature—moving from the known sight words to unknown words containing the phonic element in the beginning, middle, and end of other words. The learner will look for *st* and at least be able say it and recognize it visually wherever it appears in any word. He uses his sight memory, his auditory and visual discrimination, and his specific knowledge of *st* in words in context.

One of the key problems in all work with the word recognition growth area, and especially the phonic analysis category, is to *reduce dependence on isolated sound making and identifying*. In short, we wish to avoid such classic inaccuracies as: *b* says *buh, d* says *duh*. The word baker is not to be analyzed: *buh ay kuh*. The word is *baker*, period. It contains the phonic element *b* as in such words as ball, bounce, boy, bike, etc., and in each instance it is written the same way and it is pronounced the same way. Detailed suggestions for teaching word recognition skills appear in chapter 6.

Linguistically, teaching students to pronounce each letter in isolation is both wrong and misleading. It distorts the normal sounds of the language and does not correspond to the child's aural knowledge of the language. Also, such practice destroys meaning because it is unnatural and uncontexual.

Structural analysis. This area concerns itself with those skills that deal with identifying larger parts of words, not single letters or combinations of letters. Under structural analysis we deal with teaching such skills as syllabication, compound words, prefixes, suffixes, roots and so on. Clearly, if a student has very few phonic analysis skills, he will have difficulty trying to analyze words in terms of their roots, syllables, etc. Here again we seek to assist the student to generalize as much as possible and to move away from letter by letter analysis which easily could confuse him.

Summary of word recognition skills

The growth area of word recognition incorporates several essential skills which cause some confusion and conflict for the new reader whose knowledge of the language has been aural-oral and who is trying very hard to make the connections between the spoken sounds of the language and its printed forms, which do not always make sense. A great deal of emphasis is placed on this growth area in almost every approach to teaching reading, since most teachers seem to believe that if the child or other learner cannot master the word recognition skills, reading, and to some extent writing, is impossible. To a degree that is true, but not entirely.

The word recognition skills provide the beginning reader with analytic skills that make it possible for him to approach print with the ability to figure out how words begin, what vowel sounds appear, how to break words apart and how to fuse and blend the letters and combinations so that the words can be spoken. Some rules and principles are taught or derived and then applied to unfamiliar words the reader may encounter.

Meanings skills

The reading processes are separated only for discussions such as this, but in reality all three growth areas are interacting with each other. The meanings skills involve comprehending and recalling the literally stated facts and information. The question is no longer how to say the printed words the author wrote but, what did he say? Interpretation skills in this area of meanings involve logical and relational thinking rooted in the information presented by the author. The question is, what does he mean by what he said, by the facts and information he has presented? To what is he referring? The ability to recognize multiple meaning words, allusions, symbols, and imagery are among the components of good interpretation. But this depends on the ability to figure out the words the author wrote; it depends on the ability to recall the facts and information so that the reader can put them together to make comparisons and contrasts, to detect special uses of common words and to surmise the impact of the total context in which all of these words and facts appear. Why did the author put these facts together this way? What about his choice of words? What are his purposes, his intent? What does he want you to believe, feel, think? Why? Chapters 8 and 9 present suggestions for teaching these skills and ways of thinking.

Study skills

Study skills is the third major growth area in the reading process. It is that set of interrelated thinking skills that assist the reader to perceive the organization of nonfictional reading material and to note how the information presented fits together. Previewing gives the reader an overview of the book, article, or chapter so that he is aware of what is coming and what the author seems to be emphasizing. Finding main ideas and details gets the reader into the heart of knowing what the author is saying and what is most important in the careful reading of paragraphs. This skill leads logically into the teaching of outlining and summarizing, which are totally dependent on the reader's ability to know what is most important in history, geography, or science material. Classification is a way of logical thinking that involves grouping related facts and ideas in accord with common attributes and qualities. It appears in all kinds of nonfictional writing. The rest of the study skills assist the reader to become more and more aware of *order and relationships*. In Chapter 7 many suggestions are offered to you for teaching these useful skills.

Taken together the skills in word recognition, meanings, and study skills constitute the skills dimension of the reading process. The other dimensions of the reading process such as linguistic, cultural, psychological, and educational are subtly interwoven. We have to learn how to maintain a balance between skills instruction in the growth areas and the deeper structures of thought and feeling. If we overemphasize skills we may lose the perspective we need; if we overemphasize psychological or intellectual or physical problems we can easily forget that the learner must be able to figure out printed words. If one has developed a personal psychology of learning, a balance is less difficult to maintain. My suggestions for diagnosing and correcting reading and language problems is to establish a comfortable balance for teacher and learner in a new setting.

When learners proceed to learn the skills in word recognition, meanings, and study skills when they are taught, grade by grade, we consider this *developmental reading*. It simply means meeting expectations by age, intelligence, and cultural background. The third grade child reading third grade material, that is, material commonly read with ease by the majority of children in the third grade, is a *developmental* reader. The third grade child laboring with word recognition skills, interpretation, and vocabulary, and able to read only second grade material with any mastery needs some *corrective* work. The third grade child who can only cope with first grade material with any assurance needs *remedial* help. The distinction between corrective and remedial programs is probably unnecessary. Corrective work or remedial work generally applies the same skills we have listed under each growth area. There are no unique reading skills to be taught to any learner. The skills for all are the same; what changes in some reading programs (Aukerman, 1971) is the material to be read and the methods for teaching these skills. Some teachers use kinesthetic activities; some use more rote and drill than others; some use linguistic principles such as regular spelling patterns (mat, fat, pat, rat, hat, cat) or nonsense words to develop high speed recognition. But in all cases the reading program must teach word recognition skills, meanings, and study skills if the learner is to do what we call reading. The reader must learn not only to identify and say printed words composed of letters and letter combinations, but learn to recall the facts and information presented by these words, phrases, and sentences, and he must learn to draw conclusions, make inferences and generalize and assess the deeper meanings alluded to by the author. In addition, the reader must be able to pick up a history, geography, or science book (at any level) and quickly note its organization, structure, what is most important, and what he can expect to find in a given chapter, article, or book. In short, all of the skills in the growth areas must continually be seen in this interrelated fashion, not as ends in themselves at any level. Even the first or second grade student must not be overdosed on phonics activities. Children at these ages and levels need to be aware of meaning and of order. They may not be ready for interpretation of literary forms, but they can do work with propaganda on a low level; they can try to finish stories and explain why their endings are as good or better than the one in the book, and why; they can learn to note the overall organization of their books and begin to look at them as wholes which contain certain information or stories, without necessarily learning the names of the skills the teacher is presenting. The point simply is that *in all reading instruction, at all levels, readers must be immersed in all three growth areas almost simultaneously*. Chapter 5 offers specific illustrations of how that can be done very effectively in core concept plans.

Summary of Growth Areas

Like the learner himself, the language and the reading processes are multidimensional wholes. We have seen something of the features of language and especially of English as a medium which pervasively alters the perceptions, thinking, and personality of its users; we have also seen how learning has been interpreted by the two major schools of thought: behaviorist and Gestaltist and how either view, like language itself, alters the teacher's philosophy of learning and hence planning, and choice of methods and materials and evaluation. We have also seen how the many skills in reading any language are basically organized under the three headings of word recognition, meanings, and study skills. The interrelatedness of all these skills is the key to teaching them most effectively with developmental or corrective readers. The reading skills in the reading process, representing only one dimension of the total process, are the same for all learners. We have not *invented* any new reading skills;

what we have is a number of ways of organizing the program to include the skills. My approach is Gestaltist and therefore the skills and other dimensions of reading will be done wholistically—that is, integrating the skills inside a core concept plan of instruction. Starting with Chapter 2 on diagnosis and misdiagnosis and moving to Chapter 5 on planning core concept instruction, and then to Part 2, in which the specific word recognition, study skills and meanings skills are presented, *the attempt is to make the reading processes whole again.* Instead of following the more common approach of dealing with skills and techniques one by one and not incorporated into some clearly defined whole of content, I am offering the alternative of a wholistic approach to diagnosing and correcting reading and related language problems.

Bettleheim (1978) neatly summarizes the principles presented here when he says, "Only if the words he learns enrich his life and increase the pleasure he receives from talking will he wish to keep adding new ones to his vocabulary. New words are best learned when they have been invested first with deep emotional meaning."

REFERENCES

Aukerman, Ralph. *Approaches to beginning reading*. New York: John Wiley and Sons, Inc., 1971.

Baratz, Joan & Shuy, Roger (Eds.). *Teaching black children to read*. Washington, DC: Center for Applied Linguistics, 1969.

Bettleheim, Bruno. Learning to read: A primer for literacy. *Harper's Magazine*. April 1978, p. 56.

Brain, R. The neurology of the brain. In R. C. Oldfield & J. C. Marshall (Eds.), *Language*. Baltimore: Penguin Books, 1968.

Brown, Roger. How shall a thing be called? *Psychological Review*, vol. 65, 1958, pp. 14-21.

Chall, Jeanne. *Learning to read: the great debate*. New York: McGraw-Hill, 1967.

Chomsky, Noam. *Cartesian linguistics: a chapter in the history of rationalist thought*. New York: Harper and Row, 1966.

Dewey, John. *Experience and education*. New York: Collier Books, 1938.

Furth, Hans G. *Piaget for teachers*. Englewood Cliffs, NJ: Prentice-Hall, Inc., 1970.

Hilgard, Ernest & Bower, Gordon. *Theories of learning* (4th ed.). Englewood Cliffs, NJ: Prentice-Hall, Inc., 1975.

Labov, William. Some sources of reading problems for Negro speakers of non-standard English. In Roger Abrahams & Rudolph Troike (Eds.), *Language and cultural diversity in American education*. Englewood Cliffs, NJ: Prentice-Hall, Inc., 1972.

Lee, Doris & Van Allen, Roach. *Learning to read through experience*. New York: Appleton, Century & Crofts, 1963.

Lenneberg, Eric. *Biological foundations of language*. New York: Wiley, 1967. Lenneberg, Eric. A biological perspective of language. In Eric Lenneberg (Ed.), *New directions in the study of language*. Cambridge, MA: MIT Press, 1964.

McLuhan, Marshall. *Understanding media* (2nd ed.). New York: Signet Books, New American Library, 1964.

Pulaski, Mary Ann. *Understanding Piaget*. New York: Harper & Row, 1971.

Stauffer, Russell. *The language-experience approach to the teaching of reading*. New York: Harper & Row, 1970.

Steiner, George. *After Babel: aspects of language and translation*. London: Oxford University Press, 1975.

Vernon, M.D. *Psychology of perception* (2nd. ed.). Baltimore, MD: Penguin Books, 1971.

Warner, Sylvia Ashton. *Teacher*. New York: Simon & Schuster, 1963.

Webster's Seventh New Collegiate Dictionary. Springfield, MA: Merriam Co., 1971.

Whorf, Benjamin Lee. *Language, thought and reality: selected writings of Benjamin Lee Whorf*, John B. Carroll (Ed.). Cambridge, MA: MIT Press, 1956.

BIBLIOGRAPHY

Abrahamson, Adele. *Child language: an interdisciplinary guide to theory and research*. Baltimore, MD: University Park Press, 1977.

Bond, Guy & Dykstra, Robert. The cooperative research program in first-grade reading instruction. *Reading Research Quarterly*, Summer 1967, *2*, pp. 5-142.

Brown, Roger. *Words and things*. Free Press, 1958.

Bruner, Jerome. *The process of education*. New York: Vintage Books, 1963.

Carroll, John. *Language and thought*. Englewood Cliffs, NJ: Prentice-Hall, Inc., 1964.

Cherry, Colin. *On human communication*. New York and Cambridge, MA: John Wiley and MIT Press, published jointly, 1957.

Chomsky, Noam. *Syntactic structures*. The Hague: Mouton & Co., 1957.

Dewey, John. *Intelligence in the modern world*. Joseph Ratner (Ed.). New York: Modern Library, 1939.

Dillard, J. L. *Black English: its history and usage in the U.S.* New York: Random House, 1972.

Downing, John. *Comparative reading*. New York: Macmillan, 1973.

Ellis, W. D. (Ed.). *A sourcebook of Gestalt psychology*. (Abridged translation). New York: Harcourt Brace, 1938.

Estes, William. *Learning theory and mental development*. New York: Academic Press, 1970.

Fishbein, Justin & Emans, Robert (Eds.). *A question of competence*. Chicago: Science Research Associates, 1972.

Goodman, Kenneth. The psycholinguistic nature of the reading process. In Kenneth Goodman (Ed.), *The psycholinguistic nature of the reading process*. Detroit: Wayne State University, 1968.

Guthrie, E. R. *The psychology of learning*. New York: Harper & Row, 1935.

Kohler, W. *Gestalt psychology*. London: 1929 and 1947.

Koffka, K. *Principles of Gestalt psychology*. London, 1935.

Labov, William & Cohen, Paul. Some suggestions for teaching standard English to speakers of nonstandard and urban dialects. In Joanna DeStefano (Ed.), *Language, society and education: a profile of Black English*. Worthington, Ohio: Charles E. Jones, 1973, pp. 218-237.

Langacker, Ronald. *Language and its structure*. New York: Harcourt, Brace & World, 1968.

Lewin, Kurt. Field theory and learning. In *The psychology of learning*. National Society for the Study of Education, 41st Yearbook, Part II, pp. 215-242.

McLuhan, Marshall. *From cliche to archetype*. New York: Pocket Books, 1971.

Oldfield, R. C. & Marshall, J. C. *Language*. New York: Penguin Books, 1968.

Piaget, Jean. *The child's conception of the world*. Totowa, NJ: Littlefield, Adams Co., 1965.

Piaget, Jean. *The language of the child*. Cleveland: World Publishing Co., 1955.

Piaget, Jean. *The origins of intelligence in children*. New York: Norton, 1963.

Shannon, Claude & Weaver, W. *The mathematical theory of communication*. Urbana: University of Illinois, 1949.

Shipley, Joseph. *In praise of English: the growth and use of language*. New York: Times Books, 1977.

Skinner, B. F. *Science and human behavior*. New York: Macmillan, 1953.

Strickland, Dorothy. A program for linguistically different Black children. In *Research in the teaching of English*, Spring, 1973.

Thorndike, E. L. *Educational psychology*. New York: Lemcke & Buechner, 1903.

Thorndike, E. L. *The fundamentals of learning*. Teachers College, 1932.

Thorndike, E. L. *The psychology of learning*. (Educational Psychology, II). Teachers College, 1913.

Veatch, Jeanette, et al. *Key words to reading: the language-experience approach begins*. Columbus, OH: Charles E. Merrill, 1973.

Vygotsky, Lev. *Thought and language*. Cambridge, MA: MIT Press, 1962.

Wardaugh, Ronald. *Reading: a linguistic perspective*. New York: Harcourt, Brace & World, 1969.

Watson, J. B. *Psychology from the standpoint of a behaviorist*. Philadelphia: Lippincott, 1919.

Wertheimer, Max. *Gestalt psychology*. London, 1923.

Wertheimer, Max. *Productive thinking*. New York: Harper & Row, 1959.

Whatmough, Joshua. *Language: a modern synthesis*. New York: Mentor Books, 1956.

Wiener, Norbert. *The human use of human beings*. New York: Doubleday, 1956.

Chapter two

INTRODUCTION

This chapter and the next two, "Administering and Interpreting the Individual Diagnostic Analysis (IDA)," and "Causes of Reading and Language Problems," are closely related to each other. These topics were divided into three chapters more for the sake of convenience, reduction of bulk and, sharper focus than for the sake of their content, which directly relates to aspects of diagnosing and misdiagnosing reading and language problems.

This chapter will establish some useful diagnostic principles and practices and will take a hard look at the major types of testing and tests commonly used in the diagnosis of reading and language problems—standardized tests, criterion-referenced tests, and IDAs.

The Problem of Misdiagnosis

A critical area of concern in the classroom and the clinic is the possibility of incorrectly diagnosing students' reading and language problems because of the type of diagnostic tools we use and how we interpret the data from various types of tests. If we do not have reliable and dependable information on how students perform there is no way to establish grouping patterns, to select appropriate methods and materials for instruction, to plan an instructional program that will meet the needs of each student, or to evaluate progress. Misdiagnosis in education is as serious and detrimental as misdiagnosis in medicine or psychology, for in all instances the patient or student is misunderstood and receives the wrong prescription and treatment.

Diagnosis and misdiagnosis

How can we prevent misdiagnosis of reading and language performance? What do various tests and diagnostic instruments really measure and what do they *not* measure? How can we interpret data from several different types of data on a given student? How much data of what kind are enough, too much, not enough? How can we ascertain what certain reading errors mean and what they do not mean? Is there a more effective process for identifying weaknesses and strengths in each growth area and for gaining a more wholistic impression of the student than what we commonly use?

These and related questions will be posed and answered in this and the following two chapters so that when you have finished reading them you will be able to determine the most effective tests and other diagnostic measures and their weaknesses and strengths. You will also know how to administer an IDA, to interpret it, and to use it as the base for selecting methods and materials for instruction, for grouping, and for evaluation of student progress. When you have finished the third chapter in this trio you will also know something about the causes of reading failure. In short, these three chapters should provide you with some new tools for viewing a student as a whole person engaged in the reading/writing process, rather than as a collection of particular problems or strengths.

GENERAL DIAGNOSTIC CONCERNS

Teacher's Attitudes and Biases

In the mid-sixties during the heyday of the war on poverty, VISTA developed an advertising slogan which seems applicable here: *If you are not part of the solution, you must be part of the problem.* That may not be

a verbatim statement, but the point is very clear to all who would diagnose students for any purpose. Our own personal and professional training, experience, attitudes, and biases are as much a part of us as the air
we breathe and the food we eat, and these behaviors obviously affect
those we diagnose, vis-a-vis how we do it, and more importantly, how we
interpret someone else's performance. As we have already seen, if you
are a Gestaltist you will view and assess the performance of students
quite differently from the way in which a behaviorist would.

Somehow we must consciously reduce the amount of filtering we do
insofar as the student's performance is concerned and that requires that
we admit our own biases. It also means that we must not project our own
fears, anxieties, and models of behavior on others. Adopt a more positive
view of the student and his potential for learning. As professionals we
must maintain high expectations for all students based on our sensitivity
to their needs, interests, and abilities. We must also admit what we do
not know and not seek out glib and popular labels and solutions for complex problems.

My approach to diagnosis and teaching assumes that each learner is
smarter and more capable than he thinks he is and I try to leaven my
firmness and my demands with humor and optimism. The more common
approach to diagnosis tends to be negative, emphasizing what the student
cannot do and identifying specific skills the student does not know and
information the student does not have. Each twitch or hesitation is seen
as a noteworthy defect. Let us not miss the forest for the trees and let us
seek the student's *best* performance in any and all of our diagnostic and
instructional activity.

The Tools of Diagnosis

Generally speaking we must know what tests do and do not measure.
This chapter and particularly Chapter 3 will present numerous examples
of misdiagnosis based on poor choice of tests and even poorer interpretation of the data. For now, let it suffice to say that you should be asking
yourself such questions as, What does the Iowa Silent Reading Test measure? For whom is it most accurate, for whom less so? Any standardized
test has been standardized on what is thought to be a *representative* sample of the total population. You need to compare your own population
with that of the test population to ascertain whether it will produce fair
and accurate data.

Tests of all kinds *sample* the behavior of the learner so that you must
probe to see if the items on the test or screening instrument do indeed
provide a reasonable sample of skills and information. You also need to
check to see if the number of items measuring a particular skill like vocabulary, for instance, are representative of what the student will meet
in his reading and other language activities. For example, if the test you
have chosen measures phonic analysis skills, like consonant blends or

short vowels or digraphs with three or four or even ten items for each element, is that truly representative of the reading material the student will be exposed to? If the child misses four or five of ten items does it mean that he will not be able to deal with those elements in other words and in context?

Diagnosis is Functional

Functional diagnosis merely means continuous assessment of student strengths and weaknesses in each lesson in all areas of your instructional program. It is not possible to gather all of the diagnostic information you need with one, two, or three tests of any type. You need to add to your initial assessment actual instructional activities and performance. Most testing is done in isolation and under considerable pressure, which obviously alters the performance of the student. When functionally diagnosing students you note how the student responds to various types of questions, items, skills and activities. What does he recall? How does he connect ideas and concepts? How does he attempt to read unfamiliar words? Did he learn syllabication best when he memorized some rules or when he had to inductively derive the principle that operated? Is he more attentive aurally or visually? These and many other questions must be posed for each student in each lesson in order that you may increase your knowledge of his strengths and weaknesses in all areas of the reading process. In this way you monitor and reshape your original diagnosis and you build your instructional program in such a way that it can respond to these discoveries.

Diagnosis and Correction Are Contextual

Assessing student needs, interests, and abilities must be done in context. Testing vocabulary or phonic analysis from word lists or flash cards or other activities requiring the student to deal with individual words, letters, or combinations should be avoided. For without context there is little or no meaning, and without meaning there is no reading or communicating. Many poor readers of all ages have great difficulty reading words from word lists or flash cards, yet the same words embedded in some interesting and meaningful context are read and understood.

If your diagnosis is noncontextual then your interpretation of the results will not only be inaccurate, but they might lead you to believe the student has problems he does not have when measured in a contextual and more natural fashion. This could be an instance of the diagnostician becoming part of the problem rather than of the solution.

The corrective work you will plan on the basis of your diagnosis must also be contextual, to be in accord with the way we acquire and use our language normally. If you plan fragmented correction with the use of workbooks and dittoed sheets, and you use unrelated games and the like, you will not only bore many of your students, but you will be misleading yourself and the student. Most of us are interested in that which makes sense to us since that can have meaning. We easily lose interest and energy in those activities that are unrelated and seem to be busy work with no clear purpose. One needs only to look over the students in any public school Title I (or similar) program to discover that many of the students are recidivists who linger in these programs year after year with little or no progress. And many of these programs use noncontextual diagnostic measures like those to be discussed later in the chapter in our section on testing, and they are usually rich in workbooks and other such isolated activities. Obviously such an approach does not serve the purposes of a large number of these needy students. This book is devoted to some alternatives to such testing and teaching.

Diagnosis by Analogy

Avoid as much as possible diagnosing by analogy or any analogous reasoning that draws such conclusions as, "Doing task A means the student can do (or not do) task B," as in so many reading readiness activities in which children are taught how to identify and discriminate among various geometric shapes: squares, diamonds, rectangles, circles, etc. It is believed by many that if the child can discriminate accurately among these various shapes, i.e., see how they are alike and how they are different, then he will be able to read better. Here is why they think this: Reading requires the ability to identify and discriminate words; words are composed of letters; letters are *shapes*; therefore by analogy, if a child can discriminate and identify various *shapes* (of any kind) then it is much more likely that the child will be able to discriminate printed letters (*shapes*) in words and sentences.

This is a common fallacy and very misleading. Why? Think of it: to discriminate geometric shapes out of context and without any special emotional, affective connection cannot be compared with the discrimination of letters, none of which is a diamond shape or a rectangle, for example, and which are always related to other words and ideas, thoughts, and feelings. They have meaning and evoke emotional as well as cognitive responses. Most children do not respond to geometric forms and shapes in the same way they do to language, orally or in writing. Different mystiques and different psychologies operate in dealing with geometric shapes and with meaningful words. To deny this is to deny all meaning and the essence of language. Research shows that preschool and kindergarten children whose reading readiness programs involve (as most of them do) a fair amount of work in discriminating among various geometric shapes as preparation for learning how to read the shapes called words, do not read better or visually discriminate among letter shapes any better than children whose reading instruction excluded these activities.

The same principle holds for those code emphasis programs which stress phonics instruction almost to the exclusion of the other growth areas, on the analogous assumption that reading requires analyzing words, and words are composed of letters, and letters have spoken equivalents, therefore if the child learns to sound out words letter by letter he will be able to say words hence, he will read. Even when children have scored higher on word recognition tests there is doubt as to whether the heavy phonics emphasis in the classroom was the only or even the major reason for that success.

Analogous reasoning would conclude that heavy doses of phonics produce better readers insofar as their word recognition skill is concerned. What is left out of this, and many other analogies, is the rest of the child's personality: his or her attitudes, feelings, beliefs, knowledge, skills, and experience, the specific time and place and the person in the given situation. If we are diagnosing whole persons, then we must assess the whole person, not just specific tasks, behaviors, and reactions. Reading does require knowledge of shapes, forms, and sounds and it does require some knowledge of general rules and principles, but it requires much more, so that knowing any one or any group of things is no guarantee the student will know others like it. The IDA reduces the temptation to diagnose by analogy, whereas standardized and criterion-referenced tests tend to encourage it since they provide only minimal, noncontextual samples of performance from which we must generalize.

We allow the principle of the self-fulfilling prophecy to operate if we let ourselves get drawn into diagnosing by analogy and taking the part for the whole in the reading act, because then we directly influence the performance of our students negatively. Falling into this diagnostic trap is easier if you use standard or criterion-referenced tests than if you use the IDA, but even then it is possible. So be careful not to fragment the student's reading/writing/learning performance into small pieces. Neither the person, the material, nor the reading processes are really divisible into discrete little skills or acts.

Before we get into our description and discussion of particular tests, it may be worth noting this good summary quote from Harris and Sipay (1975, p. 132): ". . . the heart of diagnosis is not testing. It is, rather the intelligent interpretation of the facts by a person who has both the theoretical knowledge and the practical experience to know what questions to ask . . . to interpret the meaning of the findings correctly, and to comprehend the inter-relationships of these facts and meanings." I could not agree more with these remarks, even though my approach to both diagnosis and correction is quite different from theirs. These authors and almost all others would agree with the statements above, but they all still depend very heavily on standardized tests for their diagnostic data, and they all seem to be willing to interpret these testing data rather literally.

TESTS AND TESTING

We have already alluded to the three basic types of tests normally used in diagnosing reading and language problems: *standardized*, *criterion-referenced*, and *Individual Diagnostic Analyses*.* Each type of test will be discussed in terms of its definition, purposes, structure, advantages, and disadvantages. Examples will be offered, analyzed, and critiqued, so that you may select one or more of these instruments to fit your classroom or clinical needs. Relating this information on the tests with what has already been said about the wholeness of the student, learning and the processes of reading, and the summary of general diagnostic principles, should provide you with the most practical and valid assessment of each student.

The critical question of how much testing and of what type is enough can be answered only when you have decided what your purposes and objectives are and how they fit into the curricular plan of your school or grade. Obviously we all want our students, of any age, to achieve mastery of essential skills in reading and to be able to apply those to any kind of content they may encounter. In diagnosis we try to discover what students need in terms of skills in word recognition, meanings, and study skills and how we can effectively use what they already have in their experience with the world and with the language. How best to do that is dependent upon the choices you make in the area of testing and interpreting the data from such testing. All testing, whether aptitude, achievement, intelligence, or psychological, omits certain behaviors and skills.

Standardized Tests: Definition and Description

Such tests as the *California Reading Test*, the *Metropolitan Achievement Test*, the *Iowa Silent Reading Tests*, the *Stanford Diagnostic Tests* and the *Spache Diagnostic Scales* are standardized tests since they all have national norms, are timed, and are group tests typically machine-scored, providing grade placements and percentiles. All standardized tests in reading are *norm-referenced*, which means that norms or standards of performance have been established by the authors after massive national testing of students of all ages and socioeconomic backgrounds, from all over the country—rural and urban, small and large villages, cities, towns. On the basis of this testing of thousands of students, who presumably represent the total population of the country, norms are established and used to gauge any student's position or rank nationally.

---

* Individual Diagnostic Analysis (IDA) is a form of IRI (Individual Reading Inventory) of which there are a few available. IRI is a generic term for a nonstandardized, noncriterion-referenced measure of actual reading performance. The IDA is a modification of typical IRIs and is more extensive in its survey of skills, knowledge, and interests. Published IRIs include Silvaroli (1965), McCarthy (1976) Ekwall (1979), and others.

Typically, standardized tests in reading consist of several subtests such as vocabulary, comprehension (including interpretation), study skills, phonic and structural analysis, and at the lowest levels, items in readiness. The authors of the test select a limited number of test items to measure competence in each subtest, using their norms to determine the level of achievement as compared with their national sample of students in the same grade who took the test. A certain number right on a given subtest produces a grade placement score, 3.2 or 4.6 for example, and can be used to group students with similar levels of achievement.

The standardized tests come with directions for administration and scoring, so that they can be uniformly administered and scored, and hence are considered scientific and objective. Additionally, these tests are considered reliable and valid statistically. A reliable test is one that measures the same skills and knowledge each time used and a valid test is one that measures what it sets out to measure.

Purpose and objectives

Standardized tests claim to make it possible for a school or a group of schools to compare and contrast the achievement of their own students with the national norms. This is a way of assessing the curriculum of a school, student progress, and even teacher performance. One school can assess its own performance with pre- and post-testing data and that school can compare itself with the performance of other schools in its area or with schools across the country.

Grade placement scores and percentiles are useful data for such comparisons and contrasts in school and student/teacher performance. This seems to be efficient especially when these tests can be given to large groups of students at one time and can be machine scored. Using these tests to group and assess student progress is another major purpose of these instruments. Presumably the data from these tests can assist teachers and administrators in selecting the methods and instructional materials appropriate to the students in their school.

Another key objective of standardized tests has already been mentioned when we spoke of their objectivity and scientific basis which makes them both reliable and valid measures of student performance and progress.

Advantages of standardized tests

Items under purposes and objectives above are considered advantageous to a teacher and school system. Objective measures of progress, the ability to compare and contrast students with others who are said to be similar to them, the ability to group students according to achievement, administrative convenience, ease of administration to large groups at one time, and rapid scoring all are offered as advantages of these instruments. Educators are provided with a standard or norm against which to measure what is being taught and what is being learned by the students in a school system, and nationally. Subjectivity is removed and its concomitant weaknesses of teacher bias, limited sampling of knowledge and skills, and inconsistency. Uniformity is a positive result for the test makers. In addition, one can use the results of the standardized testing to decide who might require further assessment.

Disadvantages of standardized tests

Many of the stated advantages of standardized tests can be just as easily seen as disadvantages. For example, Spache (1976, pp. 254-255) remarks on establishing norms: "The collection of scores becomes known as a national norm, but because of its breadth and diversity, actually does not resemble any particular group of students to whom the test is subsequently administered . . . Hence each class or each pupil is often being compared with a standard derived from pupils *unlike* themselves."

Not only is this correct, but the age of the norms is also critical in light of the mobility of the American population, and influxes of immigrants, (Puerto Ricans, Haitians, and Vietnamese for example) significantly alter the population. How can those culturally different persons be compared intelligently with second, third, and fourth generation Americans whose first language is English and whose cultural backgrounds are so vastly different?

Furthermore, standardized test results offer general comparisons of any group of students with others in the norm population. We cannot predict with any certainty what skills or knowledge a given student must have to qualify for a particular type of instruction. The grade placement scores of 2.7, 3.6, or 4.8 tell us only how many right and wrong items a student earned on a particular subtest compared with others. These scores do *not* tell us how the student read nor why he made an error or marked the correct response; we only know that he had six correct out of fourteen items and that is equal to a certain grade placement score. The processes used by the student are lost in these numbers. Also the difference between one grade placement score and another, say 4.6 and 5.0, could be the result of one item correct. This is hardly a *representative* sampling of the total reading act.

Unless teachers perform an item analysis of these tests, they do not have such important information as how the student thought and why he missed any item. Most teachers do not have the time to do such careful item by item analysis of each test for each student. If they did the instrument would be more worthwhile diagnostically, but would reduce the efficiency of mass testing and machine scoring.

Additionally, most standardized tests measure the reading act in pieces. A limited number of skills is measured by a limited number of items, which may or may not be the most representative of the skills and knowledge needed by particular students. Furthermore, many of the skills are

measured in isolation such as most vocabulary and word recognition subtests. We need to know this and its effect when we interpret the results.
How much reading of word lists, isolated phrases, and phonic elements
do most students do in the normal course of their learning? Almost none.
Can we be sure then, that a student who can score well on a subtest that
measures vocabulary in isolation will have a large and varied vocabulary
he will use correctly in normal communication? Isolating words, letters,
and sentences produces the same distortions that teaching language in
isolation does.

All standardized testing is a sampling of the student's performance
on a given day with selected items measuring particular skills so that we
must be extremely careful not to take the results as the whole of the
student's performance, but a part of the whole.

Other concerns about a standardized testing include the actual reading levels of students in a given class. If some of the students in a fourth
grade class read below or above the fourth grade level, doesn't that affect
the quality of their performance? Surely if a fourth grade student is reading at second grade level he will have serious difficulty reading the test
items on a fourth grade test. Is the test written at a second grade level or
a fourth grade level? If you do not know the actual reading skills and
levels of your students is it not a mistake to give them all the same standard test written at the same level? Do all fourth grade children read at
fourth grade level? If they don't, *and they certainly do not*, how can you
attribute any accuracy to the test which may require third or fourth
grade reading level? And what are you measuring really, particularly for
the 20-25% of disabled readers?

Wilson (1972, p. 87) adds to Spache's (1976) and Ekwall's (1976)
criticism of standardized tests: "Standardized test scores are nearly useless for classroom diagnosis . . . that they are administered to groups necessitates multiple choice answers and encourages guessing . . . the tests'
standardizing procedures are subject to error, a fact which causes considerable concern about their reliability . . . their ability to match the child
with a given reading level is constantly under question."

My own practice has been to avoid standardized testing in reading as
much as possible, using it only in unusual cases to see if its results would
in any way clarify or amplify results from the IDA. Simply, the standardized tests now available do not seem to be able to provide us with practical and dependable information on how students read, and why they
make certain errors, or how students blend their life and language experience with their education to perform the complex act of reading. Too
much has to be inferred from standard testing about the student's skills
and knowledge in comparison with an incredibly diverse population. The
test is unnatural and noncontextual and that definitely does modify the
performance and what we can take it to mean. Why not be more direct in
your probing and use instruments which will afford a much more natural

context for the reading act? The results will certainly be more accurate insofar as how the student reads, where his weaknesses and strengths are in each growth area, and what we can use in his background to begin the corrective process.

Obviously there is widespread concern and even doubt about the value of standardized testing, yet it goes on everywhere, even by the authors who have decried them. This is certainly confusing to practitioners in classroom and clinic. If the tests have more disadvantages than advantages, and if some of the disadvantages are so serious in nature as to question their reliability and validity, why not use other diagnostic tools? Some authors recommend criterion-referenced tests or IDA's to complement standardized testing, but that logic really escapes me. If standardized tests are so limitedly useful why mix its unclear results with those of other instruments which produce different information? How can we blend the results of standardized tests with those obtained from the other types of testing? Are they comparable? How?

Criterion-Referenced Tests

Definition and description

These tests purport to measure mastery of specific reading skills according to a criterion or standard of approximately 80-90% correct for each specific skill. The skills are usually listed in a very detailed fashion under such headings as readiness, phonic analysis, structural analysis, comprehension, study skills, and reference skills. Under each heading are dozens of specific skills that will be tested and evaluated according to the criteria established for a particular test. The criterion-referenced concept merely means that each student is compared only with himself, not with others in the class, school, region, state, or nation. It also means that grade placement scores, percentiles, or other statistically derived data do not apply. What is measured are which skills in each growth area of reading the student knows and which he does not know.

Purpose and objectives of criterion-referenced tests

The major purpose and outstanding objective of these tests is to assess skills achievement in behaviorial terms in order to facilitate individualizing instruction. Another objective of the criterion-referenced test is to specifically identify skills, strengths, and weaknesses without regard to grade placements. The focus is on the individual student's knowledge and application of skills as they have been defined by the test makers. For more information on these tests, their descriptions and limitations, read Thompson and Dziuben (1973, pp. 292-294).

Advantages of criterion-referenced tests

The tests can be administered to an individual or a group and can be machine scored in some instances. It is helpful for teachers or clinicians to know which skills in each growth area students seem to know and which they do not know for individual or group instruction and to guide the selection of materials to meet individual needs. Avoiding invidious comparisons with large populations as in standardized, norm-referenced tests is a definite advantage. Monitoring student progress is somewhat easier with criterion-referenced test data since specific skills have been assessed in terms of performance at the outset. That is, if a student had difficulty and fell below the accepted criterion for coping with initial consonant blends, or picking out main ideas and details, or using context, it is fairly simple to note whether he can do these things as you progress through the materials and activities designed to overcome weaknesses.

Disadvantages of criterion-referenced tests

The small sampling of reading skills items is seriously disadvantageous. The test may have four main idea and detail items. Can we say on the basis of a student's getting three of them correct that he does not know the principle of main ideas and details? Could we say the opposite on this basis? Hardly. Criterion-referenced tests apparently share the same sampling problem that standardized tests have. How many items do we need to determine accurately if a child knows consonant digraphs, prefixes, short vowel sounds, summarizing? Certainly we need more than three, four, or five items to do this. Also, the fact is that the items measuring these specific skills are typically isolated and unnatural, much as they are in standardized tests. Connected text is available only for certain study skills items and for comprehension. Thus the related problem arises of how generalizable and how transferable are the skills measured this way. Knowing any skills in three, four, or even eight different minimal contexts does not assure us that the student can apply these skills in contexts normally encountered in the school curriculum. In short, this is also a fragmented way to measure reading skills ability. When a student makes an error on any part of this test, we still do not know *why* he made the mistake, or *how* he went about trying to respond to the item. We just know he got it right or wrong in accord with the criterion for each skill.

Another disadvantage is that the usual list of almost one hundred separate skills which emerges from criterion-referenced testing is too specific and includes skills and parts of skills that may or may not be generalizable. It is a bit unwieldy to try to keep up with each skill on the list, measuring as you go the student's mastery of it. In addition, some criterion-referenced tests contain instructional programs designed to overcome the skills weaknesses for which the teacher has a key indicating specific material and activities the student should work on. This very much limits the teaching of reading in a wholistic, integrated fashion, and emphasizes parts and pieces. Learning to read does not lend itself very well to such specificity and limitation. Skills overlap and relate to each other in numerous ways not accessible to this kind of diagnostic or corrective approach. The interrelationships of skills areas, of information, and concepts is lost and with it goes a good deal of very valuable diagnostic information.

Individual Diagnostic Analysis (IDA)

Description and definition

The IDA is an individually administered performance assessment of reading and language skills and knowledge. It differs from the IRIs available in that it derives much more information on each student and does so much more contextually and naturally. If you look at the IRIs mentioned earlier, Silvaroli (1969) and McCarthy (1976), you will notice that, like the Gray Oral, they function much more like a criterion-referenced instrument than what is described here.

The IDA measures skills performance in reading and writing in context and without time or peer pressures. It uses a modified version of a criterion-referenced standard for assessing success or failure in the process of reading, and it permits extensive questioning and follow-up questioning to uncover the dynamics of reading for a particular student. The material read is selected for each student so that it is more pertinent and interesting. If conducted like an interview, background information and interests as well as reading skill and knowledge can be gathered by the teacher or clinician.

Briefly, the IDA consists of graded materials with comprehension and interpretation, vocabulary, and concept questions, measured by a modification of the Betts (1946) criteria for establishing the instructional, independent, and frustration levels. The next chapter will discuss the administration and interpretation of IDAs in detail.

Purpose and objectives of the IDA

Simply put, the purpose and objectives of the IDA are to assess reading competencies in a natural contextual reading situation. It is designed to identify strengths and weaknesses in each growth area. The IDA enables the teacher or clinician to quickly measure the student's reading performance cognitively and affectively. It assists the teacher/clinician to establish an instructional level for each student and to group students according to various identified needs. It is also designed to assist the teacher/clinician to select the most appropriate methods and materials for instruction based on the skills data, background data, and interests of the students in the class or group.

Advantages of the IDA

The IDA provides the teacher/clinician with a much more complete profile of each student, encompassing more of the students reading/writing behavior. No guessing is necessary to interpret the performance data collected from a well administered IDA. The comparisons are essentially of one student with himself, but it can also be used to compare all of the students in a class or among classes.

The sampling of reading material in an IDA is wider and more realistic than the common sampling of testing materials in the standardized or criterion-referenced tests. Application of skills and knowledge is more easily noted in the IDA than in either of the other tests we have discussed, because the administrator can question the student until it is obvious what the student knows or does not know and how the student went about decoding words or deriving meaning from connected text.

In short then, the IDA provides more information, faster and more realistically, than either of the other types of tests we normally use in diagnosing reading and language performance.

Disadvantages of the IDA

Some critics say that the IRI or the IDA lacks uniform standards for scoring and is therefore subject to much more of the teacher/clinician's biases and subjectivity. This leads to a lack of compatibility among administrators of IDAs and hence makes it more difficult to evaluate the evaluators.

Another disadvantage critics would point out is that the IDA takes more time than either standardized or criterion-referenced tests since each IDA can take 25 to 40 minutes to administer and even more in particular cases. They would also add that since there are no norms it is almost impossible to measure progress precisely. The IDA strikes many as just too subjective to serve the needs of a school or school system.

SUMMARY OF TESTS AND TESTING

We have discussed the three most common types of diagnostic testing in reading: standardized, criterion-referenced, and Individual Diagnostic Analyses (IDA). The tests have been described and defined in terms of their purposes and objectives, and their advantages and disadvantages. My own preference is for the IDA since I take it to be *a process of interactive assessment of reading and language knowledge and skills in context*, rather than a collection of measures of specific skills, out of context. The IDA is the most comprehensive diagnostic process I know.

For a thorough discussion of standardized tests read O.K. Buros (1976), Spache (1976), and Lapp and Flood (1978).

Before we leave the topic of standardized and other testing, it may prove helpful to analyze and critique a recent standardized reading test in some detail. Since standardized tests are so commonly used in schools and other educational programs for diagnostic purposes it is important that we as teachers/clinicians fully appreciate their weaknesses and strengths, and since an entire chapter is devoted to administering and interpreting the IDA, such a detailed analysis of a standardized test will provide some balance.

THE METROPOLITAN ACHIEVEMENT TESTS—READING INSTRUCTIONAL TESTS 1978

Overview

The Psychological Corporation, publisher of the Metropolitan Achievement Tests—Reading Instructional Tests, put out a publicity brochure for the 1978 test from which I shall be quoting (MAT—Publication Announcement). The subtitle of the 1978 MAT (Metropolitan Achievement Tests—Reading Instructional Tests) is "An integrated dual-component system of norm-referenced and criterion referenced tests." The norm-referenced component meets the administrator's need for "summary information about pupils, classes, grades, buildings and system and the criterion-referenced component is specifically designed to meet the needs of classroom teachers and curriculum planners for in-depth, objective based analysis in these crucial domains. This component is also useful for administrative decision making." You can use either component or both; if you do the latter it will constitute a comprehensive system. But do administrators, teachers, and specialists have the same objectives for students? Not always.

The publicity brochure goes on to list several evaluation needs this new test meets, including: "To evaluate knowledge of specific curriculum objectives; pinpoint individual student's strengths and weaknesses; and provide diagnostic and prescriptive information to develop and maintain a program of individualized instruction."

The other needs include use for Title I, reporting to parents and school boards, and evaluating curricular programs. One of the senior authors, George A. Prescott, is quoted as saying: "Educators have traditionally thought of achievement tests simply as assessment batteries. Until now, that's all they've been. We've broadened the scope of thinking in this area with a unique systems approach to testing . . . one that merges measurement with diagnosis, so that assessing performance isn't an end, but a beginning."

This all sounds fine. I especially like the senior author's distinctions between measurement, assessment, and diagnosis, and his last remark about assessment being a beginning. Most of the remarks mentioned in this brochure really emphasize the characteristics of criterion-referenced testing, rather than the typical traits of norm-referenced testing. All well and good, if indeed the tests actually measure what they say they will, and if they measure these skills and curricular objectives *representatively* and *contextually*.

MAT (1978) measures achievement in reading, mathematics, language, science, and social studies, very much like the California Achievement Tests, and others. We shall look at the reading test only. The tests in the battery are for Kindergarten through 12.9, divided this way: Pre-primer—K.O–K.5; Primer—K.5–1.4; Primary 1—1.5–2.4; Primary—2-2.5–3.4; Elementary—3.5–4.9; Intermediate—5.0–6.9; and Advanced 1 and 2 covering 7.0–12.9.

The reading test is allotted 50 minutes for sixty items on the preprimer level; 50 minutes for thirty-seven items on the primer level; 45 minutes for fifty-five items on the primary 1 level; 40 minutes for fifty-five items on the primary 2 level; and 40 minutes for sixty items on the elementary level, etc. I am not sure how it was decided to alter the number of items from a high of sixty to a low of thirty-seven, and to alter the timing. Presumably this was determined in their massive experimentation in the field with the test and its items.

The authors claim that 250,000 children participated in the prestandardization process, and 500,000 students participated in the standardization of the tests. These figures represent a fine statistical sampling, if usual procedures were followed for determining the representativeness in terms of age, region, sex, intelligence, socioeconomic factors, ethnicity, etc. In addition to these students, ". . . over 10,000 teachers judged the importance of these objectives in terms of their relevance to local instructional programs. A panel of minority educators . . . reviewed every item for ethnic and cultural bias, and each tryout item was edited to eliminate sex-role stereotyping." The Metropolitan Achievement Test-Reading Instructional Tests (1978) and the MAT of 1970 both claim to have offered Fall and Spring norms while others offer only Fall or Spring. Presumably this would make the comparisons more realistic, and it probably does.

The claims by the test makers certainly are impressive and seem convincing, but in no test can we settle only for the author's notions of what their instrument will do. Overrating the usefulness of tests is mentioned by most leading authorities in reading as a potential weakness. In this new test the authors offer group data of great validity due to its very large sample of the population.

Now we need to look at some of the items on the tests and subtests and try to determine if they measure what they are supposed to measure, and if they do so effectively. We need to know if these tests can play a significant part in our diagnosis by providing the kind of specific information we need in order to assess a student's strengths and weaknesses, understanding, concepts, and skills in each growth area. In short, can we come away from these tests or any tests with information we can use to group, select instructional methods and materials appropriate to this whole child, stimulate the student's interest, and build both skills and concepts? If it can do these jobs, we have a fine instrument; if not, we just have another test.

Below are some sample items form the primer (k.5-1.4) level of the MAT (1978) Reading Instructional Tests, and following those are some samples from the intermediate (3.5-4.9) levels to get a fairly broad sampling of the tests.

MAT—Reading Instructional Test Primer Level

Directions for any test, especially standardized tests, are extremely important since a misunderstanding of pronunciation and vocabulary could cause the child to earn a lower score than his skills and knowledge justify. The directions for the first subtest on Visual Discrimination are rather difficult for children of this age. The children are asked to notice the wheel on the cover of the test booklet, which has several drawn animals. One animal is in a white background while the others are in a green background. The animal could be a bear or panda. The directions for the teacher indicate they want the children to call it a panda. The directions say, "Scientists cannot decide if the panda is really a bear or not. Pandas are shy, chubby animals that eat only plants. They live in the mountains of China, a country on the other side of the world from us." (MAT, Teacher's Directions, p. 5.) For middle class children in urban or suburban settings with educated parents this is not too bad; for urban or rural children with less educated parents and less access to zoos, some of the information here is more complicated than the test itself. Too many concepts are included in this direction, e.g., scientists, whether it is a bear or not, China, other side of the world. These concepts are not usually in the repertoire of most children this age. Many children this age do not always know the difference between a city, state, or country. China could be Mars, but even less familiar. I think this is a cumbersome and advanced way to explain that the children should look for the panda in the test booklet. It appears four times and never for any real purpose except to separate one subtest from another. It seems an unnecessary distraction and could easily confuse less able students, if not the others.

Subtest—visual discrimination

The first subtest is on visual discrimination. (see Exhibit 2-1.) At the top of the page are two pandas who look very much like bears with black eyes. The visual discrimination items beginning with #13 on page 3 include words like DOGS, deed, goose, FOOD, and some nonsense material like WAW, ottop, and PIDEF, mixing upper and lower case letters. The children have to look at the stimulus word and then find the same form among four other choices. It seems to measure visual discrimination, although I cannot accept the need for nonsense words or combinations. The child who is uncertain or weak and who can correctly identify the nonsense forms clearly cannot know what it means and that can be troubling. There is no point in such activity or measurement. How often do we read or hear nonsense words or forms?

DOGS	DOCS	DOGZ	DOGS	CODS
O	O	O	O	O
deed	deed	deeg	deeb	beed
O	O	O	O	O

Exhibit 2-1.   Visual discrimination. (Reproduced from the Metropolitan Achievement Tests, Reading Instructional Tests, Primer (From JI), Visual Discrimination subtest, by permission. Copyright © 1978 by Harcourt Brace Jovanovich, Inc. All rights reserved.)

Subtest—letter recognition

The next subtest is called letter recognition and contains twenty-six items. (See Exhibit 2-2.) Again there is a mix of upper and lower case letters in isolation. It may be misleading, but it does measure awareness of similar and different letter forms. The directions in the manual call for the teacher to have the children notice the row of letters, each one identified by a drawn picture (as in the 1970 version) some of which are very clear and others of which are not quite so easy to identify, like the one with bottles containing model ships in them. The teacher tells the children to mark the letter in each row, both capitals and lower case. This is letter recognition in isolation.

q	d	O	G
O	O	O	O

Exhibit 2-2.   Letter recognition. (Reproduced from the Metropolitan Achievement Tests, Reading Instructional Tests, Primer (Form JI), Letter Recognition subtest, by permission. Copyright © 1978 by Harcourt Brace Jovanovich, Inc. All rights reserved.)

Subtest—auditory discrimination

In this subtest the teacher is required to speak a word and ask the children to mark under the picture of it. (See Exhibit 2-3.) Most pictures are easily recognized; some are quite unclear and even out of the experience of many children. Also the directions tell the children to mark under the picture which the word describes, even if the word the teacher says has more than one sound, e.g., *dr*ess, *fl*ag. This could be confusing since single consonants are mixed with consonant blends or digraphs. Final sounds are being measured along with initial sounds, so let's see how good the samples are of these phonic elements included in this subtest. Starting with *l* in auditory discrimination we have single consonants, initial position: *l*, *w*, *m*, *t*, *c* (come), *r*, *d*; consonant combinations; *sh*, *st*, *tr*, *pl*; ending sounds: *t*, *g*, (frog), *b*, *p*, *s*. The next one is most confusing. They say find the picture which has the word that sounds like *more* at the end. The pictures are a *star*, *shirt*, *glass*. The sound of *star* and *more* are similar but not the same; they are obviously isolating the *urr* sound, whatever that is. This is very poor. The elements they are measuring at the ends of words include *x* as in *ax*, *ike* as in *like*, *ird* as in *bird*, *ch* in *lunch*, *th* in *tooth*, *t* as in *tent*. A fair sampling but not necessarily the most representative of the children's speaking vocabulary or of their reading.

All of these subtests do measure specific aspects of word recognition, but the conclusions one could draw from certain errors are at best doubtful since none of the words is in context. It is quite easy for youngsters to confuse sounds and symbols under time pressure and when the cues are not as clear as they might be if they had been contextualized.

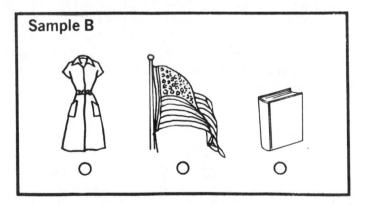

Exhibit 2-3.   Auditory discrimination. (Reproduced from the Metropolitan Achievement Tests, Reading Instructional Tests, Primer (Form JI), Auditory Discrimination subtest, by permission. Copyright © 1978 by Harcourt Brace Jovanovich, Inc. All rights reserved.)

Subtest—sight vocabulary

The next subtest on sight vocabulary contains thirty items. All of these are done in isolation as well. The sample of words included is not especially generative in that they are not common and easily related to other words in the child's immediate environment. Words such as *bump*, *oven*, *chicken*, *bark*, *paint*, and *build* are among the choices.

Subtest—phoneme/grapheme: consonants

In this subtest we get into trouble isolating sound equivalents. In the sample item (see Exhibit 2-4) a picture of a windup toy soldier is found next to three words with a little circle in front of each one. The middle word, *to*, is blacked in because it "begins with the same sound as toy." First, the picture is of a soldier and could be mistaken for it; more seriously and more likely, it encourages the children to exaggerate individual letter sounds. In this subtest, as in the 1970 version, there are several confusing picture cues such as a picture of a black and white bird with the choices *help*, *ran*, and *like*. The correct response is *ran* because it begins with the same sound as *robin*. That's confusing and misleading. If the child gets it wrong what do you conclude? Poor picture interpretation? Poor phonic skill with initial consonants? Another confusing item is a picture of a trumpet with the choices *will*, *him*, and *and*. *Him* is desired because the instrument is a *horn* and thus begins with the same sound as *him*. Then a picture of a *cat* with the choices *ready*, *keep*, and *take*. *Keep* is desired but is not spelled as is *cat* and might create confusion. All of these and other such examples could be avoided if more context was involved.

9

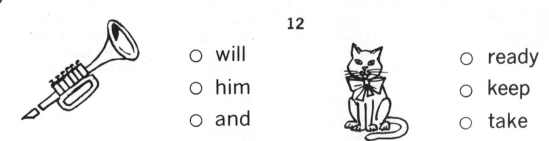

12

○ will   ○ ready

○ him   ○ keep

○ and   ○ take

Exhibit 2-4. Phoneme/grapheme: consonants. (Reproduced from the Metropolitan Achievement Tests, Reading Instructional Tests, Primer (Form JI), Phoneme/Grapheme: Consonants subtest, by permission. Copyright © 1978 by Harcourt Brace Jovanovich, Inc. All rights reserved.)

Subtest—reading comprehension: words

In the next subtest we find a picture drawn again and three words (see Exhibit 2-5). The directions for the first item say "These children are going to make some pictures. Mark the space next to the word that tells what they will do . . ." The words are *of*, *paint*, and *but*. Paint is supposed to be the correct choice. What does an error mean? Is it missing the details of a picture and understanding what is happening? Is it that the child notices three children in the picture with brushes, paper, cans, and a jar and guesses they may be drawing or painting, but does not recognize the word paint? Is it sight words we are measuring, visual discrimination, vocabulary?

1

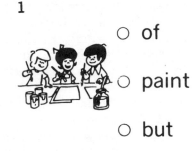
○ of

○ paint

○ but

Exhibit 2-5. Reading comprehension: words. (Reproduced from the Metropolitan Achievement Tests, Reading Instructional Tests, Primer (Form JI), Reading Comprehension: Words subtest, by permission. Copyright © 1978 by Harcourt Brace Jovanovich, Inc. All rights reserved.)

Subtest—reading comprehension: rebus

The next subtest (Exhibit 2-6) has some of the same problems of picture identification. I don't know why real pictures are not used for such items to eliminate or at least reduce the ambiguity of what is represented. Picture interpretation does measure something if the picture or sequence of pictures is very clear as in the WISC or WAIS picture arrangement subtest. But its relationship to reading performance is not entirely clear. Very young children, especially boys at this age, do not always have such mature perception. What then are you measuring? Comprehension of what? Visual identification, perception? And if so, how is that related to reading words in connected text? What can you safely predict from success or failure in such measures? Not much.

Subtest—reading comprehension: sentences

In the next subtest (see Exhibit 2-7) we find a picture and three short sentences to the right of it, and this does require reading. For example, item 18 has a picture of a girl in a boat on some water. The sentence choices are "*She rides in the boat, She rides in the car, She sits in the train*". Is this sentence comprehension or picture interpretation and matching that visually with the correct words in the correct sentence?

The dog is in the
little  .

○   ○   ○

She can see the man
painting the  .

○   ○   ○

Exhibit 2-6. Reading comprehension: rebus. (Reproduced from the Metropolitan Achievement Tests, Reading Instructional Tests, Primer (Form JI), Reading Comprehension: Rebus subtest, by permission. Copyright © 1978 by Harcourt Brace Jovanovich, Inc. All rights reserved.)

○ They want something good to eat.

○ They are painting the car yellow.

○ This goat is eating something too.

Exhibit 2-7. Reading comprehension: sentences. (Reproduced from the Metropolitan Achievement Tests, Reading Instructional Tests, Primer (Form JI), Reading Comprehension: Sentences subtest, by permission. Copyright © 1978 by Harcourt Brace Jovanovich, Inc. All rights reserved.)

Subtest—reading comprehension: stories

The last subtest contains printed stories with recall questions following. The classic problem of all standardized tests occurs when they purport to measure recall or comprehension, but the student often *re-reads* the story in order to answer the questions. That is not the same as recall.

This is not a bad test, but not much different from the 1970 version of the MAT test. It suffers from most of the same problems: some of the picture clues are badly drawn and often ambiguous; directions on some items are unclear; all of the measures are isolated; and what goes for comprehension, recall, and understanding is *re-reading*. Furthermore, all of these tests do not provide enough information to tell you as a diagnostician what the errors mean, since the test is so *un*contextual, and so unlike *reading connected test*.

MAT—Reading Instructional Test Intermediate Level

The intermediate tests in reading include Phoneme/Grapheme: Consonants; Phoneme/Grapheme: Vowels; Vocabulary in Context; Word Part Clues; Rate of Comprehension; Skimming and Scanning; and Reading Comprehension. A total of 134 minutes is required to complete the subtests according to their schedule, plus 50 minutes for distribution and collection of materials. The authors propose, as they did for the other test levels, several sittings for the test so that for the first subtest here 20 minutes of testing occur, with the longest single stretch being 40 minutes of testing and 10 minutes of distributing and collecting materials. It is not indicated whether each sitting ought to be done on different days or whether the sittings can occur within a day or two.

My guess is that more sittings would be required for the younger students and at least two, probably three, sittings for this intermediate level. That does reduce the efficiency of administration somewhat.

As in the Primary form discussed above, I find the directions fairly clear, but occasionally cumbersome and distracting. For example, at the outset of this intermediate test the children are asked to look at the cover of the test booklet and to note the wheel with the animals on it. Once again one animal is in a white background and the others in a colored background, in this case blue. The description (MAT—Reading, Intermediate, Teacher's Directions, p. 6) the teacher is supposed to give: "All of these animals are members of endangered species. Your grade is represented here by the tiger. Tigers, one of the largest members of the cat family, were originally found in almost all parts of Asia, from jungle areas to Siberia, but there are very few left in the world today." This is unnecessarily complicated in both vocabulary and sentence structure, and in content as well. There is no relationship between the information and concepts and anything on the test. Perhaps the authors thought such remarks would distract the children with interesting information so that they would not notice that they were being tested. I think it is unnecessary and only complicates the issue; it is almost indulgent on the part of the authors to do this. And as in the case of the Primary level test, the animal appears to separate the sections of the test. Spacing would have served the same purpose. Pictures of animals do not divert the children's attention from the pressure and threat of the test.

Subtest—phoneme/grapheme: consonants and vowels

Again we see that in measuring specific skills such as phoneme/grapheme: consonants and vowels the emphasis is on isolating a specific sound in the beginning of a sample of words, or at the end of a similarly small sample. Nine words are used to detect the child's knowledge of initial consonant sounds; nine for final consonant sounds, and six items purport to measure the child's knowledge of silent letters. The teacher says a word in the first two instances and the children select one of four choices (see Exhibit 2-8).

Good readers and writers will get them right and weaker readers and writers will miss many because of certain ambiguities such as tend, fake, felt. The first and last words contain consonant blends *lt* and *nd* and if the child knows this, he could become confused as to how to respond. The only way the child who does know it can get it correct is to separate each sound in an exaggerated manner. Again, these specific sounds are measured in isolation. The same process is required in doing the vowel subtest, and presents the same problems.

11. **Mark the letter for the word that ends with the same sound as** *nose . . . . nose.*

12. *Fake . . . . fake.*

13. *Yarn . . . . yarn.*

14. *Tend . . . . tend.*

15. *Felt . . . . felt.*

16. *Nick . . . . nick.*

17. *Lash . . . . lash.*

18. *Both . . . . both.*

Exhibit 2-8. Phoneme/grapheme: consonants and vowels. (Reproduced from the Metropolitan Achievement Tests, Reading Instructional Tests, Intermediate. Teacher's Directions, p. 7, by permission. Copyright © 1978 by Harcourt Brace Jovanovich, Inc. All rights reserved.)

Subtest—vocabulary in context

This subtest is a fill-in-the-blank test. Context operates minimally. Often the choices (4 for each item) contain difficult words for children in the 3.5-4.9 range, which this test (Elementary-Intermediate) is designed for. A few examples are shown in Exhibit 2-9. Choices for other items include accomplish, eventual, responsible, routinely, competition, sufficient, offensive, relatively. These are not the most common or useful words for this age group and reading level, especially when they have to be fit into a blank in a relatively short sentence. What is being measured? Ability to syllabicate, identify affixes and roots, visual discrimination, knowledge of many different words? Perhaps all of these are being measured, so what does failure mean, what does success mean? Which of these words indicates which knowledge is available to the child? Not clear, hence not very useful for diagnostic purposes, even if you were to make an item analysis when all tests are scored.

4 The _____ of the new pump kept the basement dry.

   E addition   G waterproof
   F destination   H complaint

8 The guide was chosen _____ for her ability to lead people.

   E suspiciously   G specifically
   F personality   H through

Exhibit 2-9. Vocabulary in context. (Reproduced from the Metropolitan Achievement Tests, Reading Instructional Tests, Intermediate (Form JI), Vocabulary in Context subtest, by permission. Copyright © 1978 by Harcourt Brace Jovanovich, Inc. All rights reserved.)

Subtest—word part clues

Much the same can be said of the subtest called word part clues. Here the children must fill in a blank in a sentence, but must choose from four difficult choices, as shown in Exhibit 2-10.

Sample choices from other items include apology, apologize, apologetic, apologeous; inferred, transferred, deferred, preferred; rejection, objection, dejection, projection; intracession, recession, succession, procession. I find them extremely difficult, unusual and not normally found in the vocabulary and skills knowledge of students of this age and level. Success could mean two things: the child has a very large vocabulary or he knows some roots and affixes and can figure out the choices. There are several better ways to measure those skills as you will see later in chapter 3.

1 Her _____ was needed to complete the job.

   A cooperative   C cooperatment
   B cooperate   D cooperation

Exhibit 2-10. Word part clues. (Reproduced from the Metropolitan Achievement Tests, Reading Instructional Tests, Intermediate (Form JI), Word Part Clues subtest, by permission. Copyright © 1978 by Harcourt Brace Jovanovich, Inc. All rights reserved.)

Subtest—skimming and scanning

The subtest called skimming and scanning is really a measure of the child's ability to preview. It is not a skill that is normally taught so early in the school career, since it is one of the many study skills. Furthermore, skimming and scanning is a speed reading skill which must be preceded by previewing, finding main ideas and details at least before most students (of any age and level) are ready to handle it. Why not check study skills like previewing, main ideas and details, and classification? They are more useful in most nonfictional reading, especially in the intermediate grades and above. Also the material for this subtest (on whaling) is written in small type, long sentences, and at a high reading level, at least sixth or even seventh grade level. But this test is for intermediate (elementary) students. Although the students are directed not to read it carefully most students will read some of it, since most of them do not know how to read with speed, nor do they know how to skim and scan. In fact, they do not need to know these skills until they have mastered other of the study skills. This subtest is totally inappropriate for all of these reasons. If you use this test, I would urge you to ignore this subtest. Most students below the top 5 or 10% will do poorly.

Subtest—reading comprehension

The last subtest contains eleven short selections moving from simple to quite difficult. (See Exhibit 2-11.) The problem as I have already mentioned earlier is that these measure *re-reading* more than recall or com-

Reading Comprehension

I Stories about how science might change the world of the future are called science fiction. Many of these tales are written by scientists who are making interesting guesses based on facts they already know.

We currently enjoy some useful inventions that were once only imagined by science fiction writers. Today we can watch rocket ships blast off. We delight in watching people walk in space or on the moon.

Many modern science fiction stories are about what will happen as the earth becomes more and more crowded. Will we escape to other planets or

Exhibit 2-11. Reading comprehension. (Reproduced from the Metropolitan Achievement Tests, Reading Instructional Tests, Intermediate (Form JI) Reading Comprehension Subtest, by permission. Copyright © 1978 by Harcourt Brace Jovanovich, Inc. All rights reserved.)

space platforms? Will we build enormous cities underground or perhaps even under the ocean? Nobody can be certain. Only time will tell.

1 This story says that science fiction is often written by—

A explorers   c engineers
B inventors   D scientists

2 The person who wrote this story must have read many—

E mystery stories   G science books
F science fiction stories   H poems about planets

3 Something that is true today but was only imagined thirty years ago is—

A airplanes flying across the ocean
B boats traveling under the ocean
c skyscrapers more than 80 stories high
D men walking on the moon

4 The author of this story seems to think that science fiction—

E is interesting
F is silly
G always comes true
H creates world problems

5 Science fiction describes people and things that—

A happened in the past
B are strange but true
c might happen in the future
D live only under the sea

6 In this story underground means—

E working in secret against something
F wearing away a little at a time
G on the surface of oceans
H below the surface of the earth

Exhibit 2-11 Continued

prehension. Furthermore almost all of the questions following each selection are literal recall questions. The authors include interpretation in their definition of comprehension, but there is almost no trace of such a measurement. So you get basically literal recall scores, based on some rereading of the selections by the student. The questions are weak and one dimensional. The content of the paragraphs is varied, although it is all narrative. The first three paragraphs seem fairly appropriate to children of this age, but starting with the fourth paragraph, the language and sentence structure become considerably more sophisticated. I assume the norms account for this requiring fourth graders to get only the first three or four right. But the great lack is any measure of interpretation. There are better ways to measure comprehension and interpretation and they will be explained in the section on the IDA.

SUMMARY OF THE MAT READING INSTRUCTIONAL TESTS (PRIMER AND INTERMEDIATE LEVELS)

The *MAT* was not chosen for this critique because it is especially bad or good, but because it is comparable to many other standardized tests including the *California, Stanford, Iowa,* etc. I could say many of the same things about all of them, just as other writers have. My point is that they all have serious limitations of form, time pressure, quality and uniformity of administration and scoring, content, and what is measured. The usefulness of the data for grouping children, accurately assessing strengths and weaknesses in natural reading of connected text, selecting appropriate methods and materials for instruction, further evaluation of progress, and individualizing instruction is minimal. We can get more useful and pertinent information on student performance and knowledge by other diagnostic means.

One way to use any standardized reading test is screening a large number of students quickly in order to get the lowest or highest performance. What I have done is to test say 400 students and pull out the students who score below some predetermined level, e.g., if screening sixth grade pupils, pull out all those who scored fourth grade and below. Then those persons will be given an IDA to discover what they can and cannot do in a real reading situation. With such a group, you can pull out the students who scored in the top range of the test, e.g., eighth or ninth levels. They would be screened by an IDA to verify their skills and knowledge in real reading, and then you could set up a group for the gifted or at least the best. But the remaining 70-80% of the students in between would have unclear data from the test. When you consider how long it takes to give the tests, to collect them, to send them for machine scoring, and after long delays to get the results back, it might be more efficient, or as efficient, to do IDAs on each student by each teacher. Then your results are sensible and realistic and give a good guide for grouping, planning, and teaching. Actually, most teachers could administer IDAs to their individual classes within the first week of school, which is faster than most machine-scored results come back.

REFERENCES

Harris, Albert & Sipay, Edward. *How to increase reading ability* (6th ed.). New York: David McKay, 1975.

Metropolitan Achievement Tests, Reading Instructional Tests. Copyright© 1978 by Harcourt Brace Jovanovich, Inc. All rights reserved.

Rosenthal, Robert & Jacobson, Lenore. *Pygmalion in the classroom*. New York: Holt, Rinehart & Winston, 1968.

Spache, George. *Diagnosing and correcting reading disabilities*. Boston: Allyn & Bacon, 1976.

Thompson, Richard & Dziuben, Charles. Criterion-referenced reading tests in perspective. In *The Reading Teacher*, December 1973, pp. 292-294.

Wilson, Robert. *Diagnostic and remedial reading for classroom and clinic (2nd ed.). Columbus, OH: Charles E. Merrill, 1972.*

BIBLIOGRAPHY

Betts, Emmett. *Foundations of reading instruction*. New York: American Book, 1946.

Botel, Morton. "Botel Reading Inventory." Chicago: Follette, 1962.

Buros, O. K. (Ed.). *Eighth Mental Measurements Yearbook* (Vols. I & II). Highland Park, NJ: Gryphon Press, 1978.

Buros, O. K. *Reading tests and reviews* (2nd ed.). Highland Park, NJ: Gryphon Press, 1978.

"California Reading Tests" (1970 ed.). California Test Bureau, McGraw-Hill, Del Monte Research Park, Monterey, California.

"Diagnostic Reading Scales." George Spache. Monterey, California Test Bureau, 1972.

Durrell, Donald. *Durrell analysis of reading difficulty*. New York: Harcourt, Brace & Jovanovich, 1955.

Ekwall, Eldon. *Diagnosis and remediation of the disabled reader*. Boston: Allyn & Bacon, 1976.

Ekwall, Eldon. *Ekwall reading inventory*. Boston: Allyn & Bacon, 1979.

"Gates-McKillop Diagnostic Tests." Arthur Gates & Ann McKillip. New York: Teachers College Press, 1962.

"Gilmore Oral Reading Test." John Gilmore & Eunice Gilmore. New York: Harcourt, Brace & Jovanovich, 1965.

"Gray Oral Reading Test." William Gray & Helen Robinson. Indianapolis: Bobbs-Merrill, 1967.

Harris, Albert & Sipay, Edward. *How to teach reading: a competency-based program*. New York: Longman, 1979.

"Individualized Diagnostic Reading Inventory" (rev. ed.). William McCarthy (Ed.). Cambridge, MA: Educators Publishing Service, 1976.

"Iowa Silent Reading Tests: New Edition" (rev. 1943). New York: Harcourt, Brace & World.

Lapp, Diane & Flood, James. *Teaching reading to every child*. New York: Macmillan, 1978.

Silvaroli, Nicholas. *Classroom reading inventory* (2nd ed.). Iowa: William C. Brown, Inc., 1969.

Spache, George. *Investigating the issues of reading disabilities*. Boston: Allyn & Bacon, 1976.

"Stanford Diagnostic Reading Test." Harcourt, Brace & World, 1966.

Wayne, Otto & Askov, E. Wisconsin design for reading skill development. In *Rationale and guidelines: the Wisconsin design for reading skill development*. Minneapolis: National Computer Systems, 1972.

Chapter three

INTRODUCTION AND OVERVIEW

This chapter will delve into the distinctive process called the IDA. The comparisons and contrasts in the preceding chapter highlighted the advantages of using the IDA as the major diagnostic tool in reading and language as opposed to the standardized or criterion-referenced tests. I also tried to separate the IDA from the more generic IRIs so that you could easily detect the differences between them. Since the diagnostic process is the foundation for any grouping patterns, for the selection of pertinent and appropriate methods and materials of instruction, for evaluation of progress, for functionally assessing weaknesses and strengths, and for planning instruction in an integrated and contextual fashion, it is critical that we use the most effective instrument available.

As we have noted earlier the IDA provides information about the student's background, interests, specific skill strengths and weaknesses, approach to reading and writing, concepts, experience, and feelings. The sampling of skills, vocabulary, and concepts are much more extensive and complete since they are all in connected text rather than in isolation. The personal nature of the IDA augments the diagnostician's sense of the whole student engaged in the process of reading, thinking, and feeling. Also the IDA is based much more on commonsense than either of the other types of tests since the diagnostician naturally responds to the student and his responses and reactions to the material.

When you have completed an IDA you will know a great deal about the personality of the student you have been talking and listening to for a half hour or so, and you will not get lost in a maze of numbers, such as

Adminstering and interpreting the IDA

grade placements or percentiles. Nothing will filter your impressions of the student reading. Your ability to interpret the results of the test is made easier because you can ask all the questions you may need in order to more fully understand what the student has done and why and how.

The comprehensive sampling of reading, language skills, and experience, and the individual interaction provide you with a guide to many other types of behaviorial observation not possible with any other instrument we have discussed.

Establish a Comfortable Testing Atmosphere

Before launching the student into the actual oral reading of the graded materials, try a little casual, natural conversation to reduce normal nervousness connected with any kind of reading testing. Some students dread any kind of test no matter how well disguised. Make this IDA an interview and as conversational as possible. Use your common sense, remembering that your objective is to get the *best* performance from this person. Try not to present the IDA as another test or as some special hurdle to be cleared, but rather as reading and discussing what has been read.

We do want the student's best performance because that will give us and the student the awareness of how well he can do when comfortable, so that our corrective program can start from a high point rather than a low point. Enjoy meeting a new person and collect your information with ease.

OBJECTIVES OF THE IDA

The IDA will enable you to:

1. Determine the reading level (instructional, independent, and frustration level).
2. Identify specific weaknesses and strengths in word recognition, meanings, study skills, vocabulary, and writing.
3. Observe and assess cognitive and affective behavior in a natural reading setting.
4. Uncover background information—educational, medical, family, experiential, social, etc.
5. Discover the student's interests.
6. Assess language usage and understanding aurally and orally in terms of vocabulary, sentence structure, and content.
7. Collect a writing sample for evidences of physical problems with writing and with content, form, and structure.

Experienced diagnosticians can also pick up a great deal of psychological information such as self-concept, modalities of learning, and anxieties and feelings about school, home, and friends. This far exceeds what you could derive from any standardized or criterion-referenced test.

MATERIALS FOR THE IDA

We need to have the following items to collect information about the student:

1. *Graded materials* on several levels and *several types*, e.g., social science, science, sports, literature on first, second, third, etc., levels.
2. Comprehension and interpretation questions with suggested answers and follow-up questions with answers.
3. Check sheet or report form in order to record performance.
4. Criteria by which to judge the quality of the performance in each growth area and to establish the instructional level.

This is a lot of information to gather in 25-45 minutes, but you can do it comfortably. If the first IDAs should take an hour do not worry about it; you will quickly improve and learn how to reduce the time of administration. You can adjust the IDA in several ways by adding or omitting questions, by shortening your conversational activity, and by careful selection of the content and structure of your graded materials. For example, it is often possible to just test on two graded materials if you estimate the student's level correctly at the outset and then test that level and one above it. Those two paragraphs must then be so constructed as to contain a wide variety of vocabulary and phonic and structural elements, and to come from two different content fields, for example, history, sports, or science, and a literary piece. No matter how many graded materials you may use for the IDA, be certain that they vary in content, concepts, phonic and structural elements, and vocabulary in order to have the best sampling of reading performance.

Try to select for your students materials that include content most likely to be familiar to typical students of their chronological age, type of school attended, culture, intelligence, or known or suspected physical or psychological problems. Materials for adults should certainly be of adult interest and style, not that of third grade materials designed for third grade children. Obviously your choice of these materials directly affects the interest of the reader and can alter his or her performance markedly. There is no reason why this test cannot be interesting and stimulating by presenting different levels of materials of many different contents, of both child or adult interest and style.

Where you get the graded materials does not matter as long as they meet the descriptions just offered. You can select material from magazines, newspapers, or reading series, or you can make up your own. Designing your own graded materials may require that you establish their grade levels, easily done by subjecting them to one of the many readability formulas available. In our clinical practice we will write our own materials for the IDA especially for non-English speakers, or for adults whose reading levels are very low (below third grade level), and then measure their readability. It is most important that you do not discourage the student with heavy or boring or esoteric material so far out of his or her experience and education that it becomes a major struggle. If the material is boring or too heavy in content, vocabulary, or sentence structure the student experiencing reading and language problems may very well give up and thus perform at an even lower level than usual. Information on readability is summarized later in the chapter.

QUESTIONING TO DETERMINE COMPREHENSION, INTERPRETATION, AND CONCEPTS

Perhaps equally essential to the administration of a good IDA is the questioning of the student. One of the major problems of many undergraduate and graduate students is their inability to ask probing questions of different types and to interpret answers quickly enough to generate more questions.

Questioning

Good questioning provides essential diagnostic information on reading and language performance and it can also provide us with useful information on the student's thinking, concepts, feelings, background, and experience. Probing questions concerning the text and related questions about attitudes, beliefs and knowledge add greatly to a teacher's reservoir of knowledge and understanding of the student. It provides a more comprehensive context within which to make better judgments about the person and his performance.

We must devise clearly stated, direct questions which do not give the answers away, and which are not so obtuse or esoteric that they frustrate the reader because he cannot understand what you want. Like diagnosis itself, the questions we ask must not become part of the problem. If you want to know a student's quality and level of comprehension you need questions that will reveal his ability to recall the stated facts and information in the selection. Make your questions straightforward, direct and clear-cut in plain vocabulary and simple sentence structure unless you want to measure *those* skills rather than comprehension.

When you design your questions for a particular reading selection ask yourself, *What does the student need to know* in order to answer this correctly? What skills must he have and what information and concepts does he need to respond correctly? That will tell you what you are measuring. If your question requires the student to recall the names of three generals and he does so, you have measured recall or comprehension. If your question requires the student to generalize from the stated information, you are measuring an aspect of interpretation. Examples will follow later in this section.

The Quality of the Answers is Important

In addition to knowing how many questions were answered correctly by the student, we can get considerably more information relative to the *quality* of the responses. This is almost impossible to determine from standardized or criterion-referenced tests, but is one of the major strengths of the IDA. Furthermore, with the IDA we can get many clues to how the student says the answer (syntactically, semantically and emotionally) and we can search for more clues to the way he thinks as well as what he understands or misunderstands. Also we can continue to question the student if a response is not completely clear. We can detect his logic and reasoning, his vocabulary, and his concepts and these data are extremely valuable in making an analysis of his reading and language performance. Simply, with good probing questions and an understanding of what the answers tell us about the skills he has and how he uses them in context, as well as how he thinks and reasons, we have the kind of diagnostic information we need in order to develop an effective program of correction.

The quality of answers is rarely mentioned in discussions like these and that leaves many teachers and clinicians in the position of counting how many items were right or wrong rather than with the skill to pursue the qualitative dimension. A good parallel to what I am suggesting here can be found in such tests as the WISC-R, the WAIS, and the Stanford-Binet. In these individual intelligence tests the scoring of many items on the various subtests provide for a 2 score or a 1 score or a zero score. The distinctions between a 2 and 1 score are that the former is a more general and comprehensive response while the 1 score is more limited and more specific. The 0 is usually an unrelated or totally trivial response which misses the key relationship. The answers you get from a student on an IDA can be assessed in a similar fashion so that you can differentiate those responses that are inclusive and that reveal that the student has grasped the key relationships from those which reveal that he has only repeated a statement in the selection without any analysis and ability to relate or generalize.

Obviously, any one of us can devise a test and so score it that almost everyone would fail it. If you insist on very specific, word-perfect answers and allow for no latitude in the acceptance of correct or incorrect, you could cause almost everyone to fail or to perform poorly. By the same token, we can all devise a test which would make everyone pass or score very high, again depending on the nature of the questions and what you accept for answers. How you state the question grammatically and in terms of its vocabulary and what you will or will not accept as an answer influence the scoring and the ultimate assessment of the student's performance, weaknesses and strengths, and the plan for correction and/or remediation.

Examples of Questioning (High First Grade Level)

Narration (Fiction)

Snow came down. It snowed all day. Bob and Jane were glad. They made a snowman. They worked all afternoon. The snowman was big. It was night. The snow stopped. A snowplow came. It pushed the snow away. It was morning. Bob and Jane came out. "Where is the snowman?" asked Jane. "The snowplow pushed it down," said Bob. (Northeastern University, 1968)

This is high first grade material, (1^2) and as a child would read this orally you would be noting any errors in word recognition; blends, digraphs, endings, short or long vowel problems, omissions, and substitutions. Then come the comprehension and interpretation questions, vocabulary and the check for study skills. Of course, in presenting written material to children in the primary grades, especially grades one and two, you would be concerned about the *format* of the material, particularly the size of print and ease of reading, physically. Probably a picture or two would be part of it since at this low level children may need to use some picture clues. Most important though are the questions and the answers used to judge the quality of the reading performance.

Comprehension question

The first comprehension question offered for this paragraph is "Name the children in the story." The answer could be: (a) Bob and Jane; (b) man driving the snowplow; (c) snowman. It is suggested in these questions that the examiner pursue answers by asking if the snowman is a person. This requires literal understanding of the word in this context, and it further suggests that the child be asked to compare the snowman with a human. The purpose is to disabuse the child of the answer that the snowman is one of the people in the story. Try to lead the child into dealing with some kind of classification system in order to make the comparisons and contrasts necessary to differentiate person from snowman. We might have the child list some outstanding characteristics of people: hair, eyes, nose, skin, blood, ability to walk, talk, and read, etc., and then make a list for snowmen, making the comparisons and contrasts. If one were to follow this line of probing, you might learn how much the child knows about his own body and the functions of persons, and some of the basic differences between man with mind and organic functions as compared with objects, like a snowman. But this could get very heavy, obtuse, and verbose. I would be most careful about following any lead everywhere. After all, the question and its answer should retain a close relationship to what has been read.

Most children and readers will answer the first question with (a) Bob and Jane. The question itself is clearly stated: it uses no difficult vocabulary, has simple sentence structure, and does not demand information not derivable from the story in a literal fashion.

Comprehension question

The next comprehension question is; "What was the weather like on the day the story started?" The answers offered are: (a) it was snowing; (b) it was "cold". If the child says "cold," ask him how he knows. Pursue the question. If a child said wintry or it was winter, that's a good answer, but with some children who might give such an answer I might get a bit humorous and provocative by saying: "Oh, it must be summer; I remember how it snowed last July, don't you?" or something like it, depending on the child and his or her age. If the child answered a "dark day," I'd accept that and push for more: what kind of dark day—warm, cold, grim, etc., until I get the child to really sharpen the answer with total confidence that he or she understands. This is a good question and most of the answers are acceptable.

What would be a bizarre answer to this simple, direct question "It's a bad day—why?" "It kills babies." Before jumping to possible wrong conclusions, try to find out what's in that little head that may have come out of the mouth distorted. I'd pursue that to find out what a snowy day, a snowman, snowplow (the essence of the story read) has to do with dead babies. Often it's a kind of testing that the child is doing because he hates reading; he doesn't want you to know how bad he is at it; because he wants to be out of the situation. Or he really could be sick. If such responses persisted, drop the testing and just chat to see if any kind of pattern becomes evident. You might consider a WISC-R to see if (without reading) you could elicit other symptoms that would help you understand why the child responds as he does.

So far these questions are not bad because they are clearly stated in simple English with virtually no ambiguity. A child who reads the selection without serious word recognition problems ought to be able to respond accurately to these two questions.

Comprehension question

"What did Bob and Jane make?" The answer is a snowman. Not much doubt or ambiguity here, for the story says, "They made a snowman." For the reader to answer this comprehension question correctly he or she only has to recall that clearly stated fact. That is indeed a measure of comprehension.

Comprehension question

The next question is, "How long did it take the children to make the snowman?" Answer: all afternoon. Once again, a simply stated question with no unusual vocabulary and no complicated sentence structure. It says in the story, "They worked all afternoon." Clear. Direct. Simple. The reader can respond by virtue of recall of the facts stated in the selection, and that is the essence of comprehension questions.

Comprehension question

The last comprehension question is "What happened to the snowman during the night?" The answer, is, "The snowplow pushed it down." Once again, a good question and a good answer.

If a child said, "It melted," or "Some bad kids knocked it down," I'd pursue it with the child until I could elicit the reason for his answer (which is clearly not in the story at all in any way). After getting as much of the affect and logic from the child, I might have him look back at the story to see if he could locate (or reread) the answer as stated in the last sentence.

Difference between recall and reread

It is important at this point to make the distinction between *recall* and *reread*. A basic principle in giving an IDA is to have the child read out loud, and then when she or he has completed the graded selection, we take the material away and ask our comprehension (recall) questions and interpretation questions. If the selection is in front of the child, the answer given could be the result of simple rereading and locating the information, but we are not measuring that at this point. It is important to know what you are measuring and what you are not measuring: recall is recall, not rereading or locating information. Those skills require different knowledge and technique from recall. If you do not know what you are measuring, or call one skill another, you will err in your diagnosis and its interpretation.

To return to the questions on this selection: the comprehension questions are indeed measures of literal recall since the answers are all in the story, clearly and unambiguously stated, in known vocabularies. The reader only has to recall the stated facts. Of course we could use simple material like this selection, and ask complex questions with vocabulary beyond the reader's level so that even the best readers would falter. That is not the purpose of the IDA. The purpose is to get the *best performance* you can from the reader.

Now let's look at the interpretation questions to see if we can readily detect the differences in what the reader is expected to do compared with what he needs to know and do to answer comprehension questions.

Interpretation question

The first interpretation question is Why do you think this might make a good title for the story: "The Disappearing Snowman?" In all interpretation questions and their more diverse answers *we must be able to interpret what the answers mean*. It will be more difficult than dealing with comprehension questions and their answers.

First of all, is the question a measure of interpretation or of the ability to detect a main idea or to summarize? What does it require for you to give a title to a selection like the one we are dealing with? Depending on your purpose as a writer, your title can be straightforward and informative; it can be a play on words to stimulate readers to want to read it (for example, *The National Enquirer*, headlines); it can be some form of literary allusion you expect the reader to have in his or her background and to use to enrich the material at hand (part of the interpretive process); it could be strictly symbolic. For example, the play *Equus* has a title that is literal in that it is the Latin root for horse, but is totally symbolic in that it peels back layers of meanings in terms of God, Man, worship, faith, passion; the axiom "healer heal thyself" is part of it, and it asks who indeed is sick—the psychiatrist or the patient. But the first response of most persons who have not seen or read the play is that it is about horses, and that's literal understanding and has very little to do with the impact and essence of this play's meaning and intent.

"The Doll's House" is a symbolic title for Ibsen's bold personal-political commentary on a woman who felt as if she were living like a doll, but who wanted to be liberated. "The Enemy of the People" is also a symbolic title.

These examples illustrate what choosing a title may mean and may reveal. If you ask such a question as part of your attempt to measure a reader's interpretive skill keep in mind the various layers of responses which may be given, and consider how you may weigh them in terms of quality and level.

If the reader of this little selection on the snowman says that "Disappearing Snowman" is a good title because the snowman disappeared while the children slept and it was not where they left it the night before, I take that as a good answer, but at a fairly literal level. It is in answers to questions like these that I pursue the hardest, and ask ten questions for each response so that I can see how the child thinks, perceives relationships, organizes his information and experience, and finally how he puts it into language. I would accept answers like "The Vanishing Snowman," "Death of a Snowman," "A Crime in the City," "Snowplow," "The Enemy," etc. All of these can be justified easily from the context and intent of this little selection, but most of them strike me as a bit more imaginative and at least reveal a slightly more varied vocabulary. If any of those answers were given, ask the child why he chose that one, and challenge with other title possibilities; try to get to the core of the child's reasoning in making the choice. It is worth it to pursue these questions and demand evidence from the reader; it provides you with considerably more information than whether the answer is right or wrong.

Interpretation question

The second interpretation question is, "How do you know from the story that you were supposed to feel happy when the children were out in the snow making their snowman?" One answer is, "Because it said in the story that they were glad, and if they spent all afternoon making a snowman they must have been enjoying themselves." First, if the answer is indeed stated in the story, *then that is not interpretation*, but a comprehension (recall) question, since it requires the reader only to remember the statement "Bob and Jane were glad." No thinking is required; no relationships need be seen to respond that way. It is simple recall. The second part of the answer given is a little more like an interpretation type of question and answer, for in order to answer, the reader must put together several of the facts: the children stayed out all day and worked on the snowman; they made a very big one. Then the reader must say, "If they worked so hard and so long on a cold, snowy day to make this big snowman, which required rolling balls of snow, shaping and lifting them into the right place for head, arms, etc., then they must have enjoyed it, because when I do hard work that nobody forces me to, I usually like it. Work becomes play." That kind of process, which is essential to doing any kind of interpretative work, is distinctively, qualitatively different from what is required when one merely gives one-dimensional, recall responses—the facts restated.

I don't like this kind of literal question for two reasons: first, it is too long. Why not say (if you want to ask this): "How did the children feel while they were making their snowman?" That is clearer for children. Sentences that say things like, "How do you know from the story that you are supposed to feel?" instead of "what did the story say", are a bit obtuse for many children. It could easily be misunderstood or just plain confusing. Let us not ask questions, especially of youngsters, that require more interpretation than the reading material. *Avoid passive voice statements; avoid complex sentences* for the younger children or those whose language skill is limited; *avoid unclear, obtuse statements or forms.* What is that question measuring anyway? Presumably it is thought by the questioner that part of interpretation has to do with the ability to detect feelings in characters in the story, on a superficial level. This is such a brief passage it is really difficult to expect any character or plot development—just simple statements about action, with one dimensional descriptives like glad. No imagery is used to stimulate responses which might be considered affective. The whole selection has only two descriptive adjectives: glad and big. This selection should serve as a model and principle for dealing with the writing and asking of interpretive questions and having a sense of what the answers may tell you about the reader's self and skill.

Interpretation question

The next interpretation question is "Why wouldn't Bob and Jane have been able to make a snowman if it hadn't snowed?" (Yes, that's what it says.) The answer is "Because it takes snow to build a snowman." How do you like that? Absurd, absurd, absurd!! You should be able to come up with a better question than that.

Interpretation question

The next real question says "Why do you think that if you made a snowman in the place where Bob and Jane did that the snowplow might push it down?" The answer is, "Because the snowplow plows snow out of the street, even when it has been made into a snowman." Again, the question is stated clumsily with too many words and somewhat involuted in form. How about, "If you made a snowman in the street what do you think would happen?" Then the reader must consider what happened to the snowman made by Bob and Jane, and that would include that theirs was knocked down overnight by a snowplow, and that if they made their snowman in the street (as they did) it too might be knocked down by a snowplow. I would then push, asking "Why did the snowplow knock it down anyway? Did the driver dislike kids or snowmen? Why do we hire people to do that kind of work anyway? What would have happened if the snowman had been left where they made it?" I would want the child to say things like "No, the driver of the snowplow probably does not hate children," (he might have his own), "and he probably does not hate snowmen," (he probably made snowmen as a child also), and I'd pursue the child to say also that the main reason for knocking down snowmen built in the streets is to keep them free for traffic. The next question you should ask is where the reader thinks this story took place: country, city, or suburb? Why? Why could it not take place in the country on a farm? I might then ask if the child has had any such experience and have him relate it briefly. If not, I'd move along. I do not want readers who lack some particular realm of experience to feel, as a result of my questioning, that I expect them to know things they do not know, and that I think them dumb or ill-informed. Do not let your questioning punish the child or adult, but dig out the reader's concepts.

Interpretation question

The last interpretation question is "Why would the children probably have not made their snowman in the street another time?" The answer is, "Because they would remember that the snowplow goes there." This is another poorly stated question. Why not ask it this way: "Do you think the children will build another snowman? Where? Why? Why not on the street?" Don't ask the last one if it was already answered in the question above. In taking answers, I would be certain I could get at what *ideas or concepts* the reader may have about who cleans streets; why they do that; who pays them to do it; what would happen if they were not cleared of such things as snowmen; etc. Why not make a snowman in the yard? Why didn't they?

Some Rules About Interpretation Questions

Don't use the word *why* continually. Try to state interpretation questions in a variety of ways and as follow-ups to previous questions. Keep the sentence structure simple, direct, uncluttered; use simple vocabulary. Avoid passive voice for young children and persons with limited language skill and knowledge. Make sure interpretation questions require the reader to use the facts and information in the selection and then to think about them, blending in personal experiences, knowledge, and facts from related areas, and noting any special or varied meanings of words or phrases. To interpret is to understand and to understand is to see relationships among facts, ideas, principles, and concepts.

It is important that you, as diagnostician, know which questions measure or reveal comprehension as well as interpretational skill. Don't confuse literal recall with figurative understanding of words and ideas. The key as always in any diagnostic work is what the person needs to know or needs to be able to do in order to respond correctly. Ask yourself what a wrong response tells you about the person's skill or lack of it, his knowledge, personality, etc.

A common type of diagnostic error consists in having the person read a given selection and then asking both comprehension and interpretation questions, and noting how many questions the person misses. If for example, he answers three out of ten, this comes to 70% percent comprehension—below the standard we can accept for that material. It is critical to look over the questions asked and missed to see if the reader may have answered incorrectly because of a vocabulary problem—not knowing the meaning of a word or phrase in a particular context. If this turns out to be true, it is a vocabulary problem and not, technically, a comprehension question. Of course, vocabulary is part of comprehension and interpretation, but in this case the person's specific problem is not knowing the meaning of certain words, hence missing the point in the questioning. The reason I suggest trying to analyze this way is to make correction more accurate. That is, if you note that the person clearly misunderstood the meaning of a particular word or phrase and responded correctly in terms of his misunderstanding, you know that he or she had the right process, but the wrong meaning. We can correct most vocabulary problems in several ways, one of which is to focus some attention on affixes and roots and their derivatives. That might be all this student needs, rather than a complete comprehension program. The diagnosis and correction should be as parsimonious as possible; whenever possible do the direct, simple, and sometimes obvious thing, rather than the elaborate and often theoretical or analogous activity.

Examples of Questioning—5^2 Level

Now that we have analyzed the questions and questioning process for fairly low level material, let me add more on the *art of questioning*. The following illustration (Northeastern University, 1966), using social science for content, will show how easy it is to make both comprehension and interpretation questions for almost every line in the material, and how we can probe deeper into the child's reservoir of concepts, vocabulary, and imagination.

Progress in Transportation

Automobiles and trains, airplanes and oceanliners are on the move, day and night around the clock. But this has not always been so. There was a time in which man had no vehicles and no roads. The Stone Age people used streams and lakes as roadways. And they travelled on logs, one alone, or several tied together. Logs were the first vehicles of transportation. After a while man began to use animals to pull goods along over the ground. Heavy loads were dragged on sledges. Then someone thought of putting rollers under the sledges. This led to the use of the wheel. The invention of the wheel was the most important step in the history of transportation. (Northeastern University, 1966)

The selection contains 118 words and 11 sentences. Notice that the content fits into the category of social sciences with a mix of history and technology as the focal point. The readability is fifth grade (using the Dale-Chall formula) so that we see several short and a few long sentences: the average sentence length is 10.7 words. We mentioned earlier that in general the shorter the words and the shorter the sentences in any written matter results in a lower readability, and the opposite is true.

Although this material is far from an ideal piece, it does contain a good variety of words and phonic and structural elements that serve as a fair sampling of the child's phonic and structural analysis skills, comprehension, interpretation, vocabulary, and concepts. It is a good choice for an IDA. If you were to analyze this material closely you would find polysyllabic words with good generative roots as in auto/mobile (both roots appear in scores of other common and widely used words), air/planes (note also it is a compound word), most of the consonants and vowels are represented and often repeated, e.g., *a* in *and*, *ai* in *trains*, *a* in *planes*, *a* in *ay*, *a* in *always*, *a* in other combinations besides *ay* and *ai*, as in *roadways* (*oa*), etc. The same is true of other vowels, alone and in blends and digraphs. There are numerous structural elements such as compound words, words with prefixes, roots, and suffixes (*roll*, *roller*; *auto*/*mobile*; *transportation* with trans/port/ation (prefix, root, and suffix); we also find consonant digraphs like *th* in *this* and *there*; *wh* in *which* and *wheel*; *th* in *together*, etc. Note that the elements appear in the beginning, middle, and ends of words so that the student must make the widest application of his knowledge of these phonic and structural elements. Several compound words and polysyllabic words allow for practice with syllabication. That's a lot of elements to present in order to check the student's word recognition skills. All IDA material should be at least as complete and varied as this sample. This will result in a better and more realistic sample of the reader's word recognition skills in all areas, as well as in comprehension and interpretation.

Comprehension and interpretation questions

Comprehension (literal recall) questions for the first sentence might include, "What is on the move around the clock?" or "Name some things (vehicles if you wish) which are on the move day and night." In both cases we want the literal response given in the sentence: "automobiles, trains, airplanes, and ocean liners." If the child gives one or two, press to get more by leading him with something like "Besides automobiles and trains, what else do you see moving people and goods?"

Interpretation questions for the same first sentence could include the following: "Why are these vehicles on the move around the clock?" (If the student seems a bit unsure, ask if he knows what "around the clock" means.) We want answers like, "There is a lot to move, so these vehicles have to go all the time; we move food, etc. from one part of the country to another, so the trucks, and planes have to go all the time; a lot to move to a lot of places and to a lot of people."

Whichever is given, I follow up with another qeustion: "What kinds of things do we move in these vehicles? Where do they come from and why, and where are they going and why? What would happen if we did not move them?" In other words, what is produced in various parts of the country (or world) which we send to other places because they do not have those materials, or they do not have enough. These are questions for bright kids with good backgrounds, but I would try one or two on almost any student just to see if I could tap some source of information. Sometimes this leads to a brief discussion of when certain fruits and vegetables are shipped from California and Florida to the northeast or midwest, and why such shipments of those goods would be reduced during the summer.

How far you pursue these questions depends again on the reader's background, maturity, and knowledge. But some of these follow-up questions I will ask so that I can determine if the student can or cannot give that information. Then I want to know why such information is not given—is it poor education, age, intelligence, misunderstanding the text itself, distraction, anxiety? As you probe around with such questions you will notice some clues to what may be causing the wrong response or no response. Push until you can find out.

Comprehension questions

"Has this always been true?" or "Did these vehicles move day and night always?" These are simple, clearly stated comprehension questions, as were the ones given for the first sentence; notice the vocabulary and sentence structure in these questions. These are not ambiguous and do not contain unusual vocabulary. The only word in the comprehension questions asked so far is the word vehicle, which appears in the story at least twice. If the student shows some doubt or confusion, ask him if he knows what a vehicle is and what they are talking about. Then check the word as a vocabulary item if he does not get it or can't figure it from the context.

Interpretation questions

What does this sentence mean: "This has not always been true"? What hasn't been true? Why has it not been true? What was true in the past, or long ago about vehicles? (I would use the word again as a means of assuring the child's understanding of it in several contexts.) Answers to these questions, all growing out of the one question include: In the past or long ago people did not have cars, planes, etc. People were not in touch or in contact with each other so much. In both cases I would ask the student to explain what he or she means, and I would ask follow-up questions, such as, why weren't people in touch or contact with each other in the past? How did they live (as in villages, tribes, isolated more from each other)? Then I would follow such an answer with, Where did they live? Do you know any such tribes or groups which were isolated? If in such an exchange in the questioning, answering, and follow-up questioning a concept or a word comes up which seems unclear or that the reader does not get, I follow that through with enough discussion to make it clear. Some teaching is done during diagnosis, but don't overdo it since your focus is on the reading performance in word recognition, meanings, and study skill. The reader should not be left with the feeling that he is stupid or unable to answer all the questions. As I teach a little, I discover more about what the child knows and how he uses what facts, information, concepts, and skills he does have. Yes and no answers or even lengthier ones do not reveal all that I want to get from this IDA.

The next sentence provides material for questions like these: Did man always have vehicles? (This is a comprehension question.) When didn't he have them? Why not? What did he have or use? Why? The next sentence gives part of the answer to one of the questions: What did he use? The answer: streams, lakes as roadways. But this leads to a lot of good interpretation questions and concept questions such as, How could he use streams and lakes as roadways? What does it mean to use a lake or stream as a roadway? How are the roads of today and their streams and lakes alike? Different?

In getting answers to this question just look at what concepts and previous knowledge the reader needs in order to answer correctly—relationship of road to lake or stream for moving things and people; the nature of roadway, whether cement, tar, dirt, or water, or even air—the core concept being travel from place to place on air, water, or land, wherever it might be, and irrespective of its size. This might lead into more discussion of what we now move in trucks, planes, ocean liners, cars, and what they moved, how much, how far, in what amount of time on the lakes and streams. You have certainly noticed how much more information of various types you can get on an IDA that you could ever get on any standard or criterion-referenced tests.

The next line generates questions like: How did they travel in the past? If you tie several logs together what do you call it? (Raft.) What do you suppose they tied them together with? You need something strong don't you; Why? How heavy are logs, or how round are they? Why do logs float? How do you think they used them for transportation? What could they transport on a log or a raft? (Themselves, things one could hold in one's hands; on a raft small animals might be carried, or bundles, etc.) What else did man use to move himself and heavy objects? That is, besides logs or rafts? (Answer, animals.) What kind of animals do you think they used? Why? What animals do we use today which do similar work?

(Don't use the word similar unless your student knows it; use the same word as the last phrase in the question.) Could you say that animals were like the first machines men had? Why? Why not?

The discussion would explain that anything man uses to do work and to speed it up as well as to make it easier is a kind of machine or technology. The latter word would not be used with every student. In order to further explain the question and the answer desired, I would probably show the relationship between a truck carrying lots of heavy things over the ground, and a mule dragging a heavy thing over the ground, and then ask the student how these are alike and how they are different.

The number of other questions I might ask for any of these facts always depends on what kinds of answers I get. Are the answers shallow, very limited, and literal; do they reflect a narrow background of information and experience; do they reveal limited vocabulary and concepts? As I listen to each answer to each question I am assessing all of these factors, plus any emotional reactions accompanying the answers.

Additional questions might include: What was pulled on sledges? What is a sledge? Why was it better to use a sledge than to drag a heavy object yourself, or even with an animal? Why is it easier? What makes it slide and move more rapidly, with less drag? What is drag? In order to make the sledges what else did these early men have to know about? Did using logs for transportation help them develop the sledge? How? In what ways are they alike in function, what they do? These are all concept questions, as well as questions of reasoning and previous education, but mainly the former.

What made the sledges work even better? (Rollers.) What were the rollers? How did they work? Why was that better and easier than the two runners under them? Why did that make for less drag or resistance? (I often explain drag and/or resistance with everyday examples, like skateboards, wagons, etc., or by having them drag something.) How did the invention and use of the rollers on the sledges lead to the use of the wheel? I now require the students' understanding of the interrelationships of the wheel, drag, and resistance. It also requires that they make comparisons and contrasts with moving objects by pulling them by hand, by animal or on sledges without rollers. The key is the wheel's reduction of all drag and resistance because only one small part of a wheel touches the ground at any one time, whereas the sledge has two runners which scrape along. How would your life be different if the wheel had not been invented? What would your day be like? Usually students say things like, I couldn't ride the subway, the car, bus to school, etc.; I would have to walk or ride an animal or sledge. But I pursue this because these are literal answers to an interpretation question. We get into the fact that no modern transportation could exist without a wheel in it, including motors of every kind, jet planes, racing cars, subways, etc. Without the wheel we would not be able to move ourselves and our goods from place to place; we would not know about other people, races, cultures. We would be tribal and isolated and might still believe in magic and do all our work by hand. Depending on the age and maturity of the student, we might dig even deeper into the cultural implications of no travel, no technology, and the opposite. What has technology done to us as people, a culture, etc.?

You should now be able to see the wealth of information you can get from IDA questioning. You can get comprehension and interpretation responses and measures, concept knowledge, vocabulary, educational and experiential background, basic thinking abilities, and oral communication. Notice the affective responses as well as the cognitive ones, and the mix of both, and observe test endurance, skill, knowledge, and ability to discuss. In short, you get more than what word recognition problems the student shows or percentage of comprehension and interpretation. You get an x-ray of a person performing the reading act multidimensionally.

Every question asked produces answers that generate more questions. We always want more than how many right and wrong answers to each type of question. Furthermore, what do you do with the answers? Make more questions, picking up both affective and cognitive data on many sides of a given reading performance and get more background information. Probing questions leavened with some humor produces better performance in many students because they recognize that your questioning expresses faith in their ability to respond correctly. Your questioning can also provide information so that there is a real discussion and exchange about whatever is read and that adds purpose to the reading. This is quite different from most testing, which seems to seek out what students do not know, including questions which have only one answer and that is either right or wrong and not discussable.

This should make it clearer to you how critical it is to ask good, probing questions and how to make many questions that check out the students' meanings skills and level, as well as vocabulary, concepts, thinking, and feeling about what has been read.

It has already been mentioned that I like to ask the questions as the reader goes through the material, rather than wait until the whole selection has been read. Most of my questions are interpretation and concept questions, so it does not matter much that the reader is looking at the material just read. Most students do not even look at it while I am asking my questions; there isn't time, and they become much more interested in what is being read. It is quite stale to ask the person read the whole selection, then to take the selection away and start asking five or ten comprehension questions, then five or more interpretation questions, and a couple of vocabulary questions. Since we are looking for strength and knowledge amid the weaknesses and lack of knowledge, we should allow the person tested to feel good, comfortable, and at full capacity. So we talk, joke, discuss and deal with the selections fully. You will come out with lots of specific information on the reading performance in each growth area.

CRITERIA FOR JUDGING READING PERFORMANCE

Before we do an IDA we must have some criteria for judging the quality of the reading performance. Since IDAs do not have national norms we need some guides to determining which level the student has achieved, i.e., independent level, instructional level, or frustration level. Our major concern is with the instructional level because by definition that is the level at which the student can read comfortably, making minimal errors in word recognition and maintaining good recall and interpretation. It is the level at which most people want to initiate their teaching.

The criteria given below are modifications of the original Betts (1946) criteria. They have been adjusted over the years as a result of a mass of empirical evidence with thousands of students of all ages and backgrounds. These are not norms, but are much more like the standards used for judging criterion-referenced test results. If a student scores 95% correct in word recognition on the fourth grade material, and scores 85% in comprehension and 80% in interpretation, that level could be his instructional level. Such scores indicate, and experience bears this out, that the student can easily read and understand such material at that level. If the student falls well below the criteria given below, the frustration level is reached and that is no place to begin instruction unless failure is the goal. The criteria are very helpful but are *not* to be taken so literally that you do not account for other aspects of the reading performance.

Independent Level

The Independent Level is the highest level at which the reader can read with virtually no word recognition or meanings problems. Most authors consider this level to be a year or so below the instructional level, *but I do not*. More often than not a reader who reads at the *independent level wants* to read and enjoys the material, so that it often can be a year above the instructional level, not below it. The criteria are usually given in this way:

Independent Level
98-99% correct decoding, pronunciation of words,
95% correct responses in comprehension, and
90% correct responses in interpretation.

I would leave a little more latitude by at least 5% in each growth area for this independent level. Generally, I do not specifically measure this level. When I establish the instructional level carefully and accurately, I feel comfortable in projecting that the independent level won't be lower, and probably will be higher, and the frustration level will be about one and a half to two years below the instructional level.

Instructional Level

This is the one that counts the most. This is the level at which instruction should proceed, irrespective of the grade placement or age of the student, since this is the level at which the student reads fluently in the area of word recognition, and recalls and interprets the material very well and with obvious understanding. The criteria used, with some latitude (say 5% again), are:

Word recognition

For readers fourth grade and above the correct responses should be 90%, and for children and readers under fourth grade level, 95-98%. The lower the grade of the reader, and more limited the skills of older readers, the higher the percentage should be in this growth area; the higher the grade the lower the percentage, but not below 85%.

Comprehension

Correct responses in comprehension should be 80-90%, again, dependent on age and level of the reader. The lower the age and level of the reader, the higher the percentage in comprehension should be sought.

Interpretation

Correct responses should be 75%+, dependent on age and level of student.

Study skills

It is not practical to try to establish a level here, particularly if you work with children, adolescents, or adults who read well below grade level. We don't know how to say, or what it means to say, that main ideas are at fourth grade level. It depends so much on the type of reading program being used, e.g., basal, linguistic, language experience, etc., since different programs introduce these study skills at different grades and in different ways. *It is much more important to know if the reader knows the skills and can apply them in context.* We normally just note whether the student knows a given skill in a particular context, such as history, geography, or science on certain levels.

There are many obvious and subtle problems relating to these criteria and how to apply and interpret them—such problems as the thirty-two year old man who went to school to the tenth grade, dropped out, had some legal problems, has been unemployed half the time, is divorced with three children and has a drinking problem. We must be sensitive diagnosticians to analyze the testing data with great care and some latitude. Such a person cannot be held to strict criteria for performance.

Frustration Level

The frustration level is that level at which the student is baffled and confused, inept in decoding and recalling the facts, and has little or no interpretive skill. Study skills do not exist. The key performance behavior is usually poor word recognition skills. Standardized tests like the California, Stanford, and Metropolitan tend to be at the frustration level for marginal or problem readers. That is, if you give the standard test to the student who has problems at his grade placement level (fourth grade test to a student in the fourth grade) and that student actually reads at a second grade level, that is frustration. This level is 1½ to 2 years below the instructional level. This is the level where many students of all ages are forced to work because of poor or inadequate diagnosis, choice of materials (level and content), and insensitive teaching methods and materials.

It is very important to establish the reader's *instructional level*; it's the one that counts. Once you establish that accurately, it takes very little imagination or even skill to predict the other levels. If you should be interested in determining rate of speed in reading as part of your informal diagnosis for students who are functioning above ninth or tenth grade level (speed is not for the lower levels) here's how to figure it out.

$$\text{Rate of reading (Speed):} \frac{\text{Number of words read}}{\text{Number of seconds}} \times 60 = \text{words per minute}$$

Now you have the background for why we do IDAs rather than other means of determining how a whole person performs the reading and related language acts; you know what materials you will need (graded paragraphs, comprehension and interpretation questions, and materials to check study skills) and you have some criteria by which to assess and judge at what level the reader is performing. How are reading materials graded first grade level, third, or tenth grade level? A brief survey of readability will answer your questions and help you select any materials you wish to use for an IDA.

READABILITY

Readability refers to the ways in which we measure the relative level of difficulty of reading materials. There are about 50 different readability formulas used to establish the grade levels of many textbooks and other printed matter. Generally speaking, material is readable when the reader has the essential skills to decode, recall, and interpret what is printed. The most commonly used formulas seem to be the Dale-Chall, Flesch, and Fry and Smog Index.

Which one of the formulas you choose to guide your estimates of the reading level required to read comfortably or to rewrite material to a particular level is not critical since these formulas tend to correlate rather well with each other. At the Northeastern University Reading Clinic we use the Dale-Chall formula because experience has taught us how to evaluate its results. We have used the Smog Index occasionally but have found that it overrates material, that is, if it provides a fourth grade level, many students with third grade reading skills and knowledge can handle it very easily. For a good comparison of formulas, see Dale and Chall (1958).

A study of readability formulas and concepts reveals that most of them have identified two key factors that significantly affect the relative ease or difficulty of reading matter: (1) ratio of short to long words in a given sample; (2) ratio of short to long sentences in the sample. That is, if there are many more long words than short words in your samples and if there are many more long sentences than short ones, the readability level will be higher than if you find the opposite to be true. A quick way then to estimate the level of material is to observe whether your samples of material contain many one and two syllable words in many four and five word sentences or whether there are many more three and four syllable words in ten or twelve word sentences. The former will be on a lower level while the latter will be on a much higher level.

The formulas measure these factors of word length and sentence length by identifying so-called easy words or familar words which frequently appear on special word lists. These are usually short words that are the most frequently used words in the language. The sentence length factor is easily determined by counting sample sentences in the selection and calculating the average sentence length. The samples are taken from several parts of an article or story or book so as to be as representative as possible of word choice and sentence structure.

Obviously there is much more to reading ease than word length and sentence length. These measures are only estimates based almost entirely on structure and quantitative features of written material. *What is missing in these formulas is some way to assess the meaning of the material.* For example the formulas do not provide any means of measuring the relative ease or difficulty of symbolic and imagistic usages nor do they provide any way to measure the density of ideas and concepts in any selection. But until we develop ways to measure these critical aspects of reading material, the formulas will continue to serve as *estimates* of reading level and reading difficulty. They can also be used, as I have suggested, to aid you in rewriting material from higher levels to lower levels and the reverse.

We now have *objectives*, information on *materials* needed to do an IDA, *criteria* for judging the performance, and *questioning techniques*. We now need some kind of reporting form so that a careful record of students' weaknesses and strengths in each growth area and writing may be kept. In our clinic we keep a folder on every person who comes in for diagnosis and for instruction. That folder contains pre- and post-IDAs, any standardized intelligence or other testing we might have and past medical, school, and psychological data. The folder also contains the long or short form (examples will be discussed shortly) with the specific data on the reading performance; the narrative report based on this data by the tutor; and a lesson plan with general objectives, specific objectives, procedures, and an evaluation of each lesson taught. When the term is over, the tutor does the post-IDA and fills in either the long or short form and writes a progress report and a narrative of the whole corrective program. Often tutors place into the folders selected pieces of written work done by the student.

MARKING THE IDA

Some clinicians and specialists like to use a relatively common marking system for IDAs. An example of such a system is shown in Table 3-1. You may find it helpful at the outset to use such a marking system; if you use it, try to commit it to memory so that it does not interfere with your listening to the oral reading of the student and to his responses to your questions. Your key job is to get as complete an impression of the student's performance on all levels—cognitive and affective. Report the performance with or without this marking system, or make up your own, which you will stick to consistently. Whether you use it or not, be sure to fill in your long or short form as completely and as specifically as possible. Examples of good and bad forms will be discussed shortly.

Table 3-1
INFORMAL INVENTORY MARKING

Type of ERROR	Rule for Marking
Substitutions A sensible or real word substituted for the word in the paragraph	Write in substituted word
Mispronunciations A nonsense word which may be produced by: 1. False accentuation; 2. Wrong pronunciation of vowels or consonants; or 3. Omission, addition or insertion of one or more letters.	Write in word phonetically
Words Pronounced by Examiner A word on which subject hesitates for 5 seconds. (The word is then pronounced by the examiner.)	Underline the word
Insertions (including additions) A word (or words) inserted at the beginning, in the middle or at the end of a sentence or line of the text.	Use a caret (∧) and write in the inserted word (or words).
Hesitations A pause of at least 2 seconds before pronouncing the word.	Make a check above the word on which hesitation occurs (not counted as an error)
Repetitions A word, part of a word, or group of words repeated.	Draw a wavy line beneath word (or words) repeated. (Sometimes counted as an error.)
Omissions One or more words omitted. (If a complete line is omitted, this is counted as one omission error.)	Encircle the word (or words) omitted.
Inversions The word order of two or more words is changed.	Mark as in this example: He ran there rapidly.
Self correction This reader corrects his own error without prompting.	Put parenthesis around the word or words. Not counted as an error.

Forms for Recording Reading Performance

The Northeastern University Reading Clinic uses long forms and short forms for recording a reader's performance on the IDA. Exhibit 3-1 shows the long form, which is recommended to beginners using the IDA.

Exhibit 3-1. The Long Form

Individual Diagnostic Analysis Worksheet
Long Form

Date_____

Name_____ Age_____ Sex_____ Grade_____

Home Address_____ Phone (home)_____ Other_____

Parents_____ Living_____ Divorced_____

Separated_____

Other children in family: at home_____ Age_____

_____ Age_____

_____ Age_____

not at home_____ Age_____

_____ Age_____

School now attending_____

School attended_____ When_____

Medical information_____

Referral source_____

Reason for referral_____

_____

Examiner_____ Place_____

PHYSICAL FACTORS IN READING

1. Movement: a. Restless_____ b. Nail biting_____

c. Pointing_____ d. Sub-vocalization_____

e. Fingering hair_____ f. Other_____

Comment_____

_____

2. Speech: a. Lisping_____ b. Stuttering_____

c. Articulation_____ d. Usage_____

e. Other_____

Comment_____

_____

3. General Reading Characteristics: a. Word by word reader_____

b. Cautious_____ c. Monotonous_____

d. Other_____

Comment_____

_____

SPECIFIC READING PERFORMANCE

1. Omissions (Words, letters, combinations, phrases, etc.)

_____

_____

_____

2. Substitutions (Words, letters, combinations, phrases, etc., i.e., house for horse, man for mat, etc.)

_____

_____

_____

3. Insertions (Words, letters, combinations, phrases, etc.)

_____

_____

_____

4. Repetitions (Words, letters, phrases, combinations, etc.)

_____

_____

_____

5. Mispronunciations (Words, letters, combinations, etc., i.e., mis pro noun ciation)

_____

_____

_____

   Summary and Comment_____

_____

_____

_____

WORD RECOGNITION

A. Phonic Analysis
   1. Auditory Discrimination_____

_____

   2. Visual Discrimination_____

_____

A. Phonic Analysis

   3. Does he/she use picture clues?_____

      Too much?_____ Too little?_____

   4. Does he/she have an adequate sight word vocabulary?_____

_____

_____

   5. Does he/she know phonic principles?_____

      Does he/she apply them?_____

SPECIFIC WEAKNESSES

     a. single consonants (initial, medial, and final)_____

_____

     b. consonant blends (initial, medial, and final)_____

_____

     c. consonant digraphs (initial, medial, and final)_____

_____

     d. long vowels_____

_____

     e. short vowels_____

_____

     f. r, l, and w controlled vowels_____

_____

     g. vowel digraphs_____

_____

     h. vowel blends_____

_____

     i. other_____

_____

     Comment (Percentage and level)_____

_____

_____

B. Structural Analysis

    1. Affixes

        a. Suffixes_____

_____

        b. Prefixes_____

_____

    2. Root Words_____

_____

    3. Syllabication_____

_____

    4. Compound Words_____

_____

    5. Hyphenated Words_____

_____

    6. Contractions_____

_____

    7. Use of Dictionary_____

_____

C. Meanings

    1. Comprehension (literal recall)_____

_____

_____

    2. Interpretation

        a. Ability to draw inferences_____

_____

        b. Ability to discriminate between fact and opinion_____

_____

            1. real from fantasy_____

_____

        c. Ability to detect various propaganda techniques_____

_____

        d. Ability to understand symbols in literature_____

_____

        e. Ability to understand imagery_____

_____

        f. Sensitivity to variant word meanings in context_____

_____

g. Ability to state the author's intent_____

_____

1. author's style_____

_____

Comment (percentages and level)_____

_____

_____

D. Study Skills

1. Previewing_____

2. Finding main ideas and related details_____

3. Outlining_____

4. Summarizing_____

5. Classification_____

6. Cause and effect_____

7. Sequence_____

8. Reference skills (use of library, dictionary, encyclopedias, etc.)_____

_____

9. Guide words_____

10. Following directions_____

Summary and comments (Note major problems, strengths, and recommendations.
Indicate specifically which skills can be applied
in what types of materials.)

_____

_____

_____

_____

GENERAL INFORMATION

1. Does he/she avoid assignments regularly?_____

sometimes?_____

2. Does he/she complain of inability to concentrate?_____

_____

to remember?_____

_____

3. Does he/she think or depend on rote memory?_____

_____

4. Comment on writing sample. (Attach to this report.)_____

_____

_____

5. Does he/she miss school often?_____

   Why?_____

6. Is English the language spoken at home?_____

   If not, what is?_____

7. Comments on your observations_____

_____

_____

Discussion of the long form

Review all data collected and the qualitative comments for each section of the worksheet. Determine the instructional level in reading, word recognition, and meanings. In reviewing the data, take note of any patterns in the student's responses, behavior, and performance, and discuss that. Include in the summary specific recommendations for a corrective program based on these findings. Attempt to collect all other background data on the students, for example, school records, psychological tests, reports, and interviews with parents and teachers. These data will be included in the student's file. As you work with the student daily, report on what was taught and why, materials and methods employed, progress made, a brief report on the student's performance and behavior, and an evaluation of yourself. The lesson should be evaluated as it was executed—what worked? What didn't? Why?

The long form is quite detailed, yet certainly not exhaustive; however it should suffice for our clinical purposes at this stage of the diagnostic process, for it provides an enormous amount of specific information of the reader's specific performance in each growth area: word recognition, meanings, and study skills. We want to determine whether this reader knows some of the study skills such as main ideas and details, previewing, classification, etc. Check as many of these skills as you can. However, for children below fourth grade reading level the test results could be misleading for you and frustrating for the students because most of them have not been exposed to study skills. For word recognition and meanings we can get good estimates of level of performance. Obviously, your IDA cannot cover all of the possible areas and specific skills; for example, imagery or propaganda techniques may not be possible in the context of the material the student is reading for you. You might get a clue to such skills through discussion of the material read or through your conversation. Do not expect to get every line filled in. Get the best sampling of reading performance you can for that particular person, on that day, in this particular place. Since no diagnosis is final, but is *functional*, what you miss the first time you will pick up in the first lesson or two. But this long form will provide you with a good profile of specific strengths and weaknesses in each growth area, and will guide your observations in an almost step-by-step fashion. Use it, disagree with it, know it, then alter or discard it depending on your needs. An example of a long form completely filled in is shown in Exhibit 3-2.

Discussion of the completed long form

The completed long form (Exhibit 3-2) was well done. It was done on an older version of the long form, but careful reading of this report will illustrate how much valuable diagnostic data can be gathered even by a beginner.

Whether you use the long or short form for recording a student's performance on the IDA, be absolutely certain to give *specific examples* of the errors made in each growth area. Do not just say that he or she had trouble with phonic analysis or interpretation. Give examples of the errors made at each level you test (second, third, or fifth), the percentage correct in word recognition at each level, and the percentage correct of comprehension and interpretation at the levels tested.

Exhibit 3-2. Completed Long Form

INFORMAL DIAGNOSTIC ANALYSIS WORKSHEET

NAME _C. W._ D.O.B. _6/21/62_ SEX _M_ GRADE _8_

HOME ADDRESS _162 Bellingham St., Chelsea_ PHONE _———_

PARENTS _J. W. (father)_ (Divorced) / Separated CHILDREN _3 brothers / 1 sister_

EXAMINER _M. Swiston_ EST. INSTRUCTIONAL LEVEL _Gr. 7_ DATE _2/11/77_

Used Fusoni 4A, 6B, 8A for Word Recognition and Comprehension and
PHYSICAL FACTORS IN READING _Webster's New Practical School Dictionary for / guide words, alpha. order and choosing correct def._

1. Movement   a) Restless _____ b) Nail biting _____ c) Pointing _____
   d) Lip movement _____ e) Fingering hair _____ f) Other _moved head back and forth_
   Comment _frowns from extreme effort at concentration - (nervous?)_

2. Speech   a) Lisping _none_ b) Stuttering _none_ c) Articulation _good_
   d) Vocab. _good_ e) Other _____

3. General Reading Characteristics:
   a) Word by word reader _____ b) Cautious _✓_
   c) Monotonous _✓_ d) Other _____
   Comment _Would read rapidly until coming to an unfamiliar word - did not stop or pause for any punctuation marks - did not read with expression._

SPECIFIC READING PERFORMANCE

1. Omissions (words, letters, combinations, phrases, etc.)

   4A - omitted "then"   _no accidental omissions on 8A -_
   6B - omitted "their"   _he read very slowly and asked me to_
   6B - omitted "all"   _pronounce several words for him - "devour" "deluged", "essential"_

2. Substitutions (words, letters, combinations, phrases, etc.)

   4A - read "newspaper" for "paper"   _6B - read "television" for "TV" "it is" for "its"_
   "Miss" for "Mrs." (throughout the story)   _"it is" for "that's", "we" for "we've" "other" for "others"_
   "another" for "other"   _8A - "the" for "that" "get" for "be" "use" for "uses"_

INFORMAL DIAGNOSIS

3. Insertions (words, letters, combinations, phrases, etc.)

none other than contractions mentioned above which were read as 2 words.

4. Repetitions (words, letters, combinations, phrases, etc.)

none

5. Mispronunciation (words, letters, combinations, phrases, etc.)

6B – "political" for "politics" "denty" for "deny" "explain" for "explanatory"
8A – "ploddering" for "plodding" "partly" for "partial" "silent" for "silencing"

Summary and Comment *On unfamiliar longer words he would read root word correctly then scramble the endings – needs some work on suffixes, contractions and syllabication.*

WORD RECOGNITION PROBLEMS

A. Phonic Analysis

1. Auditory Discrimination _____ *good*
2. Visual Discrimination _____ *good*
3. Does he use picture clues *didn't test* Too much? _____ Too little? _____
4. Does he have an adequate sight vocabulary? _____ *yes*

5. Does he know phonics principles? _____ *yes* Does he apply them? _____ *yes*

INFORMAL DIAGNOSIS

Specific Weaknesses:
    a) Consonants (initial, medial, final) *no problems*

        1. single, multiple *no problems*

    b) Consonant blends (initial, medial, final) *no problems*

    c) Vowel blends (initial, medial, final) *no problems*

    d) Consonant digraphs *no problems*

    e) Vowel digraphs *no problems*

    f) Long Vowels *no problems*

    g) Short vowels *no problems*

    h) r, l, w, *no problems*

    i) Other

Comment (Estimate level) *Has very adequate mastery of all phonic principles. WORD RECOGNITION - excellent at all levels - 4A - 99%; 6B - 96%; 8A - 95%.*

B. Structural Analysis

    a) Affixes
        1) Suffixes
        2) Prefixes *no problems*
        3) Roots *no problems*
    b) Syllabication *did not recognize -ity, -atory, -ing, -ial read "curious" for "curiosity", "stupid" for "stupidity", "explain" for "explanatory"*
    c) Compound Words *no problems*
    d) Hyphenated words *no problems except for "self-consciousness" which he read as "self-contained"; not due to hyphen*
    e) Contractions *read "didn't" for "don't", "it is" for "it's", "it is for "that's" "we" for "we've".*

INFORMAL DIAGNOSIS

C. Meanings

1) Comprehension (literal recall) 4A - 100% ; 6B - 80% ;
8A - 70% (had much difficulty understanding this selection).

2) Interpretation 4A - 75% - he didn't understand how the boy actually got the television he gave to Mrs. Hooks, didn't realize the boy had been fired.; 6B - 70% - he thought Alice Cooper

a) Ability to draw inferences was trying to help "Keep America Clean";
8A - 30% he understood that school was blamed for loss of curiosity but thought reason was "fooling around" by students.

b) Ability to discriminate between fact and opinion fair on 6B level -
poor on 8A level - did not recognize statement that kids are interested in sex and violence as Alice Cooper's opinion - or that children learn to become stupid in school as the author's opinion

1) real from fantasy n/a

c) Detect various propaganda techniques didn't test - however probably
poor - because when asked if above statements were necessarily true (2b) he said: "They must be because it says so here."

d) Understand symbols in literature didn't test

e) Imagery didn't test

f) Sensitivity to variant word meanings in context good

g) Can he summarize author's purpose has some difficulty - he thought
author's purpose in selection 8A was to show kids they must pay more attention in school.

1) his choice of style

Comment (estimate level) Comprehension - GR 7.

D. Study Skills

1. Previewing

2. Main Ideas Good on 4A, fair on 6B poor on 8A

3. Related details good when he had correct main idea

4. Outlining

5. Summarizing good

6. Guide Words good

INFORMAL DIAGNOSIS

7. Causal Relations poor - couldn't answer questions: "Why didn't Mrs. Hooks "Why was boy fired?" (4A)
thank the boy for the T.V.?" (4A)

8. Classification _____

9. Use of Dictionary and Reference Books ___ Good _____

10. Follow Directions _____

11. Skimming and Scanning _____

Comment (Estimate level) Indicate specifically which skills can be applied
in what types of material.

When asked to find several words in dictionary, he did so
quickly and easily - also was able to choose correct definition
to fit sentence.   Estimated level - Gr. 7.

GENERAL INFORMATION ON STUDY

1. Does he avoid assignments regularly? _____ sometimes? ___✓___

2. Does he complain of inability to concentrate? ___ no _____

To remember? _____ no _____

3. Does he think or depend on rote memory? yes, he gave many answers
as nearly word-for-word as he could.

4. Does he have difficulty writing compositions ___ sometimes _____
(Get some writing samples)

5. Is he a very slow reader? ___ no ___ Why? _____

Craig Walker   Handwriting sample -
   162 Bellingham St.

Craig Walker   Craig can write nothing other
                   than his name - he could
                   only print his address.
                   He was very embarrassed and
                   explained that even though he
                   "took" handwriting for years,
                   he'd never been able to learn
                   how.

The short form

Exhibit 3-3 illustrates the short form as used in the Northeastern University Reading Clinic which we recommend to persons who have done several IDAs and can summarize the performance data as required by this report form.

Exhibit 3-3.   The Short Form

Individual Diagnostic Analysis
Short Form

Date_____

Name_____Age_____Sex_____

School_____Grade_____

Home Address_____Brothers_____Sisters_____

Parents Names_____Living_____

Divorced_____

Separated____

Referring Source_____

Medical Information_____

Examiner_____Where Tested_____

I.   WORD RECOGNITION

A.   Phonic Analysis:

B.   Structural Analysis:

C.   Summary: Word Recognition level and skills

II. MEANINGS

    A. <u>Literal Recall</u>

    B. <u>Interpretation</u>

III. STUDY SKILLS

    1. <u>Previewing</u>

    2. <u>Finding Main Ideas and Details</u>

    3. <u>Outlining</u>

    4. <u>Summarizing</u>

    5. <u>Classification</u>

    6. <u>Cause and Effect</u>

    7. <u>Sequence</u>

    8. <u>Reference Skills</u>

    9. <u>Guide Words</u>

    10. <u>Following Directions</u>

    <u>COMMENTS</u>: Indicate key problems and key strengths and recommendations.

_____

_____

_____

Discussion of the short form

When you fill in a short form be sure to quote samples of errors made under each heading. For example, under phonic analysis if the reader said *horse* where the word *house* is printed, write *horse* for *house*, *run* for *runs*, *go* for *goes*, *hand* for *hands*, etc., just as I did on the short form for "James." Do the same for heading "structural analysis" and say such things as, he does not seem to know root words and affixes; he has difficulty with compound words and is weak on contractions. *Wherever possible give specific examples of what the reader says and does at each level on which he is being tested, and in each growth area.* Also indicate for word recognition and meanings what levels were tested and what percentage correct was achieved.

Under the heading of study skills we cannot state a grade level equivalent for such skills as previewing, finding main ideas and details, etc., but we can indicate whether we tested the skill or not, and we can indicate whether the student knew the skill and could apply it correctly. You can report this by saying the student did know how to preview a chapter in a textbook, or the student could not pick out the main ideas and details in this material, and so on. Exhibit 3-4 offers a good example of the completed short form.

Discussion of the completed short form

Presumably you could meet "James" and know what his strengths and weaknesses are specifically in each growth area; you know his level of performance, and you know that something in Jame's life has not been and still is not healthy. He attended a special school (under Title 766) for learning disabled persons for six years beginning at age 11 or 12. His almost bizarre responses to the questions on the Holt selection reflect his disturbance.

Exhibit 3-4. Completed Short Form

<u>Individual Diagnostic Analysis</u>
<u>Short Form</u>

Date_____ June 8, 1976_____

Name_____ James _____ Sex___ male ___ Age___ 19 ___

School___ Dropped out Maynard H. S. (ninth grade)_____ Grade___ W.D. ___

Home Address Maynard, Massachusetts_____ Brothers___ 2 ___ Sisters___ 3 ___

Referring Source_____ Massachusetts Rehabilitation Commission _____

Medical Information Hit by car at age of 12, concussion resulted._____

Examiner___ Dr. Melvin Howards _____ Test___ FUSONI IDA _____

Where Tested_____ Reading Clinic _____

I.   WORD RECOGNITION SKILLS

A. <u>Phonic Analysis</u> (Fusoni IDA) Levels tested: 2A, 4A and 8A

2A Errors: said <u>bug</u> for <u>guy</u>, <u>finds</u> for <u>friends</u>, <u>his</u> for <u>he</u>, <u>ran</u> for <u>run</u>, <u>jazz</u> for <u>junk</u>, <u>sanded</u> for <u>swept</u>, <u>important</u> for <u>empty</u>, <u>head</u> for <u>have</u>, <u>ticket</u> for <u>trick</u>, <u>then</u> for <u>when</u>, and could not recognize <u>choice</u>.

4A Errors: said <u>prit</u> for <u>part</u>, <u>broke</u> for <u>brought</u>, did not recognize <u>bargain</u> or <u>trade-in</u>, read <u>understood</u> as underst----d.

8A Errors: said <u>tantrum</u> for <u>themselves</u>, <u>there</u> for <u>why</u>, following for <u>few</u>, <u>last</u> for <u>least</u>, <u>that</u> for <u>them</u> and could not recognize <u>degree</u> or <u>infants</u>.

B. <u>Structural Analysis</u>

Very little evidence of knowledge of syllabication principles, compound words, affixes and roots, or contractions. If words were not recognized at once, James could not apply any of the principles in any of the areas.

C. <u>Summary: Word Recognition Level</u>   James made the same kind of errors in phonic and structural analysis at all three levels, 85-90% correct (2,4 and 8). He reads rather monotonously and word-by-word, pointing at each word. Substitutions and insertions are fairly common and of special interest. In the selection by John Holt on <u>How Children Fail</u> (8A), some unusual responses came from James. In this selection, the first sentence reads:

C. Summary: Word Recognition Level: continued

"To a great degree school is a place where children learn
to be stupid." James read as follows: "To a great de---
(he was helped with the rest of the word, gree), school is
a place where kids learn to be smart." I stopped here to
point this interesting error out, adding that perhaps he
could not believe that schools are a place where you are
made stupid. He responded by defending schools, their large
classes and children's behavior. We moved on; the next sentence read: "Infants are not stupid: children of one, two,
and three throw themselves into everything they do." James
read as follows: "Infants are not stupid: children of one,
two and three throw tantrums..."

These are not simply reading errors and will need to be pursued
in the corrective program.

II. MEANINGS

A. Literal Recall

Excellent recall on all three levels (2, 4 and 8); 90% to 100%.

B. Interpretation

Very good at all three levels. In the 85 to 95% range for each level
read. His responses were conceptually sound and gave evidence of
good relational thinking.

III. STUDY SKILLS

A. Previewing   N/A

B. Finding Main Ideas and Details

Some evidence that he can handle this at all levels tested.

C. Outlining   N/A

D. Summarizing

Some evidence that he could do this in the sample.

E. Using Key Words/Guide Words   N/A

F. Skimming and Scanning   N/A

Comments: Indicate key problems and key strengths and recommendations.

James can function at a sixth or eighth grade level, probably higher in
terms of his meanings skills. His comprehension and interpretation
are very good to excellent at all levels tested. He needs some work
in structural analysis, especially in syllabication, affixes, roots
and compound words. He needs work in phonic analysis with special
attention to substitutions and occasional insertions. James has a
good speaking vocabulary and a good aural vocabulary as well as
some grasp on relatively complex concepts, e.g., interest rates,
supply and demand. He has the intelligence, but he has personal problems which reduce his reading efficiency and confidence.

ADMINISTERING AN IDA

Determining the Reading Level

The first problem is to make a good estimate of the level you will ask the student to read. We can use as a gauge the number of years the person went to school; what kind of experience he has had; his use of the language in your casual conversation: is the vocabulary good, fair? Is it appropriate (does the student use big words in the wrong places?); how about the person's sentence structure? Good, bad? Does the person in this initial conversation before the reading is done seem to understand your language, vocabulary, ideas, and humor? Use some humor, plays on words, allusions to current events, sports, or politics, etc. The student's responses to this kind of repartee gives clues about his language and experience. Poke around to find out what the person is reading now—newspapers, magazines, books, etc. Follow up on that and question him about some of the contents just to verify that the person really does read, and that he understands what is read. After this assessment select the level of material to be read for the IDA.

It is important to try to hit the right level or just below it, because it can be awkward sometimes if you select materials above the person's ability and the reader struggles with it word by word. It's hard to say, "well, you can't handle that level; let's try something at a lower level." It would be better to say, "oh, I gave you the wrong paragraph." If you select material that is too easy it might insult older readers, but it's easier to get out of that gracefully than if you start too high. So try hard to gauge at the outset the reader's language skill and knowledge, and thus be able to put him into the right level at once. This will take time, so don't get too nervous about it if you miss a few times.

Case study: Matthew

Matthew is 32 years old, dropped out of school in the 10th grade, has a family now, an uneven work record, a bit of a drinking problem, and a poor self image, which sometimes makes him shy and at other times makes him furious and quite aggressive. When he was in school he did erratic work, sometimes very good, other times very poor in the same subject. But in your conversation with him you find out that he keeps up with the news, mainly on TV, and occasionally he reads a paper. He appears to be somewhat familiar with what's happening. Matthew has strong, generally unsupported opinions about politicians, coaches of football teams, employers—"others" who have made it. But he seems to want to learn and has exposed himself to the point where he has come to you for a diagnosis and some instruction. His vocabulary, although sprinkled with "you knows" and some uneven grammar, is understandable and quite direct. So, where do we begin? I'd try eighth grade material in an area of Matt's interest like sports or politics.

Matt reads from an eighth grade paragraph while I listen and make notes on errors he makes. I have of course told him what we were going to do: "I am going to listen to you read and I'll ask some questions so we can find out where to start our instruction. We don't want to spend time doing things you already know. I'll make some notes because I can't remember everything." So he reads; I make notes on his performance; for example, he says house for horse, device for devise, etc. *If he reads the first two or three sentences almost flawlessly or with only one or two minor errors, I let him read the rest silently*. Otherwise, I let him read the entire eighth grade selection aloud, in order to get a full sample of his reading behavior and skills. When he finishes the reading of the material, I ask him several questions, perhaps ten comprehension questions and five interpretation questions (or more). Before he answers the questions, take the printed materials away so that he has to answer from memory— that's what comprehension is, literal recall, not rereading. I always ask questions while the student reads because I get more information that way. But if you do it that way, be sure your questions are being answered from recall and interpretation, not from the reader looking for the answers. If you want to measure rereading or locating answer skills then let him go back through the material, *but* we want to measure comprehension.

Let's say Matt reads the eighth grade selection with perhaps ten errors out of 150 words in the selection ($1/15$ or 7% wrong). That's 93% correct in word recognition; and if he answers nine of the ten comprehension questions correctly, that's 90%; and if he gets four of the five interpretation questions correct, that's 80%. These scores, this performance, meet the criteria for his *instructional level*. He can handle eighth grade material comfortably and independently. What now? Have him read a ninth grade selection, unless he seemed uncomfortable or embarrassed during the work on the eighth grade material. You could cajole him and support his efforts positively, and move into the ninth grade material. If at that level he also meets the criteria, move up to the tenth grade, unless of course he reacted negatively and appeared to struggle with the ninth grade material. (Generally, people will go along and if you treat them right, like adults—no fake enthusiasm, but honest comments on the reading performance and some encouragement to keep trying—they will go along and perform well.) If on the other hand Matt read the ninth grade material and his word recognition problems caused him to score about 80% correct, and his comprehension dropped to 70% and his interpretation stayed at 80%, I'd consider his instructional level to be between eighth and ninth grade, or 8^2.

In addition to the check on word recognition and meanings, ask the reader to suggest titles for the material he read, or, if the material contained ideas and facts in sequence, ask for the sequence. Level is not important; for now, find out whether the reader knows how to summarize, deal with main ideas, follow a sequence, classify, etc.

During the reading and questioning, record not only the number of right and wrong answers, but more importantly, record any qualitative information, such as how he answered emotionally and intellectually, and any gesture or other behavioral acts. We are interested not just in the percentage correct and the specific errors made, but in who made these errors and how, because we want to know why.

Case study: Roger

Suppose a young boy of ten years in the fourth grade has a history of reading and writing problems. His name is Roger. He is sloppy; he makes some reversals it is said; he reads below grade level; he seems uninterested and sometimes in another world; but he seems bright enough. (This is a fairly typical description of many boys who often get classified as learning disabled. Try to ignore that kind of diagnosis until after you do yours; try to avoid starting with too many biases against the student. Assume he really doesn't have all the problems stated, and when we analyze and make comparative diagnoses of such cases, you'll see why I say this.)

Roger's mother and teacher feel he can do better, and he needs to in order to keep up with his classmates. As far as the boy is concerned, both mother and teacher have become part of the problem. In this kind of etiology, it doesn't matter what is really true objectively, but it does matter what the child thinks and feels because that's what controls his behavior.

My approach is powerfully, aggressively positive—in essence I try to convey to him that I don't care about the past; that I know he *can* read and write; that I like him, but I will take no nonsense. I use humor; I probe his interest and challenge his knowledge about things he says he likes and knows about. I take the lead, giving and taking, with direction and purpose. We are not just rambling, but discovering and uncovering a little about each other. I ask him questions when he seems to know something and have him give me information. I listen. Now we read.

I'd probably start Roger on third grade level (3^1) in content which may be of interest to him (hockey, rocks, dinosaurs, etc.). He reads orally. I make notes; I keep asking questions as he reads—some funny, some serious. Then I follow the scoring and decide whether to go up to fourth grade level. If he reads the 3^1 selection just below the criteria, for example, 85% in word recognition, 80-95% in comprehension, and 70% in interpretation, I might start him at that level, 3^1, or more conservatively go down to 2^2. If he is not too nervous after he completes the 3^1 performance, I might push him to a higher level, 4^1, in a different kind of material just to see what I can find out.

Sometimes, children and adults score the same at several levels, or even score higher on higher level material than on the lower level. The content, of course, affects that; his confidence in you as a tester counts; and the materials are not always that different between say 3^1 and 4^1, that is, the phonic and structural analysis skills may not involve many more skills at the higher level. When to try the next higher level depends very much on the person being tested and the kind of relationship you have with him or her. If you have any inkling that you can get more out of the reader, push. One has to move with *bold caution and sensitivity*. In fact, if you get a good relationship going in this IDA, you can really do a lot of things at various levels. You can come up with an incredible amount of reading information and also personal information, which comes forth as you progress in your questioning about the material and its possible relationship to the reader's life and experience.

Along the way, as the person is reading orally and misses a word, always give the person a chance to self-correct. Say, "I'm sorry, what did you say?" or "I didn't hear that, could you repeat it." or "What?" If you want to find out only how bad a person's reading is, if you diagnose negatively by seeking problems, you won't allow for self-corrections; you will merely count the errors. Keep a casual tone during the process. A little humor, a smile, a "good" now and then (but not too much praise), and a little sharing of yourself—this is a human process of diagnosis.

The manner in which an IDA is administered can very much negate its normally valuable results. If you keep the IDA informal you will get all the information you need on the performance in each growth area; you will note both strengths and weaknesses; and you will get some of the readers' interests, background, and problems.

The IDA can be projective in the sense that the WISC or WAIS can be. It is revealing of performance and personality, a glimpse into a life. Don't settle for less. Use this informal diagnostic process as an interview with a person, one whose symptoms or problems are in reading and writing. If you expand the context of your diagnosis you will get much more valid and useful information in terms of planning and executing a successful corrective program that really meets the needs of the student.

Any diagnosis that depends on lengthy written accounts, reports, and studies, and relatively little on the person must be distorted and will probably produce negative results. I prefer to get information from my observations and interactions with the person, and then note what others have said and reported. The fewer the filters between me and my student, the better, and the truer the analysis will be.

EXAMPLES OF IDAs

Following are some examples of real IDAs done by students in clinical courses at Northeastern University—some bad, some good—with my analysis and criticism of each. When you read the report on the short form, think about it in terms of what you would do if you had this report in your hands and tomorrow the student walked in for help. Do you have enough information about him as a person? As a reader? Where would you begin with skills and what would you use as a focal point (content center) of your lessons? What content? What level? What strengths and weaknesses? After reading the analysis and criticism and comparing and contrasting them with your own feelings and views, you'll have a good idea of how to administer an IDA and how to begin to use the information for grouping, planning, and implementing an instructional program. The short forms will appear first, followed by an analysis and criticism. Exhibit 3-5 illustrates the IDA short form on *Robert*.

Analysis and Critique of the Individual Diagnostic Analysis Short Form on *Robert* by Marjorie

The boy's age should be in years and months; the date must always be written (as a basic rule date and make copies of everything). This form does include a place for medical information and referral source; however, there is no information in either place on the form. This kind of information may be very helpful later on and should be included.

Part I: Word Recognition

Section A. Phonic analysis. Marjorie fails to give us any specific examples of the kinds of mistakes Robert made which would lead to her statement that he recognizes consonants and blends—vowels. Does he recognize all consonants, in all positions (initial, final, and medial)? Does he know all blends, both consonant and vowel blends? Does he know all vowel sounds and combinations? Did he make any phonic analysis errors in his reading? If so, give examples: house for horse, place for palace, etc.

Section B. Structural analysis. We get a similarly vague, general comment on Robert's performance. Are there some prefixes and suffixes he does not know that you discovered in the selection he read? Which ones? He knows the principle of compound words but does he know all of them? What about his skill in syllabicating, one of the most essential and basic structural analysis skills—can he or can't he, and give examples of what he actually did. Can he handle roots of words and does he understand their meanings and that they can be found in many other words called derivatives. Prefixes and suffixes are good to know, but they are virtually useless unless the student can identify root words and know that the prefix will usually change the meaning of the roots meaning,

Exhibit 3-5. IDA Short Form on *Robert*

Individual Diagnostic Analysis
Short Form

Date_____

Name_____Robert_____ Sex_Male__ Age__16____

School____Sycamore High School_____ Grade_10____

Home address_172 Vaughn Lane___ Brothers__none___ Sisters__none____

Referring source_____

Medical information_____

Examiner_____Marjory_____ Test_____

Where tested__Sycamore High School_____

I. WORD RECOGNITION

   A. Phonic Analysis

      Recognizes consonants and blends - vowels.

   B. Structural Analysis

      Knows most prefixes and suffixes - compound words.

   C. Summary: Word Recognition Level

      Can sound out most words. Does not always have exact meaning. Gets
      meaning from context. Will guess rather than look up a word.

II. MEANINGS

   A. Comprehension

      Level: 10th grade. Schrammel - Gray Standard Test.

   B. Interpretation

      Level: 9th grade level - answered questions at end of stories in
      text - "Adventures Bound."

   C. Meanings

      Gets meanings and interprets stories well - Does not want to bother
      to read anything unless on sports or adventure.

III. STUDY SKILLS (Previewing, Main Ideas, Details, Outlining, Reference Skills)

      Have not tested him on these skills yet.

      Comments: (Indicate key problems, key strengths, and recommendations)

      Robert is in a shop program - a sophomore - sixteen years old -
      chubby, good-natured boy. Easily distracted by others. Sees no
      reason to read. Would rather spend time in shop or running errands.
      Does like sports and is interested in high school football team
      games. Not athletic himself. Textbook used for this group of boys in
      shop program is Adventure Bound by Jewett, Edman, McKee - Houghton
      Mifflin Co., 1961. Is one of a reading-for-meaning series. It is
      recommended for ninth grade and stories are well chosen for varied
      interests among students.

      Robert handles vocabulary and meaning very well. Motivating him to
      read is the main problem and because he has not read too widely his
      knowledge is limited. I kept skipping around in the book. Find
      sports stories interest him the most.

while the suffix will normally (not always) reveal what part of speech the word is in that particular sentence. This is not clear from Marjorie's statement.

Section C. Word recognition level. We expect a summary of the major errors in phonics and structural analysis, and we want some evidence of any patterns of errors, and we want *level*. But Marjorie didn't record Robert's level of word recognition skills. It could have been fourth, sixth, or tenth. She says, "Can sound out most words." At what level— fourth, eighth, tenth? What kinds of words does he have trouble with? Multisyllabic ones, which? Her statement is not specific enough. Then she says, "Does not always have exact meaning." Is that a problem of word recognition or of vocabulary? Obviously, there is some relationship between these reading acts, but vocabulary, which focuses on the meanings of words in and out of context, is not the same act as being able to syllabicate a word, or to pronounce initial consonant blends like bl, gr, st, etc. Then she goes on, still in her own context, with "Get's meaning from context."It sounds here like a problem, rather than what it is, a useful skill. But she is still talking about vocabulary and telling us that Robert does not always have the exact, real dictionary meaning and then he gets meaning from context (said almost negatively).

Then she says "Will guess rather than look up word." If he guesses rather than looking up words and if anything she has said in this statement is true, Robert *does* use context to get the meanings of some words. That's good; it's a strength. But to call the use of context guessing is wrong and inaccurate. To use context is to use the structure and the vocabulary one has to narrow the meaning and function of the word in doubt. For example, if I ask you what *heuristic* means and you say, "I don't know, then I put it into a sentence, into context: "*I have a heuristic mind, while she is prosaic.*" Even if you don't know heuristic and prosaic, you do know that heuristic is an adjective modifying the word mind, and you also know from context that prosiac must be different from, perhaps the opposite of heuristic. If you know the word prosaic (as in prose— aic), you might "guess" that heuristic as the opposite would be something creative, imaginative, poetic. These are all logical antonyms. And right too. Is that whole process guessing? No. It is using several cues: grammar, antonyms and synonyms, maybe even roots and affixes to narrow the possible meaning of the unknown words. We all do this and it is a good skill.

Part II: Meanings

Section A. Comprehension. Marjorie mistakenly gave a standardized test at the tenth grade level (probably because Robert was in the tenth grade) and she reports the results. Why is it a mistake or inappropriate to do this in the middle of an IDA? We give the IDA to determine accurately what level and with what strengths and weaknesses a person performs the reading act; when we discover his level, we can give a standard test at the level at which he performed on the IDA, *not at grade level*. Furthermore, the Gray-Schrammel test measures more than comprehension, but she ignores this. Never do this.

Section B. Interpretation. Marjorie decided to test Robert's interpretation skill and level with questions taken from a textbook he uses in school. This is not good practice because Robert may have used the book the year before or may be using it currently so that he could be very familiar with it. Another problem with using certain school texts is that often the questions at the end of each chapter tend to be comprehension questions, not interpretation questions. We must make the distinction between these two.

Section C. Meanings. Marjorie reports that Robert "gets meaning and interprets stories well." Note the contradictions in her report relative to some of her other remarks about Robert's use of context and guessing at the meaning of words. Marjorie does not seem to be able to understand that using context to guess or estimate the meaning of words of phrases is not wild and haphazard, but is directed and requires understanding most of the context in which the unfamiliar word or phrase appears. She does not seem to want to credit Robert with very much understanding throughout most of this report. She then says that Robert "Does not want to *bother* to read anything unless on sports or adventure. What do you make of the word bother underscored? Obviously she does not consider reading sports or adventure stories *real* reading. Somehow it is lower level, lower quality to her. This is negative, narrowminded, and short-sighted. It really does not matter what a student likes or wants to read; if he or she likes anything, then we can teach reading and writing. Whether you like the material or have biases about what is good and bad reading material is irrelevant. At this stage of diagnosis, we'll take any cues we can and use everything the reader brings to us, so that we can teach him where he is.

Robert did take the Gray-Schrammel test, but we don't know how he did. Marjorie asked what she thought were interpretation questions taken from a ninth grade anthology. We don't know how well he did, but apparently he didn't miss them all. Marjorie did not summarize the findings in the growth area, nor did she give a grade level. Marjorie did not test study skills.

Comments

Please never say condescending things about people like: "chubby, good-natured boy." It's saying, he hasn't much going for him, but he's good natured. Do not damn with faint praise.

The distraction she mentions in this case was partly true because the test was given in a large room where others were moving in and out. Robert noticed this. The next sentence, "Sees no reason to read," could be conjecture. Is that what he told her, or is that what she reported? He likes adventure and sports stories, that's motivation enough. But she does not think that's real reading, not literary, not substantial enough. The only dependable statements in this summary are what book was used, that Robert is in a shop program, and that his vocabulary is good. This is a very poor report.

Exhibit 3-6 illustrates the IDA short form on *Jeff*.

Analysis and Critique of the Individual Diagnostic Short Form on *Jeff* by Nancy

Skim over the report on Jeff by Nancy and compare it with the report on Robert. As you look at it, consider that you will meet Jeff and have to teach him on the basis of the data provided in the report. Can you do it? What's missing? What do you know of his strengths as well as his weaknesses, interests, etc.

Part I: Word Recognition

Section A. Phonic analysis.   Although we do not know this at the outset, Jeff is apparently almost a nonreader at fifteen years, six months, according to Nancy's report on the results of the Botel Inventory. This standardized test is designed for persons functioning below fourth grade level—the lower the better. The test requires the student to listen to a list of words, one at a time, and to write the first letter of each word he hears. On the first subtest, Jeff missed only one of nineteen items. In other words, his listening or auditory discrimination for single consonants in the initial position is good. Note the next part of the Botel: Jeff missed 18 of 19 in trying to hear and then write the first two letters of each word. (These are all initial consonant blends, *gr*ow, *pl*ay, *st*op, etc.) He could not get them and this is quite common for persons taking this test who are almost nonreaders. He did worse in the remainder of the Botel items. This was to be expected because if he couldn't handle initial consonant blends, which tend to be quite regular, then certainly we could expect him to have more difficulty with irregular elements like consonant digraphs (sh and wh, for example). Jeff did not do too badly on the last item of the Botel where he was given in print one word, *ball*, and asked to write at least three other words that rhyme with it.

Why is this an acceptable procedure for a very poor reader, perhaps a nonreader? Because it is basic to be able to handle auditory and visual discrimination tasks very early in the reading process. These subtests do not require that Jeff read—just listen, hear, and record minimally what he picked up. Now there is something else Nancy should have done here with a student in Jeff's condition, and that is to check out his sight vocabulary, which is critical to any formal instruction. She apparently did not do that, or she did not report it. To check sight vocabulary with a boy his age is easy. List common, everyday words like men, women, stop, go,

Exhibit 3-6. IDA Short Form on *Jeff*

Individual Diagnostic Analysis
Short Form

Date_____

Name____Jeff_____ Sex__Male__ Age_15-6_____

School___Washington High School_____ Grade__*8_____

Home address__Waltham, Mass._____ Brothers___9__ Sisters___4_____

Referring source__High School Guidance Counselor_____

Medical information__Normal except for artificial left eye._____

Examiner__Nancy_____ Test_____

Where tested_____Washington High School_____

I. WORD RECOGNITION

   A. Phonic Analysis

   Botel Analysis – Level A
   1 error out of 18 on beginning consonants
   18 errors out of 19 on consonant blends
   4 errors out of 5 on beginning digraphs
   4 rhyming words for ball; 4 for make; 1 for get; 2 for will

   B. Structural Analysis

   Cannot blend phonic elements to form a total word.

   C. Summary: Word Recognition Level

   Pre-primer in isolation. In meaningful context – perhaps a first
   reader.

II. MEANINGS

   A. Comprehension

   Level: Oral work – grade 8; silent reading – grade 2.

   B. Interpretation

   Level: Oral – grade 9; silent reading – grade 2.

   C. Meanings

   Level: Oral – grade 8; silent – grade 2.

III. STUDY SKILLS (Previewing, Main Ideas, Details, Outlining, Reference
                    Skills)

Level: Grade 3

Comments: (Indicate key problems, key strengths, and recommendations)

Jeff has a good speaking vocabulary and is well accepted by his peers.
He has a strong interest in cars and engines. His biggest problem is
that although he seems to know phonic elements, he cannot blend them
into a word. He experiences a glottal stop between each individual
phoneme which blocks his forming them into a word. His sight vocabulary in context is good on long words. He confuses smaller words such
as them, the, these, his, she, etc. – even in meaningful context. From
a completely garbled question, however, he can give a correct answer.
He seems to sense what the question asks although he cannot read it
meaningfully.

walk, car, Dodge, Ford, the student's address, nearby street names, Stop and Shop, bank, etc. These are words he had to have seen many times and which he probably recognizes on sight by memory. It is very important in such a case to have some feel for his store of sight words because it will be these that serve as the foundation for building stories from which we will develop, in context, the phonic and structural analysis skills the reader needs to know.

Section B. Structural analysis. Nancy reports that Jeff can't blend phonic elements to form a word. Good statement, but no examples. An example could have been *global*, which Jeff attacks in this way: he says, with help, *gl* (*guh*, *luh*), then *o, bal*; then when asked to put them together to say the word, he repeats *gl o bal* but cannot get it all together to say glóbal or even globál. Inability to blend phonic elements to form a word is a serious problem found often in nonreaders. The solution is easy, as you will see later.

Section C. Summary of word recognition level. Nancy gives the level as "preprimer in isolation," meaning that Jeff can attack unrelated words on a list, e.g., Dolch, but that in small sentences (context) Jeff might handle some first grade material. And that is not at all uncommon with persons of this age or older whose reading is so low. Their life and other language experience somehow fill in the gaps and can make much of few clues. Note the next section of Nancy's report as an example of that phenomenon.

Part II: Meanings

Section A. Comprehension. Nancy very cleverly did two measures of Jeff. Since he obviously cannot read on his own, and since she wants to know his strengths as well as his weakness, she read to him at a much higher level: eighth grade. His aural comprehension is at the eighth grade level—that's a strength we'll use in the corrective program; on his own, in context, Jeff reads second grade material with good comprehension. The phenomenon of older students and adults who possess few word recognition skills but who are able to recall and interpret material written on much higher levels, is quite common as this case illustrates.

Section B. Interpretation. Nancy repeated the procedure to measure Jeff's interpretation skills. She read ninth grade material to him, and his aural comprehension was fine. Again she tried to see what he could do with language in context, and he was able to handle second grade material on his own. So, in Meanings, Nancy did two sensitive things: (1) She read to him at a much higher level than his own skills would permit, in order to identify some of his aural strengths; and (2) She had him read, in context, so that he could use whatever clues he could discover.

Comments

Nancy gives him appropriate credit for both his aural and silent comprehension and interpretation. This is a good model for testing persons at such very low levels, and particularly for older adolescents and adults. She accents the positives; good vocabulary, interest in cars and engines. He knows phonic elements in isolation, but can't blend (that is good information and we can solve that problem fairly easily, and did in fact). The next sentence is of questionable value: "I merely attribute that behavior to nervousness." We never found that to be a part of his problem in learning to read and write, and we taught him. The rest of her summary is meaty, to the point, and most helpful for one who would plan an instructional program for Jeff. Nancy did a clever thing in giving a garbled question to Jeff to see what he could do with it, in this case because she had evidence from him of a good vocabulary and a good rapport. Jeff's ability to interpret a garbled question, make it straight, and then answer it, is a strength which is most useful in correction. Apparently he thinks well and expresses himself well. He needs work in word recognition but he has strengths in vocabulary and reasoning, and a real interest in cars and engines.

Case Study: Example of IDA for Ed

Here is another example for an IDA done on a young man I'd never met. (We did this for twenty-four observers.)

Ed, nineteen years old, divorced or separated, daughter of two years; up from New York City, apparently living with his sister; didn't want to say anything about number or nature of brothers or sisters during the IDA, so I dropped it, to find out later he has a reported twenty-two siblings. In the midst of questioning about a paragraph he had read on which I deliberately made a little digression, he blurted out that he had been on his own, in the streets, at twelve years of age. This sort of information is revealed if your IDA seeks out that kind of affective information above and beyond how many words and questions, right and wrong.

The IDA can have the effect of a good interview educationally and psychologically. Ed's interview did. He read an eighth grade selection on automobiles, accidents, and teenagers' symbolic uses of the car. I thought the content would be more interesting than others I had on hand. It was a badly written paragraph using expressions like "the under 20 driver," when it should have said simply and directly "the driver under 20," which Ed would have understood at once instead of struggling. Poor readers who have had bad or little formal schooling need material stated plainly and directly. Ed read aloud in front of twenty-four strangers and me. Throughout, his problem was the same: inability to read multisyllabic words. He'd get one or two syllables, guess the rest from configuration clues, and then fuse, or blend the parts incorrectly. Usually, after I told him the word, he'd show signs that he understood the word, except the word *illegitmacy.* He decoded that something like *il leg . . . ill eg,* and he mumbled the rest. I told him the word and then asked if he knew the meaning; he did not. That did surprise me a bit. For *annually,* he read *anormally;* with the word *approximately* he could not get beyond *app.*

I questioned him continually in comprehension and interpretation and he scored between 80% and 90%. So I tried him on a lower level to see if his word recognition would improve noticeably. It did not improve; he continued to get the beginning of a word and then guess the rest using context and configuration, thus following the common pattern of older students scoring much higher on comprehension and interpretation than on word recognition. Ed made as many, and the same, mistakes on the sixth grade material as he did on the eighth. His comprehension and interpretation were the same or 5% higher at the sixth grade level.

In Ed's case, and in other cases like his, one or two basic skills are missing or badly developed (e.g., multisyllabic words and vocabulary), and when they are taught, they soar to higher levels, but without help they perform as Ed did.

Ed came to me at the end of this session (more than one hour in front of the group) and asked if I really could help him with that syllabication and vocabulary; I said I could. Ed came in for another session, this time for instruction, in front of this group. He wanted some of my materials and I said I'd bring them at the next session of the group (a workshop group). A few minutes later, through his sister, he reminded me that the next meeting was off because of a holiday and would I remember the session after that. I did. He took the material and came for instruction.

THE IMPORTANCE OF EARLY ADMINISTRATION OF THE IDA

A good IDA administered to each student in the public schools would save teachers (and the children) many weeks of time by revealing what the children know and what they need in reading and language skills. Usually it takes weeks for most teachers to know each child's true strengths and weaknesses in a class of twenty-five or thirty-five children. The good and bad readers show up early, while the mass in the middle (at least 70%) is not known to the teacher, but is hidden under standardized test scores like 3.2 in vocabulary, 3.5 in comprehension. These scores mean almost nothing in practical and specific terms because they do not tell which phonic elements the child knows or does not know; the child's vocabulary; his knowledge of roots and prefixes; and so on. Standardized test scores by themselves tend to hide children and their actual reading performance.

The IDA, done right, reveals exactly what a child does when he reads; what mistakes he makes and why; what principles he knows in phonic and structural analysis, and which ones he uses and which he does not; and how his thinking and logic processes operate when he responds to a barrage of comprehension and interpretation questions.

Before any standard language testing is done, I urge that the IDA be administered to establish the actual instructional level of the child. Then, if you must, give the standard test at that level, not at the child's grade placement level. Furthermore, the IDA done correctly generates a great deal of affective information about the person being tested. It's almost like a WAIS or other psychological test requiring some projection; you get a sampling of behavior and feeling, which is as important as the factual material on the student's strengths and weaknesses. The nature of the interview and interviewer greatly affects the output by the student.

SUMMARY OF STEPS IN ADMINISTERING THE IDA

1. Talk to the student casually and warmly to reduce tension, fear, and anxiety. Observe his use of vocabulary, sentence structure, concepts, feelings, interests, and experience. Explain that he will be reading orally and silently and discussing what was read and what it means, so that you can quickly discover what he can and cannot do.

2. Add to this information as much as possible about the reader's background so that you can select material for the IDA very close to his ability. Often you can start the testing with graded material about a year or year and a half below current grade placement, or last grade attended, depending on what you pick up in #1

3. Have several types of reading material with you, e.g., history, science, sports, and fiction at several levels (second grade, fourth grade, sixth, eighth, and tenth grade levels). It is most desirable to have two or three graded selections at each of the levels representing different content fields.

4. Let the student start reading *orally* at the lowest level you have chosen. If the reading at that level in that type of material is fluent after the first two or three sentences, let the reader complete the piece silently. If the oral reading is labored and filled with errors, let him read the entire selection orally so that you can record the errors. If the reading is really difficult, after a couple of sentences say, "Oh, I gave you the wrong selection; here's the one I wanted," and then present a selection from a lower level. If the reading of this first selection is slow but reasonably accurate, let the student read the whole selection orally. You might have him read another selection at the same level.

5. Ask your prepared comprehension, interpretation, vocabulary, and concept questions either at the end of the oral or silent reading, or interspersed throughout the selection. If the material is at fourth grade level and above, and the student is in the fourth grade level or above, ask study skills questions.

6. On the long or short form, record errors made in the oral reading under each heading: word recognition, meanings, and study skills. Except for study skills, you should list examples of specific errors made and the percentages correct at each level tested. Calculate percentages as the reading proceeds so that you do not have to stop and compute after each selection read.

(a) If the student scores within the criteria in word recognition at a particular level (90% and above with self-corrections) and not below 70% in interpretation and not below 75–80% in comprehension, move to the next higher level, e.g., from 4^1 to 4^2 or 5^1.

(b) When the student begins to struggle with the material and makes more word recognition errors and begins missing comprehension questions regularly, stop the reading part of the IDA and get a writing sample. The writing sample can be a brief paragraph on the student himself, an interpretation of a proverb, or what the student expects from the program. For very low level students, the writing sample can be writing their name and address. Get something in writing.

7. Study the long or short form you have been filling out and notice if the errors made in word recognition fall into patterns, e.g., cannot handle initial consonant blends, or drops endings (some or all), cannot recognize medial vowel digraphs. Check comprehension and interpretation answers for their shallowness or literalness and for their relationship to the material read. Try to detect whether older students are responding to your questions on the basis of what they read or what they know from their experience.

8. Establish the *instructional level* on the basis of the criteria. Generally, we want a balance between word recognition performance and skill and meanings. High word recognition scores coupled with low meanings scores dictate that we start closer to the word recognition level; high meanings scores with low word recognition scores suggest that we can begin successful instruction at least a half year above the word recognition score, and this is especially true of older students and adults. When in doubt, start closer to the word recognition score.

Note—When dealing with older students and especially adults who are nonreaders or at first or low second grade level in reading, we may use the language-experience approach. If you use this approach, their actual level is less important, since you would use their own language, experiences, and knowledge as the raw material for instruction.

9. Write up the recommendations for the instructional program on the long or short form, and then write a narrative summary of the whole IDA in terms of the performance, patterns of errors, strengths, interests, and background.

10. Using the student's interests and background and the diagnosed strengths and weaknesses on the IDA, plan two or three core concept plans in general (see Chapter 5). In each instructional session continue diagnosing strengths and weaknesses and adjust your materials and methods accordingly.

CASE STUDIES

Now that we have discussed, analyzed, and critiqued the IDA process and practices, let's look at two case studies that seem to typify common diagnostic practice. Standardized tests of several types are reported by the diagnosticians and their interpretations of these data are included.

After each case report I shall offer my own analysis and interpretation of the diagnostic data collected. The first case is Mark (see Exhibit 3–7).

Critique and Analysis of Report on Mark

I want to take this apart almost line by line to illustrate as tangibly as possible that many diagnoses look just like this. I cannot mention the names of all the institutions and individuals who have made diagnoses like these, but I can say they cover a wide range of outstanding medical institutions, universities, and private neurologists and consulting psychologists, among others. For illustrations of more serious misdiagnoses especially for children called hyperactive or learning disabled, or minimally brain damaged, read Peter Schrag's (1975), *The Myth of the Hyperactive Child*. It is frightening and so true.

Introduction

The first phrase, "a suspected underachiever suffering from possible delays in perceptual-motor development," is classic and common statement. What is a "suspected underachiever"? Who suspects him and on what grounds? What evidence is there for such a suspicion? And, aren't we all underachievers? And how can one suffer from a *possible* delay? Either you suffer from an ailment, disease, disability, or you don't. The paragraph refers to "probable cause of his underachievement," which was not proven yet. Immediately Mark is being classified as having a perceptual-motor handicap in reading—on the basis of what? Nothing. He was, in fact, *diagnosed before he came for the testing*.

The next paragraph is supposed to soften the anticipated blows, and is true but meaningless in this context.

Intelligence testing

Mark was given the WISC, (WISC has been revised and is now WISC-R) a perfectly good test in the hands of the right administrator of

Exhibit 3-7. Case study on *Mark*

<u>Language Disability Tests Report</u>

Re: Mark
Age: 12
Grade: 7
Parents: Mr. and Mrs. Sam
Address: Massachusetts

Remarks:

<u>Introduction:</u>

Mark came to the testing center from Mrs. C. as a <u>suspected underachiever suffering</u> from <u>possible delays in perceptual-motor development</u>. A number of tests have been given to assess the probable cause of his underachievement. The results appear below.

Mark is a brown-haired male of 12 years, 10 months at the time of testing. He is a nice looking, well dressed young man. He was very cooperative and followed directions well in the testing situation.

<u>Intelligence Testing</u>

<u>Since realistic expectations for any child must be related to his intelligence potential</u>, the Wechsler Intelligence Scale for Children (WISC) was administered. This is an individual test requiring approximately 1½ hours to administer, and consists of 12 subtests measuring both Verbal and Performance abilities. The WISC differs from group-IQ tests often given by schools since <u>almost no reading is required</u>. Questions are asked and answered orally, and non-verbal tasks are performed with objects or symbols. Children with learning disabilities frequently score 15 or more points higher on the WISC than on group-IQ tests. It is usually considered to be a more accurate estimate of intelligence than the group tests.

On the WISC, Mark scored as follows: Verbal Score, Above Average; Performance Score, Average; and Full-Scale Score, High Average. Verbal scores were 14 scaled points higher than Performance scores. Highest scores were obtained on subtests of Digit Span and Coding. This is a pattern frequently seen in the case of children with learning disabilities, and is considered to be a symptom of a perceptual-motor deficit.

The scores obtained on the above IQ test would suggest that <u>underachievement probably is not related to Mark's intelligence</u> since normal ability is present.

Specific scores on the IQ test given will be sent on request to schools or other institutions requesting them.

<u>Perceptual-Motor Skills Tests</u>

<u>Visual</u>

The way in which a person is able to see and hear and to integrate these sensory stimuli into his central nervous system processes may have a profound effect on his ability to learn the language arts and to achieve in school. Therefore, a number of perceptual tests are given to measure both visual and auditory acuity, and to determine whether there may be a disability in discrimination, organization, and memory for visual and auditory stimuli.

To test visual skills, the Keystone Visual Skills Tests were given to determine both visual acuity and ocular-motor control. On these tests, Mark failed the near fusion subtest. <u>Such visual difficulty is often linked with underachievement</u>.

Persons with learning disabilities often have difficulty integrating what they see into central nervous system functions. Therefore, a number of tests of perceptual functioning were given to determine whether Mark is having difficulty with integrating and remembering what he sees. One instrument for measuring visual organization and memory at the central nervous system level is a visual-motor gestalt test, containing a number of geometric forms which the subject is asked to observe and draw.

On the Berea Visual Motor Gestalt Test, which is ordinarily used with subjects from seven years of age through adolescence, Mark had some difficulty with reproducing the figures, and organization was quite poor for his age. Memory for designs was also found to be poor.

Auditory

Auditory acuity, discrimination and organization are considered by many investigators to be even more important than visual perception in reading. A number of auditory tests were given with the following results.

An Audiometric Test was given to check hearing acuity. Results on this test indicate that Mark has normal hearing acuity, without any hearing loss. In addition to the audiometric check, which determines whether the child is able to hear pure tones or not, other auditory tests were given.

The testing center's Auditory Discrimination Test measures the ability of a subject to hear the difference between words that are nearly alike in sound but different in meaning, e.g., fan/van, pen/pin, clove/clothe. On this test, Mark showed some loss of ability, but not to a major extent.

On a test of Blending Ability, in which the pupil is asked to listen to the sound of each letter in a short word and then identify the word, Mark showed a major difficulty.

Motor

Recent research indicates a relationship between motor development and language arts skills. Not only were specific motor tests given but observations were maintained throughout the testing period in order to assess motor functions.

On the Gesell Double Commands Test, Mark was able to execute hand movements in a manner appropriate to his age.

Language Arts Tests

Since school achievement is so dependent on reading, writing, and spelling, Mark was given a number of language arts tests to determine whether normal language development has taken place.

When asked to write the alphabet in both capitals and lower case letters, the responses indicate that Mark is able to perform this task without difficulty and within normal time limits.

On a test of visual word memory in which the child is asked to copy words seen for five seconds on a flash card, Mark's performance was normal.

To determine reading ability, the Durrell Analysis of Reading Difficulty was administered. This is a test battery that includes oral and silent reading, listening comprehension and others. This instrument measures speed, accuracy, and comprehension in reading. On oral reading, for example, the pupil begins with a very simple, first grade paragraph and he reads progressively more difficult passages until it is no longer possible for him to read or to score with anything like normal ability.

On the Durrell, Mark scored at the low fourth grade level in oral reading, the high fourth grade level in silent reading, and the fifth grade level in listening comprehension. His oral reading was marked by incorrect phrasing, monotonous tone, inadequate word-analysis ability, and ignoring word errors and reading on. While Mark showed considerable difficulty with the oral reading process, his comprehension ability was at the fifth grade level.

A spelling test was given to determine Mark's ability to produce normal sound-symbol relationships. On this test, he showed a spelling disability, misspelling 5 of the 24 words dictated.

On a list of words that must be spelled by rules or learned memory, Mark was functioning at an upper elementary level. In addition to the spelling list, Mark was also asked to write down a dictated paragraph appropriate to his grade level. In this test, he exhibited the same bizarre spelling patterns obtained in the spelling test above. He also showed considerable difficulty with this task and very poor auditory memory. On this same test, handwriting was judged to be poorly developed for his age.

On tests of grammatical usage, Mark showed normal development for his grade level and age. Oral language patterns also indicate normal development.

Projective Testing

Some children are underachievers because of emotional problems. It is, therefore, important to determine whether there is any emotional basis or component in the underachievement. This is normally accomplished through the administration of a number of tests. Results from these tests indicate that Mark is within normal personality development limits, and it is doubtful whether personality factors are a major consideration in his language disability.

Conclusions

Mark is a child with high average intelligence who is currently underachieving in the language arts field. There are evidences of a perceptual-motor disability which undoubtedly is contributing to underachievement in the language arts areas.

The late and irregular development of perceptual-motor skills is particularly noticeable as a global problem involving both visual and auditory functions. This is seen in the visual areas where he has a typical visual skills problem, some difficulty remembering geometric designs, and copying of simple figures is very difficult for him. This is also apparent in the auditory areas where he has difficulty blending sounds into words and a severe difficulty remembering a sequence of numbers; and in the motor areas where his handwriting is somewhat immature. Language arts skills are found to be extremely retarded for Mark's age and IQ.

All of these results suggest that Mark is suffering from perceptual-motor difficulties leading to a learning disability. Such a condition often is referred to as "dyslexia" or a "specific learning disability."

Recommendations

Mark should be recognized as an adolescent with a perceptual-motor disability which is interfering with his ability to achieve in school. If his school has a program for dyslexic pupils, or if the school anticipates setting up such a program, Mark should be considered a candidate

A perceptual-motor training program is advised.

Mark should be able to make normal progress with specialized help. We would recommend that he be tutored at least three times per week. This tutoring should emphasize the structure and pattern of the language and involve not only reading, but spelling and writing as well.

We would also recommend specialized help with handwriting in order that Mark may develop at least a legible hand. We will be glad to make more specific recommendations in this area if requested to do so.

A summer program structured for dyslexic pupils would be very helpful for Mark.

tests; otherwise, it too can be misused and misinterpreted as can any test. All is well in this paragraph until the next to the last sentence when out of the galaxy comes this remark about children with learning disabilities, which says almost nothing, except that it puts Mark in the class of learning disabled children. Even if six out of ten disabled readers score fifteen points higher on the WISC than on group IQ tests it certainly does not mean that Mark will, because we do not know that he is disabled at all, in any way. He is very much suspected though. Also, where is the proof that disabled children (legitimately diagnosed) score higher on WISC than on group IQ tests? Most children I have tested also score higher on the individual intelligence test, because of the individual quality of the test and its conversational mode and because it requires no reading. The test itself is part of the reason for the variation in scores; it is not necessarily true that learning disabled children score higher on WISC because they are learning disabled. Furthermore, inserting that sentence in this paragraph sets the reader and parent up for his performance on the WISC. It also clearly maintains the air that this boy is learning disabled, ipso facto.

Next come the results on the WISC. *His pattern of scoring is not at all unusual.* We do not get the exact results anyway, so it is difficult to tell just how well he did on the various subtests. Again we get the insidious and unrelated remark about children with learning disabilities. This report is on Mark and no one else. The examiner again refers to perceptual-motor development, without data to support it. *A low score on digits and coding do not assure motor discoordination, and even if it did, it is not clear that such discoordination affects reading skill significantly,* or that it does so in Mark. This kind of reporting is nonprofessional. The conclusion was reached before the child was met and tested, and the data from the test are largely ignored.

Perceptual/motor skills tests

Now we move to the reports on other kinds of diagnostic measures to determine the learning disability which is expected. Nothing on the WISC gave any major indication of a need to pursue perceptual, visual, or auditory testing. Usually, these can very easily and quickly be checked without formal testing.

Visual.   In the visual screening paragraph we read that the ability to integrate sensory stimuli into the central nervous system *may* affect reading and language arts. It may not. And this visual test is not able to tell us whether there is appropriate neural integration. *The Keystone Visual Skills test does not measure, nor does it purport to measure, neural integration.* Mark's visual acuity score is normal anyway, except in one subtest. Can one fusion subtest measure the ability to fuse in a wide array of visual environments? No. And again, the last sentence slips in the underachievement note. *One poor score on one subtest, fusion in this case,*

*does not correlate with overall underachievement, and there is not legiti-
mate research that shows it.*

Then we jump into a paragraph beginning with "Persons with learning disabilities. . . " Back goes Mark into the category of perceptual-motor problems in spite of the evidence presented to the contrary. On the
visual-motor test Mark did alright but had some difficulty (not identified
in detail) with organization and memory for designs. Where is the evidence that either of these functions (measured as they are on this one
test) is directly related to reading ability? There is none.

Auditory. Mark's auditory skills all seem to be intact and normal
even by these tests. The measurement of such specific elements in words
as blends may not be an accurate indicator of reading skill.

Motor. My own experience denies the insinuations. The final line
on Mark's motor development says he is adequately developed for his
age, even though the paragraph started with some *imagined relationship
between motor development and the language arts.* I have no idea what
research is alluded to, and have not yet found any fitting that description.
Furthermore, even some aphasics and cerebral palsy victims can and do
learn to read in spite of massive brain and nervous system dysfunctions.

Language arts

Now onto the language arts tests on which Mark did well, except on
the Durrell, and even there they found his comprehension at a higher
level than his oral reading. Generally, Mark was fairly average on their
tests, which they administered, scored, and interpreted.

Conclusions

Mark is also a normal personality by their own admission. Now to
the conclusions of their testing. We have evidences of the perceptual-motor difficulty suspected in the first paragraph. He has it! How could he
miss? What is the basis for this conclusion: he had minor difficulty with
coding and digits on the WISC; he fell below average on near fusion; his
organization of figures and his memory for designs were poor according
to them; he was below grade score on the Durrell in phonics. This is the
gist of it. *A flimsy collection of data to support the conclusion of perceptual-motor disability, learning disability, and underachievement.* If you
cut out the conclusions without data, you are left with almost no hard
data on how Mark does read, on what kinds of reading errors he makes,
and on his stengths, weaknesses, and real performance levels in reading
and writing.

Recommendations

*In the recommendations we have Mark all labeled and ready for ship-
ping to the never-never land of learning disability.* Naturally he is advised
to take perceptual-motor training which this group can offer for a fee. I

cannot condemn this sort of diagnosis enough, especially since I have tested boys like Mark and have found no such behavior. I did test Mark with an IDA and the report on that follows this. Compare and contrast these diagnostic approaches and the results and conclusions reached.

The diagnosis of Mark's reading and language related problems turns out to be, as so many of them do, full of subjective probes laced through with non sequiturs—conclusions drawn that don't follow from the premises and evidence presented. In short, it does appear that the diagnosticians in this case devised and imagined their hypotheses about Mark from very little if any evidence and then tested him formally (and for too long a setting—three hours) to try to prove their initial conclusions. If this is an honest error of diagnostic skill and judgment, and interpretation, it is still not acceptable.

Neurological Diagnoses

I must add this note about some of the testing results I have seen on people tested at various hospitals and private groups. A neurological diagnosis is done by a neurologist at the hospital or wherever, and *in almost every single case the neurological findings are reported as negative* i.e., they could find nothing wrong, unusual, abnormal, or deviant in the functioning of the person's nervous system or brain, yet, these same neurological reports conclude (using the ever-popular non sequitur) that although the findings are negative, we believe that Joe, Mark, etc., is suffering from a form of dyslexia, or perceptual-motor handicaps. Why bother doing an EEG, and other neurological tests, if you deny the results you get from them, and draw conclusions not warranted by your own data?

IDA of Mark

Individual Diagnostic Analysis

Mark will be thirteen next month, and is currently completing seventh grade. He came with his mother, and with Mr. and Mrs. B. and their son, Skippy. Both boys have been fully or partially evaluated at the Testing Center and were classified as "dyslexics."

Mark is an excellent physical specimen and revealed no signs of any physical difficulty of any kind. Once relaxed, he displayed an excellent sense of humor and he frequently offered answers or comments on the reading he was doing without any specific encouragement from the examiner. As part of a normal reading analysis the examiner engaged Mark in conversation, as a means of putting him at ease and to reduce the anxiety he obviously felt at being tested again, and as a means of estimating his vocabulary level and his general intellectual functioning. On the basis of his conversation, the examiner gave Mark a copy of the Time Life series book on Evolution, which is written at a 7-8th grade level. Mark handled the material quite comfortably with a few exceptions. He knows his word recognition skills quite well and generally applies the basic principles; however, he does have some difficulty with pronunciation of words like capable, which he pronounces as <u>cap-a-ble</u>, stressing the first syllable and treating the <u>a</u> as short. He looked at the word <u>evolution</u> and seemed a bit thrown, but when asked to break it into syllables, he did so after a couple of attempts and pronounced it correctly. <u>He needs more work in syllabication, particularly as it relates to changing the pronunciation of some vowel sounds.</u> He had similar difficulty with the word <u>success</u> and the name <u>Ethan</u>, where he used the short <u>e</u> sound rather than the long sound. He was questioned very closely on the material in two different selections from the book, and his comprehension (literal recall) was excellent. When questioned for interpretation he also displayed great awareness and accuracy of understanding of the context. In fact, Mark's comrehension of this scientific material was at grade level or a little above, and the same was true of his interpretation; it would be stated as 7^2 - 8^1.

In spite of these errors in syllabication indicated above, Mark would still rate between 7^1 and 7^2 in word recognition skills. He is a perfectly capable boy, and with <u>a little bit of help in the area of structural analysis, he should readily overcome this difficulty he is experiencing.</u> For, in fact, he measures at least 90 percent accurate pronunciation in the material at his own or just above his own grade level. His instructional level (the level at which he is capable and comfortable reading independently and with good understanding) is 7^2. He is not a retarded reader. He has a specific <u>problem with syllabication, which with some prodding he can usually correct himself.</u> I recommend he have a professionally trained and experienced teacher work with him in this area, but <u>using interesting material</u> (science particularly) and <u>not teaching rules or skills in isolation.</u> His hearing and vision and his general sensory motor activity gives no evidence of any physical problem. He needs to be treated like the bright young man that he is, and stimulated to think more and recite less.

After I gave Mark's mother this diagnosis and corrective plan, I never saw her or Mark again. This has happened too many times to count; it is part of what I call the cherished ailment. They seem to like the ailment or problem they paid heavily for, and don't trust any free or inexpensive advice given by any other professional, and they may need the problem for other reasons as well.

Case Study: Jane

Here are the test results (Exhibit 3–8) as I received them from the child's father, who came seeking help and advice about the reports and what they meant. Some of the testing was administered by a bright, capable young woman who works in a large university speech and hearing clinic as a therapist.

Analysis and Critique of Reports on Jane

The three standardized tests used—Peabody, Frostig, and ITPA—are rather commonly used in diagnosing some reading and most suspected learning disability or perceptual cases. In all of the ITPA subtests, except Auditory Closure and Memory and Visual Association, Jane scored average or just below average or just above. Nothing significant or major. Her composite score has her at 7 years 10 months; the child was born June 19, 1968 making her at the time of the test (6/1/75), almost exactly 7 years old! So what's the problem?

Exhibit 3-8. Case study on *Jane*

Summary of Evaluation done by the Speech and Hearing Clinic
on Jane

I saw Jane for an evaluation on May 13, 1975, at the request of her parents. Following
is a summary of the results that I discussed with you by phone a few days ago.

Three standardized tests were administered: The Peabody Picture Vocabulary Test (Form
B), The Illinois Test of Psycholinguistic Abilities (ITPA), and the Developmental Test
of Visual Perception (Marianne Frostig). On the Peabody Picture Vocabulary Test Jane
achieved a receptive vocabulary age of 8 years 2 months placing her above the 78% for
children of her chronological age. The results of the Illinois Test of Psycholinguistic
Abilities were as follows:

Subtest	Raw Score	Age Score	Scaled Score
Auditory Reception	32	7 yrs. 6 mos.	40
Visual Reception	29	9 yrs. 10 mos.	43
Auditory Association	28	7 yrs. 11 mos.	42
Visual Association	22	6 yrs. 6 mos.	35
Auditory Memory	16	4 yrs. 8 mos.	27
Visual Memory	24	10 yrs. 5 mos.	46
Visual Closure	30	8 yrs. 9 mos.	46
Grammatic Closure	25	8 yrs. 2 mos.	44
Verbal Expression	29	7 yrs. 5 mos.	39
Manual Expression	32	above norms	46

Supplementary Tests

Auditory Closure	17	5 yrs. 9 mos.	32
Sound Blending	22	above norms	46

Composite Psycholinguistic Age - 7 yrs. 10 mos.
Mean Scaled Score - 40.8   The standrd Mean Score for children of Jane's
Median Scaled Score - 42.5   chronological age is 36)

The scaled scores provide a method of determining Jane's strengths and weaknesses
without comapring her to her peer group. In Jane's case the Median Scaled Score was
used as a basis for comparison since her scores differed in one direction only. Significant weaknesses (-10 or more points from the median scaled score) were seen in the
areas of Auditory Sequential Memory (-15) and Auditory Closure (-10). A bordering
weakness (-7 to -10 points below the median) was noted in the area of Visual Association (-7). Even though none of the other subtests showed significant weaknesses
when comparing the scores of the median, Jane's pattern of errors indicated possible
areas of difficulty. For example, on the Visual Reception subtest (a test in which the
child must look at a picture and then find a picture belonging to the same category on
the next page) Jane frequently picked a picture with the same outline shape rather than
one in the same conceptual category. Also on the Visual Sequential Memory Subtest (a
test in which a child must put designed chips in a sequence after seeing a model) Jane
was able to reproduce the correct sequence of chips but the design of the chips was
often placed in the wrong direction. For example, if the chip model were / Jane would
place the chip in a different direction.

The Developmental Test of Visual Perception showed similar results. On the Figure-
Ground subtest Jane did not have difficulty picking out a complete figure if it overlapped with a similar figure. In such cases she was able to

The Developmental Test of Visual Perception showed similar results. On the Figure-
Ground subtest Jane did not have difficulty picking out a figure from a very different
background. However, she had significant difficulty picking out a complete figure if it
overlapped with a similar figure. In such cases she was able to pick out only the
general outline, not the overlapping detail. During her attempts at such items she

frequently made remarks such as "I can't see another one." Or "I can't see the rest of it." When attempting to outline the overlapping detail she tended to begin outlining another figure. Her errors on the Form Constancy, Position in Space, and Spatial Relations subtests also indicated that she was attending visually to general outlines rather than focusing on internal differences. The Eye-Motor Coordination subtest was also difficult for Jane. She frequently extended her lines above and below the required track. It is my opinion that the visual perceptual portion of this task was difficult for Jane rather than the motor portion.

It is my opinion that the test findings clearly indicate visual perceptual difficulties particularly in the area of perceiving internal similarities and differences. Such perceptual problems often make it difficult for a child to perceive differences between similar letters such as e and o or words with similar outlines such as then and them. Also her significant weakness in auditory sequential memory skills (she cannot recite the days of the week or the months of the year by rote) would make it difficult for her to retain a series of sounds in the appropriate sequence to correctly "sound out" a word. Her additional weakness in the area of auditory closure would make it difficult for her to anticipate a whole word from hearing or sounding out part of it.

Based on these findings it would be my strong recommendation that Jane be seen by a Learning Disabilities specialist (with a Master's Degree in Learning Disabilities) daily to work on improving both the visual and auditory skills. I would also recommend that further visual perceptual testing be completed by such a specialist. In a telephone conversation with Dr. B. (an educational optometrist who has evaluated Jane) he discussed similar findings and endorsed the idea of a Learning Disabilities resource opportunity for Jane. I would recommend your contacting him for a complete report of his findings. If I may be of any further assistance please do not hesitate to contact me.

Speech and Hearing Examiner

Public School Reading Center
Reading Evaluation

Date of Report April 15, 1975

Name   Jane   Grade   1   Date of Birth 6/19/69

Teacher   Ms. L.   Reading Specialist   Ms. F.

Reason for Referral

Jane was referred by her teacher because of her slow progress in reading. She is to be evaluated at a speech and hearing clinic.

Informal Tests

Word Recognition failed pre-primer (BOTEL)

Phonics Inventory

Consonants 16/18   Blends   13/24   Vowels

Vowel Combinations   Syllables

Accent

Total 29/42

Standardized Tests

Slingerland Pre-Reading Screening Test   11 errors
Showed difficulty in Test V in visual recall and in the formation of numbers 4 and 9.

Summary and Recommendations

Jane is making slow, steady progress in her reading program. She has needed a great de
deal of time to master her letter names and consonant sounds. She has made good gains
in her auditory perception of consonant and blends and is beginning to apply her sounds
to the graphemic bases of Level # of the Ginn 360 Series. She can now recognize 48/58
of the words in this level. In the Slingerland Test she showed some difficulty with
visual memory. She was able to follow directions very well and gave her attention to
the tasks that were required of her.

Public School
Pupil Personnel Services and Special Education

REPORT OF INDIVIDUAL TESTING

Student Jane   Psychologist_____

School_____ Grade 1   Date of Birth   6/19/69

                                                Date of Test   4/15/75

TEST: WISC-R, Bender   Verbal IQ: 103   Performance IQ 112   Full Scale IQ 108

Reason for Referral: Reading below grade level; difficulty in working independently;
inconsistency in performance.

Observations: Jane speaks with a slur and with difficulty in pronouncing some letters.
She was outgoing, cooperative and tended to work and answer questions quickly.

Test Results:

Average verbally, and bright normal in the performance scale. The verbal scores were
very inconsistent. They range from extremely poor in background of factual information
to excellent in understanding reality situations. She was average in ability to conceptualize, in arithmetic and above average in vocabulary.

In the performance area she showed excellent ability to perceive missing details and to
understand sequence in a social situation. Her sense of spatial relationships was
poor.

The Bender test was just within the lowest limit for her age group. There were many
distortions in the drawings, but they were placed in a logical order on the page.

Summary:

Jane responded in an erratic manner in the test, which seems to be the pattern of her
learning in the first grade.

She has been going to the Reading Center two to three times a week for help and has made
steady gains. She will continue to receive reading assistance in the second grade and
will be watched and re-evaluated to make sure her gains continue in a satisfactory
manner.

Scores:

Verbal		Performance	
Information	5	Picture Completion	14
Similarities	10	Picture Arrangement	14
Arithmetic	10	Block Design	8
Vocabulary	13	Object Assembly	11
Comprehension	15	Coding	12
Digit Span	8		

(Letter to Jane's parents)

June 22, 1975

To Jane's Parents:

The purpose of this letter is to summarize Jane's progress in school this year and to let you know, officially that Jane will be in Grade 2, Room 1 next year.

Academically, Jane's overall growth has been slow. In two years, I have observed a learning pattern in Jane which has consisted of a period of growth, followed by a plateau, followed by another period of growth. She seems to reach a plateau after each new concept or skill she grasps, and long periods of time have passed before she seemed ready to take the next step. In her growth periods, Jane has needed much reinforcement and review of each skill before she masters it. Her performance is not consistent on a day to day basis; e.i., one day she can read a particular word, the next day she has no recollection of it.

Jane has made measurable progress since she began kindergarten. She came to school knowing only 7 letter names, and had no concept of sound/symbol association, her visual discrimination and small motor skills were not developed nearly to the point one would expect in a child her age, she had weak math concepts and lacked one to one correspondence, and she had a very short attention span and found it difficult to stick to a task. An inventory of her abilities at this point shows: 1. written mastery of 31 phonic sounds, 2. mastery of a sight word vocabulary at the Pre-Primer level, with a score of 45% at Primer level on the Botel Word Inventory, 3. mastery of level 3 of the Ginn 360 reading program, 4. good story comprehension, 5. good inflection in oral reading, 6. mastery of one to one correspondence and a good understanding of addition and subtraction, and 7. (and this is the most important) a great deal of motivation to work at learning for much longer periods of time.

The areas in which her performance in reading is weak are: building a sight vocabulary, transferring the phonics skills she has mastered to the process of decoding, hearing medial sounds and sequencing sounds. In math, she will need work in: non-rote counting (i.e., "count from 13 to 21" or "what comes after 26"?), understanding missing addends, reading and writing numbers above 30, and understanding grouping in tens.

Because acquiring skills seemed to be very difficult for Jane, her day to day performance was inconsistent, and she seems to have made little progress in the last term of school, I referred Jane for an evaluation by the reading specialist and the school psychologist. I had a meeting with them when they completed their testing, and they concurred with my opinion that Jane's overall development is proceeding at a rate that is slower than what we should expect, given her inherent ability. The psychologist's tests show Jane as being average verbally, average in ability to conceptualize and in arithmetic, above average in vocabulary, and in the bright/normal range in performance. The tests did not zero in on the specific factors contributing to Jane's slow progress. However, the tests which were administered to Jane at your request by the Speech and Language Pathologist, did identify both auditory and visual problems which are consistently evident in Jane's performance as I've observed her in the classroom. Jane is, therefore, being considered for tutoring next year with the learning disabilities teacher at school. She will be avaluated and tested in the fall, and I have strongly recommended her placement in the learning disabilities program.

Jane will need a lot of special attention, support, and understanding in the classroom as well. She is a very cooperative student, is highly motivated to perform, and socially functions well with her peers. However, she is becoming increasingly aware that other children are performing at a higher level than she, and I think it's extremely important to be sensitive to this, or she could lose her motivation to learn. She will need help in learning to work independently; she's been given a great deal of one to one tutoring in the classroom this year. She will require much individualized planning to develop a program that will fit her seeming need to go slowly, one step at a time, and that will be consistent with her learning disabilities program.

I know from experience that working with Jane will be a very rewarding task, for she is an absolutely delightful young lady. She's warm and affectionate and enthusiastic. She has a great sense of humor (very sophisticated at times), loves to tease and be teased. She can be a real character -- and is a marvelous actress. (She often gets so engrossed in stories I read, I'll look up to find her acting out the story as I'm reading it.) She gets a great deal of satisfaction from her accomplishments. We'll just have to keep in mind where Jane is, and make sure we don't overwhelm her, at the same time we try to give her every opportunity to progress as fast as possible.

Obviously, I've enjoyed working with Jane immensely. I appreciate the sincere interest you have shown in her development, and feel confident that with the learning disabilities program and much support and patience, Jane will "get it all together," and school can continue to be a positive experience for her.

Copies of the reports written by the reading specialist, the school psychologist, and the speech and hearing evaluation have been placed in the learning disabilities program,

Copies of the reports written by the reading specialist, the school psychologist, and the speech and hearing evaluation have been placed in Jane's folder. If there is any way that I can be of help in following through on my recommendation that Jane be placed in the learning disabilities program, please don't hesitate to call on me.

Ms. L. Classroom teacher

This report reiterates and boldy underlines what I have been saying throughout this whole discussion of diagnosis: *When anyone isolates specific functions, task, operations, and skills through standard testing, the tendency is to exaggerate and distort the importance of that single factor, behavior, attitude, etc., and most standard testing has the tendency (much more than the IDA) to pull behavior apart into little pieces, and then to focus considerable attention on one element, and to conclude that it is important—apart from its relationship to the rest of the person's behavior or performance.* It is just like looking at a painting by Seurat (the pointilist) and paying special attention to one group of his color dots and ignoring the total effect of the thousands of color dots he has arranged (without formal line) to create the impression of a landscape or a portrait. In short, one must guard against missing the forest for the trees—the old part-whole problem or in Gestalt terms, the figure-ground relationship.

The other critical problem with this kind of testing done on Jane (and others) is diagnosing and interpreting by analogy. The visual association subtest on the ITPA has items like this: Which one of these things (point to hammer and sock) goes with this (shoe)? Answer they want: Sock goes with shoe because they both go on the feet. We have here stimulus pictures of objects like shoe, sock, hammer, etc., and the respondent has to indicate which things go together. In another test item, the answer desired is, cup goes with spoon because we use them both when we drink coffee.

Visual motor association

The subtest is called Visual-Motor Association and they say it is measured by showing stimulus pictures and having the child say what goes with what. Is that measuring *only* visual discrimination (distinguishing and recognizing common objects and seeing similarities and differences)? The child is expected to say that these objects (2—as in sock and shoe, rather than hammer and sock) go together *because* both relate to, or are used in conjunction with shoe. Now that requires something other than visual and/or motor association. Pointing to an object is very minimally a motor act anyway.

What is required for the child to respond correctly to such items? The child must know something of common, everyday practice—a certain sense of social correctness in dress, for example. He must also have some inkling of what things do not go together, e.g., hammer and sock. The ability to know "what goes together" implies a sense of wholeness, a context within which the child makes basic associations; but visual and motor are the least significant of those associations, for underlying the ability to say that sock goes with shoe, or cup goes with spoon is a very similar skill to that which is measured in the WISC under comprehension.

The testers say that if children can respond correctly to common objects in the world, and can say which two go together under normal circumstances, this indicates visual-motor association abilities. The rest of the reasoning then continues: if children can handle this task they will therefore have an easier time in reading and writing, which require the ability to make visual-motor associations between the word and its printed form. That's an enormous leap. How does identifying common objects that people use really relate to the skills, sensitivities, perceptions, and understandings required in dealing with letters, words, and meaningful utterances in language as spoken, written, and read? The analogy is assumed, and the fit is forced. The child who can do what this subtest requires will not necessarily be able to do the visual-motor associational activities we require in most reading and writing activities; and the converse is also true, i.e., if the child cannot do those items it does not mean that he will fail in those tasks in language requiring visual-motor associations. There are many types, levels, and qualities of both visual and motor associations; they are not all the same; they are not related in any one to one fashion with other activities.

Auditory memory subtest

Auditory memory was found to be a couple of years below the norm for Jane's age (she scored 4 years, 8 months on the subtest called Auditory Memory and Auditory Closure subtest, both described in the report). The test writers standardized this test on 700 children in Decatur, Illinois. It is not clear just how representative this sample was to justify such broad generalizations about children all over the country, irrespective of sex, IQ, ethnic background, rural, urban, and socio-economic levels.

The examiner perfectly illustrated my point about diagnosis by analogy when she describes her opinion of the test findings, i.e., "Also her significant weakness in auditory sequential memory skills (she cannot recite the days of the week or the months of the year by rote) would make it difficult for her to retain a series of sounds in the appropriate sequence to correctly 'sound out' a word. Her additional weakness in the area of auditory closure would make it difficult for her to anticipate a whole word from hearing or sounding out part of it."

How do the skills necessary for a person to recite the days of the week and months of the year relate to each other? Superficially, there is a sequence (Monday, Tuesday, Wednesday, etc., and January, February, March, etc.) but a sequence with no affect, just established, conventional form, no real meaning. How is that memory related to whatever it takes to recall the sequences of letters in words which do indeed have meaning and evoke many types of responses? Is memory devoid of its content? How then can we compare the ability to recall a sequence of names of the days and months, with emotionally loaded and meaningful (in different ways) sequences of words and sentences? I do not believe they are analogous except in the most superficial way: they both deal with sequence.

My classroom and clinical experience, and the experience of my students and colleagues, do not support such interpretations. All standard tests, whether psycholinguistic (ITPA), perceptual (Frostig), achievement (California, Stanford, Iowa, Metropolitan, etc.), aptitude, intelligence (both individual and group), are all caught in the same bind: first, what is intelligence or aptitude, or neurosis, or reading level? Second, how can we measure these things so that they are as true as possible to what people do when they think, reason, emote, and read? And finally, the standard tests are all based on analogous reasoning, i.e., if you can respond correctly to this type of item or task, then you can do something else which *appears to be similar* to it.

My answer is relatively clear and simple: *if you want to get an understanding of a person's reading, writing, and other language abilities and skills, measure them in the most normal, natural way—reading and writing in context.* The IDA is the major way to discover directly what a person can and cannot do, and how the person tries to do what is needed in reading and writing. You do not have to translate from one instrument or test to another, or to reason by analogy that since Skill A requires sequencing, therefore all other activities requiring any kind of sequencing will be related and affected by each other. Nonsense! My ability to draw squares, rectangles, and diamonds, or to recall the days of the week, phone numbers, people's names, in no way assures my ability to read, write, or think logically and in sequence. I remember words, names, places because I want to, so I have worked out my own set of sensitivities to such information and I deliberately work on keeping it in my head by relating it to emotional, personal, and other factors *in context*. As I pointed out earlier, the research shows preschool, prereading children who have been taught how to discriminate various geometric shapes from each other have not been any better at learning tasks than those children who were not.

Often persons who diagnose learning disabilities or dyslexia make much of the child's clumsiness as a sign of motor or perceptual difficulty. A child can be a klutz, with an unzipped fly, runny nose, and badly laced shoes, tripping over his own feet, maintaining disorder and chaos in his room and desk, and writing sloppily, but still be able to read and write very well with excellent understanding and control of the essential principles; and the opposite can also be true. We must not take one, two, or three symptoms, pieces of behavior, or performance and make a total diagnosis. We must not diagnose by analogy.

All of this testing and pursuit by Jane's parents make it seem as if the child has major problems that will impede her learning and deform her personality. Not so. The tests are so different from each other, it is impossible to make valid comparisons. How does the child respond to the concerns—the nervousness and anxiety—of her parents? Such concentrated emotion and activity on the parents' parts is certainly contagious, and that cannot help the child to perform at higher levels. Even though these parents, and many others, are filled with good intentions and want the best for their children, such persistence in finding out what is *wrong* with the child contributes significantly to the problem.

By way of summary in relation to diagnosing by analogy, ask yourself as diagnostician (or parent) what the person taking the test has to do in order to respond correctly? How are those skills necessary to answer correctly related to other tasks? For example, if the child's ability to recall four or five numbers spoken at one or two second intervals (forward and backward) is low, what does it mean in and of itself as a measure of recall of neutral material in sequence, and then what does that have to do with remembering meaningful, emotional words and sentences? Can these be compared? Does doing one task well mean you can do the other task well? Not likely. If you want to test reading skills measure them as directly as possible, in the most normal and natural context possible, i.e., an IDA.

SUMMARY

We have noted some common sense diagnostic principles, processes, and practices so far. We have also compared and contrasted various types of testing such as standardized, criterion-referenced, and IDAs. Advantages and disadvantages have been discussed and my preference for IDAs has been explained. Many illustrations of how to give and interpret IDAs, along with the most useful reporting and recording forms, have also been presented. Throughout I have tried to be as fair, but as critical, as I could so that the values of individual diagnosis as we do it in our Reading Clinic would be as clear as possible, offering you a valid alternative to standard testing procedures.

Good diagnosis is dependent upon an open, practical, and sensitive mind embedded in a whole person seeking the best performance from each student. The misdiagnosis of Mark and Jane will follow them through school; they will be labeled and stigmatized from without and within, and this will set up the chain reaction of failure feeding failure. I have emphasized and pleaded for much more qualitative than quantitative information in all educational diagnosis; I have also pleaded for a much more wholistic view of the student, the reading processes, and the language. Earlier I referred you to Schrag's (1975) work; I remind you to read it again since it exposes much of the fallacious reasoning, diagnosis, and prescription for children with any kind of learning problems.

The key to any good diagnosis, whether it be educational, psychological, or medical, is the ability to interpret the behavior of the student, client, and patient, and to do that most validly requires that all observations and measures be contextualized, not fragmented and isolated for easier viewing. Relationships among parts is crucial in such interpretation. The best way to do that is to do the IDA as I have suggested it. Overtesting students with achievement, intelligence, perceptual, and reading tests is like giving a patient several drugs each with its own special side effects which often cause more difficulty than the presenting ailment. Tests, like drugs, are not all compatible or comparable and more often than not do counterbalance each other. *The less testing the better in most cases; the more natural observation and natural assessment of performance and behavior the better.*

REFERENCES

Dale, Edgar & Chall, Jeanne. *Readability: an appraisal of research and application.* Columbus, OH: Ohio State University Press, 1958.

Northeastern University Diagnostic Analysis. John Maguire (Ed.). 1968.

Northeastern University Individual Diagnostic Analysis (IDA). Progress in transportation. Leslie Burg (Ed.). 1966.

Schrag, Peter & Divoky, Diane. *The myth of the hyperactive child; and other means of child control.* New York: Dell, 1975.

BIBLIOGRAPHY

Betts, Emmett. *Foundations of reading instruction*. New York: American Books, 1946.

Flesch, Rudolph. *The art of readable writing*. 25th Anniversary Ed., rev. and enlarged. New York: Harper & Row, 1974.

McLaughlin, G. Harry. Smog reading. In *Journal of Reading,* IRA, May 1969, p. 639.

Rupley, William & Blair, Timothy. *Reading diagnosis and remediation: a primer for classroom and clinic*. Chicago: Rand McNally College Publishing Co., 1979.

Spache, George. Problems in primary book selection: the selection of pre-primers . . . supplementary preprimers . . . primers and supplemental primers . . . first, second readers. In *Elementary English Review,* Jan., Feb., April, and May, 1941, pp. 5–12, 52–59, 139–48, 175–81.

Fry, Edward. *Teaching faster reading: a manual*. Cambridge: University Press, 1963.

Chapter four

INTRODUCTION AND OVERVIEW

Questions that ask why some people do not learn to read at all, or why they read as well as we might expect, or how we can determine what causes may be most influential in producing failure in reading, may be answered by investigating *physical, educational,* and *psychological* factors. Under these three broad areas of causation we can include almost all of the known reasons for reading and language failures, certainly enough to be practically useful in classroom or clinic diagnosis.

These three broad areas of causation are interrelated and interdependent. In effect, one cannot speak of any one of the areas without implicating the others significantly. How could a major hearing loss, for example, not affect the educational program of the student, and how could such a loss not deeply affect the attitudes, feelings, and behavior of the student, the teachers, fellow students, family, and friends? Obviously, this single loss or handicap affects the total behavior of the person afflicted including how he learns, reads, or does not read.

Try to separate emotional and pyschological forces from one's physical and physiological responses or from attitudes toward self and the learning process and you find yourself trying to draw a line where the river runs into the sea and the sea into the ocean. Impossible. Because the causes of reading and language failure are so interwoven and overlapped it becomes speculative to say why the diagnosed problem does exist and exactly how it is affecting the learning. In extreme cases it may be easier to detect the root of the difficulty, but in many cases in classroom and clinic, the boundaries of each area of causation are much fainter.

152

Causes of reading and language problems

The point is that you do not need to be unduly concerned with which cause or area of causation may be responsible for the reading failure. What you need to know is how this particular person deals with language, learning, the reading processes, and the world in which he lives as a whole human being. Some people with severe physical problems have no difficulty learning to read and write their language skillfully, while others with no physical handicap or impediment, a good home, a nice neighborhood, and good teachers, do not learn to read as well as we might expect them to. So do not belabor the search for *the* cause or causes of a particular reading problem. Most of them will not be revealed by any one test or group of tests, but will expose themselves as you work with the student and functionally diagnose his problems within the context of a stimulating program of instruction and a warm personal relationship. Too many professionals seem to be attracted to labels for reading and language problems and for their causes, but that almost never improves either the quality of the diagnosis or correction.

Another problem with pursuing causes of reading failure in practical classroom or even clinical settings is that we must often *infer* both the causes and behavior from various tests and tasks on the basis of *analogous reasoning*. Analogous reasoning has its shortcomings, which was illustrated in the preceding chapter. Furthermore, the validity of the inferences we make is dependent upon the types of tests we have administered. *Many tests are not compatible nor are they comparable in what they are measuring, how they measure it, and how these data can be logically interpreted.* For example, the Metropolitan or California reading tests are not comparable or compatible with the Illinois Test of Psycholinguistics, and neither of these is sensibly related to the Botel Inventory or the Gray

Oral Reading Test. To verify this for yourself merely read the reviews and discussions of these tests and their manuals. Then take the tests or parts of them so that you can understand firsthand what is required of the person taking these examinations.

Learning disabilities and special needs* clinicians and teachers often overtest with similarly incompatible and incomparable instruments so that their conclusions and inferences are subject to serious question. Many reading teachers, specialists, and clinicians also succumb to the promise of valid and useful diagnostic data made by many test makers. If we misdiagnose a student on the basis of such incompatible and often contradictory data, we set him up for labeling and its acommpanying stigma, and we set teachers' expectations on the wrong course. The diagnostician must not become part of the problem.

One value in seeking causes of reading and language failure is to know what *not* to do in the instructional program. For example, if we discover a student has a very limited vocabulary because of limited intelligence or too minimal experience with language, there is no point in trying to increase his vocabulary through crossword puzzles or games, which require a more extensive vocabulary. Many corrective programs for remedial readers involve materials, exercises, activities, and teacher expectations which are almost identical to the developmental program in which the student failed.

Some special needs or remedial students receive special attention and engage in activities such as walking on balance boards, rhythm exericses, tracing, and other equally unrelated and scientifically unsupported routines. But in the main, these handicapped students receive the same kind of reading program as others, but only *more of the same, more slowly* including large doses of isolated phonics activities, fill-in-the-blank exercises, matching pictures and other symbols, drill, and repetition. This type of correction may be useful for the retarded, but what of the vast majority of students labeled "LD" or "special needs" who have normal or above normal intelligence and no physical handicaps or emotional disturbance?

It is also worthy of note here that the corrective programs which contain some or all these special learning activities claim success because of their program, without considering the powerful effect of smaller group or individual instruction on the students, or of the powerful effect of the special relationship the students may have forged with a particular teacher or clinician. All of this casts shadows and considerable doubt on the entire process.

I have spent this much time on special needs since these special education professionals have become deeply involved in many diagnostic

---

* Special Needs are needs of students who have physical, emotional, intellectual, and learning problems. The federal government's legislation, Public Law 91.142, defines this large and varied group of problems and provides funds for assessment and remedial instruction as needed.

and corrective activities normally assigned to reading teachers and specialists, historically. *Both sets of professionals must share knowledge with each other* so that LD and special needs teachers have more experience with the diagnosing and teaching of reading and writing than most of them do presently, and that reading professionals become more familiar with the particular problems of the mentally retarded, emotionally disturbed, and multiply handicapped. Because this interdisciplinary sharing is not happening to the extent that it should, some LD and special needs teachers are teaching reading and language skills for which they have little preparation and supervised experience, and some reading specialists and classroom teachers are working with serious special needs students with whom they have had too little training and experience. All of this directly affects the quality of the diagnostic and corrective work made available to students of all ages and backgrounds who are experiencing serious difficulty learning how to read, write, and communicate.

The division among the professionals leads to less effective diagnostic and corrective measures, labeling, and the proliferation of terms and definitions, thus confusing students, parents, and teachers. McCarthy (1969) summarizes the shifting definitions and approaches to diagnosing and correcting reading and language and so-called special needs problems:

> Methodologically, we started with visual perception, then went to sensorimotor training, then to ocular pursuit, then to the establishment of cerebral dominance, then to stimulus reduction, then to auditory perceptual or language training, then to multisensory training, then to integration of sensory stimuli, then to an analytic approach, and then to behavior modification. Academically, we have gone from Orton to Fernald to Gillingham to Spaulding to SRA to BRL, to Phonovisual, to the Language Master, to ITA, and not to any reading method which has a decoding emphasis. The focus of remediation has been passed from the social worker to the pediatrician to the psychiatrist to the psychologist to the neurologist to the endocrinologist and now back to the teachers.

Have the teachers really regained their role in diagnosing and correcting some of these problems? Teachers and prosepective teachers should prepare themselves by acquiring knowledge and skills from both reading and special education in order to provide the best for each student.

The shifting from approach to approach and definition to definition which McCarthy has pointed out detrimentally affects the attitudes and behavior of all professionals involved with students. We need common definitions and more lucid descriptions of what we are doing diagnostically and correctively.

The confusion and lack of clarity regarding special needs, LD, and dyslexic students is highlighted by Hallahan and Cruickshank (1973, pp. ix, 8–9).

> Reading problems, emotional problems, management problems, intellectual problems, speech problems, handwriting problems, and others, irrespective of their etiology or symptomatology are found grouped together on the premise that each is a learning problem . . . Thus, the practical result of the new term went far beyond its original conceptualization . . . Indeed, the popularization and misuse of the term could easily undermine its usefulness . . . Confusion is everywhere.

My purpose in the preceding chapters, especially chapters 2 and 3, has been to offer some alternative modes of diagnosing and interpreting diagnostic data much more wholistically than is common. My hope is that reading professionals and special educators, and those of you preparing for either field, will balance the current situation with some of the suggestions in these chapters.

Let's turn now to brief discussion of the three basic areas of causation of reading and language failure.

PHYSICAL CAUSES

Included in this group are all auditory and visual problems: physiological factors in the organism, especially the brain and nervous system, which are defective or dysfunctioning—in short, any measurable, locatable physical defect. Brain damage, neurological dysfunctions, perceptual anomalies, retardation, cerebral palsy, aphasia, and alexia are all physical problems which have been studied for their relationship to reading and other language disabilities. To a degree many of these defects are related to each other so that it becomes increasingly difficult to say with certainty that this type of brain damage in this part of the brain produces that particular reading, language, or communication problem. With certain forms of aphasia and alexia researchers seem more definite about the location and extent of the lesions or other damage and their resultant language problem, but in most instances this is not possible yet. Little is known about the brain and all of its neurological interactions and effects at this time. It does appear that more researchers are beginning to accept a more wholistic approach to some of these physical/physiological behaviors and are searching for their interrelationships rather than their own specific activity apart from the rest of the organism.

If you think of such severely handicapped people as Helen Keller, who was deaf, blind, and for a time mute, and who learned to read Braille and speak, and James Thurber and James Joyce, who were both legally blind, you realize that even with such massive physical deficits some people can communicate effectively on several levels. Some 70% of cerebral palsy victims, who have normal or above normal intelligence and whose brain and neurological damage is massive and measurable, have learned to read well. Others with arteriosclerosis of the brain still read well, even when their speech is thick and difficult to understand; and some aphasics have also learned to read in spite of a major physiological defect. At our clinic we have had some aphasic students and have, with time and a good program of instruction, taught them to read and write passably. For example, George appeared one June for help in reading.

From his mother, we learned that George, about 23 years old, had had two major brain operations 3 months earlier. Most of the Wernicke's area of the brain was removed. George worked with us during the summer and following school year. Doctors at the hospital where the operation was performed felt that George's situation was so severe and irreversible that they did not recommend any educational therapy. They did not feel he could learn to read and write.

George did learn, so that by the end of the school year he could name things and places and recall the names later; he mastered some of the word recognition skills so that he could figure out words and then recall them later; he wrote a little and it was readable. When George returned to the hospital a few months after working with us and reported to them what was happening and what he could do, they expressed considerable surprise and pleasure.

Here was a case of measurable and tangible brain damage and dysfunction, yet George was able to learn visual and auditory symbols and sound relationships, to recall them, and to apply the skills to other words to a degree not expected in such serious cases of physical damage. Of course, not all cases of aphasia or alexia are curable, but probably many more could learn to read and write than currently do, partly because we don't think they can and we don't try *qualitatively different* instructional approaches. We should act as if handicapped children can be taught and try everything until no choices are left.

In another case a man entered a hospital with brain cancer in the left hemisphere, the main source of thinking. He was given the choice to live with his cancer or to have an operation that would remove the whole left hemisphere. The operation had been performed very few times and the risks were enormous. The man agreed to have the operation. It was done. He lived for 18 months and he learned how to speak and read and write almost as well as before, well enough to be understood and to understand others in speech and written form.

What made it possible for this man and for George to learn to read and write? There is a tendency in making diagnoses to make one-to-one matches of a symptom or a syndrome and specific behavior. It doesn't work that well, because, in spite of everything, a human being is an organism, *a totally interrelated and interdependent whole.* We must not forget that; we must not fall prey to the easier notions of dealing with parts of a human being whether physical or psychological. There is no dependable one-to-one relationship between a specific brain damage, or neurological damage, and a specific reading or writing problem. The aphasics and alexics come closest to it, but many of them are amenable to treatment which somehow overcomes the damage.

In this class of physical causes we must mention the use of drugs and other biochemical interventions designed to alter behavior. In a sense these therapies fit as much into psychological causes as they do here because of the intimate interrelationship between the physical and the psychological; they are inseparable. Schrag (1975) reported in his book on the hyperactive child that many abuses have occurred and continue to occur with such drugs as Ritalin and Cylert. Much too little data is available on the long-term effects on the biochemical balance in the body. The removal of a couple of symptoms does not assure the end of the problem. And since so much diagnostic work—medically, educationally, and psychologically—is still fairly limited and imprecise, I caution against any and all medication as a therapy for poor reading and writing performance. We are not doctors and doctors are not teachers or reading specialists, and parents are neither. The three parties have little in common for sharing some of the knowledge needed, some of which is only inferred anyway.

The quality of reading and language skills performance does not seem to be highly correlated with the vast majority of physical defects, including the kind of real brain damage evidenced in cerebral palsy or arteriosclerosis of the brain. Of course the degree of these problems matters, but *short of total immobility and dysfunction of brain, nervous system, and sensory organs, most physical handicaps do not prevent learning how to read and write.*

Probably 95–98% of the physical damages will still permit us to teach with some degree of success. We are not yet able to localize learning functions within the brain and nervous system so precisely as to say that damage in part x of the brain or destruction of n number of these or those nerve cells will result in inability to remember two- or three-syllable words or endings or whatever.

In all physical problems the degree of damage, as well as location, is certainly important and can directly limit performance, but a lot less than we have been led to believe by piecemeal diagnostic procedures and interpretations. If Pribram is correct, then the brain and nervous system function holographically, rather than in the old stimulus-reflex arc. In essence, the brain operates three-dimensionally and is much less specialized in its functions and malfunctions than we have been led to believe. Pribram (1979) points out that "2% of the fibers in a particular system would retain that system's functions." His argument about memory refutes behaviorist concepts, and diminishes the magnitude of the accepted notions of brain and nervous system specialization.

Clearly, the mentally retarded cannot handle certain kinds of rules, principles, concepts, and generalizations. But we have discovered that many mentally retarded persons can learn more than we thought. The one thing rarely considered in cases where physical defects seem insurmountable is the psychological powers we all have to alter our behavior. Doctors are amazed when certain patients they have labeled moribund pull out of the fatal ailment and survive. Such cases abound, and that is not because doctors don't know what they're talking about or have made a bad diagnosis or provided an ineffectual therapy. It seems that we have strength and power in us we rarely use and when that is mustered and our will to live becomes prominent, we can overcome major physical distress.

We have mainly spoken of brain and neurological damage with a few words about drugs and other biochemical interventions. We have not really mentioned the whole complex area of perception which plays such a large role in many diagnostic and corrective programs. Familiar names like Orton (1928), Gillingham (1966), Fernald (1943), and Frostig (1966) come immediately to mind as spokesmen for neurological assumptions about learning to read and write and perceptual training programs for corrections. Their work began in the 1920s and achieved a certain celebrity into the thirties and early forties, then faded, and seems to have returned in the past 15 years or so. Many of their assumptions about learning disabled, dyslexic, and strephosymbolic (mixed letters) students have filtered into special needs programs. Both their assumptions and their corrective suggestions seem to verify their belief that a one-to-one correspondence exists in the brain and nervous system of people so that it is possible to determine which area is damaged and exactly how that will affect reading/language performance and how to cure it. Their results have been largely concealed or unimpressive to many professionals, but their influence is still very much alive particularly in the field of LD and special needs.

In chapter 1 we spoke of perception and learning and cited the work of M. D. Vernon and others which refutes this behavioristic mechanistic analysis. Vernon's arguments strongly support the organismic nature of human perception integrating cognition, affect, and experience. In essence, she is saying, as are many others, that perception involves the organism in its total environment. There is no way to separate parts of the perceptual process, nor to assume that they are discrete acts of a robot. Perception is a constantly shifting process of interpreting the world about us; it is not composed of static objects, people, properties.

If perception and the functions of the brain and nervous system are indeed organismic acts of thought, feeling, experience, education and the culture which structures all of these, then a great deal of the work of the authors mentioned above is of dubious value. The examples I have given in this chapter further support the organismic nature of human perception, learning, and behavior.

Are there no physical causes of reading/language disability? Certainly there are but they are much fewer and much less pervasive than many authors and practicing professionals are willing to accept at this time. Mental retardation is certainly a physical cause of reading failure, as is blindness, and to some extent deafness. But many blind people have learned Braille and successfully completed undergraduate and graduate studies, as have many deaf persons. In essence, it is my view that relatively few, probably less than 5% of the population, have such massive and debilitating physical defects as to make learning to read and write impossible. As diagnosticians we must continue to gather data on any student's physical condition and history, but we must use that data with caution and with the knowledge that almost none of the physical problems we encounter in classroom and even in clinics are so massive as to prevent teaching and learning.

EDUCATIONAL CAUSES

In this group is included what schools, teachers, administrators, curricula, parents, community, and society do to us in the name of education. What impact does a particular type of curriculum have on your learning? How does the medium of curriculum affect and alter the message we get? How do certain personalities in the classroom directly affect our motivation, our desire, our understanding? How do books and other instructional materials used in the curriculum, the evaluation system, and the grouping arrangements, affect our sense of what we are and are not? Can we, as John Holt (1970) suggests, make children stupid in school? Do the complaints of disciplinary problems and delinquents and drop-outs mean anything when they say they were bored, treated like dirt, had to learn things that made no sense to them; that the school, the teacher, did not care about them or what they were doing? Obviously, all of these factors make some difference. We simply cannot believe that any one is all right or all wrong in these circumstances. The schools have been put upon by a society that keeps specializing its functions and the schools have picked up or had forced upon them many tasks they are not equipped to handle. Schools cannot be homes, churches, employers, parents; their role has to be redefined and limited or as now, the schools, the children, and the parents will be unhappy and looking for a scapegoat. The protests, the costumes, the drugs, communal living were all seen in the '60s as the direct result of schools and the kind of permissive teaching and disciplining going on. Some say that if the schools had not been so easy, so permissive, the kids would not have protested and dropped out of the mainstream of society. They would have been like us—their parents, stable, solid, law abiding, conforming, and generally nice and likable.

This leads to the age-old controversy over whether the school should teach more and more of less and less, emphasizing phonics and the "basics," or whether they should emphasize the meaning of what is read and taught. This either/or set up is phony; most reading programs have always done a little of both—some phonics and some whole word learning. Jeanne Chall's (1967) study and Nila Banton Smith's (1965) classic, present a broader perspective on how reading instruction has grown and developed and responded to religious, political, and educational needs as perceived in different periods of our history. Clearly, this book urges a meaning emphasis in diagnosis and teaching.

Perhaps the most serious problem in this group of educational causes of reading failure has already been alluded to in our discussion of testing and diagnosing students: we are failing to do the kind of job we could because of our approach to assessing pupil performance and progress. Our diagnoses mislead us into faulty grouping patterns, faulty selection of methods and materials and in appropriate curricula, and inaccurate evaluation of progress.

We have been stubborn about such changes and we, the schools and teachers, then tend to blame parents and the community for pressuring us into teaching some things in some ways. But that is only partly true. Parents and the community are entitled to more discussion of what kinds of reading, math and science programs are being taught and why; what the benefits are; and what the weaknesses and strengths are compared with other programs and approaches. These topics should be openly and honestly discussed. What generally happens is that a school board intimidates the administration of the school to emphasize certain things in the curriculum, or the administration intimidates the public into believing that it knows what is best. Both approaches are wrong and doomed. The publishers of instructional materials are another force which has to be dealt with. Salesmen have almost as much to say about which reading program will be adopted as most teachers do in some school districts.

Where to begin to reduce the negative impact of the educational programs on the public is not clear, since *like most major problems or ailments, everything is related to everything else.* We cannot improve the quality of teaching unless we improve the quality of colleges and universities training future teachers. We cannot improve curriculum if teachers and administrators have only textbook knowledge of ideas about curriculum, we cannot improve communication among teachers, administrators, parents, and the community by wishing it so.

Practically, schools and communities can share more of the successful alternatives in education insofar as diagnosing, grouping, curriculum, and teaching are concerned. More and closer contact with the schools and their communities in this manner can help. By this I mean *coordinated, informed,* and *concerned cooperation* of the segments of the society touched by what we do or do not do in our schools. The problems which schools have that no other professional institution or group has, is that *we teach everyone:* prospective doctors, lawyers, teachers, criminals, prostitutes, actors, congressmen, researchers, space men, and garbagemen. *Our population is the whole,* not a selected part.

It is clear that schools have become a major part of learning problems, and nowhere more noticeably than in the area of reading and writing. Everyone is up in arms about how badly children read and write. National magazines devote sizable portions to writing problems or reading failures. *If teachers are misdiagnosing as I have shown, then their teaching will fall far short of the mark; children will be hurt and made stupid, angry, and failures.* It is estimated that 20–25% of public school children are having problems learning to read and write acceptably. Some twenty million American adults are functional or total illiterates; the high school drop-out rate is estimated between 20–30%, and for some groups like American Indians and Mexican Americans, it is at least double that. No point in cataloging all of the problems. Schools cannot fix all of these, but they can alter their current diagnostic, grouping, and curricular approaches to increase interest and understanding. We can get off the behaviorist bandwagon with its pseudoscientific rituals presumed to be reliable because they are numbered and measured.

In short, the problems of the schools and the educational system in all its dimensions are matched by problems of the society as a whole, so I do not intend here to extract the schools from the context in which they are born, grow, develop, and decline. If I were to cite data relative to the divorce rate, the crime rate, the unemployment rate, the number of unnecessary or health threatening operations, the millions of defective automobiles produced, one could become discouraged about our entire political, social, and economic behavior. The schools are certainly part of these major problems—causing some, contributing to some, and fighting others.

One could add massive life-long doses of television viewing to the list of factors that affect the amount and quality of reading youngsters now do. It is estimated that youngsters spend about 15,000 hours watching television compared with some 12,000 hours attending school, from kindergarten through twelfth grade. Certainly this medium affects the viewers in numerous ways, but I do not believe that the schools can afford to just notice such data and wait for a change.

Can schools and educational programs really effect social, political, and economic change? People like Illich (1971) and Freire (1971) have proposed major changes in the way a society could and should educate its people. They call for somewhat revolutionary activities, including Illich's notion that we "de-school" society entirely and depend upon informal and selected networks of persons and institutions to bear the brunt of teaching people what they want to learn. He proposes closing schools as we know them. Freire uses what appears to be Marxist ideology to educate illiterate peasants and to make them conscious of their condition and to organize and inform themselves to change it. Since Illich's notions have not become popular we do not know if they would work. Freire's activities have produced results according to him but have not been widely accepted as an alternative to the way we educate our children and adults.

In the past two decades we have seen many experiments with open classrooms, alternative schools, and variations of those themes. At the outset they are greeted with hope and offer great promise. Soon they fade from the picture and are replaced by another variation of another theme with the same hoopla and the same fate.

What then can we say about educational causes of reading and language problems that seem to handicap and cripple so many millions of our population? Primarily, what we can say is that the educational program and system is a part of a much larger whole—society—and that change must permeate every cell in the entire system and social structure. However, this does not deny the potential of a single institution, such as schools, which deal with so many people, to initiate some movement toward change of attitudes, behavior, and visions. Schools do not have to wait for other segments of the society to urge them to change unilaterally. Parents and the community support schools and have ultimate control over them, so why can't schools do so much more with various types of adult education and information so that parents could make better informed choices about curriculum, personnel, goals, and the like?

The educational causes of reading and language problems can be attacked at the college and university level where teachers and specialists are educated, and in in-service activity which could incorporate some new concepts of diagnosing and teaching students and of qualitatively different curricular plans.

In short, schools will remain a major cause of reading failures unless university professors of education, elementary, and secondary school teachers; school administrators; parents and the community; and the state departments of education come together on a more regular basis to focus on improving the learning environment for students. Issues relating to turf must be subsumed to the needs of the students and the community. Also overspecialization in all segments of the educational enterprise will have to give way to more interdisciplinary thinking and planning. We must help our fellows and former students develop reasonable expectations from us and from other institutions.

PSYCHOLOGICAL CAUSES

In this group all else merges. Our cognitive activities are permeated with affect, and our affective responses are somewhat altered by our cognition. Emotions such as pride, fear, anxiety, trust, love, and hate are powerful undercurrents pulling us unexpectedly. It is difficult to identify the exact emotion which may be affecting us at a given time, and it is even more difficult to say just how much anxiety or fear, for example, may be distracting us from our tasks. Measuring which emotions are operating at any moment in us and exactly what they cause us to do has escaped our skill. We know tht emotions do directly affect all learning and behavior, and in extreme cases we can even come close to naming the emotions and their effects, but feelings evade measurement and controlled study. Because emotions are so pervasive in each of us and because they fluctuate, many psychologists and educators omit them from direct measurement in their diagnostic work.

Some behaviorists, however, apply their theories of behavior and learning to emotions just as they do to cognitive activity. This treatment is called behavior modification (BM) and is being used with many disturbed and other special needs students across the country. The gist of the BM therapy is that behavior can be modified by designing a program of selected rewards and punishments applied at the appropriate time in a learning task. This system of rewards and punishments consistently applied is supposed to condition and control the responses of the learner. The rewards can include *m & m* candies, free time, little gifts like pocket radios, gold stars, free books, and the like. Punishments can include anything the group or class has identified as undesirable.

When such BM programs are reported, success is claimed when some overt behavior is measurably changed by their criteria. But what is left out of the entire process is exactly why a student accepts or rejects the reward system. *Since all behavior/learning is the result of the total personality functioning in a context, with its past and present interacting on several levels simultaneously and imagining its future,* the problem of isolating one or two specific emotions as causes of specific behavior becomes even more complicated. But the fact remains that we must be cognizant of and alert to emotional tides flowing through any student and altering his responses.

For these reasons I have offered a different approach to diagnosis and its interpretation, as well as to planning and teaching. This wholistic, individualized approach to diagnosis should provide us with much more cognitive and affective information in a more natural reading/language context. If it does so, then my suggestions in the following chapters for planning integrated lessons and for teaching the word recognition, meanings, study skills, and vocabulary and writing within such lessons should assist us in incorporating these affective behaviors. At the least, such an organismic approach to both diagnosis and teaching avoids some of the major pitfalls of behavioristic assessment and instruction.

Any discussion of psychological causes and influences on reading and language learning must consider perception foundational.

Perception

Many reading and special needs specialists, as well as psychologists, include diagnostic and corrective measures and activities in perception. In fact, identification and correction of perceptual difficulties represent the bulk of the assessment and teaching for such authorities as Orton, Gillingham, and Fernald. Their views, as has been pointed out earlier in this chapter, are largely rooted in behaviors. What is the alternative?

In chapter 1 perception was defined as "the ways in which we filter all of our experiences, feelings, knowledge through each other and through our total personality." Perception is the bulwark of our sense of stability in and around us, clarifying for us the patterns of shapes, forms, colors, textures, and sounds. Perception, in short, is much more than the ability of children, for example, to discriminate between *b* and *p* visually and aurally, or circle from diamond, or big from small, or rough from smooth. The perceptual process also involves the cognitive, conceptual interpretation of sensory and other data as well as the emotional and affective overtones. If we attempt to divide the perceptual processes and interactions into manageable units of activity as too many professionals are doing, we shall miss the forest for the trees. Perception is whole, integrated and integrating; it is holographic.

Once again we need to turn to one of the world's leading experts on perception, M. D. Vernon (1971, pp. 19, 20), for some guidance. She tells us that perception is a developmental process beginning at birth when the physiological structures of the eyes and optic nerves are already fairly well developed and are very similar to that of adults. Although infants make almost no distinctions in their sensory impressions, by the time they reach two months of age ". . . the infant begins to realize that certain of these events recur regularly, and in particular that some of them frequently occur together, at the same time and in the same place or direction." She goes on with this line of reasoning: "There is also evidence that during the early months infants begin to realize that certain sensory patterns belong together."

Perception of patterns in sensory and other experiences grows and develops rapidly in children and provides them with the sense of order and stability and permanence in their internal and external worlds. The wholeness of perception is further expressed by Vernon (1971, p. 23) in this excerpt: "A further difficulty for the young child is that he tends to perceive situations as a whole. Objects are seen as part of the settings in which they most frequently occur, and the qualities which characterize their identity cannot be differentiated from other non-essential qualities . . . Thus a familiar person may not be recognized if he appears in new and unfamiliar clothes; or he may seem different if he is encountered in a different place."

Note her emphasis on the wholeness of perceptual acts, the patterning of early perception and the importance of the context in which all perception occurs.

Vernon goes on to relate perception and probability which help us all to reconstruct reality in terms of shapes, forms, colors, textures, and sounds as well as situations and events. We can and do anticipate or guess what we have seen or heard or what someone intended in a particular context, and this is intimately related to our discussion in chapter 1 of probability in language.

The Gestalt psychologists agree with Vernon on the wholeness of perception and on the patterning of the fields of experience, as does Lenneberg (1967, p. 279) who adds: "Perceptually, the child reacts also to whole patterns rather than to small segments, and so the intonation pattern of a sentence is the more immediate input rather than the individual phonemes." Hence we must ask reading teachers, specialists, special needs personnel, and classroom teachers: Why is there so much isolated activity with letters, sounds, individual words—why the flash cards, word lists, workbook exercises? Such activity seems to fly in the face of this research on perception by reputable and acknowledged scholars.

No discussion of child growth and development would be complete without some words from Piaget (1966, pp. 60–61): "We are bound to admit how well founded are the descriptions given by Gestalt Psychology. The essential "wholeness" of mental structures (perceptual as well as intelligent), the existence of the "good Gestalt" and its laws, the reduction of variations of structure to forms of equilibrium, etc., are justified by so many experimental studies that these concepts have acquired the right to be quoted throughout contemporary psychology. In particular, the method of analysis that consists in always interpreting facts in terms of a total field is alone justifiable, since reduction to atomistic elements always impairs the unity of reality."

Perhaps this quotation makes the case for the wholeness of perception well enough for our purposes. My concern now is that we all use this data as part of our diagnostic assessments and their interpretation, and that we then plan instruction to accommodate these truths about perception and learning. That is what the next chapter attempts.

So far we have discussed the problem with psychological factors and forces as causative agents in learning to read and write by pointing out that emotions and feelings are so pervasive as to make their measurement and control extremely difficult, if not impossible. We have seen that perception is indeed whole, patterned and hence somewhat predictable. We have also seen that perception must always be seen in context, never in isolated acts or responses. The wholeness of person, the language, and the learning process described in chapter 1 are now reinforced. Clearly we must always seek the psychological concomitants to any learning activity, particularly reading and writing, since our society places so much emphasis on literacy. Not to read and write intelligibly produces a vortex which pulls the poor reader/writer swiftly down to failure and the accompanying frustration, despair, and anger we have all met in our classrooms and clinics. To ignore psychological factors and to ignore their relationship to perception and learning is to misdiagnose and to design failure into your corrective work.

Symbolizing

At the root of certain perceptual problems are not only physical or physiological defects or malfunctions, or just the curriculum, or teachers, and materials alone, but the *symbolic nature of all human behavior*. Obviously, our symbolizing interacts with, directly affects, and is affected by, our perceptions, experiences, and knowledge. *We are what we perceive and we perceive what we are* and it is not possible to separate one from another.

Since this topic covers so vast an area of inquiry, this discussion is limited to those aspects most directly related to reading and language learning. Chapter 1 discussed at some length what Marshall McLuhan and others have to say about our symbolic nature, especially as evidenced by use of the technology of language and by its effects on us. We saw that the language we use for our varied purposes also exerts control over our behavior, including as it does our feelings, thoughts, perceptions, and experiences. McLuhan's message in part was that all of the technologies devised by man represent or symbolize extensions of himself into the world. When he described his concept of the effects of a particular language, ideographic or alphabetic, on the reality of the users, he pointed out the wholeness of ideographic languages as contrasted with the partness of the alphabetic languages. This explained for him the essential differences in the cultures using one or the other language system. Thus, alphabetic cultures like our own specialize and fragment work, thinking, and feelings as if we were dividing words into syllables composed of individual letters. That is one major aspect of our symbolizing which does permeate almost all of our behavior, but I want to uncover some other aspects of the process.

We have already seen how emotions and feelings merge and pervade all of our thinking and perception, and we have said that the physiological activity of our organisms is interrelated with our psyches. We are psycho-biological creatures like no other on the planet that we know. We do use many languages such as English, music, mathematics, color, physical movements, and art to communicate symbolically with those sharing our culture's needs, desires, hopes, fears, and the like. In all languages, symbols represent and embellish our meaning and intention. Whether we use letters of an alphabet, or symbols for square root, or convergent lines to create the illusion of perspective in a drawing or painting, we are symbolizing thoughts and feelings for others. Conversely, those who do not use the language of their culutre in a commonly acceptable way suffer the consequences of being different or even not normal, producing frustration, anger, alienation, even guilt. Clearly such feelings alter behavior and self-concept quite negatively, thus generating more variation and failure.

Put another way: *Nothing succeeds like success and nothing fails like failure.* The point I wish to make here is not just that some people fail and some succeed at learning how to communicate with their fellows in an acceptable fashion, but that *many students need to fail as much as some need to succeed.* I take much reading and language failure to contain a large dose of this *need-to-fail syndrome.* It sometimes appears as the need of the student to call attention to himself to distracted or inattentive parents; it sometimes appears as unruly behavior in school and rebellious behavior at home, either to call attention to the self or to punish the parents. Sometimes this failure syndrome is a disguised cry for help, for affection, for a push. In the classroom or clinic the poor reader can give the impression superficially of not caring about the work, or claiming that it is too easy. If you take these symptoms literally and do not probe to find the symbolic meaning of the acts, you will miss a great deal and will therefore misinterpret the student.

How do we symbolize daily? Freud's *Psychopathology of Everyday Life* is a good general study of common actions and errors we all make which derive from deeper, unconscious needs, desires, fears, and guilts. But the best source to help us understand more about how we symbolize is the field of psychosomatic medicine. Unfortunately, the diagnosis and correction of reading and language problems generally omit any consideration of these personality dynamics. I know of no reading or special educational authority who deals with psychosomatics as part of the discussion of diagnosing and interpreting reading/language performance. This seems a glaring omission of valuable data in any diagnostic process. How can we hope to interpret the performance and general behavior of anyone without some attention to this type of symbolizing which produces either sickness or failing behavior?

Psychosomatics

The simplest definition of psychosomatic medicine states that it concerns itself with *the dynamic interactions of mind in body.* This approach to somatic illnesses depends upon an understanding of personality and how we all *transform* basic emotions and needs into overt behavior that often appears perverse or at least contradictory. That is, if you really want love, attention, and affection as a means of building trust and confidence in self and others, why rebel and fight with those most capable of providing what you need? How can failing in reading and writing achieve your ends? When I encounter a student with normal or above normal intelligence who is performing miserably in reading and writing I want to know what his family is like, what demands they place on him, or what demands *he thinks* they are placing on him. What does he need to do to get the affection and attention he wants within his family? What is he trying to say in this symbolic way? Obviously, some students fail because they lack intellectual stimulation at home, or learn that intellectual pursuits are not important, or the parents are so defensive as to need the child's failure. This of course is not normally a conscious decision on the part of the parents. I want to know about these possibilities as part of my diagnosis. Just teaching skills to a student so enmeshed in these emotions and feelings will not produce the positive results we seek. We need the foreground and background emotions in perspective.

This is not a call for all of us to become psychologists or therapists, but rather it is a call to alert us all to the possibility that the failing student is failing for more reasons than our testing may uncover.

Psychosomatic Medicine

What do the researchers in psychosomatic medicine have to say which we might use in our own diagnosis and its interpretation? They point out that many physically identifiable bodily ailments such as heart problems, asthma, certain forms of cancer, ulcers, and a host of others, are accompanied by distinctive emotional factors are in fact psychogenic. (Psychogenic-psychological and emotional factors cause the behavior, in this case reading failure). On the basis of their research they urge doctors to include this dimension in their diagnosis and treatment—that is, they recommend that doctors diagnose the physical and psychological problems as inseparable. I urge the same to you, since so much failure in reading and language is *not* attributable to physical causes alone, nor to intelligence, sex, school, or socio-economic level. What is it that the student is using the failure for? Why does he project himself as a trouble maker, rebel, and failure?

The research and experience of those engaged in the field of psychosomatic medicine has direct applicability to our own diagnostic and corrective work. It adds a dimension we almost always neglect or omit as evidenced by the widespread, almost universal use of standardized testing instruments in reading and language which are neither designed for, nor to be interpreted as offering this kind of perspective. Use of the IDA overcomes some of the problem in testing and diagnosing students because it permits a much more comprehensive assessment of cognitive and affective performance. Let me summarize the basic concepts of psychosomatic medicine.

Good sources for a background on psychosomatic medicine are Alexander (1950), Dunbar (1955), and Grinker and Robbins (1953). These sources will acquaint you with the processes operating in most phsycial ailments; how emotion and physiology converge, merge, and interact on many levels.

Alexander says that personality is the expression of the unity (or disunity) of the organism. He, like most of the others, tries to show correspondences between certain personality traits and particular physical ailments. He cites Freud, who said that bodily symptoms develop in response to chronic emotional conflicts. Most practitioners and researchers in the field agree with that basic concept. Alexander emphasizes the importance of the doctor-patient relationship, especially in its emotional dimension.

Dunbar speaks of "emotional contagion" as a significant force in the development of physical symptoms of sickness. She emphasizes this as a critical etiological factor. She says we select our symptoms as one might select clothes, in keeping with our personality. At the root of psychosomatic ailments she says is the emotional need for illness, for love and attention. (Many psychoanalysts would agree with this.) She goes on to give examples of specific personality characteristics and the physical ailments she correlates with them, as for example in ulcers and other digestive ailments, respiratory ailments and the psychological concomitants, and cardiovascular problems and their psychological concomitants. She goes as far as to spell out a syndrome of psychological behaviors, fears, and needs for love and attention with particular types of sickness.

The Grinker and Robbins *Casebook* is filled with fascinating cases of physical ailments and their psychological concomitants. The mother-child relationship on all of its levels runs through their etiologies, as it does with the others. They say that life experiences can and often do alter physiological processes. They point out more than other researchers the symbolic connections we tend to make with organs of the body like the eye and hand.

Grinker and Robbins maintain that *there is a natural interaction between thought, feeling, and behavior.* How we feel phsyically is very much affected by our psychological state. Our psychological state, which triggers endocrinal secretions and which affects major control organs like the thyroid gland and adrenal gland, has direct relationships to our susceptibility to ailment. The will to live referred to earlier is closely related to this phenomenon of the psychological conditions altering phsyiological processes. Personality traits and patterns of some people seem to correlate very highly with certain types of diseases. We all have some sense that certain types of people who are ambitious and driven might be more susceptible to ulcers or heart problems than others.

My experience in clinical work in education, particularly in reading and language problems, has uncovered many cases of children, adolescents, and adults who exhibit many psychosomatic patterns of behavior. We need to explore this realm much more closely than we have. How do the psychological state and personality transform feeling, needs, fears, and desires into physiological correlates and how do they directly affect reading and language ability? The phenomenon of the "pygmalion in the classroom"—of the relationship between teacher expectation and pupil performance, is intimately related to this discussion. How does the process described by Alexander (1950, p. 68) in the quote below bear on our diagnostic concerns, and the interpretation of the behavior we note in the reading and language activity?

> . . . every emotional state has its own physiological syndrome. Increased blood pressure and accelerated heart action are a constituent part of rage and fear. Increased stomach secretion may be a regressive response to an emergency attack of asthma which is correlated with an unconscious suppressed impulse to cry for mother's help.

Alexander (p. 74) goes on to say:

> . . . chronically sustained hostile impulses can be correlated with a chronic elevation of blood pressure while dependent help-seeking trends go with increased gastric secretion.

And what about such severe psychiatric problems as autism? Are such people, especially children, saying something through noncommunication? Many of us think so; many think that autism is the ultimate communication by a particular kind of personality which cannot and finally will not communicate any more due to the emotional climate in which it finds itself.

What the people in psychosomatic medicine, psychoanalysis, and psychiatry do is very much like what McLuhan did with his concepts of language as technology. In both cases these people interpret human behavior symbolically because they see us as symbol makers and users. *Like words, we too have many possible meanings,* depending on the context in which we are placed. Like words, not only our specific meaning is affected by the context, but our function (noun, verb, and adjective) is affected by where we are placed in the sentence. Can we be seen through this metaphor? Do you become subject or object in certain relationships; are you a noun or an adjective at certain times with certain people? Yes, to all of them.

Obviously much more could be said about these very important and almost always neglected components of good diagnosis and its interpretation. Let this serve as an appetizer for you. Do not settle for the one and two dimensional discussions of causes of reading failure, their diagnosis, and interpretation found in almost every major text in the field. Broaden your base, probe other dimensions, and seek more relationships. A good diagnosis and a good interpretation of it must consider this symbolic aspect of human behavior.

SUMMARY

The question which started this chapter was, Why do students fail in learning to read and write? We looked at three broad areas of causation: physical, educational, and psychological, noting that they were intimately related and interdependent upon each other, inseparable and indivisible. I urged that reading professionals and special educators share the content and experiences of their education and training so that they can assist each other much more than they currently do. I decried the general trend by both groups of professionals, and others, to specialize to the extent that they tend to see only parts of a person or problem and then prescribe and treat them in isolation and piecemeal. The wholeness of the diagnostic and corrective processes was reiterated in this context.

A very brief historical survey of the changes in diagnosis and correction was presented as a way of decreasing our tendency to make either-or distinctions and to caution us against fads in research and practice. Then we discussed certain physical causes of reading/language failure and concluded that a very small percentage of problems are the result of physical abnormalities, so that the current overemphasis on such defects is leading us astray. In this connection some contrasts between the Orton school's concepts of perception and learning were opposed by the work of M.D. Vernon and others.

Educational causes were described in terms of teachers, administrators, parents and community, the curriculum, and the society as a whole. The conclusion was drawn that reading/language failure occurred as a result of such things as misdiagnosis, misinterpretation of diagnostic data, the resultant inadequate grouping patterns, choice of materials and instructional methods, and evaluation. The role of the school in society was briefly touched upon and lead us to the conclusion that changing schools will require concomitant changes in other segments of the society that control and direct them. More parent education and information was called for in order to provide some guidance to any changes in schools.

The last broad area of causation discussed was the psychological. The nature of perception was presented from the standpoint of such people as Vernon, Lenneberg, and Piaget. Their views can be characterized as Gestaltist. The implications for this view of perception were then related to causes of reading/language failures. It was pointed out that emotional and affective responses merge and permeate each other so that it is extremely difficult for any diagnostician to assess them individually. But without an awareness of these powerful forces in all of us and how they affect our self-concept, our reading/language performance, and all of our behavior, we miss many meaningful cues in our diagnostic and corrective work.

The logical extension of these concerns was presented under the heading of psychosomatics. How we all transform certain basic emotions into physical ailments or school failure was briefly described. The awareness of the symbolic dimension of human behavior was considered essential to the entire process of diagnosing and teaching students. The principles of psychosomatic medicine were expressed by such authorities in the field as Alexander, Dunbar, Grinker and Robbins, and they were applied to reading and language problems. I strongly urged all specialists in reading and special education to familiarize themselves more fully with some of these concepts and principles as a means of expanding their diagnosis and its interpretation.

This completes the triad of chapters on diagnosis and misdiagnosis: testing and tests; administering and interpreting the IDA and the causes of reading and language problems. Now we are ready to move on to planning reading/language instruction in a wholistic and integrated manner.

REFERENCES

Chall, Jeanne. *Learning to read: the great debate*. New York: McGraw-Hill, 1967.

Fernald, Grace. *Remedial techniques in basic school subjects*. New York: McGraw-Hill, 1943.

Freire, Paulo. *Pedagogy of the oppressed*. New York: Hurder & Hurder, 1971.

Frostig, Marianne & Miller, Ann-Marie & Horne, David. *Developmental program in visual perception*. Chicago: Follett, 1966.

Gillingham, Anna & Stillman, Bessie. *Remedial training for children with specific difficulty in reading, spelling, and penmanship* (7th ed.). Cambridge, MA: Educators Publishing Service, 1966.

Hallahan, Daniel & Cruickshank, William. *Psycho-educational foundations of learning disabilities*. Englewood Cliffs, NJ: Prentice-Hall, 1973.

Holt, John. *How children fail*. New York: Pitman, 1970.

Illich, Ivan. *De-schooling society* (1st ed.). New York: Harper & Row, 1971.

Lenneberg, Eric. *Biological foundations of language*. New York: Wiley, 1967.

McCarthy, J. M. Learning disabilities: where have we been? where are we going? In *Learning disabilities: selected conference papers*. Arlington, VA: Council for Exceptional Children, 1969, pp. 33–39.

Orton, Samuel. *Reading, writing and speech problems in children.* New York: W. W. Norton, 1937.

Piaget, Jean. *The psychology of intelligence.* Totowa, NJ: Littlefield Adams, 1966.

Pribram, Karl. Holographic memory. In *Psychology Today,* Feb. 1979, p. 72.

Smith, Nila. *American reading instruction.* Newark, DE: IRA, 1965.

Vernon, M. D. *Psychology of perception* (2nd ed.). Baltimore: Penguin Books, 1971.

Bibliography

Alexander, Franz. *Psychosomatic medicine.* New York: Norton, 1950.

Dunbar, Flanders. *Mind and body: psychosomatic medicine (rev. ed.).* New York: Random House, 1955.

Freud, Sigmund. *Psychopathology of everyday life.* A. A. Brill (Ed.). New York: Random House, 1966.

Grinker, R. R. & Robbins, F. P. *Psychosomatic casebook.* New York: Blakiston, 1953.

McLuhan, Marshall. *Understanding media.* New York: New American Library, 1964.

Schrag, Peter & Divoky, Diane. *The myth of the hyperactive child: and other means of child control.* New York: Dell, 1975.

Chapter five

INTRODUCTION

After we have ascertained the quality of the student's reading and language performance, the level, weaknesses and strengths, and interests and background, we can plan interesting and relevant groups of lessons using the student's strengths and interests. We know how students read, and perhaps we even have some insight into why they read as they do, so that we have the raw material necessary to build a program emphasizing the positive

A key question in planning any kind of instruction for individuals or groups is how we can relate content and skills in each lesson and among lessons. We want to avoid teaching skills in word recognition, meanings, study skills, and vocabulary in isolation out of workbooks or worksheets. Rather, we prefer teaching skills within some content so that any phonic analysis skills which may be needed—blends, digraphs, and short and long vowels—are derived from words appearing in the integrated content which is the focus of the entire corrective program. In short, all of the reading/language skills will be taught within a *core concept* plan that integrates content from several subjects and that provides the meaning for all of the skills.

Core concept planning

In this chapter many illustrations of actual lessons will be presented, analyzed, and interpreted to exemplify how a core concept plan is made and how the needed skills are taught and practiced within this context. The sequencing of skills in each growth area is not overemphasized since we are not positive that teaching the initial consonant m should come before the initial consonant b; or whether the root *path* should come before the root *ced*. As you will see, such choices are dependent upon which consonants or roots are *most regular, most common,* and *most generalizable*. If a child did not learn x or z and their particular variations, it would not be too serious since these letters appear in very few words in our language, while $b, m, d,$ and p appear in thousands. The same applies to root words; we seek in all cases those words, letters, roots, and affixes most commonly found in the language and especially in the type and level of reading the student is most likely to encounter.

Planning instruction (developmental or corrective) should be whole and integrated, based as much as possible on the needs and interests the student brings to you. The reading and related language skills are taught as a means of learning more about the content, and they are easily taught within the core concept plan. Hence the skills become an integral part of the entire reading process, not just a useful appendage; *any skills can be taught in any core concept plan of instruction*. This wholistic approach to planning and teaching is quite different from most reading programs, which still reflect diagnostic and corrective work in fragments.

Once you and your students have selected a core concept, you will functionally diagnose in each lesson and you will adjust your instruction in accord with this information. No matter how well you do your IDA you will not learn all you need to know about each student.

ESSENTIAL COMPONENTS OF GOOD LESSONS

Focus, continuity, coherence, creativity and *pace* are among the most critical components of good lessons. Like a well written paragraph a good lesson has its main idea and related details, or like good music, painting, sculpture, or dance, a good lesson and a good group of lessons has this kind of wholeness, this special interrelatedness and interdependence of its parts.

Since our goal will be to develop core concept plans for many connected lessons bearing on the same content or theme, each lesson must be seen in that context and related closely to it. Each lesson must be whole and must be directly related to the core concept which guides the development of both skills and content. How do we weave the thread of content and concepts throughout many lessons and still teach the necessary reading and language skills? Just as in drawing a picture, writing a story, or choosing a wardrobe, we must consider the whole first when we plan instruction and then decide which parts to include, where, when and in what proportion. We do *not* plan one lesson at a time with several different and unrelated elements, skills, and content. Most students who have reading/language problems have already been subjected to that kind of teaching. Planning is *order*: a logically structured set of relationships among facts, ideas, concepts, and skills. The key to understanding this core concept notion is the word *relationship*: how do the elements in a lesson or among lessons relate to each other on how many different levels? Let's get back to the specific elements of good lessons, starting with *focus*.

Focus

The dictionary definition is helpful (*Webster's Seventh New Collegiate Dictionary*, p. 323): "A point at which rays converge or from which they diverge or appear to diverge. . ." The definition also contains such synonyms as "concentrate," and "converge." How does a lesson concentrate or serve as a point of convergence and divergence of rays (skills, content, and activities)? A lesson having focus does indeed concentrate the skills and content so that they relate in natural and logical ways. A given core concept plan of instruction gives both meaning and direction to all of the facts, ideas, concepts, and skills needed. It is the road map that student and teacher use to easily follow from one point to another. Whatever the core concept is, it makes use of all the word recognition, meanings, and study skills so that the words which come up are used to teach the word recognition skills needed by the students as well as to teach vocabulary. The study skills are taught (as needed) in order to improve comprehension and the sense of organization of the material read. Interpretation is taught within this framework as is writing. All skills and content converge, focus on the core concept, and when mastered in this meaningful context, diverge to any other reading material the student may encounter.

The focus of each lesson is on the content—the information, ideas, concepts, and the skills are taught to assist the student in gathering the information in an organized, related fashion, which enhances the meaning of everything read and discussed. Concept plan focus is relatively easy since all of the lessons are concerned with one major concept and its closely related subconcepts; content does not vary from lesson to lesson, book to book, activity to activity. Students' attention is thus drawn to the core concept and does not wander as easily as in usual instruction; the student always knows what is being studied and why; he knows the various skills are useful tools, not ends in themselves.

Unfocused lessons present too much information about too many different topics and insert skills in a rigidly sequenced fashion, confusing most students who have experienced difficulty in reading and writing. Many examples of good core concept, focused planning, and instruction will follow this section and perhaps the best illustration of well focused, core concept plans is the one on *Migration*. Everything read, written, heard, and spoken about for the 16-week period in which this concept was studied was related directly to aspects of migration in people and animals. Focus in these lessons is analogous to focus in a fine camera which produces a picture with excellent definition; unfocused planning and instruction produces fuzzy images and unclear relationships.

Continuity

Continuity is another critical component of good planning. It is the result of individually focused lessons that relate to each other. Continuity within a single lesson is produced when the lesson has a clear focus on both content and skills, and in which movement from activity to activity and skill to skill is smooth because it all converges on the content. Isolated words, facts, or skills do not appear in such a lesson. The words read in the context serve to maintain a functional diagnosis of the student's word recognition skills and vocabulary, and the context serves as the source of both comprehension and interpretation. Study skills, if appropriate, are easily checked as the student goes through the material for that lesson. If the content is *Migration* then the previewing, finding main ideas and details, classification, etc. are checked in that material, not in workbooks which have little or no content. This constant reinforcement of the content makes the skills much less obtrusive and much more sensible. The application of skills inside the core concept makes it much easier to maintain a sense of continuity in the lesson and among all of the lessons which are part of the corrective program. Each lesson hangs together logically, and groups of lessons more readily link with each other when this kind of planning is implemented. Application of skills and understanding is the goal of instruction and that happens best when students see the relationships embedded in any core concept.

Creativity

Creativity is another component of good planning even though that may sound a bit paradoxical. After all, how do you plan creatively for creativity? One aspect of creativity has already been expressed indirectly when we spoke of focus and continuity. It certainly is true that well focused and continuous lessons could be prosaic and dull, but creative lessons cannot fail to have both focus and continuity. Creativity always evokes the sense of wholeness and interrelatedness that core concept lessons are designed to produce. It is creative to put together several elements, forms, sounds, shapes, textures, and ideas into a pleasing and meaningful whole which enhances the understanding and satisfaction of the student. The student or observer of creative acts enjoys knowing what he did, why he did it, that it can be done again, and that he can anticipate what is yet to come. Focused and continuous lessons provide the base for this kind of anticipation and relational thinking and feeling. But creative lessons do more: they encourage *novelty*, and the making of new connections and relationships among people, ideas, words, and concepts.

Wholeness, which is the crux of creative work and planning, is much more satisfying than fragmentation, which means that it can stimulate much better performance from students of all ages and backgrounds than the typical remedial program of disparate parts. Besides, many of the students who fail in reading and language skills have had more than their share of fragmentation in the curriculum and in materials such as workbooks, boxes of cards, word lists, etc. For whatever reasons, these students do not respond successfully to this fragmented approach, so why do more of the same when correcting their problems? Why not try a new way of structuring the learning environment, which is focused, continuous, and creative—in short, whole?

Obviously not everyone is capable of the same quality of creativity, but we are all capable of more than we think we are. Most of us unfortunately have been subjected to behavioristically designed, fragmented instruction so that we may feel a bit uncomfortable with Gestalt type planning, such as the core concept. But I urge you to try it and to discover in yourselves and your students much greater creativity and success. *More of the same* in diagnosis and correction makes no sense; it is part of the problem, not part of the solution.

Coherence

Coherence is closely related to both continuity and focus since it deals with how things hang together and relate to each other. Once more the dictionary (*Websters*, p. 161) offers the best definition I can find for what I mean: "to hold together firmly as parts of the same mass. . . to become united in principles, relationships, or interests. . .to be logically or aesthetically consistent." When a lesson is coherent it relates all of the content, skills, and concepts to a focal point. All of the parts of the lesson stick together because of the principles and relationships being developed in word recognition, meanings, and study skills, and because the core concept serves as an organizing principle, a magnet. The last part of the definition, "logically or aesthetically consistent," is the gist of good planning — it is artistic.

Pacing

Pacing is another important aspect of all planning and teaching. How much material and information, and how many skills, ideas, and concepts should be included in each lesson? Is it too slow, too fast? Pacing must be determined by the information you collect on your IDAs which should guide you in determining how much each child can handle and at what levels, both cognitively and affectively. Additionally one must consider not only skills levels, but level of anxiety, embarrassment, and hostility. Pacing is also part of your own personality. In any kind of planning, the key is *balance* within each lesson and among them. Like a fine piece of music, some parts of lessons can be played staccato, some fortissimo, some crescendo. You can judge that from your IDA and continuing observations of the students and your own reactions to the learners and the material to be taught. Pacing can destroy a lesson by racing through too much material too fast or by lingering on the same note too long.

Plan more than you expect to need, but don't use everything you plan unless the lesson really flows swiftly. You should have an alternate or supplementary plan for each lesson so that if things are too difficult or too dull for the day, you can shift to another activity quickly. Nothing is worse than dragging out limited material and activity or running out of material and activity before your session ends.

I have presented some simple notions about focus, continuity, creativity, coherence, and pacing as an introduction to the process of core concept planning. Obviously when one speaks of planning instruction one must include some remarks about methods and materials, and objectives, but I shall not say much here since what is most pertinent about them will emerge in the examples of core concept planning. Methods and materials are not separated from such integrated planning. Objectives are derived from the IDA and the functional diagnostic work done during each lesson. By placing all of these factors into a core concept plan you avoid the complications so often encountered in fragmented planning and teaching. In sum, all of the components of a lesson must be kept in focus and balanced in accord with the student's performance.

THE CONCEPT OF "CONCEPT"

Since concepts are at the heart of all learning, it is essential that we define and discuss them in some detail before we look at actual plans. Once again let's go to the dictionary for an overview of concepts (*Webster's*, p. 171): "an abstract idea generalized from particular instances. . . the sum of a person's ideas and beliefs concerning something." Carroll (1964) has written extensively on the subject of concepts and concept formation: "In brief, concepts are properties of organismic experience—more particularly, they are the abstracted and often cognitively structured class of 'mental' experience learned by organisms in the course of their life histories."

The key words here are *organismic*, which means a totally integrated organism like man, a monkey, a tree; an interdependent set of cells, membrances, tissues, and organs within a unique individual. It is wholeness—integrated, purposeful wholeness like all of Nature. Carroll is telling us that concepts are comprehensive experiences taken out of other (but related) thoughts and experiences. They are used like tools by your mind, which has sorted and interpreted all of the experiences you have day by day throughout your life. You keep adding, subtracting, and shaping your concepts as you have more experiences. Carroll (1964) goes on to say:

> One necessary condition for the formation of a concept is that the individual must have a series of experiences that are in one or more respects similar; the constellation of "respects" in which they are similar constitutes the "concept" that underlies them. . .The infant acquires "concepts" of many kinds even before he attains anything like language. One kind of concept that is acquired by an infant quite early is the concept embodied in the experience of a particular object—a favorite toy, for example. As the toy is introduced to the infant, it is experienced in different ways—it is seen at different angles, at different distances, and in different illuminations. It is felt in different positions and with different parts of the body, and experienced with still other sense-modalities—taste, smell. But underlying all these experiences are common elements sufficient for the infant to make an identifying response to the particular toy in question—perhaps to the point that he will accept only the particular specimen that is the least bit different."

We could add to Carroll's discussion of the child's development of concepts related to a favorite toy. He has emphasized sensory-based concepts without considering the feelings the child has in relation to these sensations of touch, taste, and smell. One cannot separate and omit feelings from concepts at any stage of their acquisition; the child's feelings and emotions evoked by the toy are an integral part of the concept. Also, Carroll did not mention the toy itself insofar as what the child is thinking and feeling as he plays with it, imagines it in other contexts, and separates it from less desirable toy and from nontoy. What are the toy's symbolic qualities to the child? The favorite stuffed animal, truck, or blanket will be carried everywhere especially when the child is in transit or in some unfamiliar place to serve as a reassurance and a re-creation of familiar surroundings and feelings. Thus the concept of toy (or any other) is constructed with psychological materials, physical/sensory materials and experiences, and personality factors all interacting in several ways and on several levels simultaneously. The concept of toy is a generalization of other related generalizations. It is fun, play, object, love, security, an appendage, a friend, etc. The whole of this concept is greater than the sum of its parts.

Carroll (1964) clarifies his notion of concepts:

> "My concept of "stone" may not be precisely your concept of "stone" because my experiences with stones may have included work with pieces of a peculiar kind of vitreous rock that you have seldom seen. To a large extent, how I sort out my experiences is my own business and may not lead to the same sortings as yours. Nevertheless, I can specify the way I sort out my experiences by noting the *critical attributes* that differentiate them."

Many students of concept development would agree with much that Carroll has said so there is no need to cite them here, but rather for me to modify these notions as a way of explaining how core concept planning and teaching operates. The key to understanding concepts and concept formation is that our experiences and feelings build and shape all of our concepts. As our experiences are organized and classified in our minds as a result of detecting the critical attributes of objects and events and other concepts, we form and alter the concepts we have. We build generalizations that group experiences, ideas, information, and feelings. Each new experience we have is considered in light of the concepts we already have and we decide whether it fits in that class or group. We look for similarities and differences in each new experience; we make comparisons and contrasts, and we note the positive and negative aspects of each concept. For example, to understand a concept like justice we must be aware of both just and unjust acts in particular contexts and all of this is filtered through our own unique personality.

Concepts are a kind of shorthand notation that help us to recall and rearrange the data we have and continue to gather. Concepts integrate, organize, and uncover the relationships among ideas, abstractions, and first-hand experiences. All of us who are of normal intelligence have thousands of concepts in our minds and we can sort them, reflect on them, and alter them through new or old experiences seen from a new angle and with new feelings, while the mentally retarded or the psychotic are unable to organize their thoughts or to deal with several ideas or feelings at the same time. The retarded have a very limited supply of concepts since they are, by definition, unable to make generalizations or to make many comparisons and contrasts and to uncover patterns. The highly intelligent are so characterized by us because they have many concepts and therefore can make many more relationships and projections than most of us can. They see patterns and predict and interpret more data from more sources faster than most of us.

Example of a Concept: Taxes

Perhaps a more concrete example of conceptualizing would help us in our thinking and then in the core concept planning presented shortly. Let's take taxes as a concept to understand and which we could easily make into a core concept set of plans for our students.

If we were trying to understand taxes and taxation, what would we have to know and think about? We might ask what types of taxes there are. To that we could answer income, excise, sales, estate, inheritance, property, capital gains, etc. For each one, we could find out who pays these taxes, how they pay, when, to whom, and for what purposes. The answers to these questions are all part of the concept of taxes, which is rooted in the concept of people paying to support their governments: local, state, and federal.

Why we pay taxes is related to the way we support our governments so that they in turn can provide us all with certain essential services including health and medical care, education, welfare, sanitation, police and fire protection, the civil service, and armed forces. For each of the services rendered by the government we could make comparisons and contrasts with other governments around the world that operate similarly and differently. The economic and political forces impinging upon government support could be studied as part of this core concept. The historical, social, and cultural aspects of the ways in which peoples support their government would also be looked at, depending upon the age and maturity of your group. The whole system of taxation, both its negative and positive aspects, would be discussed and read about as a way of expanding the concept of taxes. For planning purposes one could expand this concept for students of very high levels of skill and knowledge or restrict it for those whose age, maturity, and background are much more limited. But in both instances, the concept and related subconcepts of taxes would be viewed from all angles and aspects to produce fuller understanding of the interrelationships of forces and conditions that alter taxation. In the wake of Proposition 13 many states are reacting politically as well as economically and socially. All of these factors and forces would be woven into the study of this concept, or any concept that might be studied at any level.

Even this brief sketch of taxes only skims the surface of the nature of concepts, although we could use such a concept for extensive long-range planning and teaching. In dealing with this concept, or any other, it is clear that we must organize and classify many different facts and types of information so that we can abstract and generalize from them to other concepts. Relationships are uncovered in their wholeness so that students are never merely collecting data at random. Their focus throughout such a study is always very clear and it guides them at every step of the way.

Example of a Concept: Redness

How do we develop the ability to note that red is not the property of one object, but rather a quality attached to many different objects in many different places of many different sizes, shapes, textures, and uses? If Piaget, Carroll, and others are right the very young child first attaches red to a specific object in his immediate environment: the red chair or red toy. Other objects which are red are not seen as such for a time, at least until the child can generalize enough to identify the "critical attribute" red. The child has to notice that the color has a certain brilliance and hue on all objects like the flower, dress, curtain, scarf, face, paint, blood, car, house, even a sunset. The child separates thingness from redness, a process requiring experiences with many objects in many contexts, then the ability to classify these, noting similarities and differences and what is constant and what is not. All of this sorting and comparing is the essence of concept formation in us all and it occurs over a long period of time like all learning.

The more the child sees red and is told it is red in many different contexts the sooner he is likely to realize that red is red no matter where or when it appears. This generalizing, this conceptualizing is what we must do more of as teachers and clinicians. All concepts develop similarly and are altered throughout life by our experiences and our thinking about our experiences and feelings. Since all of our experiences are filtered through our personalities, that special psychological interaction must be included in any understanding of concept formation and development: it is simply not a purely cognitive act, but a blending of the cognitive and affective.

Thus the development of concepts is the hallmark of humanity and its intelligence and learning. In core concept planning, we take full advantage of this process to structure the learning environment in as natural a way as possible.

PLANNING CORE CONCEPT PROGRAMS

How does the core concept work? How can we teach all of the reading and language skills a student or group of students might need in such a curriculum? And how can we be sure to teach the reading and writing skills when we seem to be focusing on concepts and content? The following examples come from direct experience with students of all ages and backgrounds all over the country. Let's start slowly and work into more complete core concept plans, discussing how methods and materials are included, how we might group and so on.

There is no problem in choosing reading materials for a core concept plan, nor is there any problem in offering fascinating reading materials, teaching needed skills in all of the growth areas, doing work in writing and drawing or even making a book on it. This is certainly better than prosy, uninspired, literal material found in most basal readers and other commonly used instructional materials. And it pleases the students and inspires their best effort, concentration, and involvement. One problem I have not mentioned here is that in core concept planning one may encounter material that is over the heads of your students. The *only* thing to do is to translate the material downward (in accord with a readability formula like Dale-Chall or Spache) so that your students will be able to read the information themselves at their own instructional level.

Suggested Topics for Core Concept Programs

Some of the following core concepts are very common choices among the students who come to our clinic at Northeastern University: *witches, magic, cooking, space, animals (especially dinosaurs), jobs, transportation,* or just *cars* or *jets*, to name just a few. Any one of these provides our tutors with a focus of content and interest, even experience, which is then developed into a series of 10, 15, even 20 lessons which tie together whatever word recognition, meanings, study skills, vocabulary, writing skills, and activities the students may need. The students have fun, they bring to bear what they know or are curious about, and they get the kind of painless help in dealing with the reading and writing activities that foster motivation and conscious progress. There are no special word lists and no special materials; even methodology sometimes takes a back seat. For in fact, the methodology and the materials are appendages to the process of building and developing the core concept jointly with the learner, and flexibility is built in with controls since the core concept can move several ways and onto various levels. It can always be adjusted logically and coherently to the students' intellectual, academic, and emotional needs, which are monitored functionally in each lesson.

LANGUAGE EXPERIENCE AND CORE CONCEPT PLANNING

Language Experience

The language-experience (L-E) approach offers many advantages not found in other approaches, particularly for very poor readers, beginning readers of all ages (especially older adolescents), and adults who are functionally or totally illiterate. First, it provides a coherent limited context within which to develop the word recognition skills, meanings and study skills, and vocabulary and writing skills. This context is taken from the students' own life experiences, feelings, and needs, thus increasing its motivational power. The content of the language-experience stories and activities is not only rooted in the needs, interests, and experiences of the student, but it serves as an integrating force in what is spoken, read, and written. No matter what level of skill in English the student may possess, he can help direct his own learning in familiar materials, often self-constructed.

Another distinct advantage of the language-experience approach is that it individualizes the instruction and presentation of skills and content in accord with the student's needs and abilities. The student is the best guide to his own vocabulary, information, and skills. We can start where he is and move on much more easily than if we subjected such a student to a prescribed, rather rigid sequencing of skills. We do not need to depend on isolated phonics activities, flash cards, workbook drills, word lists, or any arbitrary scope and sequence of skills. Our instruction can attend directly and constantly to the student's interests, skills, and content needs.

We have found in both classroom and clinic, that most students whose reading and writing skills are minimal can tell a story or relate some facts, and then "read" what has been spoken. That student can then copy what was written, and then read that. This provides us with the raw material for the basic phonic and structural analysis skills derived from material of interest to the student. This kind of dictated material does not seem to threaten or embarrass the student, especially the older students or non-English speakers as much as the usual published series or programs.

As you will see in the examples in the remainder of this chapter, there are many ways to initiate a language-experience type of lesson so as to involve the students fully and positively. Several things happen to the students which create a distinctively different learning climate: the students are rewarded for what they *do* know and care about, their own language and knowledge serves as the medium of instruction, they find they can read something, and they discover reading is not so remote from their lives. All of these factors improve their attitudes towards themselves and the reading processes. The teacher is constantly monitoring the student's progress and can more easily adjust the presentation of skills and content. As the profession moves into competency-based instruction it will require more approaches to teaching and assessing reading and language skills performance like this.

To use the L-E approach you can use a variety of techniques for getting the material from the student in his own language. You may not even use printed materials at the outset, just his own spoken language about some interest or experience. You can use everyday materials to start with, like pictures from magazines, books, or newspapers; a film or filmstrip to generate some conversation; an experiment in science; a visit to a museum or aquarium. You can use TV shows; the person's own neighborhood with its street signs, names on stores or mailboxes. In short, almost anything can be used to launch a discussion that will result in a joint plan of instruction—a core concept.

A good example of the L-E approach using some older printed materials may be a good place to begin. The John Day publishers in 1965 produced a group of photo albums in two series: *Urban Education Studies* and *Rural Education Studies*. These albums contain large photographs (about 18" × 18") organized into topics with themes such as Friends, Family, etc. Each album contains a scene of people or animals revealing some aspect of the overall theme of that particular album. For example, in the album on Family one picture shows some puppies with their mother. None of the pictures in any of the albums has any words with it. The point of showing the pictures is to stimulate some conversation about them and to pose questions to the students that will start them thinking about families, friends, etc. The discussion leads to an L-E dictated chart with simple sentences related to what the students see and feel about the picture. The students read what each one has said, and then they each copy from the board what the teacher said and wrote. Thus they see, hear, read, and write these simple sentences dealing with this picture.

Suppose for example the dictated chart looked like this in response to viewing the pictures of the puppies and their mother:

Puppies are sitting with their mother.
The puppies are brown and white.
They are soft and cute.
The mother takes care of the puppies.
She feeds them and takes care of them

A smart teacher or clinician could guide the children or adults in their choice of language and even in thinking about what to say about the picture. Instead of getting just a factual set of statements about what is in the picture, one can lure remarks of affect, anticipation, imagery, and relationships out of the picture. Let us say, though, that this group of youngsters produces the above language experience story. What can you do with it instructionally?

Word recognition

If the children are in the first grade, some are reading at preprimer level, some at primer level, some at first grade level, some at second grade level, and maybe a couple are reading at third grade level. The teacher should have done some homogeneous skills grouping so that all of the children are not engaged in the same activity too often. But let us assume for now that the students are heterogeneously grouped for this activity so that you must account for several levels of skill in word recognition. Before using any kind of material or activity such as this, go through it to discover what phonic and structural analysis elements appear and what may come out of the discussion in response to the album. If you know your students need particular practice on certain phonic elements, you may guide their discussion of what they see so that you can get some of the words which contain these elements out of them, and make them part of the dictated story. The story doesn't just happen—it is fathered.

In this little story some phonic elements are repeated, such as initial *p*, medial *p*, *th*, *m* in the initial position, and *m* in the final position, *sh* as an initial digraph, and many others including silent *e*, short *e*, digraph *wh*, long *i*, syllabication in *mother*, *protect*, *puppies*, and so on. Obviously, all of these phonic and structural elements cannot be taught in one or two lessons—that's bad planning or pacing. So one decides which elements will be emphasized and worked on in each lesson, and those will be determined by what you know about the students from their IDAs and also by which of the needed elements are the *most generalizable* and *generative*. In pulling out phonic and structural elements, numerous exercises and practices can be used (see Lee and Allen (1963) and Stauffer (1970) for specifics) such as working with phonograms related to words in the story, e.g., *other* in *mother*, *akes* in *takes*, *eeds* in *deeds*. One can do some vocabulary work on synonyms and antonyms, and, if possible, with roots, prefixes, and suffixes (depending on the language in your story). Of course, you can pull out the *th* in *their*, *the*, *they*, and *them* which appears in this story and make sure the student's auditory and visual discrimination of the element is known (it is repeated nine times—once in the final position, wi*th*; once in the medial position, mo*th*er; and six times in the initial position, *th*em). In only one instance is the sound different as in wi*th* (voiced and voiceless). Otherwise, the *th* digraph in this story maintains consistency in sound and sight, auditorily and visually. The words are also in context and they were evoked from the students—not placed on a worksheet, out of context, and without an interesting stimulus.

How many elements you work with in a lesson depends on your students' needs and abilities. But whatever their word recognition needs, they can be introduced, developed, and practiced in a much more contextual and interesting fashion this way. For those students who know these skills, one can use the same story as a take-off for writing a longer story, for developing vocabulary, and for introducing some literary skill in use of imagery—describe how the littlest puppy feels nuzzled into its mother's side. How does the puppy see? touch? feel? taste his mother? his brothers and sisters? How many ways do you know to say *protects them*. Describe the texture of their fur, the shapes, etc.

Meanings

This same little story about the picture seen and discussed provides enough matter for you to ask comprehension and interpretation questions. For example, under comprehension (literal recall), you could ask, Where are the puppies? What colors are the puppies? Puppies are able to take care of themselves—yes or no? For interpretation questions, you could ask, How does the mother protect and feed her puppies? What other animals do the same? What animals do not care for their babies? Why? What kind of dogs will these puppies be when they grow up? Will they look just like their mother? Why? Why not?

You see one of the problems with lower level written matter: it is difficult to ask too many good and thought provoking questions. But you can ask some. At higher levels of performance, you will get longer dictated stories, and hence, have more to ask. Still, you can measure the performance in the meanings area with such questions as given above. Also, in the case where you use pictures or similar devices to launch discussion as the base for the language experience story, you can use the picture itself to evoke some interpretational responses. For example, in the scene where the mother dog sits with her pups, what season is it? Where do you think this picture was taken? Why? These questions can lead to further discussion and other questions, as well as giving you more information on the children's knowledge and reasoning and experience.

Study Skills

For children in the first grade, you will not need to make a full scale approach to study skills, but I suggest laying some of the foundations for these skills very early. For example, you get a title for the picture, and then discuss three or four possibilities for why the students chose the title they did. This activity is also a beginning of interpretation and when you direct the children's attention to the scene and ask for summary of what's in it, you touch on a study skill. Previewing pictures and other material can also be initiated, as when you show them the album on Friends or Family so that they can get an overview of what is likely to appear in the album. In leading such a discussion, I always mention something which would not fit into such a book, and encourage the children to see if they agree with me or not, and why. At higher levels, of course, you can get much more out of the study skills in this process.

Vocabulary has been mentioned as one of the skills to be derived and developed from even a simple chart like the one we have. Obviously, with more matter and more varied concepts and language, pulling out root words, prefixes, suffixes, synonyms, antonyms, and some imagery is easier to do.

Writing

Writing is also part of this simple, low level chart activity. Children should say the line they contributed about what they have seen in the picture and what they have heard in the discussion. Then they should read it after you have written it on the board. When all the lines to the story are on the board, and each author has read his line, have others read the lines, and then copy them in their own book. If you use something like the Urban or Rural Education Studies material, or make your own album, the children can be writing the copy for each picture and hence create a book for their own use. This is a good writing practice and gives them material they are familiar with. They could be encouraged after such a set of lessons to pick their own picture from a book or magazine, and write their own captions or small stories. They could draw the pictures and follow the same process in an organized way.

When the stories have been copied and reread, and the skills work in phonics structural analysis, and so on have been completed, children should move simultaneously to reading simple printed books related to the theme, say of "Friends" or "Family," taken from the initial lesson. This helps maintain some continuity among the lessons, some articulation. Work in spelling, grammar, and sentence structure as well as oral presentation accompanies this type of approach. Thus, the language skills—reading, writing, speaking, and listening—are aimed at a focal point of interest.

Sequencing Skills

Determining the sequence of skills is accomplished by closely following each child's weaknesses, strengths, and interests, and by using some common sense. Usually most children have more difficulty with consonant digraphs than with vowel digraphs; initial single consonants of the regular variety (b,d,f,l,m,n,p,r,s,t, and v) are taught before the irregular ones (or, rather the more irregular ones) such as c,g,h,k,j,q,z,x, and y (y and w, which are sometimes vowels). It may not be so terribly important to follow a prescribed and rigid sequencing of skills. In general, most students have less trouble with consonant blends like bl, pr, and st, and more trouble with consonant digraphs such as sh, wh, ch, and th. Pay more attention, however, to the specific student, or group of students, when planning the instructional sequences. Basal readers, in fact most printed materials in series, including isolated phonics programs like *Phonetic Keys to Beginning Reading*, all offer variations of the same basic theme on what word recognition skills to teach, and in what sequence or order. It is preferable to *derive* the skills needed and the order in which to teach them from the students as much as possible. Respond to their weaknesses, strengths, and interests personally and directly, not to some arbitrary listing of what ought to be taught and when to masses of students. Besides, a good teacher who is a good functional diagnostician, who daily observes and collects performance data on each student in each lesson, does not need to rely so heavily on pre-established orders or sequences for teaching.

Summary of the Family Core Concept Planning

This illustration of planning in which we use a single, simple picture as a focal point for developing a concept (Family) with the students allow us opportunities to teach skills in all of the growth areas in reading, and link all of the reading and language skills. Putting the parts together so that the pacing is correct is the only problem. It is directly related to the data from the IDA of the students involved, knowing how much they can take and give, and in what period of time. More can be done, though, by way of variety of related skills, in focused lessons like the one we have been discussing than in typical lessons. At least the content is clear and generative for students and teacher alike, and the skills then fit into the context much more comfortably than if one were jumping all over the lot with content and skills. Here they are related clearly.

The next step in planning such a lesson as we have just seen would involve sketching four or five (preferably more) lessons bearing on the concept of Family. If you use the John Day materials, you will find several large photographs of different types of families in the one album. You will find people families and animal families. After doing lessons like the one illustrated, in which many related reading and language skills were taught contextually, we lead the students into broadening and deepening the concept and subconcepts deriving from Family (and, as developed limitedly in the picture of mother dog and her pups). What we want is the fuller context within which to teach all the skills and understandings that are at the heart of reading and communicating. For example, if we discuss another picture in the Family album showing three or four children, a mother and a father, and a house in the background, we take the children through a discussion of what they see, who the poeple are, and how they are related (brother, sister, mother, father, home). We make charts and stories about these in whatever detail we feel the students can handle. You can make it very simple for young children:

> This is a picture of a family.
> There is a mother and father,
> two sisters and a brother.
> They are standing in front of
> their house in the city(country).

You could follow most of the same procedures we did in the preceding picture of the dog and her pups insofar as skills instruction goes, but here you could add the dimension in thought of how the two kinds of families (dogs and people) are alike or different, and what they do to protect, care for, feed, and educate their young. Exhibit 5-1 illustrates the way in which categories can be compared and contrasted.

Exhibit   5-1

	Animals	People
Protection		
Food		
Homes		
Learning		
Play		

How much and how thoroughly this kind of activity is developed depends only on your students, their skill, and their knowledge. The thread through all of the activities as you move into the rest of the album is, What is a family? Any kind of family? Do they live differently in different places? Why? How? All of the relationships among people or animal groups can be uncovered in readings and discussion to enrich the concept of family, the focal point of all the lessons. In dealing with the other pictures, stories, and discussions in this process, we make with the students a context of ideas, facts, relationships, and experiences which feed the concept of family. Any skills that need to be taught are easily inserted into the context, as we saw in the previous illustration, and will be made clearer in the next illustration.

What is the point? Simple. Here is a process for planning and implementing lessons utilizing all that has been presented in terms of the language, the learner, the reading processes, the diagnosis, and its interpretations. All of that is essential for anyone in making plans.

The notion of a core concept is the principle which ties the lessons together, linking skills instruction and elaborating the concepts we want students to learn and use in all of their learning. Using this integrating principle, we follow nature and common sense logic of what goes with what. We avoid arbitrary and rigid sequences and irrelevant planning and we avoid boredom—a major cause of learning problems. Furthermore, the core concept and integrated planning we see in these brief examples focuses on meaning and understanding, emphasizing relationships among facts.

Communication

One of my favorite core concept launching lessons is illustrated in Exhibit 5-2. Without comment, I put on the board the illustrated items, then I ask the students what they see and what any of these items means to them. I get a few specific answers like addition, money sign, music, swastika, cross, foreign language, or some variation of these. Then I ask questions: What do these things mean to you? What do these things tell you? What are all these marks and signs? Someone always says symbols. What are symbols? We finally decide they are signs or marks that represent something else. I ask what they represent to them—what ideas, people, places, times, and feelings. We try to synthesize: These marks are symbols that represent certain thoughts, feelings, ideas, and processes.

Exhibit 5-2

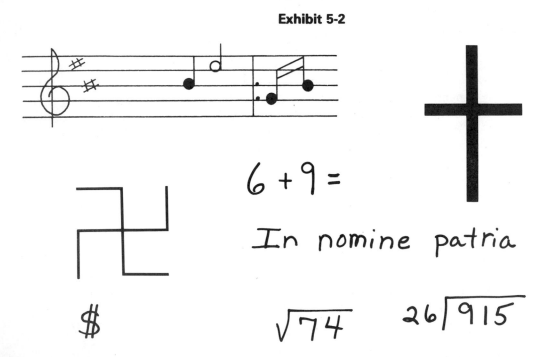

Can you give me a name for it? Usually after a couple of attempts, we agree that these are forms of language. Then we pursue that concept to produce a definition of language: a standard symbolic code for transmitting information, feelings, and ideas from person to person. Language, we agree, can have two forms: verbal (using words) and nonverbal (everything but words). We agree both verbal and nonverbal language serve the same end: to communicate with words, symbols, gestures, movements, color, sound, form, and shape in order to let someone else know what you think, how you feel, and what you want. I might insert some unfamiliar or unexpected sounds in order to illustrate that not all sounds are language or music, but only sounds put together in certain standard ways are language. We talk about misspelling or bad syntax as problems which confuse or break down communication.

Depending on the age of the group, I try to get them to demonstrate some of this nonverbal behavior, like dance, or making faces, or bodily gestures to transmit feelings and attitudes. We may do some verbal gestures which add meaning to a normal utterance, like "Oh," said in a drawn out fashion and with a smirk on the face, usually meaning doubt; and then we'll say "Oh" as in surprise, shock, or joy. If there is time, we may go on to discuss communication in terms of various types of languages including foreign languages and what they are like, how they resemble ours, how they differ; different dialects and the problems they may cause us (liberally salted with examples). We might talk about how animals and machines communicate and how that differs from our form of communication and how it is alike. We'll talk about movies, TV, radio, paintings, dolphins, bees, music, and dance in terms of communication, language, and symbols—how messages are sent and received. We look at other cultures and their communication systems. Always we talk about technology or science and communication. We talk about instruments such as telephone, stereo, tape decks, records, films, and other such mechanical media and discuss how they have affected communication and language and how they use symbols, and for older students, how the media affect the messages they send.

With all of this discussion behind us, we have indeed laid the conceptual foundation for a plan of study which integrates all of the major subject matters normally taught; It also provides the context for teaching all of the reading, writing, and other language skills. I have often recommended that the core concept of *communication* would be most useful for the first three grades, since that is when the typical school curriculum imposes language and forms of communication on students in a dry and stultifying manner. Why not make the content identical with the processes we usually teach in those grades? Children like to know where language came from, who spoke it, wrote it, where and when. They like to hear and read stories about different people around the world at various times in the world's history, just as they love dinosaurs and cave men. Why settle on workbooks and stories about trivia? If language instruction is the heart of the curriculum, why not focus on it for the content of our curriculum so that while children get the background of language and communication, they use other forms of communication and language to directly experience it?

Adults and "ESL" Students

Another type of illustration of integrated planning using the language experience approach comes from real life, as do all of the other illustrations here. But this was perhaps more unusual than most of my experiences. We are in Western Colorado, a town of about 3000 people, predominantly white, the remainder Chicano (Mexican-American). Most of the group is transient, part of the migrant stream which starts each year in El Paso, Texas and moves with the seasons and crops north through Colorado to Idaho, west to Washington, and south to Oregon and California, and then eastward back to El Paso. Many such migrant groups, largely Mexican-American, largely illiterate or functionally illiterate in both English and Spanish and largely unschooled, were involved in programs using the language-experience core concept approach.

Planning integrated, useful educational programs, especially in ESL and literacy, is most difficult since so little time is available and so much cultural conflict is rooted in the system. However, using core concepts, staff and students experienced a great deal of success. The students were adults who had been in the migrant "stream" all or most of their lives so that their educational problems were linguistic, cultural, and social, as well as educational. Never being in one place for more than two or three months does not make for the most secure type of environment. It means few attachments, little emotional involvement in any area or with any group of people, and scraping out a subsistence living while on the run, and returning to where the migrants' lives began in the same state of existence and hope (or lack of hope).

Rainy Day Program: Survival Course

The "rainy day" curriculum was an offshoot of the core concept curriculum, but designed for one day, two days, a week, or more of survival life skills, utilizing all the reading and language skills rooted in the needs of every day life.

The rainy day program was designed to provide money to the migrants on those days when they could not go into the fields to pick and for which they would not be paid. The whole educational process was condensed into a day; if it were a rainy day, the migrants would be brought into town to the educational center. There they would be screened by an IDA in reading and math; then grouped according to those data; then scheduled for the day in a core concept such as *The Law and You, Health and Safety, Transportation,* or *Consumers.* Each core concept provided within a single day (or group of days) reading, writing, math, social studies, and possibly some science. Individuals like the sheriff, police chief, a lawyer, a doctor, a public health official, a nurse, or a manager of a big store had been asked if we could count on their assistance in the event of rain. Such persons would come in to give first-hand information about the particular topic.

Each single day, then, came to the students whole and tied together—not as in most programs, in programmed bits and pieces, unrelated, unreal.

This was a special educational program that involved training, teaching, and tutoring the migrants when they were not in the fields, or for those who had settled in the community. Here we have a large group of twenty-five to thirty functionally and totally illiterate persons with very little time to devote to even minimal survival education. Where do we begin? I arranged with the two supermarket managers in the town to permit me to take some people to the store for a project we were going to do. One cloudy day the townspeople stared at us as we walked down the main street of this town toward the first supermarket. Despite the shock on the manager's face, the thirty of us entered his neat store.

The students had been told before the trip to go through the store with pencils and paper to mark down the names of products they used, liked, or didn't know about. I circulated throughout, asking them why they bought such and such a product and they replied with answers like, they knew the box, the color, the shape, and had been told it was a good soap, cereal, vegetable, etc. Most of the students could not read the labels or the price on the products. Using clues like color, shape, size, maybe a letter or two, or location in a certain store, they would choose what to buy with the incredibly limited amount of information at their disposal.

After they had circulated around the supermarket making notes, we went across the street to the other supermarket, receiving the same chilly, incredulous stares. We went through this store, listing prices for some of the goods in order to compare them later. We finally left, laden with names of products, prices, some comparisons, and a collective sense of madness.

When we got back to class, after about an hour and a half, we made lists of products we had seen and from whose containers we had copied the name of the product and anything else we could find on the box or package—a list of things like Ajax, Wheaties, Dial, Hunt's Tomato Juice, Heinz Catsup, Wonder Bread, Dole Pineapple, Cheerios, Ivory Snow, SOS Pads. We wrote these all down, read them (several of us for each item), and copied them into a notebook. Then we talked about how these products are organized and laid out on the shelves and racks in the stores. This is simple classification requiring the ability to see relationships. Our categories were *Meats, Vegetables, Soaps, Cereals, Produce,*

Desserts, Coffee and Beverages, Bread and Cake, etc. Under each of these newly formed, spoken categories we entered the specific products we had listed earlier, discussing why a product goes under its particular category. When we finished we had a fairly well organized list of supermarket items properly categorized under major headings. Then we moved onto reading the prices and making comparisons between the two stores to ascertain the most economical product.

Now we had a core concept—an integrated curricular plan rooted in the language as they knew it and derived from their desperate need to survive in this foreign country. In addition to using the language of the stores and their products, we used street names, names of buildings, the court, the schools, lawyers, doctors, police, fire, etc. All of these words became part of the sight and spoken vocabulary, and the base for auditory and visual discrimination practices (all readiness activities). All teaching was taken from the language around them and in them. By using the world they found themselves in, the choice of words and their concepts were made easier and much more significant to them. If you can stir up some emotion in this overall process, all the better.

They responded excellently in this program. They spoke the names of products, wrote them, and read them. Many such words were developed into sight words, as were the names of important streets and offices, for example, *stop, go, walk, don't walk, in, out, exit, entrance, men, women, ESSO, Texaco*—the language around all of us all the time, basic survival language. If the rain continued beyond one day, the concept served to organize the curriculum for any period needed since that is the essence of core concept and its way of integrating information and skills. For each core concept, plans were made for about 8-10 consecutive days so that we had available integrated plans for at least four or five key concepts of a survival nature. We managed the best of both worlds; the real, survival world and the academic support for it. The sense of wholeness of information and ideas in the real world made good sense to these people.

Rainy Day Core Concept: Health and Safety

On the first day all students were screened by individual diagnostic analyses in reading and math (cf. Indian material), grouped homogeneously for reading and for math (separate groupings) and scheduled for the day, given instruction in core concept, with wrap-up and review at the end of the day.

We'll sketch out the day for nonreaders, third grade readers, and a higher level, say seventh graders in terms of the word recognition skills and principles to be taught within the context of Health and Safety, meanings skills and study skills, vocabulary and speaking and writing skills and activities. I will not detail this day, or any of these days, hour by hour, with specific activities, but will rather give the feel and sense of the day and the integration of skills as taught within this framework, this planning schema.

Nonreaders, Primer Level:

Have a doctor or a nurse come in and talk about some common health and safety problems such as washing hands before meals, and how unwashed hands carry certain bacteria (germs) which can cause a variety of ailments; eating the right foods and what can happen when you eat the wrong foods or an unbalanced diet; or seeing a doctor or public health nurse when certain symptoms appear. Students ask questions about these topics and see pictures, perhaps slides or public health films on diseases and smoking, and basic safety precautions around the house, in the fields, and in the car. All of this information can be deliberately preplanned so as to present the facts of health and safety in categories or other logical arrays, e.g., health and safety in the home, health and safety in work (the fields and factories, etc.), diet, cleanliness, and so on. The speaker, films, slides, and discussion should be organized so that they generate clearly defined and simple sentence patterns—hence, keeping the focus on just two or three key factors in health and safety limiting the vocabulary needed to express it. Parts of the presentation and accompanying discussion should be written on the board in simple sentences so that the connections can be established between what is being said and how it looks in English writing. You might have each student make a little handbook on health and safety, which includes his copied statements from the discussion that was put on the board. The students can clip pictures from newspapers and magazines and write captions. The little handbook would be organized like a book with chapters or other divisional headings so that organization and relationship is built right into the entire language and thinking process.

In addition to the talking, listening, and copying of content into the handbook on the subject of health and safety, we try to make much of the information direct and first hand. The students see a heart model while hearing how it works and what its parts are, or a chart on the human body with its bones, muscles, veins, arteries, and key organs. For non-English speakers or those whose English is very limited, concrete experiences help considerably in clarifying what is being discussed in the foreign tongue: it takes very little for most students to learn the word heart, for example, when they see the model, and then see the word, and tie that into what is being said about what it does and how it does it (concepts). Obviously, with students whose English is minimal it may require some translating into the native tongue and then back into English, e.g., corazon for heart. Most often, though, such concrete experiences do not require so much translating when you find there is no accurate way to make it clear in English what process is happening. When dealing with older children, adolescents, and adults with such language problems, it is a good principle to use as often as possible live, real, concrete objects or events as the place to begin vocabulary development (auditorily and then visually), then conceptually.

On the first day, we have had a formal presentation by a doctor or a nurse about the subject of health and safety. Concrete experience with models, and films have helped clarify the language being applied to them. Some simple sentences have been put on the board, read by several students, and then copied into a little handbook for their own use.

The words used over and over again in discussing this topic, e.g., *doctor*, *nurse*, *sick*, *temperature*, *pills*, *vitamins*, *diet*, *first aid*, *bandage*, *hospital*, *ambulance*, *medicine*, etc., have been spoken several times each in several meaningful contexts so that they become part of the listening and speaking vocabulary of the students. This is accompanied by writing some of these words down and making the connection among the modes: speaking, listening, writing, and seeing and touching of models brought in. These same words related to the discussion of health and safety also become sight words for reading, and are used in the simple writing in the handbook. Hence, the same group of words are used in several contexts and through several modes, establishing them as listening, speaking, reading, and writing vocabulary—and all in an important, useful, meaningful context!

With some base of sight words built up, and it would certainly take more than one day of teaching to build up a significant reservoir, we can move into developing phonic and structural analysis skills in word recognition. Using the sight words, we try to get words from the students that sound the same in the beginning, e.g., what words sound like *doctor* does in the beginning? (*d*o, *d*oor, *d*ime, *d*ay, etc.) Then ask for the words which contain that same initial consonant at the end, such as in en*d*, di*d*, wel*d*, han*d*. Finally, the same sound, *d*, in the middle of words. These are done both visually and auditorily in order to establish the connections between what is said, how it looks, and how to write it. As the sight word vocabulary is being increased in each instructional session (auditorily, visually, and in writing), phonic and structural elements are singled out and studied for similarities and differences with known words. This is the beginning of the whole process of making phonic generalizations and sharpening auditory and visual discrimination for the words in the new language.

In terms of meanings skills, it takes little to see how we would question students about the content of the presentation, films, and discussion of health and safety. We'd ask basic literal recall comprehension questions about the information, and we would pursue interpretation of the facts, principles, and concepts relating to health and safety. Insofar as study skills are concerned, with virtual nonreaders it is not possible to use the skills in dealing with written matter, but it is possible and most desirable to introduce some of the organizational notions of what is the main idea of this picture, film, or of our discussion. What kinds of illnesses and diseases are there, etc.? This takes us into summary, main ideas, and details, and into the discussion of what conditions, behavior, and medicine cure them. Even though the reading level is so low, older children and adults have a great deal of life experience and many concepts (no matter what their native tongue) and we have to try to use these fully. No matter what the word may be for an ailment, or a cure, or a problem, the ailment is the same in any language—pain and suffering hurt everyone equally.

Writing will be done in this day as described. How much you will worry about spelling, sentence structure, grammar, and punctuation depends on their specific needs and abilities. But they will write what they have heard, seen, and talked about. The topics are very important to their daily lives so there is no problem of interest or motivation. Pacing of all the skills in such a situation as this is obviously very important. For one, it may be a challenge to deal with many words, ideas, facts, and principles. For another, it is totally discouraging.

Vocabulary development will come out of this context. With medical language there is the advantage of being able to help students locate roots and prefixes and suffixes (some of which will be like the words in their own native tongue) as a means of expanding the vocabulary without isolated word lists. All of the vocabulary will come from the core concept under study so that a deeper level of relationship and wholeness is built right into the learning process. It certainly is more meaningful than learning from word lists or isolated phonics.

The focus of this lesson and all that follows is health and safety; how to stay healthy, how we get sick, why; what we can do to prevent illness; what to do when we get ill; how to prevent accidents at home, at work in the fields, in school, and on the streets. When completed, such a concept plan produces knowledge of some sicknesses, their causes, effects and cures; common safety hazards and how to avoid them, what to do when you can't avoid them, and what resources are available in the community to assist a person, in the event of sickness or accident.

The content focus is clear from one lesson to another; the skills needed are woven into the fabric as illustrated. In short, one does not need separate, special lessons to deal with phonics, structural analysis, vocabulary, writing, speaking, listening, reading, and content.

For these persons who are virtually nonliterate we use their life and language experience to deal with a major daily life concern, in this case health and safety, to focus their attention. Within this live context they learn the language, in all levels and modes, needed to understand the problems and cures. It is survival on at least three levels: (a) developing some literacy to be able to deal more independently with institutions, persons, and problems they may not be too familiar with; (b) survival value of knowing about health and safety; (c) confidence that one can learn to deal with the language problem as a beginning to dealing with the social, political, economic, and personal problems. And it works on all levels.

Third Grade level

What did we do with those persons who read at third grade or seventh grade level*? (For adults these levels do not mean much but we have little else to use at the moment.) For the third grade readers we did work in word recognition usually needed on such a level: a review of some phonic principles and a great deal of work in structural analysis; more vocabulary development especially in terms of prefixes, suffixes, and roots; more independent writing, along with some discussion and dictated matter for guiding the uncertain and unconfident; comprehension and interpretation skills woven easily into the reading. Some higher level written matter may need to be rewritten at third grade level, so that the students can read more on their own, in material that is interesting and related to whatever core concept you are developing. Study skills would be more evident in terms of actual application to some of the reading matter, e.g., previewing *News for You* or some of the *Scholastic* materials that may be pertinent to the core concept. Main ideas and details and classification skills are also easily applied. If the students are to write their own books or stories, it may be easy to teach these study skills as a means of helping them organize their thoughts and their writing. For example, the book they write with pictures and captions could have a table of contents (which, correctly done, is really an outline); headings and subheadings within each chapter; illustrations; and a glossary. Students making their own books and reading materials like them to be as much like "real" books as possible. This gives you every opportunity to teach the essential study skills as concrete guides to organizing thoughts and information.

Seventh Grade Level

At the seventh grade level what do we do on this day and on those days which may follow in our "rainy day" core concept planning and curriculum? It's much easier than the other levels. At the seventh grade level, you have virtually no need for concern about the first growth area in reading: word recognition. So you devote your time and energy to building up study skills as applied in a wide variety of books and materials that bear on your core concept, and you teach comprehension and interpretation skills more fully. You can move into critical reading skills such as (and particularly) detecting propaganda techniques and becoming aware of the use of words in a variety of other ways as in simile and metaphor (which can be derived at the outset from their own spoken lan-

---

* See Appendix A for detailed definition of grade level.

guage). You can continue to work on vocabulary by using some of their own language. In short, *the same core concept can be taught to individuals (or groups) reading at any level from nonreader to college graduate*; all the skills needed by the students are taught in that context and are appropriate to each student's ability to cope. But we use the students' life and language experience as much as possible, particularly at the lower levels.

SUMMARY OF CORE CONCEPT PLANNING

My concept of planning (and curriculum) is wholeness which integrates skills and content using the students' life and language experience as much as possible, particularly for students who have had trouble with reading and writing. They need to feel that this corrective or remedial program is different qualitatively from what they have undergone. We need to change the context of learning for them, just as words change meaning and even function when they are immersed in a different context. Different context here *does not* mean undergoing the workbook activity routine, flipping colored cards in a box, talking or listening to plastic tapes, responding to flash cards, or learning isolated rules and lists. For troubled persons and poor readers of all types, ages, and backgrounds this wholistic, experiential approach is most effective in changing the students' attitudes toward self, others, and the whole communication process. It is more interesting and motivating to such students; it is natural, logical, and practical. You can use whatever is in your environment and in yourself and your students. You do not need equipment, and a lot of material. You may need to work hard to get good material written at the level of your students, but you can translate down to their level of reading ability. That's not as hard as it seems if you subject the material to a readability measure for level.

THE LAB SCHOOL CURRICULUM: CORE CONCEPT ON MIGRATION

The Lab School was the educational component of the Boston Neighborhood Youth Program for three and half years. The students were 16-22 year old high school dropouts, and the Lab School serviced more than 1200 of them during its existence. Its most outstanding features were its excellent staff and their ability to use core concept curriculum so effectively.

The faculty, administration, and students helped make the core concept curriculum for our Lab School; it was not, as most curricula are, preplanned for the students, but rather with them. We needed something qualitatively distinctive for this population of Boston high school dropouts who had many problems, including their educational ones. We had delinquents, drug addicts, and everything in between. We knew most of the reasons for their school failure and were determined not to make the same curricular mistakes again; nor would we present our material in the same fragmented, meaningless way. We would, and we did, use the students' life and language experience, and their vocational needs and knowledge to fashion a whole curriculum that would weave skills and content into real cloth . . . for them.

Introduction

Let me quote some excerpts from the Lab School Curriculum, (Northeastern University) published in April, 1968:

"One of the major purposes of the Laboratory School is to provide youth who have dropped out of school with either basic education, ranging in reading levels from non-reader, or non-English speaking, to 6th grade level, or to provide high school level work for those who have completed 8th grade and who are functioning on the 7th grade level. Employability is the goal of the Neighborhood Youth Corps and this directly affects the school program and philosophy . . . The philosophy of the school has been and remains organic and experience-oriented in that we encourage the students to begin their work with us on the basis of their experiential backgrounds, their knowledge, perceptions or insights. From these beginnings we move with the students to higher levels of concern with problems of our society and world. Basically, we integrate subject matters around key concepts, e.g., *Conflict, Migration, People Who Made America*, etc. This means. . .that reading, writing and language skills (spelling, grammar, punctuation, literature) are all taught within the context of the core concept. Some of the science is woven into the strands of the core concept so that the student gets a multi-dimensional, multi-disciplinary view of the concept under study."

The chart which appears in Appendix B is similar to the charting we used in this publication of the Lab School Curriculum. It is the simplest and most direct way we found to share this process with others. After brief explanation for our headings in the chart, we can discuss the process as a means of planning and teaching wholistically. Under the first heading, *Concept Development*, are included the subconcepts most directly converging upon and diverging from *Migration* as the core concept. Under *Factual Content* we included key facts and information (but not all that would be covered). Under *Skills* we included the reading skills (word recognition, meanings, and study skills), vocabulary, and writing that the particular group needed. These skills needs were adjusted to whatever group might work on Migration. *Activities* are self-explanatory as are *Readings* and *Materials*. Again, these are key sources and activities, not all of which might be included in the program. Each of these core concept plans was designed for 16 weeks of instruction, 9 hours per week.

For each core concept, a full bibliography was published, as you will see in this illustration of the Migration core concept in its three phases. Note that the sequences of time and place, and all related concepts, are built into the linked phases of the concept of migration. This is 48 weeks worth of integrated skills and content instruction, focused on a universal concept.

Launching Core Concept: *Migration*

We launched this particular core concept when two new youngsters appeared into a group of about eight or nine students. They were introduced to the group and were asked where they came from. The two boys had come from Georgia and Mississippi. The teacher, ever alert to prospects for discussion and development of ideas, asked why they had come and where they lived in Boston. This brought forth information which explained some reasons for their move—one largely economic, the other personal. The teacher questioned some of the old timers in the class about where they were from originally, and why they had moved. This opened a fountain of conversation. The teacher threaded herself subtly through the discussion with well-placed questions and even offered her own story of migration.

After this type of discussion had progressed and seemed headed for boredom or for a new direction, the teacher led the class into talking (in categories) about reasons for migration, once that word had been introduced and thoroughly discussed. They came up with personal, social, economic, and political. Under each category, they began to list some subpoints to provide more detail. After a little more discussion, an assignment was given for the next class: jot down the names of people in your building, your street, names from windows in the stores, etc., and bring them to class. This of course produced more than a dozen different national backgrounds, including Syrian, Lebanese, Irish, Jewish, Greek, American, Italian. Many of the students lived in the South Dnd, an area which contained, at that time, about 30 different national groups in a one-square-mile area of some 30,000 people. The teacher used this information derived from everyday material to continue building the core concept migration. There were more questions about why so many different types of people came to the United States, and particularly to Boston. When did they come? How were things where they were? How did it go when they got here? What problems did they face and do they still face? Why? What about differences in language and culture; the whole process of assimilation? What evidences are there in the community that this diversity exists in it? Special occasions, celebrations? What do they mean? And so on. All of this discussion helped organize the ways and means of dealing with and planning the curriculum.

This kind of interchange, done almost impromptu, is one of the many ways to launch core concepts. But at the heart of this cooperative process of curriculum building is an imaginative and sensitive teacher who helps lead the way.

I am enclosing everything appearing in the Lab School Curriculum publication on Migration so that you can see how it was developed for each 16-week term and how the content and skills were integrated, etc. The principle here is the same one I've been illustrating throughout the chapter; here it is more advanced and more complete. But the principle guiding its development and its implementation are the same, and the process is the same. No two groups would work it exactly the same way, but all of the groups pursuing this Migration concept would ultimately come up with the same massive information from all sides of the curriculum. They would have the opportunity to work on the skills they needed to deal with all of the material. The first group in the school to develop this core concept, Migration, was reading at about the seventh grade level, so some of the materials had to be rewritten down to their level.

Exhibit 5-3 illustrates how content from various fields is drawn into the study of the core concept *Migration*. Facts, information, and concepts are developed in relation to migration. If one were to understand migration one would have to know its history, where it occurred geographically, why it happened—the political, social, economic, religious, and other factors that caused people to move from place to place at certain times and in particular circumstances. Sociological, anthropological, psychological, and literary forces implicated in various migrations need to be studied. What was happening in a particular country at a particular time on all these levels directly affected who moved, and when and where. A study of migration must also include how many moved and what happened to them when they arrived in their new homes. This multidisciplinary study of any concept highlights all of the relationships contributing to the event and its effects.

Such a study is both longitudinal and cross-cultural, which is the best way to enrich concepts and understanding. Such an approach adds great interest to the usually dull and unclear factual presentations. A conceptual approach of this type has worked extremely well with persons of all ages and backgrounds in our clinic for the past ten years, even with very young students and very poor readers. It makes sense and it is so different from the typical curricular approach to any subject that it stimulates even bored and indifferent students.

Instead of just learning how many people moved from one country to another at a certain time, we try to discover as much about their lives as we can in order to comprehend what they did and why. Core concepts provide a context within which all of the facts, information, and concepts are woven together in a logical fashion. For example, if one were studying in the usual fashion the migration of the Irish to America in the 1840s and 1850s, one would learn of the potato famine as a major cause of the migration. How much more was going on in Ireland at that same time!

Exhibit 5-3

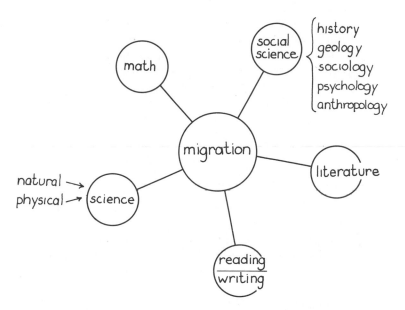

The political and economic strangulation by Britain must be included in the investigation of this mass migration to the new world; it simply was not just potato famine.

Reading, writing, listening, and speaking activities are interwoven in this core concept since all that is read and written about and discussed is related to this multidimensional concept of migration. No need for isolated workbook activities, flash cards, or unrelated writing assignments. The content is clear and all of the skills needed by the group are taught within it. Hence, everything learned relates to everything else being read and discussed. Teaching the various subjects like history, geography, literature, composition, and reading is simpler since they do not each have their own focus and content; they all focus on migration, or whatever the core is. The only problem could be mathematics since it does not have the same flexibility as the other subjects do. Mathematics does have its own inviolable sequences of skills so that work in this area does not always fit as neatly as we'd like. However, if the students are functioning at a level at which they can compute, then some mathematics work related to migration can be taught comfortably as when one speaks of percentages of persons of different types who came or settled in a certain place; distances can be computed and compared; all of the computational skills can be practiced in this context. We have often taught our mathematics separately for those students whose skills were more advanced. Whenever possible, though, we would try to tie in these skills with the concept development occurring in the remainder of the core program.

Hence, contributing to the core concept are facts, information, concepts, and skills from the entire curriculum. It focuses all of this information for the student on one major concept like migration or conflict or family, etc. All reading, writing, speaking, listening, and content information is related. Hence, the understanding of the various aspects of migration are much more clearly revealed; understanding of the concepts is enhanced as in no other curricular plan.

The following material is from the Northeastern University Laboratory School Curriculum "Core Concept—Migration," pp. 70-93.

<u>Core Concept: Migration</u>

<u>Curriculum Organization</u>

We have chosen the concept approach to curriculum organization because it provides wholeness and longitudinal perspective as opposed to segmentation and confinement through such organizing dimensions as time, space and separate disciplines; for it is not possible in any study to comprehend the part without comprehending the whole.

<u>MIGRATION—A Theme</u>

The theme of migration has been selected as the organizing concept for units of study in American History and English. Our outlines of the material to be covered in each of the three areas will be presented separately, but the activities in the areas will be integrated in class projects and activities.

<u>American History—Two Units</u>

The theme of migration lends itself particularly well to the study of American history, as migration is the story of American history. We have chosen to study migration as related to American history in three major phases.

1. Migration as evidenced in present day Boston
2. Migration to America (1600 to present)
3. Migration within America (late 1700's to present)

The first section of our unit will deal with migration as evidenced in contemporary Boston. We have chosen to begin here for two reasons:

1. We are the products of migration and if we are to approach the study of migration with understanding and enthusiasm, we must first try to understand the significance of our location in the Boston area.
2. Boston presents a wealth of immediate and tangible resources for dealing first hand with the forces engendered by migration—its implications, significance and results.

From our work in the present, we will move back into the colonial period, applying many of the themes that have been established in our study of contemporary Boston. Phase three of the unit will mesh in part with phase two.

The first half of phase two moves us through the colonial period. At this point we will begin or work simultaneously with two phases of migration (across the ocean and within the United States).

Phase three will deal with major movements within the United States—their many causes and end results. The completion of phase three will bring us back to the present for a study and evaluation of the concepts of restrictions and expansion of migration.

Migration I (one unit in American history to be taught in a sixteen week period) will include the period from 1600-1800. Historically, the periods covered in this unit will be colonization and expansion.

Migration II (a second unit in American History to be taught in a sixteen week period) will include the period from 1800 to the present. Historically the periods covered will deal with expansion and development within the United States. Migration I will be a prerequisite for Migration II.

As basic texts for phase one, we have selected Kennedy's <u>Nation of Immigrants</u>, Muzzey and Link's <u>Our Country's History</u>, Madgic's <u>Rebels vs. Royalists</u>, and pamphlets on the Boston area, particularly the South End in which there are an estimated forty different ethnic groups. The basic texts for the second phase will include the above plus Seaberg's <u>Pioneer vs. the Wilderness.</u> In addition, two books by the Pulitzer Prize winner and Harvard historian Oscar Handlin, <u>The Americans and Immigration as a Factor in American History,</u> will be used for individual assignments by high achieving students. Handlin views history as the process of migration. Basic texts for phase three will be <u>The Immigrant in American History</u> by Marcus Lee Hansen and the final chapters of <u>Immigration as a Factor in American History</u> and <u>The Americans.</u>

English Overview

Not only are we concerned with the historical aspect of migration, but with the literary one as well. The English unit, in addition to the mechanics of English, will consist of reading, discussing and writing about American novels, poetry, essays, and plays. Each work will pertain to that particular period of history under consideration, and will be intimately related to the migration theme.

The literature, selected for both literary and historical merit, will be read as a class and independently. The former group will be dealt with from an historical point of view insofar as relating to migratory events. From a literary point of view, the students will learn to interpret a work of art, to note an author's style, and to sense the significance of the work itself. Biographical material will be read to understand writers as real people.

With independent reading, the student will combine writing skills with those of reading. The written literary assignments will vary from book reports dealing with particular problems, to comparisons of works and styles of different authors. Students will be encouraged to read a number of works by the same author, as well as other authors writing in the same areas.

One week of intensive work in reading and language skills will precede these activities so that all students will be better equipped to function effectively in the planned program.

Summary

We followed the same process for all of the core concepts we developed and implemented in the three-and-a-half-year history of the Lab School, from which a number, perhaps 60 to 70 students, went on to college. Many of them have graduated with degrees, and one is completing a doctorate at a major university near Boston. Others went on to technical training, others to jobs, and others back to the streets. Unfortunately, funds for the program were discontinued.*

BLACKFEET INDIAN EDUCATION PROJECT: A TOTALLY INTEGRATED PROGRAM FOR A WHOLE CLASS USING THE CORE CONCEPT CURRICULUM

Perhaps enough illustrations of various ways of making integrated lessons and plans have been discussed so that most of the essential principles and concepts are clear. We have seen clinical situations in which planning and implementation of lessons were developed for a single case, and some general discussion of instances in which wholistic, integrated planning and implementation have worked effectively with groups. Now I'd like to share one of the great instances in my own professional life which involved a total curricular change using the principles presented here. Because of the length of the materials produced in this outstanding

---

*The average gain in reading for each 16-week term for each student, irrespective of level, was 9 months. For students in the upper level groups, gains averaged 1 year for the 16-week term. The students spent 9½ hours per week in this program.

instance of wholistic education, I shall summarize it so that you can get a feel for it and experience some of the process yourself. This particular application of the theories, principles, and concepts was unusually successful under minimal, if not negative circumstances. It can serve as a good summary of everything we have discussed about diagnosis, planning, and correction in context—natural, relevant, and completely participatory.

Background

We are on the Blackfeet Indian Reservation in northwestern Montana, adjacent to the Glacier National Park. It is isolated, vast, and as deprived as Indian Reservations are in America. We are in a three room school house, and our authors are in a combined sixth, seventh, and eighth grade class. There are twenty-three students filling the room to capacity, and a smattering of old books and some maps, but not much else since the room is so full of children. The teacher, a White from the midwest, is also principal, and really cares about his students. He has never been involved in anything like a curriculum innovation and he knows little about the presentation and planning of lessons and activities for teaching basic skills in reading and language inside an integrated context. But he is eager and he is willing. After 30 years of professional teaching and education, I respect those qualities above the verbalisms, "conceptualizations," and theoretical propositions of many of my colleagues. This teacher and I had a common goal: to make education for these children—who have been left out of serious consideration by most of the American society—pertinent, alive, coherent, and hence, *qualitatively* different from what they had known, and also to make it fun. Qualitative change in planning and in implementation is rare; typical innovations, changes in planning, curriculum, methodology, and materials, are more often than not a mere renaming phenomenon. Rarely do we see and experience a new way of looking, seeing, and thinking, which should be at the root of instructional change. This was our basic goal—a qualitative change which would yield new behaviors, attitudes, and skills in students.

In this class of sixth, seventh, and eighth grade students we discovered through an IDA on each student, that the range of reading ability was from second to about tenth grade—each child was almost a level of his own. So our plan, like all plans, had to include not only diagnostic measures, but plans for grouping students to individualize the program as much as possible. We needed a focus for the plans, some sense of how long we would have available, and related notions about scheduling. All of these critical components of planning were easily accommodated in our final decision.

Steps in planning

First, it was decided that the plan for instruction would be on the basis of core concept planning and that it would last for 12 weeks, using a 3-hour block of time (more or less), 5 days a week for the entire 12-week period. Such a block of time allows for a great deal of latitude in grouping, instruction, and integration of content and skills.

Second, we decided to make a small curricular leap at first. The focal point for all content and skills instruction was to be the state of Montana, since that was a course required by the state Department of Education. The available textbook which had been used for ages turned out to be quite biased and anti-Indian in several places, so it would be used only minimally in this process of writing a book on Montana, which might serve other students. This concept developed more slowly than this paragraph suggests, but the decision to use Montana as a focus for all the instruction during this 12-week period, about 3 hours a day, was made by students and teachers.

Third, materials were also a problem, mainly because there was almost none available to make a core plan operate well and to give the students the kind of variety they needed. So a campaign was launched in several cities around the country to get contributions from Boston, Kansas City, Missouri, Boulder, New York, Los Angeles, and Denver; several other cities sent boxes of books donated by college and high school students. We got about forty cartons of books, some of which were very useful for our particular purposes.

Grouping and Scheduling

Fourth, we had to plan types of groupings to meet individual needs and group needs in the skills areas. (See Exhibit 5-4.) We decided on a simple arrangement allowing for individual, small, and large group activity and instruction, and would meet the needs we uncovered in our IDAs. Large group sessions (heterogeneous) with all twenty-three students participating would be used for such activities as sharing information collected in the readings done about some aspect of Montana; discussion about a particularly interesting or controversial matter; instruction in generic skills identified as needed by all levels of reading and writing ability such as sentence structure and certain grammatical and spelling problems and study skills such as previewing, main ideas and details, outlining and summarizing, classification, etc. In short, the whole group sessions would be held as needed, functionally, and sometimes would be planned ahead so that certain key elements in reading and writing would be shared by all simultaneously.

Small groups would be basically homogeneous based on reading and language skills levels and needs. In these small, homogeneous groups specific instruction and help would be provided for students, so that the students in the lowest group reading second grade level would be working on material directly related to the focus on Montana (like everyone else), and they would be reading material written at a second grade level and would be getting the help they needed in word recognition skills. This material was rewritten and measured by the Dale-Chall readability formula.

A third type of informal grouping was invented by the students. It allowed time for kids to work on individual projects or on a group project like the mural painted by four or five of them. Some individual projects included making a model of an Indian Days celebration with hand-carved and hand-made people, tepees, and other components of the celebration. Time for this became more available as the 12 weeks wore on and the higher level students did not require as much small group instruction. These informal groupings produced the art and music of this integrated curriculum and provided just enough freedom for the students to produce a fine balance in the entire program. Hence, large group sessions provided students with opportunities to share information they had discovered and it provided them with the opportunity to work together on common, generic skills needs. The small group sessions focused on improving

Exhibit 5-4.

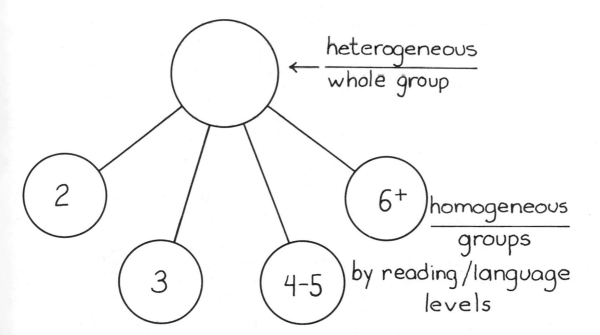

specific reading and language needs and the third groupings which were more informal were self-selected and provided enrichment activities, art, and music as it related to the multilevel study of Montana.

In essence, for 12 weeks these twenty-three multileveled students collected information through reading, writing, speaking, and listening in a variety of sources, and they applied the appropriate reading and language skills within a context. They produced a book with illustrations, and some projects which also related to the overall plan. Everything was about Montana—the history, geography, science, reading and writing, some culture, art—in short, most of the typical curriculum was totally integrated in this project.

A word on scheduling. With roughly a 3-hour block available each day, a good deal of latitude existed. Some days 1½ hours might be set aside for the whole group session of sharing ideas, information, discussion, and work on some common problem like sentence structure, and the remainder of the time might be allocated to small-group, intensive skills work in reading and writing. As time progressed, the first 1½ hours of Monday, Wednesday, and Friday might be set aside for a block schedule like this, and the remainder for skills instruction. Tuesday and Thursday might be scheduled for small-group instruction—about 1 or 1½ hours, depending on the needs. Some of that time might be spent on just getting information for the particular assignment each student had in the preparation of each chapter of their book on Montana, and a small segment, perhaps 45 minutes on those days for projects. Of course, there were many variations in the scheduling since it was functionally adjusted to students' progress and needs. But a basic schedule was fairly well maintained in that a large group session occurred at least three times per week; small group skills instruction took place at least four times a week, generally five, especially for those with remedial problems in reading and writing. Project time increased toward the end of the 12-week segment, particularly for the students who were functioning at or above level. Hence we managed a good flow of time in order to maintain continuity and pacing and to meet their needs.

After lunch, time was left to the principal–teacher to do what the state department of education required. Mathematics was one of those needs which had to appear separately. But the mornings were ours to engage in clearly defined activities with clearly defined responsibilities. Each student was assigned two, three, maybe four articles for one or more of the chapters in the book. This article would be turned into the editors or assistant editor for checking. If the sentence structure, spelling, punctuation, or logic, was poor, it had to be rewritten and then handed back corrected. The teacher oversaw the entire operation and determined from the assignments which generic skills would be taught in the large group sessions, and it also gave him a functional diagnostic tool to deal with specific problems in the small groups.

Materials—Montana

The cover, note to the reader, and introduction are shown in Exhibit 5-5. Chapter outlines, headings, and some other material follow, but not the entire book on Montana.

The cover for the book on Montana was of course drawn by a student. *To the Reader* was written by the teacher-principal and it says a great deal so I shall not add or subtract from it except to say this was his first attempt at such a massive curricular and planning change. I respect him for his attitudes and work in this situation. He has my professional respect just as he had the respect of his students and most of the community of East Glacier Park, Montana. The Introduction written by the editor is clear. Remember it, for when you read the introduction written for the second book this group wrote, I think you will learn how to spell confidence and learning.

Now let's look at the overall plan of organization these students worked out: I. Prehistoric Montana; II. The Indian Times; III. After the White Man Arrived. As you will see, each chapter has headings and subheadings like a real book. Now in order for these students to make a chapter outline and decide on headings and subheadings required some knowledge of basic study skills like previewing. Also, in collecting the information on each topic and writing them up (or giving oral presentations) they needed to know about main ideas and details and something about outlining and summarizing, even classification (the key study skills). The study skills instruction was woven into the fabric painlessly in response to the needs of the students to collect information, organize it and transmit it, and all within the context of Montana. That is integrating skills into content.

Here is their outline as they made it:

I. Pre-Historic Montana
   A. Land Forms
      1. The Lewis Overthrust
   B. Plants
      1. Plants out of the past
      2. More about plants
   C. Prehistoric Animals
      1. Pterodactylus
      2. Triceratops
   D. Climate
      1. Weather
   E. Chart of Geologic Time

Not bad; not good; but a start toward learning how to organize large amounts of information. I personally would have worked on these skills more as part of the initial discussions of the topics so that the outline

Exhibit 5-5. Core Concept Curriculum Project: *Montana*

MONTANA

Exhibit 5-5

<u>TO THE READER</u>

This book is the culmination of a twelve-week unit on Montana by 23 sixth, seventh and eighth graders. It is the product of a core program at East Glacier Park Grade School. Reading, English, Social Studies, Art and and Science were all blended together to try to make language a meaningful challenge.

Too often, an individual subject, standing alone, has little practical meaning to the student. However, as part of a total project, the same subject can be related to something practical by the student and there-by gain relevance.

The class as a whole developed the outline upon which the book was based. The three major chapters (Prehistoric, During the Indian Times, and After White Man Arrived) were their idea.

Each student researched and wrote on two different subjects from the outline. These were checked and suggestions for improvement made by the student editor and the teacher. They were then rewritten by the student. The final draft was accepted and published as the student turned it in. Each reflects the student's abilities and talents in certain skills. Some are very original; some not quite so.

Learning took place in more than just the particular subject area covered by the student. Reading played a major role in the original research. English came into play as the student wrote and rewrote his particular paper. Social Studies and Science were the written subject matter.

After all the writing was finished, each student selected a visual project, relating to some part of the unit, to work on. In this phase, he used and developed his art talent. These projects scanned the history of Montana all the way from primitive Indian villages to models of modern strip-farming methods.

Organization, working together and a sense of responsibility to others in the group were important

Exhibit 5-5. Continued.

objectives of our unit. You are now about to read the
creative end product of our 12 weeks' work. We hope
you enjoy it, but we know that the real experiences
were working together doing it.

W. T. H.
Teacher

INTRODUCTION

This book was written and published by the sixth,
seventh, and eighth grades in the East Glacier Park
Elementary School located in East Glacier Park, Montana.
This book was a twelve week project.

The sixth, seventh, and eighth graders decided to
write their own textbook about Montana. They surveyed
all of Montana's past and present. In some parts it
tells how the land was formed, how Indians and white
men came, and the development of Montana until today.

-The Editor

would have been tighter, but these kids learned without my help in this
regard.

II. Arrival of Early Man
   1. Houses
   2. Food
   3. Weapons and Tools
   4. Religion
   5. Transportation
   6. Culture
   7. Communication
   8. Education
   9. Clothing

The bulk of what appears in the chapter is related directly to Blackfeet
culture, food, language, etc., and includes some general information. This
is quite different from the state-required textbook, which referred to the
Blackfeet Indians as "savages who roamed the plains." Clearly, this outline of the chapter leaves much to be desired in terms of helping the students make relationships more effectively. They needed help in making
an outline, which means they needed more study skills work before mak-

ing this one so that it could have been tighter. But again this is the first attempt at anything so bold for these students and their teacher. When one considers where they were academically and personally when they started this book one cannot but applaud their every move. But I still would have pushed them harder toward a better organization and outline. I have to remind myself that to each person discovering the wheel or inventing fire, it is the first time and it is of galaxial import, and each of us is entitled to discovering his own wheel, even if that slows down Man's learning and his progress toward wholeness.

III. Development of Montana
    A. Transportation
        1. Horses and foot Travel
        2. Riverboats
        3. Railroads
        4. Automobiles
        5. Airplanes
    B. Economy
        1. Ranching
        2. Farming
        3. Trapping
    C. Conservation
        1. Wildlife
        2. Plant life
        3. Soil
    D. Religion
    E. People
        1. Indians
        2. White
    F. Education
    G. Organization
        1. State
        2. County
    H. Cities

You see, they almost did it this time. They almost made a good chapter outline with more detail and a little less overlap in key topics and headings.

Throughout, there are good illustrations drawn by the students as part of their third grouping arrangement. All students read, wrote, spoke, and listened to the history, geography, science, and culture of Montana in the past and present. They collected their own information, read it, digested it, and then wrote their own articles. They corrected their spelling, grammar, and other errors for the final draft. They spent 12 weeks, 3 hours each day, thinking, talking, reading, and writing about

Exhibit 5-6.   Core Concept Curriculum Project: *Rivers and Cities*

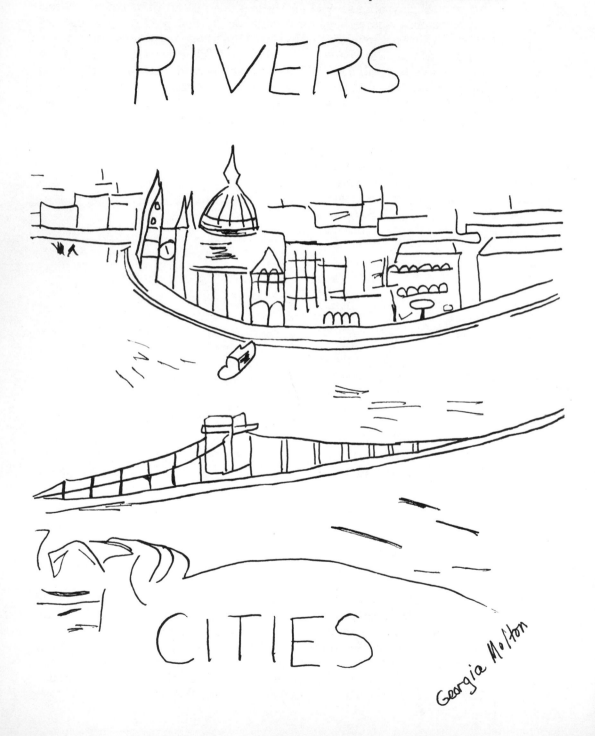

Montana. They had large and small group instruction and sharing and they did individual work and projects. They made a book which they dittoed and which I had printed on an offset press so that it would look more like a real book, and then I gave them copies of it. They loved it, and their parents loved it. Then the kids decided to do another book for the next 12 weeks using the same concept of planning and instruction they had just experienced with such success.

Materials—Rivers and Cities

The second book produced by these youngsters was their curriculum for the next 12 weeks. It was a much larger book (*Montana* had about 58 pages; *Rivers and Their Cities* contained 105 pages). The cover is shown in Exhibit 5-6.

Several other changes are evident in book two: first, on the back of the cover page we find, in splendid arrogance and pride:

OTHER BOOKS BY THE SAME AUTHORS

MONTANA

At the bottom of the page we see:

Published by the East Glacier Elementary Grade School

East Glacier Park, Montana

MCMLXIX

and behold, Roman numerals, yet! It spells confidence, a sense of mastery, and knowing what one is doing and why. Add that to the content and skills learned in making the book on Montana and you have what I call success and innovation—qualitative change in these students.

INTRODUCTION

"Til taught by pain
Men really know not what water's worth."
                    -Byron

Water. The substances of life. Ponce de Leon
could have saved himself a long, hard journey in looking for the Fountain of Life. He passed many of them.

The scientific H_2O started life. It not only
conceived life but probably limited it (in this solar
system) to this planet alone. Mercury is far too hot
to contain water. Venus and Mars may have some vapor
and Mars has polar caps. All the other planets must
have either frozen water or no water at all.

Some one celled animals can do without air, but
no plant or animal can go without water. Man himself
is 65-70% water. The brain is 74.5%, and the bone
22% water. A man has about 50 quarts (100 pounds) of
water in him. He must replace 2½ quarts of this every
day. Drinking returns about 1½ quarts of this. Water
in food about 1 quart and an extra ½ quart comes in
"dry" foods. Man can live without food for 2 months,
but will die without water in a week. The donkey, like
like few gifted animals, can store water and live for
some time on it. On the desert, the donkey can go
without water for 4 days, losing about 30% of its
body weight; 15% would dehydrate a person. But the
donkey is a very long, fast drinker. He can drink 5
gallons of water in 2 minutes.

A jellyfish must remain submerged, for it is 95%
water. A kangaroo rat, which lives in the desert where
water is scarce, gets along with 65% of its body
weight as water, while the weevil is only 48% water.
Chicken, a delicious dish, is 74% water. In the
plant kingdom, tomatoes are 95% water, corn is 70%
water, and the sunflower seed is 5% water.

In the human body, 1 pint of water is lost in
breathing, 1 pint in perspiration, and 1½ quarts in
excretion. There are also 2 million sweat glands
used to cool the blood when exercising.

According to all laws of Physical Behavior, ice shouldn't float. But it does! Its lopsidedness is why--two hydrogen atoms and one oxygen atom. When a drop forms, it becomes round because of the pull of the hydrogen atoms pulling inward. Water determines the climate, soil, plant life, animal life, and types and amounts of land. It does this by coming in three forms: vapor, liquid, and snow or ice. It is odorless, colorless, and tasteless. It lubricates your eyes, cleaning and allowing the lid to close over the eye. It is a carrier of waste and life, a cooler of the blood carrying the heat and waste out of 2 million sweat glands all over the body. It carries out the salt your body cannot use, as too much would probably do the human kidneys in, as they cannot cope with more than 2.2% in the urine. Some animals can come with a lot more, like the camel (6%) and the kangaroo rat (7%).

So, as you can see, you will treat your body far more with a glass of water than a candy bar. The water still cools bodies and the earth. It still supports life and destroys life. It comes in three forms, vapor, liquids, and solids. It is still not and cold. All animals and plants use it. The only thing that is different is that we know more about it now. And wonder of wonders how it is still here from centuries ago.

-C.Y.

Dear Readers:

We hope you will enjoy this enlightening edition of of "Rivers and Their Cities". It was a twelve week project done completely by the 6th, 7th and 8th grades of the East Glacier Park Elementary School.

If the Reader should notice some obvious omissions of important cities or rivers, this can be blamed on the Hong-Kong Flu which hit our class full force in the middle of the project.

In writing this book, we have gained information on the cultures of many people and the way they live, also on the backgrounds of these people, their cities and their rivers.

-The Editors

Discussion

The introduction is *not* written by the teacher; nothing is in this book. Look at the "Dear Readers"; direct, bold, arrogant—by implication they tell us that if they had not been hit by Hong-Kong Flu in the midst of this undertaking, no omissions would have occurred. That's arrogant—a most non-Indian trait, but healthy in this context. Note the Introduction by another student, preceded by a quote from none other than the most arrogant Mr. Byron. The substance itself is fairly sophisticated and a good backdrop for a study of Rivers and Their Cities. The whole thing is a conscious attempt to sound as good, as mature, as sophisticated as possible. That is a byproduct of the process of doing the book on Montana—of wholeness, full-scale participation and responsibility for one's work within a known context. The medium (integrated curriculum) does indeed affect the message (learning, attitudes, etc.). Book II on Rivers already reveals a great deal of growth on the part of these students.

As to the content, the key focus is geographic insofar as rivers and their locations, cities, towns, and continents are highlighted. Within this they managed history, science, social studies, and of course all the reading and writing skills and activities necessary to getting the information, organizing it, writing, and speaking it. Again, this book is well illustrated with maps, charts, and other drawings.

Outlines are a little more precise this time, and although there are more subheads, they are tighter, less diverse, and better focused. The bulk of information here is a bit textbookish, but this is still just the beginning for these kids in such an academic adventure. Too little appears which shows evidence of dealing with or understanding of concepts and principles. Personally, I would have worked this quite differently, putting much more emphasis on the role rivers have had in history, especially in terms of how the earliest known civilizations rose up at their sides as in India, China, Egypt, and Mesopotamia, etc. I would have followed more of the cultural path in this and used more of Gordon Childe's (1954) approach. But again, I cannot be too harsh in my criticism of this teacher and these students. They did integrate their curriculum and focus it on their theme of Rivers and Their Cities; they did weave skills and content together; they did get the instruction they needed in multi-group arrangements; they did enjoy it and do it all with real pride and a sense of confidence in their own ability to carry out such a large project.

SUMMARY

We have just seen two examples of student participation in the planning and implementation of an integrated, whole curriculum in which they learned skills and content in a new mode, and did so most successfully and with pride and joy. It certainly beats the usual system of dealing with fragmented, piecemeal curriculum which has its 40 minutes of history dealing with the American Revolution; followed by 40 minutes of geography concerning the rice, wheat, and barley production of Brazil 20 years ago; followed by 40 minutes of science concerning clouds and weather in general; followed by 40 minutes of . . . .etc. In such a set up, the most common practice in our schools, the student is buffeted by facts and information presented in isolation and related mainly to themselves. They appear to have little meaning because these facts are not organized so that their relationships on several levels (multidimensionally) will be revealed or discovered. The sense of wholeness which the two books produced for these students made recall of facts and information much easier because they had learned to seek relationships among them, and to try to fit them into a context.

This model of an integrated curriculum, such as these two books illustrate, has been utilized in other settings. The Lab School curriculum was another illustration of the process of interrelating content and skills into a context which helps produce deeper understanding and a clearer sense of what goes with what and why. This process does not deny any skills development or hinder sequencing skills or concept development no matter what specific approach you might choose. The medium of integrated, whole curriculum affects the message (learning and behavior) in ways that increase self-concept, sense of confidence, and willingness to try. It makes most students, whether they are big-city drop outs, Indians, Mexican-Americans, or average suburban kids, feel good and somewhat in charge of what they are doing and learning. And all the while they understand the skills and the ideas; they make decisions and live with the consequences, to some degree. They are not just receptacles for collecting the facts, ideas, thoughts of others. They are not objects of instruction; they become subject and verb, and that directly affects their attitudes, behavior, and performance. They read and wrote more and spoke and listened more to each other, to the facts and experience which make concepts and principles.

Perhaps we have had enough illustration in this chapter to clarify for you the many ways and means for making your own planning whole and integrated rather than fragmented and disjointed. These principles apply to clinical instruction or classroom instruction, to normal students, corrective or remedial problems. Consider this approach as an alternative to the host of programs and approaches on the market like SRA, Tactics in Reading, linguistics based programs (like Merrill), basals and individualized programs (which are largely programmed). Compare and contrast the core concept curriculum with its language experience approach with the others; try to see if you find what I have found time and time again, everywhere in this country. Start thinking whole; think relationships; think and enjoy learning and teaching.

Now you can plan one coherent, integrated lesson or five of them or fifty of them for one student, a small group, or a whole class. You have seen and understood something of the nature of language, the learner, the learning process, the reading process and dimensions of diagnosis and misdiagnosis. Add all of this to the work in planning and you are ready for Part 2—the how to of teaching many of the word recognition, meanings, and study skills, as well as vocabulary and writing within a core concept.

REFERENCES

Bruner, Jerome. *The process of education.* New York: Vintage Books, 1963.

Carroll, John. Words, meanings and concepts. In *Harvard Educational Review,* Summer 1964, pp. 178-202.

Childe, V. Gordon. *What happened in history* (Revised ed.). New York: Penguin Books, 1954.

Lee, Doris & Van Allen, Roach. *Learning to read through experience.* New York: Appleton, Century & Croft, 1963.

Northeastern University Laboratory School Curriculum. Compiled under the direction of Melvin Howards, Director and James Clay, Principal. Boston, MA, 1968.

Stauffer, Russell. *The language-experience approach to reading.* New York: Harper & Row, 1970.

Webster's Seventh New Collegiate Dictionary. Springfield, MA: Merriam, 1971.

BIBLIOGRAPHY

Allison, M.L. (Comp.). New educational materials; pre-k through grade 12. *Scholastic.* New York: Citation Press, 1967.

Aukerman, Ralph. *Approaches to beginning reading.* New York: Wiley, 1971.

Moffett, James & Wagner, Betty Jane. *Student-centered language arts and reading, k-13: a handbook for teachers* (2nd ed.). Boston: Houghton-Mifflin, 1976.

News for you. Syracuse: Laubach Literacy, Inc.

Niles, Olive; Bracken, Dorothy; Daugherty, Mildred, & Kinder, Robert. *Tactics in reading.* Chicago: Scott, Foresman, 1961.

Sloop, Cornelia; Garrison, Harrell; & Creekmore, Mildred. *Phonetic keys to reading.* Oklahoma City: The Economy Company Schoolbook Publishers.

Van Allen, Roach, *Language-experiences in communication.* Boston: Houghton, Mifflin, 1976.

Van Allen, Roach & Allen, Claryce. *Language-experience activities.* Boston: Houghton, Mifflin, 1976.

Wright, Betty (Ed.). *Urban education studies album.* New York: John Day, 1965.

Part two
Applications

Chapter six

INTRODUCTION AND OVERVIEW

Chapter 6 is the beginning of more detailed discussions of how to teach word recognition, meanings, and study skills. This chapter will focus attention on:

1. what the word recognition skills are;
2. how they relate to each other and to other skills;
3. how to teach them contextually.

The basic principles for teaching these skills include *functional diagnosis* in each lesson of the skills and content taught; teaching all skills in each growth area *in context* (no isolated phonics activities involving single letters and single sounds or words from word lists); and teaching all skills as *inductively* as possible, that is, leading students to discover and develop their own rules and generalizations rather than to memorize rules. These principles are particularly important in the teaching of word recognition skills, because learning these skills can be duller than learning most other skills and because they involve beginning reading activity for the learner, which can be imbued with a certain mystery and uncertainty.

Following is an outline of word recognition growth areas:

The Growth Areas in Reading

    I. Word Recognition
       A. Readiness Skills
          1. sight words
          2. auditory and visual discrimination

Teaching word recognition skills

3. picture and other context clues
B. Phonic Analysis
   1. Single consonants in the initial, final and medial positions
   2. single vowels (short then long sounds) in the initial, final and medial positions
   3. blends (two letters, two sounds)
      a. consonant: st, br, gr, dr, tr, bl, cl, gl, sl, etc.
      b. vowel: oi, ai, ou, ew, au, etc.
   4. digraphs (two letters, one sound or a new sound)
      a. consonant: sh, wh, ch, th, ph, ng, etc.
      b. vowel: ee, ie, ei, ea, ae, oo, etc.
   5. vowels followed by l, r and w producing neither a long nor short sound.
C. Structural Analysis
   1. compound words: break fast, some thing, base ball, no where, etc.
   2. syllabication: hop/ing, de/light/ful, hap/py, etc.
   3. affixes
      a. prefixes: in, un, de, pre, im, a, anti, etc.
      b. suffixes: ly, ic, ate, ed, ion, etc.
   4. root words: path, ced, mort, anim, port, path, cred, etc.
   5. hyphenated words
   6. contractions
D. Using the dictionary as an aid in learning
   1. syllabication
   2. etymology
   3. accent

          4. pronunciation
          5. common meanings
          6. synonyms and antonyms

II. Meanings
    A. Comprehension
        1. literal recall: who, what, where, when, how many
           a. facts, names, places, etc.
    B. Interpretation and Critical Reading
        1. drawing conclusions
        2. making inferences
        3. making generalizations
        4. detecting propaganda techniques
           a. glad names
           b. bad names
           c. testimonial
           d. transfer
           e. plain folks
           f. card stacking
           g. bandwagon
        5. interpreting imagery and figures of speech: simile, meta-
               phor, symbols
        6. interpreting satire, allegory, etc.

III. Study Skills
    A. Previewing
    B. Finding main ideas and details
    C. Outlining and summarizing
    D. Classification
    E. Using guide words
    F. Patterns
        1. question-answer
        2. cause and effect
        3. sequence
        4. fact-opinion
    G. Following Directions

This summary of the essential word recognition skills illustrates what all reading programs include when teaching beginning reading to anyone. Most reading programs devote considerable, sometimes excessive amounts of time to presenting and practicing these skills in the first three or four years of school. Mastery of these interrelated skills is accompanied by varying amounts of work with meanings skills, with some programs giving only minimal attention to understanding what is read in favor of assuring mechanical skill in figuring printed words out.

In the mid 1950s, Rudolf Flesch (1954) spurred a back to phonics movement which faded in the sixties, but which is now back in vogue in the guise of "back to basics." Such overemphasis on these word recognition skills, usually out of context and out of the range of interests of many students, tends to make the process mechanical, and it can become an end in itself. Because of the nature of the language, the learner, and the processes of reading such overemphasis and exaggerated attention to specific phonic or structural elements distorts the language and the act of reading. We must see these word recognition skills as related to each other and assisting the beginning reader to detect whatever patterns exist in both spoken sounds and in their written equivalents. No one skill or small group of these skills can be isolated without causing distortion in the normal use of the language.

One basic fact about phonics which is rarely heard is that consonants in English do not have spoken equivalants unless you add a vowel sound, e.g., *b* is usually pronounced *bee* or *buh*. In the first instance we have added the long sound of the vowel *e* and in the second instance we have used the *schwa* sound (uh). So teaching consonants in isolated fashion is misleading and unnecessary. Vowels in English make it possible for us to open our mouths since vowels cannot be reproduced without opening the mouth: try saying *bkfst* without vowel sounds. One must therefore avoid isolating letters and sounds.

Many students of all ages and backgrounds experience considerable difficulty learning these word recognition skills because of the variations in English itself, because of variant pronunciations, and often, because of undue concern of some teachers in presenting these skills. At least 75 - 80% of students do learn these word recognition skills fairly easily, and those who do not rarely benefit from intensive, isolated phonics programs. Like all else in human learning, *relationship is the key*, and so in teaching word recognition we must not emphasize the letter or its spoken equivalents, sound by distorted sound, but rather emphasize words and the meanings of what is written. At the end of this chapter is a list of sources on word recognition skills including Harris and Sipay (1975), Lapp and Flood (1978) which provide extensive and very specific scope and sequence charts for presenting these skills. Personally, I do not recommend obedient adherence to any scope and sequence chart since it can mislead you into believing that if you present the word recognition (or other reading) skills in a particular order you are teaching reading. Furthermore, following any scope and sequence chart rigidly tends to isolate phonic elements or other skills. Very little evidence exists to support the idea that if you present initial consonant *m* after initial consonant *b* you are right or wrong. What you can derive from reading the sources is a general sense that single consonants which tend to be more regular—that is, written as they are usually spoken—are taught first since they will usually be easier to learn. Irregular consonants such as c, k, w, x, y, and z normally and sensibly should come later. But there is no magic in any specific sequence of these skills.

SEQUENCE FOR PHONICS INSTRUCTION

While Harris and Sipay (1975) provide the most extensive scope and sequence chart for phonics instruction, Dallman, Rouch, Char, DeBoer, 1978, p. 150) present the most succinct suggestions:

A Sequence for Phonics Instruction

1. Provide needed work on auditory and visual discrimination.
2. Teach the sound of consonants before those of vowels. Start with the single consonant sounds that have but one sound, namely, b, h, j, l, m, p, t, and v. Teach them as they occur in initial and then in final positions in words, before teaching them in medial positions. Later teach common consonant digraphs, then two letter consonant blends, and then, three letter consonant blends.
3. Teach the vowel sounds with the short sounds first and then the long.
4. Teach vowel digraphs and diphthongs and silent letters.
5. Teach rules governing long and short vowels.

The outline presented at the beginning of this chapter serves my purposes perfectly well. Since altering the sequence offered by any author will not necessarily confuse students, do not get caught up in rigid sequencing. In the list above the authors speak of teaching rules, which conflicts with my suggestion that you encourage students to detect patterns of sounds and letters in meaningful contexts so that they can discover and develop, inductively, their own rules. Such principles will work best for them since they understand why certain letters and combinations produce the sound equivalents they do. If you keep your focus on the meaning of the content to be read, distortions will be eliminated and these mechanical word recognition skills will be more interesting.

Another major problem with teaching rules in word recognition is not only that students often forget or misunderstand them, but that many of the rules simply do not work as well as we'd like to believe. Clymer's study makes this point very well. Following are the results of his investigation into the usefulness of common phonics generalizations (Clymer, 1963).

"The Utility of Phonic Generalizations in the Primary Grades," Dr. Theodore Clymer.

GENERALIZATION*	No. of Words Conforming	No. of Words Exceptions	Percent of Utility
1. When there are two vowels side by side, the long sound of the first one is heard and the second is usually silent.	309 (bead)**	377 (chief)**	45
2. When a vowel is in the middle of a one-syllable word, the vowel is short.	408	249	62

"The Utility of Phonic Generalizations in the Primary Grades," Dr. Theodore Clymer.

GENERALIZATION*	No. of Words Conforming	No. of Words Exceptions	Percent of Utility
middle letter	191 (dress)	84 (scold)	69
one of the middle two letters in a word of four letters	191 (rest)	135 (told)	59
one vowel *within* a word of more than four letters	26 (splash)	30 (fight)	16
3. If the only vowel letter is at the end of a word, the letter usually stands for a long sound.	23 (he)	8 (to)	74
4. When there are two vowels, one of which is final *e*, the first vowel is long and the *e* is silent.	180 (bone)	108 (done)	63
*5. The *r* gives the preceding vowel a sound that is neither long nor short.	484 (horn)	134 (wire)	78
6. The first vowel is usually long and the second silent in the digraphs *ai*, *ea*, *oa* and *ui*.	179	92	66
ai	43 (nail)	24 (said)	64
ea	101 (bead)	51 (head)	66
oa	34 (boat)	1 (cupboard)	97
ui	1 (suit)	16 (build)	6
7. In the phonogram *ie*, the *i* is silent and the *e* has a long sound.	8 (field)	39 (friend)	17
*8. Words having double *e* usually have the long *e* sound.	85 (seem)	2 (been)	98
9. When words end with silent *e*, the preceding *a* or *i* is long.	164 (cake)	108 (have)	60
*10. In *ay* the *y* is silent and gives *a* its long sound.	36 (play)	10 (always)	78
11. When the letter *i* is followed by the letters *gh*, the *i* usually stands for its long sound and the *gh* is silent.	22 (high)	9 (neighbor)	71
12. When *a* follows *w* in a word, it usually has the sound *a* as in *was*.	15 (watch)	32 (swam)	32
13. When *e* is followed by *w*, the vowel sound is the same as represented by *oo*.	9 (blew)	17 (sew)	35
14. The two letters *ow* make the long *o* sound.	50 (own)	35 (down)	59
15. *W* is sometimes a vowel and follows the vowel digraph rule.	50 (crow)	75 (threw)	40
*16. When *y* is the final letter in a word, it usually has a vowel sound.	169 (dry)	32 (tray)	84
17. When *y* is used as a vowel in words, it sometimes has the sound of long *i*.	29 (fly)	170 (funny)	15
18. The letter *a* has the same sound (o) when followed by *l*, *w*, and u.	61 (all)	65 (canal)	48

* Generalizations marked with an asterisk were found "useful" according to the criteria.
** Words in parentheses are examples—either of words which conform or of exceptions, depending on the column.

"The Utility of Phonic Generalizations in the Primary Grades," Dr. Theodore Clymer.

GENERALIZATION*	No. of Words Conforming	No. of Words Exceptions	Percent of Utility
19. When *a* is followed by *r* and final *e*, we expect to hear the sound heard in care.	9 (date)	1 (are)	90
*20. When *c* and *h* are next to each other, they make only one sound.	103 (peach)	0	100
*21. *Ch* is usually pronounced as it is in *catch*, *kitchen*, and *chair*, not like *sh*.	99 (catch)	5 (machine)	95
*22. When *c* is followed by *e* or *i*, the sound of *s* is likely to be heard.	66 (cent)	3 (ocean)	96
*23. When the letter *c* is followed by *o* or *a* the sound of *k* is likely to be heard.	143 (camp)	0	100
24. The letter *g* often has a sound similar to that of *j* in *jump* when it precedes the letter *i* or *e*.	49 (engine)	28 (give)	64
*25. When *igh* is seen in a word, *gh* is silent.	30 (fight)	0	100
26. When a word begins *kn*, the *k* is silent.	10 (knife)	0	100
27. When a word begins with *wr*, the *w* is silent.	8 (write)	0	100
*28. When two of the same consonants are side by side, only one is heard.	334 (carry)	3 (suggest)	99
29. When a word ends in *ck*, it has the same last sound as in *look*.	46 (brick)	0	100
30. In most two-syllable words, the first syllable is accented.	828 (famous)	140 (polite)	85
31. If *a*, *in*, *re*, *em*, *de*, or *be* is the first syllable in a word, it is usually unaccented.	86 (belong)	18 (insect)	87
32. In most two-syllable words that end in a consonant followed by *y*, the first syllable is accented and the last is unaccented.	101 (baby)	4 (supply)	96
33. One vowel letter in an accented syllable has its short sound.	547 (city)	256 (lady)	61
34. When *y* or *ey* is seen in the last syllable that is not accented, the long sound of *e* is heard.	0	157 (baby)	0
35. When *true* is the final syllable in a word, it is unaccented.	4 (picture)	0	100
36. When *tion* is the final syllable in a word, it is unaccented.	5 (station)	0	100
37. In many two- and three-syllable words, the final *e* lengthens the vowel in the last syllable.	52 (invite)	62 (gasoline)	46
38. If the first vowel sound in a word is followed by two consonants, the first syllable usually ends with the first of the two consonants.	404 (bullet)	159 (singer)	72
39. If the first vowel sound in a word is followed by a single consonant, that consonant usually begins the second syllable.	190 (over)	237 (oven)	44
*40. If the syllable of a word ends in *le*, the consonant preceding the *le* usually begins the last syllable.	62 (tumble)	2 (buckle)	97
*41. When the first vowel element in a word is followed by *th*, *ch*, or *sh*, these symbols are not broken when the word is divided into	30 (dishes)	0	100

syllables and may go with either the first or second syllable.

42.	In a word of more than one syllable, the letter *v* usually goes with the preceding vowel to form a syllable.	35 (cover) 20 (clover)	73
43.	When a word has only one vowel letter, the vowel sound is likely to be short.	433 (hid) 322 (kind)	57
*44.	When there is one *e* in a word that ends in a consonant, the *e* usually has a short sound.	85 (let) 27 (blew)	76
*45.	When the last syllable is the sound *r*, it is unaccented.	188 (butter) 9 (appear)	95

Clymer's study questioned the value of teaching children in beginning reading programs to memorize phonics rules or generalizations to try to figure out how to pronounce printed words. Clymer used a basic word list of 2600 words taken from commonly used basal readers for grades one through four and from basic word lists. Then he went through basal readers to ascertain if the rules usually taught in phonics were useful in figuring out the words in those books. You see what he found out about some of the primary teachers' favorite rules, e.g., When there are two vowels side by side, the long sound of the first one is heard and the second is usually silent (two vowels go walking, ... etc.). If a child knows this classic phonics rule, he would find in most basal readers (for the first four grades) that 309 words would follow the rule like the word *bead*, but that 377 would not follow it like the word *chief*. Clymer calculated what he called the per cent of utility, or usefulness. He found for this particular rule the per cent of utility is 45%. In other words, one could flip a coin and have more chance of randomly guessing which pronunciation was correct.

Another rule with many exceptions is, When *e* is followed by *w*, the vowel sound is the same as represented by *oo*. This "rule" works in nine words in Clymer's sampling, and does not work in 17 cases! That's 35% utility. Of course, that's an extreme example of what he found; there were rules having 60, 70, 80, and 90% utility. But the point is that many of these rules, the more reliable and useful ones, as well as the unreliable ones, are taught as if they were gospel in many schools. Obviously, we cannot depend on such "rules" as the foundation of our word recognition teaching.

THE FIRST STEPS: LANGUAGE ACQUISITION AND READINESS

Auditory and visual discrimination are companion skills in learning to speak, read, and write the language. How shall we present them in an instructional program? Let's take whatever cues we can from the normal process of language acquisition in children as they learn to hear, speak, and generate their own language. What are some of the components of that language acquisition? We have seen that scholars like Chomsky and Lenneberg believe that language is biological. Language is written on the cells of those creatures called human; they *must* generate language just as they must eat, drink, sleep, reproduce, and excrete. These same people put less emphasis on the importance of imitation as a major means of acquiring language, implying that developing activities and exercises which depend on imitation heavily will not serve our purposes.

When they speak of imitation in acquiring language, most experts refer to the idea that children and non-English speakers pick up the language by mimicking what they hear. If a child mispronounces a word or misuses a word in a particular sentence, someone corrects the child, perhaps even repeating the word several times and having the child do the same. This is thought to eventually produce the correct pronunciation or usage. To a minimal degree that is true, but that omits a great deal of meaning and feeling in language usage and it denies the biological nature of language and language learning.

Language Acquisition

How do children naturally and normally learn their language? They do so in the presence of loving parents and in an environment relatively responsive to their needs physically and psychologically. There is love, support, concern, attention, and praise. Mother does not pull words out of the hat and say to the one year old, "Today we will learn how to say or hear words beginning with the consonant *b* or *p* or *d*." Parents and others around the child speak fairly normally in context about things, people, places, ideas, and feelings. Practices and drills are not held to sharpen pronunciation or hearing. Corrections are made, but in the context of the spoken message and made by someone the child needs and depends on for love and care. Quizzes are not given to the child to see if he has developed the correct auditory or visual discrimination or oral expression. All corrections are made over time in a variety of contexts all embedded in the family life and ordinary daily occurrences. Those parents who overdo language development consciously and in intellectual and verbal ways often end up with children who speak as they do, with proper pronunciation in correct sentences and with varied vocabulary. Many adults take such verbalization for intelligence, when in fact it is only skill in reproducing sound forms and sentence forms. I am not convinced that oververbalizing for small children in the preschool years is at all valuable, but rather may be destructive and misguided. Even if such highly verbal children read correctly and early, I want to probe to see if their reading is more than mere mechanical skill and fluency. Where is the interpretive skill?

This issue is very important for parents and teachers, so let's look at it for a moment.

In the normal process of language acquisition we have seen that normal development is much like the coming and going of tides: slow, regular, subtly overlapping waves moving into shore or away from it. Each wave of the incoming tide does not go an even distance onto the beach; the waves move in a more undulating motion, with one wave rolling pretty far up on the sand, the next not quite so far, the third almost as far, between the first two, the next wave coming farther in, and so on.

Language acquisition, in fact all learning, is tidal in that way. Hence there is no need to outdo nature in regard to language acquisition. We know language is biological and will come forth; it needs some stimulation and nurturing to be sure, but it does not need to be programmed for adult level communication. After all, a two year old child is still a two year old in all kinds of ways: physiologically, intellectually, emotionally, and experientially. Making adult noises in adult ways is not a sign of more rapid maturity or greater intelligence. Children (all of us actually) can say much more than we know; we can say words and combinations of words for which we have no or very limited conceptual support. Lack of conceptual support is of course related to the lack of broadly based and carefully sifted and suffered experiences with a variety of people, places, ideas, and feelings, etc. There is no substitute for normal childhood and its discoveries, inventions, and play—its experiences and the meanings derived from their relations.

When we try to by-pass childish play and activity, we deny nature her time; that cannot be done without serious consequences. Language inserted into little inexperienced heads can be a short-cut, an abstraction from experience and reality. Words are not things, people, feelings, and textures. They are words: *standard sound arrays in syntactic groupings pointing to some meaning*. But meaning is not in the words; meaning is in the space between the print, the reader, the writer, and their culture. The space is filled with experiences and the concepts built on them, not on other words; words are not well defined by other words unless the synonym is rooted in a clearly defined concept which capsulizes a host of related experiences.

Preschool children need first-hand experiences of various types on various levels during the years of their childhood. They need to make their own concepts out of their experiences and the relationships they can find among them; they need to compare and contrast characteristics of objects, people, places, ideas, and other concepts. They will make their own language and they need time and many experiences to enrich it; they do not need words to substitute for real experience so early. Words are abstractions, pointers to experiences and to the concepts they are part of. I cannot re-create for you a great painting, musical piece, reaction to first flowering or a fleeting moment of love or the like. In teaching or parenting I strongly urge you not to oververbalize, making mynah birds of children, but let them experience as much of the world as possible, first hand;

they will then have reason to want to communicate in language.

Heavy-handed, however well-intentioned, doses of language instruction by parents deprive that child of experience and feelings never again available to him.

Reading Readiness

Auditory discrimination

Auditory discrimination merely means the ability to hear the similarities and differences in spoken language—*b* from *p* or *d*, for example. At home or in school the idea is to provide the child with many opportunities to give evidence that he can identify and discriminate spoken sounds correctly. It is a way of sensitizing the child to listen more carefully and with greater accuracy of discrimination. Most children seem to be able to do that quite naturally in the usual course of learning to hear and speak the language prior to school entry. Many authorities believe that sharpening the child's skill in listening to similar and different spoken sounds will assist him when he has to make the connections between the spoken sounds (phonemes) and their written equivalents (graphemes).

Visual discrimination

Visual discrimination has similar goals in the readiness program, that is, to sharpen the child's skill in noticing similarities and differences in printed letters, so that we don't get reversals like *b* and *d*, *p* and *q*, etc. Incidentally, it is not uncommon for normal children to make reversals of this type with letters and some words like *was* and *saw* up to age 10 or so. It varies with the child, and boys take longer to straighten out than most girls, so do not get too concerned about it in first, second, or even third grade boys. Help them of course, but don't call such reversals some form of brain damage, LD, or dyslexia.

Many reading readiness programs use geometric forms to test and train children's visual discrimination and perception. It is generally useless and often causes teachers and clinicians to isolate a weakness in this area as a visual problem or a perceptual problem, thus misdiagnosing what could well be a normal, maturational event.

> "In general, the research (. . .) is in harmony with long established findings about transfer of training, which have shown that the more closely a learning activity resembles the activity to which transfer of learning is desired, the more likely it is for useful transfer to take place. Thus visual discrimination practice using letters and words is more transferable to reading than discrimination of geometric forms . . ." (Harris and Sipay, 1975, p. 50)

I agree that children need to sharpen their visual discrimination as a prelude to reading, and expect that both auditory and visual discrimination activities and experiences will be continually woven into early reading lessons so that they are reinforced in some meaningful context and not in isolation. We hear and see words and phrases, not one letter or one sound. Auditory and visual discrimination should be handled the way we handle mispronunciation, that is, in context, so that meaning aids in correct pronunciation.

Auditory and visual discrimination activities and skills then should, like all other skills, be part of meaningful, interesting language usage, whether spoken or written. Always keep in mind that the semantic dimension of words is a constant companion to the morphological aspect of printed matter. *A constant interaction must be going on among form, sound, and meaning.*

Sight words

Accompanying the work in auditory and visual discrimination is the development of a stock of *sight words* in almost all beginning reading programs in the area of word recognition. Sight words are just that: words learned by memory and by visual recognition, and are identifiable by the student without benefit of phonic or structural analysis skills. Some reading programs build up a stock of 50, 100, or 150 sight words prior to working on the skills in phonics and structural analysis. The number of sight words is not critical, and it varies with the student as to how many might be useful as a base for starting the process of generalizing certain phonic elements from these sight words. You can start phonic analysis instruction from a base of as small as only a dozen sight words.

The purpose of starting with a stock of sight words in almost every current reading program is to provide the learner with something known automatically and to use this stock of known sight words as the core of words to develop the ability to generalize about initial consonants, medial vowels, blends and digraphs. It also builds confidence in the beginning reader.

Some linguistic programs don't do this but rather leap into spelling patterns, e.g., dan, fan, man, pan, can, etc. However, I have always found it easier to *start with some sight words derived from each student's life and language experience* and then to move into the technical work of learning about the sounds and combinations of sounds which appear in these words. Examples will appear later in this chapter on some ways to build from sight words to phonics generalizations and structural analysis.

Learning sight words while simultaneously working on auditory and visual discrimination in these early stages of beginning reading prepares the student to tackle the more systematic approach to figuring out words in print.

When we move from sight words and continuing reinforcement of auditory and visual discrimination activities related to them into phonic analysis we must maintain our awareness of the interrelationship among these readiness skills and activities and the content we are trying to read. Let's sketch the contents of phonic and structural analysis before we show some ways to teach all of these word recognition skills in some interesting content, because done in isolation, using flash cards, language masters, workbooks, etc., phonic and structural analysis can be boring to most students of all ages. Our only hope for maintaining interest and motivation is to embed the words which matter to the student in a context that stimulates him.

Phonic Analysis

Phonic analysis deals specifically with those skills of analysis and synthesis that students need in order to pronounce written material. If students can pronounce the words in print they may have that word in their listening and/or speaking vocabulary and will therefore be able to attach meaning to it. When they can do that they have taken a significant step toward associating spoken and written forms, which is essential to beginning reading. Knowing the word in context in normal speech makes the letter by letter analysis more sensible to the student and makes synthesizing the spoken equivalents of the printed letters much easier and more meaningful than the too common practice of attempting to analyze a word letter by letter and sound by sound. Harris and Sipay (1979) offer a detailed listing of grapheme-phoneme relationships in English which you may find helpful for background knowledge.

Single consonants

The single consonants are taught in the initial, final, and medial positions in that sequence as when we teach the consonant *m* in words like *m* other, *m* ake, *m* uch, *m* ore, and then we present words like ri*m*, ha*m*, mo*m* and finally we present words (in context) like ma*mm*a, mu*mm*y, ski*mm*ing. We start with the most regular consonants, that is, those with one spoken equivalent and save less regular consonants like *c, g, x, z* for later. The consonant *m* tends to have only one spoken equivalent no matter what word it is, in but the consonant *c* can produce the spoken equivalents in such words as *c*ent, *c*ut. The first spoken equivalent of the *c* is *s* and the second is *k*, although in both instances we write the same letter. This is the reason for teaching all of these word recognition skills in context; meaning is a useful guide to pronunciation. Also, in English one quickly runs out of regular consonants or blends or vowels.

Consonant blends

Most reading programs teach consonant blends after work with single consonants and either short or long vowels. Consonant blends normally do not cause much difficulty for most readers; because the combinations are spoken, i.e., *bl*, *gr*, *st*, one hears the spoken equivalent of each letter as in words like bread, play, stop. Since one does hear each letter, this skill of blending follows work with regular single consonants rather logically. As before, regular and generative blends are presented first and then those which are less regular such as *sc* and for some students the *pl* combination at the end of words like apple. After the regular consonant blends are presented, in context, in the initial, final and medial positions and the irregular ones are presented as needed, we move to teaching consonant digraphs such as *wh*, *sh*, *ch*, and *th* which do cause many students considerable difficulty. The consonant digraphs combine two or more letters in such a way that we do not say the combination as we would each separate letter, for example one does not say the *w* and the *h* in the word where. If we did we would pronounce the word where as *wuh-h-ear* (or *air*). A mess to be sure, since the digraph cannot be broken up that way and the *ere* is not pronounced that way in any other word the young student is likely to know.

Vowels

Programs vary greatly but generally the next step in developing word recognition skills under the subheading of phonic analysis is the presentation of vowels, usually single short vowels first and then long vowels, followed by vowel blends and vowel digraphs. Vowels cause many problems for beginning or troubled readers since they can be equivalent to two spoken forms (long and short) and often vowels produce a schwa sound. Trying to teach vowels singly or in combination in isolation is next to impossible. Look at some of the variations in vowels:

a as in bake is long; *a* in cat is short; *a* in about is schwa. (This omits the other sound equivalents of *a*, such as father, car, hall, etc.)

e in deep is long; *e* in bed is short; *e* in never can produce a schwa sound in the mouth of an Easterner who says *nev-uh*.

i in die is long; *i* in did is short

o in go is long; *o* in hot is short

u in due is long; *u* in under is short—like schwa

Sometimes *y* and *w* are vowels, and as a vowel, *y* has two equivalents:

in happy the *y* is long because it sounds like long *e*

in gym, the *y* is short because it sounds like short *i*

w is a vowel in words like vowel or few because it fuses or blends with the vowel

The next step after presenting long and short vowels singly is to offer them in combinations, like vowel blends. A vowel blend is merely two or more vowels written together in which you hear a little of each vowel sound. This is not nearly as easy as it sounds. Some of the vowel blends are oi, ai, ou, au, aw, eu, ew, and oy. Say them to yourself and try to discriminate different vowel sounds. It is not easy, especially for a young-ster who is not accustomed to making such refined distinctions. A lot of children have trouble with this process at this stage.

Digraphs

After consonant and vowel blends have been taught and practiced, most phonics programs move into *digraphs*. A digraph is a combination of two or more letters making one sound or at least a sound different from either of the letters in it. Here are some consonant digraphs: ch, wh, ng, sh, gn, ck, pn, th, ph, gh. Here are some vowel digraphs: ee, ea, ie, oo, ae, and ei.

Most students by this time in their phonics program have almost gotten the idea of learning to write what they hear—that what they read is speech in printed form. They have struggled with many of the excep-tions and then they are faced with digraphs and become confused. They want to write what they hear, and if they hear one sound they want to write one letter. Generally, consonant blends are easy while vowel blends are difficult; and consonant digraphs are difficult while vowel digraphs are a bit easier to figure out.

For each of these phonic elements and combinations many activities are planned and executed which are designed to give the child much prac-tice in discriminating visually and auditorily. Also some writing is done, but usually not enough. For instance, the student hears a word, visual-izes it (perhaps sees it in print as well), and then writes it. If he can see, hear, and write at the same time, some think he will learn it better. And, some do learn better using more than one sense mode at a time; others do not. Some students are much better able to learn something by ear or by eye or by some other single sensory mode, e.g., touch.

Structural Analysis

The second major area under word recognition is structural analysis, which involves learning how to deal with larger parts of words rather than with single letters or combinations. The areas of study in structural analysis include:

1. compound words (break/fast, some/where, no/thing)
2. contractions (don't, can't, won't, I'll)
3. affixes: prefixes (pre-, in-, im-, il-); suffixes (-ing, -ly, -less, -ed, -able)
4. root words (path, cred, mort)
5. hyphenated words (in-service, jack-in-the-box)
6. syllabication—breaking longer words into parts for spelling and pro-nunciation (tap/ping, let/ter)

The skills needed for structural analysis depend to a large extent on the preceding work on individual elements and combinations presented and practiced in phonic analysis, and reinforce previous skills and extend them. For example, compound words are usually quite easy to handle in that they merely represent putting two one-syllable words together. For example, the words *break* and *fast* are probably already known either as sight words or in terms of the student's ability to pronounce them using learned phonics skills. Learning to handle compound words is primarily a visual skill, seeing that two known words are stuck together. If it is not apparent to the reader that this is so, he can fall back on the ability to pronounce each printed letter and combination, e.g., *br* is seen as the blend which appears in many words like break, brick, and brought, so that sound is recalled; *eak* is a bit harder, and would not lend itself to a letter by letter analysis. This is one of the key problems with teaching isolated phonics lessons, letter by letter since spoken and written forms just don't correspond too well in our language. *Ea* ought to sound like it does in *leak*, but it could sound like the *ea* in *bread* or *lead* (pronounced led), etc. With compound words it is better in most cases to point out the whole words first, e.g., *break*, and *fast* even though neither word is pronounced this way in any other word the student knows. What he does know from experience is that you say it *breck fast*, and there is no apparent reason for it. Students usually accept that from us, even after we have lectured them on being logical.

Compound words lead to work in syllabication, since to discover compound words is to break them into syllables: break/fast, no/where, some/time. *Each syllable has a spoken vowel sound no matter how many vowels there are.*

As one learns to break words into syllables, one discovers that prefixes (pre = before; fix = to place) are syllables you stick on the front of a word and suffixes are syllables you stick on the end of words. Of course, there are some confusing exceptions to the fact that affixes may be one syllable, e.g., *anti* is two syllables; *able* is two syllables. And finally one can be taught that what remains in most words is called a root or stem. Some words, especially long ones, may have two or three prefixes, two or three roots, and two or three suffixes, but if the student has been shown this simple structural analysis skill he will quickly discover that big words are just that because you do indeed add pieces before and after the root. The word *indefatigably* seen at a glance frightens most people because it looks unfamiliar and somewhat terrifying because of its length. The good reader, utilizing phonic skills to sound out letters and combinations of letters and structural analysis skills, figures out that the word comes apart like this: in/de/fat/i/ga/bly and that the *in* is a prefix as is *de*, both of which mean not or away from. The reader then notices (if taught to do so) that there is a suffix: *ably*, meaning able to, just the way it looks, and that what is left is *fatig*, which looks like fatigue, meaning tired. So this enormous word, broken into syllables (its basic structure) means not able to be tired, or tireless. That's all. Most words work out well when subjected to this kind of analysis so that these structural skills are very well worth learning. Breaking words into syllables helps you to pronounce them and perhaps remember having heard them in some context, and helps you to figure out the meaning if you do not have the word in your speaking vocabulary. Learning affixes and roots is a very effective way to expand one's vocabulary since many of the roots (Latin, Greek, French, German, and Anglo-Saxon) are found in thousands of other words. This gives the student a generalized skill. For example, if the student learns the root *path*, meaning either feeling or suffering, he can usually figure out words like empathy, sympathy, antipathy, apathy, or pathology. The last word might confuse the student because path is being used in its alternate meaning of suffering, but even so the student would be better off with that guess than with no guide at all.

James Brown (1962, pp. 120–121) of the University of Minnesota did a study of fourteen Latin roots and traced them to their derivatives (other words with the same root, having the same or a similar meaning in each word). He found that with a knowledge of these fourteen roots and twenty-one common prefixes you could get the meaning and pronunciation of some 14,000 words in English. Following is a table of these roots and prefixes.

Words	Prefix	Common Meaning	Root	Common Meaning
precept	pre-	(before)	capere	(take, seize)
detain	de-	(away, from)	tenere	(hold, have)
intermittent	inter-	(between)	mittere	(send)
offer	ob-	(against)	ferre	(bear, carry)
insist	in-	(into)	stare	(stand)
monograph	mono-	(alone, one)	graphein	(write)
epilogue	epi-	(upon)	legein	(say, study of)
aspect	ad-	(to, toward)	specere	(see)
uncomplicated	un-	(not)	plicare	(fold)
	com-	(together, with)		
nonextended	non-	(not)	tendere	(stretch)
	ex-	(out of)		
reproduction	re-	(back, again)	ducere	(lead)
	pro-	(forward)		
indisposed	in-	(not)	ponere	(put, place)
	dis-	(apart from)		
oversufficient	over-	(above)	facere	(make, do)
	sub-	(under)		
mistranscribe	mis-	(wrong)	scribere	(write)
	trans-	(across, beyond)		

Later we shall use all of these phonic and structural analysis skills in actual activities, experiences, and practices with which you can help your student regardless of his grade in school.

Other structural analysis skills include learning about hyphenated words. Many words formerly hyphenated are no longer hyphenated. Words like co-operative, in-service, and anti-perspirant are disappearing in that form. They are being spelled as one whole word: cooperative, in-service, antiperspirant. What is a hyphenated word? It is merely putting two words together, often used as a compound adjective. You actually change the normal usage of each word, e.g., *in* usually is a preposition which introduces a phrase or which is used as an adverb to indicate where or direction; the word *service* is usually a noun, or sometimes an adjective as in *service man*, or it could be a verb. Putting *in* and *service* together mixes two usually separate ideas, and changes the function of the words. They usually become an adjective as in *in-service* training. There is no particular rush to teach hyphenated words in this much detail because, as you see, it relates to grammar, or how words are used and what they do in different contexts. They are rare and getting more so.

In summary, structural analysis is a major subdivision in the word recognition growth area. It is usually taught after most of the basic work in phonic analysis is taught since it deals with larger parts of words like syllables and compound words. Structural analysis also leads into vocabulary development and expansion, as well as into grammar in terms of how words change their functions, e.g., from noun to adjective. Structural analysis also helps students to recognize parts of words by blending phonic elements.

Words, Words, Words

Obviously we cannot master any language if we concentrate our efforts exclusively on the spoken equivalents of individual letters and combinations of letters. We must shift the emphasis to words and phrases, the more meaningful units of communication, and we must be aware of the interrelationship among the four dimensions of all language: the phonological, the syntactic, and the statistical, and the semantic. If you separate these aspects of words and utterances and focus considerable attention on any one to the exclusion of the others you can easily distort pronunciation, meaning, and function in a given utterance.

Phonological dimension

Phonology refers to the sound system of any language, that is, how you pronounce the sounds of your language individually and in combination to evoke intelligent responses in listeners or readers. Every language has its own rules and customs which are standardized among those who speak and understand the language. When persons mispronounce words or parts of words as do dialect speakers or foreign language speakers, it affects all of the other dimensions of the language. Phonological distortions or errors can cause problems in reading and writing if the speaker tries to write exactly what he has said or heard.

Syntactic dimension

Syntactics has to do with word order and what is acceptable as a phrase, clause, or sentence. Defying the rules of grammar and syntax easily can distort meaning and produce noise rather than communication. You cannot say "Man love I is John" in English since our word order tends to follow the subject-verb-object pattern. Each language has its own order; for example in German, the verb usually must be the second word in the sentence, but that is understood by the speakers of that language; it is not transferrable to another language system operating under different rules.

Statistical dimension

As indicated in chapter 1, the statistical dimension of language refers to the expectations and predictability of language usage. As we acquire our language and internalize its rules, principles and patterns we come to know what to expect of most utterances that are written or spoken. Knowing the phonological and syntactic rules and practices, we can anticipate or predict much of what will be said or written. Variations of the rules either confounds us or signals some novel or unusual meanings on the part of the speaker or writer. Good literature often bends the common rules and practices so that we must alter our perceptions as is true of these lines of poetry:

> somewhere i have never travelled, gladly
> beyond any experience
> your eyes have their silence. . .
> (cummings, 1965, p. 88)

and

> Altarwise by owl-light in the half-way house
> The gentleman lay graveward with his furies;
> Abbadon in the hangnail cracked from Adam,
> And, from his fork, a dog among the fairies,
> The atlas-eater with a jaw for news,
> Bit out the mandrake with to-morrow's scream.
> Then penny-eyed, that gentleman of wounds,
> Old cock from nowheres and the heaven's egg,
> With bones unbuttoned to the half-way winds,
> Hatched from the windy salvage on one leg,
> Scraped at my cradle in a walking word
> That night of time under the Christward shelter:
> I am the long world's gentleman, he said,
> And share my bed with Capricorn and Cancer.
> (Thomas, 1953)

Clearly these examples illustrate variations on normal syntax and semantics which no word-for-word translation could possibly reveal. Here we see statistically improbable, unlikely juxtapositions of words that alter our perceptions to the core and which enhance meaning and feeling. Although we might never speak or write this way, we are able to enjoy and understand much creative use of syntax and semantics.

Semantic dimension

Included in this dimension of language are the literal (denotative) and figurative (connotative) meanings of words and phrases, multiple meaning words like play, bank, act, puns, and double entendres. Since many words do not have a single meaning, we must attend to the context in which they are used in order to determine their particular meaning or shade of meaning, as well as to note the effect of altered syntax on them. In short, everything we do with words bears on this dimension since the purpose of all communication is to be understood by others who share your culture. Rearranging word order, altering pronunciation, and including the unexpected all directly affect the meaning of any utterance spoken or written.

SUMMARY

In sum, the interrelationships among the four dimensions of language require us to broaden our concept of word recognition skills. We must get beyond isolated letters, blends, digraphs, and syllables to words and sensible utterances. Context determines phonology to some extent, directs the syntax and thus establishes the probabilities, the expectations of any given message and imbues it all with meaning.

We have also discussed the difficulties generated by teaching word recognition skills in isolation as in the case of the vowel *a* with its seven spoken equivalents or the *ough* and its seven possible spoken equivalents. We also noted that vowels in English have at least two spoken equivalents and many have three (long, short, and schwa).

TEACHING THE WORD RECOGNITION SKILLS

We have spoken of the basic word recognition skills and have presented some useful general principles for presenting them. Now we can look at more specific ways to teach word recognition skills in a more interesting and meaningful way than often occurs. I shall focus my suggestions for teaching on a language experience, core concept approach to the skills and on the inductive mode of generalizing certain patterns and "rules."

Included in Chapter five are some ways of making a language experience story from a picture (the John Day materials for example), and how we could take some of the words in a dictated story and build more sight words, and then do the phonic and structural analysis activities necessary to develop greater independence.

Building Sight Vocabulary

Here are some examples of how we might work with a group of (or individual) adults who are almost nonreaders, at a primer level, or at a low first grade reading level. You might start a discussion with your group about the purpose of the center, the educational program, the goals and objectives, and the students' needs and desires. After some conversation has occurred you might write down several sentences that have been spoken by members of the group. After you write a sentence, ask the person who said it if he can read it. Chances are, he can. If not, perhaps someone else can; in any event, you could read it correctly after the students have tried.

After you have written several sentences on the board and had them read correctly, ask the students to write them in their notebooks. Have them underline words they cannot say or figure out. Most of the other words then will probably be their sight words. Almost everyone has a stock of sight words. Usually the larger the stock of sight words, the easier it will be to begin formal instruction in phonics. In any case, you will be assisting the students to build a larger and larger stock of sight words in these early sessions. You can develop a stock of sight words from dictated sentences and you can make a general list of words which you suspect almost everyone in that area might have seen many times, for example, *stop, go, in, out, men, women, up, down, children, store, grocer, liquor, cigarettes*, etc. All the students should make their own personal dictionary in which they keep sight words, and to which they will add new sight or other words they want to know. This notebook should be set up alphabetically as in a dictionary, with the words listed under the proper letter heading, and preferably with at least one definition for it and the word used in a sentence. This is one way to help the students become aware of the alphabet if they are not already. It also encourages closer observation of the use of complete sentences.

Another activity in the readiness and sight word stage of development of basic reading skills is to let each student make a name card for himself, including his first and last name. The students will wear their name, if it does not embarrass them, long enough so that each one in the group can read by sight all the other names. Some people like to make labels or cards with the names of objects in the room: window, chair, desk, chalk board, calendar, door, floor, lights, etc. Be sure when you try things like this that your group is not being embarrassed by them, for if they are, these activities will not work, no matter how good they sound to you.

To help students develop sight words related to time have them make calendars, either for the current month or for a whole year or season of the year. If they make a one month calendar, have them list the days of each week with the appropriate number; also include holidays or birthdays, etc. Don't put too much into any one lesson. Insure success by presenting small, meaningful parts. Another activity is to have everyone make birthday or anniversary cards for each other. The cards can include snapshots or hand-drawn pictures and words. The nice thing about making cards of this type is that such occasions require a fairly limited vocabulary and thus give you better control over the number of difficult phonic and structural elements to be presented. Such activity also is filled with emotion and that is always valuable.

Whichever of the above activities you are involved in, be certain that the *students say what it is they have to say* and *then see it written down* and *then write it themselves and read it*. Always keep reading and writing activities as closely related as possible.

A related approach would be to talk about a particular topic for a given period of time, for example, tools, places, special people, family, holidays. In discussing any one of the those topics you limit the vocabulary used to carry it on. After your students have developed some fifty or sixty sight words that they can read automatically, you can begin more formal instruction in phonic analysis. You can begin to show them that these words they can speak and now read are composed of letters and combinations of letters, and if they learn these they can then read many other words without help. The whole point in developing sight words is to provide them with a core of familiar words from which you can teach them to generalize, e.g., if the student knows *rain* as a sight word, you can help him to discover that the word begins with the same letter and sound as the words red, rich, rat, and that *ain* is a rhyming element (phonogram) found in many other words like pain, gain, drain, plain, and so on. However, do *not* teach this kind of generalizing by merely saying it and making lists of words. It is much more effective and enjoyable to the students if they figure them out by themselves. For example, you might ask the person who knows rain as a sight word what other words he knows that begins the way rain does. Let him say the words beginning with the *r*. Then you might ask if he knows words that have the *r* at the end of the word like never, far, poor and repeat the procedure for *r* in the middle of words. If the student is ready for it, you could then deal with the *ain* and elicit words with that element in it.

After a number of words have been listed, discussed and read with the consonant *r* in the beginning, middle, and end of words and after the *ain* has been identified in other words, you could show them that by substituting a consonant or consonant blend at the beginning of the word you can make many words with the *ain* in it. This is a first step toward generalizing phonic and structural elements.

Here are some suggested topics with the appropriate vocabulary for a language-experience approach:

Time	Weather	Holidays	Work
minutes	hot	Independence Day	job
seconds	cold	Christmas	police man
hours	snow	Easter	fireman
days	rain	Halloween	farmer
weeks	hail	Valentine's Day	plumber
months	sleet	birthdays	carpenter
years	windy	*cultural*	secretary
night	summer	Chinese, Greek,	Army, Navy, etc.
yesterday	winter	Black American, etc.	Factory-different types
last night	fall	national holidays	lawyer
tomorrow	spring	religious holidays	doctor
before	seasons		teacher
after	clouds		electrician

For younger children or beginning readers of any age, such simple classification systems help them and you to organize the content and to generate the key words necessary for each grouping. These words and the concepts they point to provide you the raw material for teaching all of the reading, phonic and structural analysis skills in an organized fashion. Such an approach also provides you with many opportunities for vocabulary development and expansion. Beginning readers can be learning that certain jobs have something in common or that certain facts about weather are related to each other. You can achieve several objectives in a single lesson planned this way, i.e., you can be building the sight vocabulary in context, not just off a list of unrelated words; you are building in repetition of a stock of words in speaking, listening, reading, and writing; you have added meaning so that all of the words will be more readily learned and understood. You have in short, built a rational context within which to teach word recognition, meanings, study skills, vocabulary, and writing.

The best way to increase the value of a language-experience approach is to develop the students' interest into a core concept which easily moves in several directions and on several levels as was seen in Chapter 5. This combination of the language-experience approach and the core concept plan guarantees your students that they will be learning about things which they know and care about, that all of the facts, information, and concepts will be related for greater meaning and understanding, and it also provides control over the vocabulary. All of this adds up to greater focus in each lesson and among all of your lessons. It also insures that the students will encounter similar words many times, but in context, and will receive all of the repetition and practice they may need to master the word recognition and other reading skills.

Once beginning or low level readers have built up a stock of generative sight words in the context of their language-experience, core-concept lessons, we move easily into working on phonic analysis and structural analysis so that they can generalize from their sight words to many others containing the same or similar elements. We can also write our language-experience stories, read them, and then find synonyms and antonyms for some of our words. We can check both comprehension and interpretation on these stories, and we can build in the appropriate study skills.

Although many low level readers may not be able to read fluently we can introduce them to the idea of study skills if not the skills themselves. In the Northeastern University Reading Clinic we have had many students who have written little books during a quarter of instruction. These little books were language-experience stories on a particular topic such as animals, cars, monsters, and the like. Often we have the student decide (with teacher's help) what kind of cars he knows about. We get, finally, such headings as racing cars, sports cars, family cars, stock cars, etc. Then under each type of car we generate the words which fit such as names of racing cars or family cars (Buick, Dodge, etc.). We may even have the student alphabetize these if that skill is needed. We discuss different racing or family cars to find out how they are alike and how they are different, and we use that language as part of the stories for our books. The student may decide then to organize his book according to one type of car only, for example, racing cars. If he decides to do this, we then decide which cars and then we write a little story about each one, including a picture, drawn or from a magazine. Under this picture the story will appear. The story is developed from the child's other reading, if he can do it alone, and from readings you do. For each car you may decide to tell about the name of the car, where it is made, how fast it goes, and special features of it. That could produce four or five sentences which will be dictated by the student, read by the student and then written by the student. So for each type of car four facts will be stated. This guides the child's thinking and reduces his anxiety about what to say. He knows he will tell the same facts about each car in his book; he knows he will be comparing and contrasting their features.

To write such a book the student discovers that you could have a title, the author's name, a table of contents. To do these correctly he has to have at least an idea of some of the basic study skills. When he has completed each story about his racing cars he will be asked comprehension and interpretation questions about the car, where it was made, etc. The content from geography, science, and even history could be woven into this type of project to insure that the student develops and expands concepts, not just word recognition skills.

STARTING AN L-E LESSON

There are several ways to generate a language-experience discussions:

1. Discussion of current events like the blizzard of '78 in the Northeast; war in the Middle East; gas shortage, baseball, etc.
2. Using a film on a particular topic such as science, nature, history, or literature.
3. Using material from favorite television shows.
4. Listening to pop music, key stars, lyrics, and the like.
,5. Performing experiments, for instance, using ammonium dichloride to make a volcanic eruption.
6. Having a guest speaker.
7. Taking a trip to the aquarium or museum of science or art and focusing on some aspect of it such as animals, space equipment, prehistoric creatures, etc.

Be on the look-out for such opportunities to develop some incipient interest or curiosity into a full blown core concept plan for students. I have often developed a core concept curriculum as a result of the IDA itself, e.g., the transportation selection in Chapter 3.

Two Language-Experience, Core Concept Word Recognition Lessons

These lessons reveal how I developed a similar core concept with two different children functioning at different levels and who had very different intellectual and social backgrounds. Both had word recognition problems. Charlene was 7½ years old when I began working with her. She had been working with an undergraduate tutor for 4 or 5 weeks on giraffes. Presumably the tutor intended to make her version of a core-concept set of plans for this instruction based on learning about giraffes. In the four or five instructional sessions that had occurred, very little had been learned about giraffes or word recognition and other skills.

Case study—Charlene

Charlene was diagnosed on the IDA as reading on a primer level. She needed work in readiness, phonics, structural analysis skills, and vocabulary. In the preceding lessons the teacher tried to get Charlene to read material on giraffes (and look at a few other pictures of animals) from a book written on at least a fourth or fifth grade level. I intervened because the tutor and I and the supervisor who had been observing the sessions agreed that this set of lessons was going nowhere. Additionally, the tutor had the impression that Charlene was trying to learn but seemed to be having some serious difficulties remembering what she was taught and in general understanding some of the content of the lessons.

So why start with giraffes? Giraffes are not only fairly rare animals, but the word contains unusual and relatively uncommon phonic elements. Even if Charlene could learn giraffe how could she then generalize most of the phonic elements in the word? How many words in English, for example, contain *affe*? How many the *gir* combination? A handful at most. So that even if she had learned the word, no real generalizing could be done that would help her figure out and analyze other words.

Do not, therefore, select such words or content for troubled, beginning readers. Pick material containing a good variety of phonic and structural elements, and elements that are as common as possible so that the transfer or the generalizing will be expedited. You should choose words with the letters *m*, *b*, *d*, *p*; common consonant and vowel blends such as *br*, *pl*, *st*, *ai*, *ou*; digraphs; common prefixes *in*, *un*, *im*, *de*, *anti*; suffixes *able*, *ous*, *tion*, *sion*; and roots like *cred*, *mort*, *port*, etc. In language-experience work one should plan ahead to make sure the student is exposed to words that will assist in building the generalizations most useful in reading at his level and just above.

When I met with Charlene for the first time, I started by trying to get a better sense of what Charlene knew of the content that her tutor had presented to her; what skills she might have been taught or at least introduced to; some sense of her own knowledge, background, concepts, vocabulary, and thinking. I took a picture of a giraffe she had drawn and whose parts she had labeled—horns, legs, neck, ears, etc., and asked her to read them one by one. She made only one error; when she saw *hoofs*, she said *feet*. When asked to look again, she noted the *h* but could not fuse the other letters into the word. I told her *hoofs* and asked what they were, how they might be like feet. When she read *horns*, correctly, I asked playfully, did she have horns? Why not? What are horns for? She was not too clear, responding that she thought they might be for signaling. In this initial diagnostic probe, it was clear that she had little factual information about giraffes or horns, and her responses up to this point were shallow and off the mark by much. She tended to drift into unrelated conversation, remotely (if at all) connected with what we were doing. I pulled her back quickly but gently.

After we had gone over the labels she had put on the giraffe picture, we turned to a book about African animals. Excellent pictures, but with difficult text, were included. The captions were in small print and the sentences long, using a fairly high level vocabulary. This material was obviously way beyond this child's decoding skills and way beyond her conceptual skills—a very poor choice of material for this student. However, I stuck with it. We started through the book, stopping at each page to look at the picture, to check her idea of what was in the picture and what it might mean—the mother zebra having a baby, wild dogs chasing some zebras, a flock of birds flying. This was an attempt to check her use of picture clues, and more on her knowledge and understanding of the content, which were both sadly lacking. We joked and had a pleasant visit all through these activities.

We moved on and I pretended not to know how to spell giraffe (which was put on the board). She gave me a couple of versions including *gerggfe*, *geraffe*, *geru*. I finally had her look at the picture and the words and read me the spelling, which she did proudly. I pretended surprise and had her double check the book spelling with what was written (both auditory and visual discrimination review). Then, to condense this, we picked out several of the animals: zebra, wild dogs, birds, and wildebeast (she got the latter word right with one self-correction). Each word was put on the board, then she took the pen and put the same animal names on a pad in front of her. She checked my spellings after she picked the name of the animal from the book. I wrote it, she read it, and then she wrote it, and then she read it again. This went rather well, although she needed some help. I kept up a flow of conversation about Africa and asked her if she knew where it was, how to get there, what other animals lived there, and if she thought a kitten would fit on our list of African animals (which was made earlier). To the last question, she said no, and I asked why. She said it was too small and it was a pet. We tried pursuing the idea of pet and wild animal to little avail.

After ten animals had been listed by both of us, I suggested that she might want to write a book about African animals. She said yes, and asked if she could keep it in our Clinic library. I said of course. Then we tried to decide what we should include in this book on African animals. She needed much help in this stage of the language experience development. I asked, What would other children who read your book want to know about these animals? What did she want to know? So I managed to elicit: *what they eat*, *how they get their food*, *their size*, and *what they do*. A brief but useful classification.

The lesson ended shortly thereafter. As we went through the text it was clear that she had almost no word recognition skills, little recall, no interpretation, and a limited vocabulary. She was in fact dull intellectually. I had made a point throughout the lesson to repeat and review and to put things into several similar contexts in order to be sure she could recall what we were doing and why we were doing it, and to recall the names of the animals we were seeing, discussing, and writing about.

What followed with her tutor was the writing of the book on African animals (almost entirely a language experience approach here). On each page she cut out or drew a picture of the animal, like the zebra. Under it she would talk about the animal and the tutor would talk about and read to her about what the animal ate, how it got its food, etc. Hence each little story about each animal already had its structure by stating something about each item, based on the simple classification system. For a child like this with a limited intelligence, almost no background of knowledge and concepts, minute recall, and no interpretation ability, it is especially helpful to work out of the language experience program such a schema of characteristics or types of animals, food, etc., so that each written section is already laid out and can be easily filled in by the student. The story to be told about each animal is the same, because you are asking for the same facts: what it eats, its size, how it gets its food, etc. This produces four or five sentences containing similar words with similar phonic and structural elements, for example:

The zebra is as big as a horse.
The zebra eats grass and leaves.
The zebra gets its food in the fields.
The zebra runs across the fields.

For Charlene this was fine. For more capable students, of course, you would encourage and get more varied sentence patterns and a little more variety in vocabulary. But for Charlene this provided almost enough repetition of words and elements so that sight words were developed and reviewed, especially going from animal to animal and finding many of the same words in each story. That kind of internal repetition is best.

The tutor ensures that sight words are being accumulated in the reading of the little stories and then when the child writes them down herself it also reinforces auditory and visual discrimination.

In Charlene's little story about the zebra, she had responded to my question of what a zebra looks like. It looks like a horse. She then thought it was a horse, and I added, no, it was *like* a cousin to the horse. Did she have cousins? Yes, many. Anyway, the key word recognition skills were woven into each of the following lessons derived from each little story with its predetermined four or five sentences. There was plenty of opportunity to reinforce auditory and visual discrimination and to build up a stock of sight words from which would be developed the phonics generalizations. There was also much repetition of words and elements. Simple sentence patterning was built in to aid in her own sentence structure.

This brief and incomplete summary of my first encounter with Charlene perhaps gives enough clues for you to see how we initiate at this very low level the basic word recognition skills. For purposes of building the generalizations on the words from these stories let me illustrate. Again be sure to select for phonic and structural analysis words containing the most regular and common letters and letter combinations. Words like zebra and giraffe were put aside because their phonic elements are rare and not as generative as those in lion, tiger, or wild dog. We might focus on the word lion, which would appear four or five times in the little story about lions. I asked Charlene to notice how the word lion sounds in the beginning (*l*)—just like what other words? She answered finally, *lady, like, look,* which were written on the board with the initial *l* underlined. I checked to see if she would notice that they are all spelled the same way. I added three or four more words here with one or two wrong words just to check Charlene's perception:

*l*ight
*l*ady
*t*ell
*l*ife

I pronounced these words without too much exaggeration, while she looked at them, so that she could hear the sound that the letter *l* represents. With somewhat better students, one could then move into dealing with the single *l* in the final and even medial positions:

hill
until
will
thrill

underlining the final *l*, saying it in each case.

This process is common and useful in dealing with the early stages of phonic analysis from language experience stories. Care in directing the development of language experience stories can increase the rate of learning the phonic or structural elements needed by the student. In the case above, the language was severely limited because of Charlene's own limitations, but she did learn some of these elements and did learn to generalize some of them. For children or adults like Charlene, I avoid certain core concepts so that I can reduce the vocabulary and the concept load. Keep such material simple, tangible, and easily digested.

Case study—Louis

Louis is a fourth grade student who attended the Clinic. He was reading at a 3^2 level with some word recognition problems, primarily in structural analysis. His mother speaks Spanish, but Louis seemed not to know Spanish. As a result of my observations and the supervisor's observations, we decided to try to show the tutor how to get the lessons going and how to insert more effectively the word recognition and study skills into these lessons. Louis was interested in wild animals or at least animals. His tutor had chosen a book called *Zoo Animals*. My intervention began with an attempt to see where the tutor had been, what Louis knew about the content of the five or six lessons he had had, and how I could direct the future lessons inside a more clearly defined core concept with appropriate skills inserted. Since Louis did not have massive word recognition problems and was reading at about a high third grade level (by which time most word recognition skills have been taught and learned) the corrective program should be involved in introducing study skills and certainly increasing vocabulary, writing, and the all-important interpretation skills. None of this was really happening. In fact, little was happening in word recognition except isolated activities—flash cards and fill-in-the-blank work sheets.

Louis and I looked at his book on zoo animals and I asked him what he thought it was about. We looked at the title, author, table of contents—in fact did a mini-preview of the book, taking particular note of the picture of a squirrel on the cover. I asked Louis if he thought squirrels were zoo animals. He said no. Why? He said, as if he couldn't believe my asking such a dumb question, because they don't have enough trees in the zoo. He then added that squirrels were everywhere and were not wild and did not need to be put in cages in the zoo. He understood all the essential concepts. I asked him why anyone writing such a book would put that picture on the cover. Louis agreed it was a poor choice because the book was not about common, unwild animals like squirrels. We decided a lion or elephant would have been better.

As we went through the introduction and table of contents, I questioned him continually, asking such questions as, What do you think will be discussed in this part? Why? Why not? while throwing in near-correct possibilities, even funny and wrong possibilities to make sure the child knows that what he says is so and why it is so.

After we discussed the table of contents, made some brief comments about the author, and looked at the back where there was no index or glossary, we checked out the two or three animals he had read about. Louis named some zoo animals he knows as we previewed the book.

After I put the word "Introduction" on the board and Louis double-checked my spelling, I broke it into syllables, saying each as I separated it. He followed me and said it in parts. Then I wrote *lion* on the board in syllables: *li/on*, telling him that it comes in parts just as the longer word *introduction* does, and many others do. He knew the parts are called syllables. What makes a syllable? He said that it needed a vowel. I added a vowel *sound*. I asked if he knew Spanish or his mother spoke it at home; no to both questions. I wanted to use it to show its phonetic qualities but there was no chance to do so. Then I put *ti/ger* on the board. He got it and showed me that there were two vowels and two vowel sounds; the latter was emphasized. Then we moved to the word *elephant*, which his tutor had apparently tried to present earlier. We broke it up: *el/e/phant*. He was uncertain about the *ph* but we reviewed his knowledge of consonant digraphs like *ph*, which do make a distinct, single sound. He got the point, and we moved along. When we encountered some other multisyllabic words, I put each one on the board or we just syllabicated from the text. He got the idea.

Then we moved to the table of contents. He had difficulty with the word *ones*. We looked at *one* and then added the *s* and he saw it. The word *zoo* took us off the preview for a minute, but I pursued it to delve into his concepts and to evoke as much as I could from him about his knowledge and language. Louis is a shy 8-year-old. He seems so much older than he is because of his pale complexion and dark circles under his eyes. He seems uncertain with people so he holds back. I wanted to get him out in the open, talking and laughing, even as we worked on several skills at once: syllabication, auditory and visual discrimination, previewing. He misread "other" for "over," and I got him to self-correct easily. We took *over* apart and broke it into syllables; he hit it immediately as he did with other words in the text.

After the table of contents review and discussion of how it tells what is in the book, and where to find it, we talked about the animal book Charlene made. He was interested in making one, too, about zoo animals. We talked about which animals he would include and which ones he would not. He decided we would not include cats, dogs, and squirrels. I asked if he had gone to the circus and he had not, so I briefly told him about some of the zoo animals there and what they did.

Then we discussed how he would write his book, how he would organize it so that it would look like the book we were reading and previewing. I asked him what the most important things are about zoo animals. He said they are hunted down. Then I asked when they would attack us. When they are scared or hungry. We talked more about wildness and what it means and how it differs from not wild. He went to the board to write the plan of the book. He decided to call it Wild Animals. He spelled it right, but had some trouble with the word *animals*. He struggled, but finally got it right. Then he wrote: *This book is about wild animals.* He seemed unsure of the word *about*, so I asked him how many syllables or parts it has? He said one. We tried again, he missed again, so I told him. Then I asked him what he will tell about these wild animals. He says they have sharp teeth. He then writes it as a sentence like the one in the book's introduction. *Some of these animals are:* He writes this correctly after some effort and assistance. For example, he wrote *af* for *of*, but self-corrected. He named *lions*, *tigers*, and *elephants* as some of the animals he would include in his book. We went over each of these and syllabicated it and then put each in a simple sentence which he wrote on the board. I mentioned something about commas, since he does not seem to know how to use them or why. Then after this work, I asked if there was any other wild animal he wanted to add to his book. He says yes, he wanted to add *bison*. We described it as a cow with big horns, and we divided the word into syllables. He wrote:

> This book is about wild animals. Some of the animals are lions,
> tigers, zebras, elephants and gorillas.

We discussed his title and I asked if I wanted to know about kangaroos would I read his book. He said no, and I asked why not? He said it is not in the book and it is not the same kind of wild animal as the others. Then we talked about putting his name as author on the book. We talked about the table of contents he has read in the real book and what his will have in it and why. Next I wrote; he told me what goes in it. Chapter I. He helped spell it. Lions. Then we include the things we listed: wild, food, dangerous, etc. We would have a picture of lion and tell all about him. Then we skimmed over the others the same way.

We would keep his book in the clinic. We always keep copies of their books; it pleases us and it certainly pleases them.

In both cases, Charlene and Louis, we can see how to build up a core concept about animals, utilizing a language-experience approach to elicit the language and ideas from them and to direct their future reading. When they start writing these books, they will know what they are going to write about: which animals and what important things about them. They also know, as does the tutor, that each story will contain a sentence for each trait listed: what they eat, their size, etc. This is such a simple guide for readers of all ages who are struggling or who are functionally or totally illiterate. They know exactly what they are doing and what they are going to do. The thinking is directed and limited to each animal and each trait, lesson by lesson. Choosing words with necessary phonic and structural elements is easy and because they don't come from an isolated list, they have meaning and feeling from the story. Students of all ages seem to enjoy working this way at the outset and you can easily find stories with the words containing the critical phonic and structural elements from which you want to make generalizations. Comprehension and interpretation are done right along with the story reading, writing, and talking; and basic study skills such as classification, sequence, previewing, main ideas, and details are easily woven into the work done in reading and then turned over into guides for good writing.

More suggestions

Obviously it is not so difficult in a 40 to 50 minute session to build in word recognition skills, in this case mainly structural analysis, study skills, comprehension and interpretation, and vocabulary and writing, but all of these can be checked in each lesson and some specific skill within each area can be presented or reviewed. With Louis it was clear that he had done some previewing before, so a brief review of it was quickly done; then we moved into main ideas and details in a few of the short stories about each zoo animal. Later in the lesson those skills, if learned well, will become a guide to writing a good paragraph. That is, once Louis can pick out several main ideas and note how the details relate to it and once he can justify each, we can ask him to take a main idea and write three or four (no more at the outset) details relating to that main idea. In that way we generalize those study skills and make them tangible guides for writing nonfictional material. We do the same with outlining and especially summarizing. All the while we can check his word recognition skills, especially syllabication.

It is easy in this kind of planning to check comprehension and interpretation for each story about each animal, and it is easy to work in synonyms and antonyms, perhaps even some prefixes, suffixes, and roots in the words arising from the stories. Then we have integrated the essential word recognition, meanings, and study skills, plus writing and vocabulary into the content—core concept of zoo animals or whatever. This was the process used in working through all of the core concepts discussed in Chapter 5.

You must go through the materials you intend to use, noting which phonic and structural elements will appear in the words in the material. Do they give the student ample opportunity to practice what he knows about the elements and generalizations? Is the material at the level at which the student can read with some confidence (instructional level)? Is the vocabulary and language usage real and not too literary, not too technical? How does the content and the language in the material fit into your plan and the student's knowledge, weaknesses, strengths, and interests? All of these factors must be considered simultaneously, or the lesson will go askew.

Word recognition skills

In teaching word recognition skills, use as many words from the reading matter as possible. Let's say the student is having difficulties with words ending in silent *e*. I'll take one, two, or three words from whatever is being read and written, for example, hate, lute, bite. Plan for this or be ready to get into this activity spontaneously if needed. I put these on the board or pad:

```
hat --------------------------------------------------- hate
cut ---------------------------------------------------cute
bit--------------------------------------------------- bite
dot ---------------------------------------------------dote
```

Then I ask the student to read each list vertically, then horizontally. Depending on responses, I might ask him to read the pair *hat* and *hate*, and tell what is different in the way it looks and the way it sounds (auditory and visual discrimination). Most kids will say *hate* has a long *a* sound and *hat* has a short *a* sound. As long as the student hears and sees the similarities and differences and can pronounce them correctly, you can tell him one is short $\breve{a}$ and one is long $\bar{a}$. Then have the student check out each pair of words and tell sentence by sentence what he can about them, e.g., they are all one syllable words; the *e* is silent in the second column, since we do not say hat-$\bar{e}$; and finally with some discussion you will come up with: *in one syllable words ending in a silent e, the first vowel is long*. Depending on the student's skill and confidence, ask for more pairs, or offer a few yourself. Also ask for exceptions. What we have is a very simple, commonsense process for making our own rules. Now they don't work any better than the printed rules we saw earlier in this chapter, but the student is being sensitized to note common and uncommon elements in words and to try to figure out how things relate and that is critical. In essence, *we are helping the student understand the concept of rules, or patterns*.

As we encounter the less regular words and elements such as in *ough* or *ea* words, we laugh about them and work on making them sight words since they will not fit into any pattern. Your careful reading of materials to be used will help you work out well in advance several activities for developing such rules inductively. In the area of word recognition it is especially important for you to try out your reading material and all activities and questions before you do them, so that you will get a better feel for what kinds of responses you'll get or problems your students might encounter. Thus, you can have other plans, activities, and exercises ready for emergency and not have to force one approach onto the student.

Word Recognition Games

My biases about games for teaching or even practicing any reading skills have been mentioned but I feel the need to talk a little more about them since they are often used in teaching word recognition skills. I don't like them because they deal primarily with phonic or structural elements, or words in isolation, and because so many of them require skills not mastered by the student. Certainly the games describe which skills are being practiced, but they often leave out other factors also operating.

Games are for winning

Games of all kinds whether they be for instructional purposes or for "fun" like Monopoly, are usually very competitive and hence anxiety-producing. Some anxiety of certain types in certain circumstances can assist the learning process, but we know that anxiety can also (and very often does) debilitate the learner and hence hinder learning and recall. In addition to this aspect of games, the key for students is that they must win; *games are for winning*, especially in a learning situation since the stated objective of learning games is *to practice skills supposedly known by the player*. If you must use games for your own reasons or needs, be sure the student can win the game because he has the knowledge, skills, and desire to win it. Poor readers usually feel dumb, incompetent, and frustrated by what they cannot do, and they perceive themselves as persons who fail. Another failing experience, no matter how nicely dressed, is still failure—that black pit of agony and embarrassment.

Do not use a game to introduce a new skill or concept. Use it, if you must, to practice or reinforce known skills and concepts. If you have ever tried the New York Times crossword puzzles, you may have experienced frustration with your lack of knowledge of esoteric and rare words, ideas, or facts required to do them correctly. Your student feels that way about many games and for the same reasons. The game can be fun only if the student can win it without too much effort. However, it cannot be a pushover or the student will probably spot your motives and your low estimate of his skill and knowledge. *The game has to be worth winning.*

The key as always in all teaching is, What must the student know (skills, knowledge, concepts, etc.) in order to play it and win? Before you play a game with any student, play it yourself and observe very carefully and specifically whether the directions are clear, whether the skills needed to win are in this student's repertoire, and whether the other knowledge needed to win is in his background. With little effort, we can give students a variety of practices and activities that will enhance their ability to apply skills and knowledge already learned and mastered which do not involve games at all.

Sample word recognition game

Since I had not seen this particular game before, I went through it before writing this so that I could detect what is required at all levels. The game is called "Full House," one of a group of phonics games from the series called *Phonics We Use Learning Games Kit* (Lyons and Carnahan, 1968). Let us see what the game makers think this game will do and how they think it will be accomplished.

Directions:
Game Equipment: 8 large cards, each with 10 picture squares and 2 Free spaces. Picture squares also show symbols for the vowel or vowel combination sound contained in each picture name. 80 small picture squares (cover cards). Picture name in print contains vowel or vowel combinations that correspond with symbols on large cards. 16 Free cards (cover cards).
Players: 4 to 8

How to Play:
1. One large card is given to each player.
2. Have dealer shuffle the cover cards and deal five to each player.
3. Place remaining cover cards in stack, face down, in center of table, with one card turned face up and set apart to start the discards.
4. Player to the left of dealer begins turn by drawing one cover card from face-down center pile.
5. Player matches any card he now holds with picture names on his large card in *both sound and symbol*. (On cover cards whose picture names have more than one syllable, the syllable containing vowel combination to be matched is underscored.)

6. Any *Free Cards* received in the deal must be played on the Free Spaces in the first turn. Any that cannot be used must be discarded.
7. Player places any matching cover cards on large card in appropriate places, stating each play, as for example, "I play *pail* on *snail*."
8. Player then draws from face-up discards any cover cards he is able to play, each time stating the play. (Player may draw one or more discards only if he is able to play them.)

There are 6 more directions, but they do not affect the object of the game; only its procedures.

Obviously one skill that could be claimed (the game makers do not) is following directions, probably oral directions. That's alright. It is one way to do it, even though it is a bit confusing, particularly for younger students (third or fourth grade and below, and for older students who read below fourth grade level). Notice that the game makers added the caveat that the teacher should be sure the players can at least *recognize* (that's all they require) the elements the game emphasizes: *vowels, vowel digraphs,* and *diphthongs.* If the students can recognize these difficult and variable phonic elements in terms of what you have been teaching, why move away from your content for this unrelated practice? This game has nothing to do with the information, ideas, and concepts you should have been teaching. It is isolated practice.

In the section of the directions on how to play the game some serious confusion could arise, especially in relation to the point of the game which is stated in item 5. See Exhibit 6–1 for an illustration of some of the game cards. Some of the pictures on the cards could cause students problems in identification alone. For example, a student could say *shade* in response to the picture of the awning; or *fingers* for hand or rib of meat. Whether the student can identify the drawings as intended by the game depends very much on the student's knowledge and background. The pictures on some of the other cards are even more confusing. Age and maturity play a major role in this kind of game; the child's experience with some of these objects and their own particular way of naming them plays a part in their response to the items. This game, and others, in no way accounts for Black dialect, or for bilingual or culturally different students.

Notice the randomly chosen smaller cards in Exhibit 6–1. These are the cover cards. The first one has a confusing picture of what must be an oyster (not very widely known among students, especially those in land-locked states). Under the picture is the word oysters. The *oy* combination (vowel blend or diphthong) is underscored. According to the rules of this game, the student should take this cover card, oyster, say the word, and place it over the picture of the boy's head under which appears the dipthong *oy*. Presumably the student is doing both auditory and visual dis-

Exhibit 6-1

FULL HOUSE

ĕ	FREE SPACE	ee	**2**
ow	aw	FREE SPACE	
oy	ī	ei	
ă	ĭ	ea	

breakfast

oysters

field

spray

crimination as part of his decision to put the cover card on that picture. That's another way to reinforce auditory and visual discrimination, although I don't think it is the best way since it is so disjunctive: what have boy and oyster in common? Only the *oy* in the word, and in one word it is in the beginning and in the other it is at the end. Notice, the next cover card showing a glass, piece of toast and jelly(?), fork, knife, and spoon, and a plate with eggs and bacon (not too clear) on it. Under it the word <u>break</u>fast.

Break is usually pronounced *breck*, not *break*(ē) or short *e* as if no *a* were there. Now I can decide whether to put this little card on the picture of the rib roast of *meat*, because *ea* is in the word *meat*, but it is not pronounced the way it is in *break*fast. The rule for the game says you must place the small cover card over the picture on the large card which matches in terms of *both sound and symbol*. Well, the breakfast card does have a similar symbol, *ea* as meat does, but the sound is different. Most students would be tempted to place the *breakfast* card on the *meat* card because of visual similarity. It could be confusing.

The next card has a picture of an aerosol spray can, but it is not perfectly clear. One must find on the large card a word and picture that look and sound like the *ay* in *spray*. There are none. Discard. Another small cover card (not illustrated here) has a picture of a towel and the word towel under it, with the *ow* underscored. This card is to be placed over the picture of the clown on the big card.

Notice the next card showing, unclearly, what looks like corn or something green growing in rows. This is a confusing picture: one could respond with *field*, *corn*, or *plant*. Now one looks for a word on the large card with some vowel or vowel combination that sounds and looks like the *ie* in *field*. Two possibilities: the wheel picture with *ee* under it since it is equivalent to the *ē* sound in field, or if one were a bit confused, the *ei* in receiver (the picture of which, on the large card, could be confused with telephone). According to game rules neither is right and this field card should be discarded. But you can see some of the ambiguity and confusion which might be engendered by this card. Actually, it would confuse players since it deals with variations of sounds represented by different spelling patterns. Unless a student were solidly in control of his phonics skills, I would not subject him to such ambiguities and variations in the early stages of the learning of these phonic elements. And still none of it makes any particular sense. It's like filling in blanks except that there is no attempt at meaning in this game at all. In fill-ins at least there is minimal context, a sentence, as a guide. We should question what the student knows if he gets the right answer and wins.

Cautions on the use of games

It should be clear that there are some serious concerns about using any game, especially for word recognition activity: problems with pictures and the ambiguities they can stir up in the player's head; the isolation of letters or sounds; some distortions in pronunciation; and the basic senselessness of the game except to fill up a card. Perhaps the best general rule for games is not to use them with corrective or remedial readers since they would be most likely to fall prey to any ambiguities either in the pictures or the sound equivalents, or spelling patterns. I have played a few games with some young students with minimal word recognition problems and encountered several of these problems. We just changed the rules to clarify what was needed, otherwise the students were confused as to what was intended and why such variations of vowel sounds did not match spelling patterns.

Obviously, the teacher must make sure that her students know all of these vowels and vowel combinations before they play the game. *And clearly the game, even played well, assures no wider application of these vowel identification skills.* Unless this game were followed up with contextual readings utilizing other words with these elements, the game would be a dead-end activity. Also the confusion still remains with sound/symbol variations as indicated. And are these words on the game cards, small and large, chosen to be more generative in the sense that many other common words will be recognized because of the knowledge of these isolated elements? Maybe. But since no meaning is involved in this game, or any of them that I can see, the likelihood of getting the widest range of application to unfamiliar words seems limited.

I don't like such artificial and contrived means for getting students involved, interested, or motivated to learn, because when those props are removed most students fall back into boredom and lack of interest. If we are involved in the art of teaching reading and its joys and skills, then let's do that as directly as possible; let us not use gimmicks and external motivations of such limited applicability. Poor readers know (and so do the others) that reading is not a game; that it is very important to them in school whether they like it or not, and that you can't fool them into believing it's fun with ambiguous and isolated "game" activities. To learn the word recognition (or other) skills in reading, read; to learn how to write, write. Reading is done in books, magazines, or papers, in connected text—not on cards or in boxes.

Let us make the reading and writing more interesting, stimulating, exciting, humorous, and beautiful, and most of the word recognition problems can be handled meaningfully and contextually as in our language-experience, core concept illustrations. Then the reason for reading and for figuring out the sounds of letters and combinations, syllables, etc., is obvious. Bettleheim says:

> If the stories we use in teaching our children to read do not reflect purpose . . . if they do not give the child immediate pleasure, and add meaning to his life by opening up new perspec-

tives—if, in short, these stories fail to provide the child with deep satisfactions—then they also unintentionally belittle reading itself.

We want them all to want to read and to understand. Games help accentuate the mechanical aspects of reading and that is not good for any reader. The beauty of the language, metaphors, similes, unusual vocabulary, or a good turn of phrase will not emerge from these isolated activities. Tie all word recognition skills activities into the core concept you are working with, since therein lies a source of motivation and pure desire to learn something which is both interesting and which makes sense to you as learner.

Vocabulary

Another aspect of word recognition skills is vocabulary development. Various authors place vocabulary skills and development in different places in their own charts of reading skills; I put it here from the standpoint of its structural aspects. Clearly, vocabulary is significant in all other aspects of reading (meanings and study skills) but I place it here after the decoding skills since I shall offer an approach which best fits here for first step vocabulary development.

Developing speaking, listening, reading, and writing vocabularies is, like concept development, a life long activity for most of us. We add to, subtract from, and shape our particular vocabularies in keeping with our special life and language experiences. Vocabularies serve several purposes for all of us: educational, social, political, and literary. All of us have several vocabularies at our disposal: several speaking vocabularies and several writing vocabularies, and usually our reading vocabulary is larger than our writing vocabulary, and our listening vocabularies may be the largest of all. We never use all the words we know or have heard.

In the normal course of a day you may speak and listen to your mother, siblings, friends, teachers, employers, strangers, in short, persons of various ages and educational and social backgrounds. Your language then reflects your and their relative position to each other and to the larger context within which you deal with each other. These factors shape your language usage. Most of us speak with our parents in a particular manner, utilizing particular words and phrases derived from the special history you share with them; your language with friends certainly differs if in no other way than in ratio of vulgarity and slang as compared with that used with your parents; the language you use for teachers or professors will differ from both these modes, and your language usage will differ from all of those in the context of your job, and definitely in your relations with your lover, wife, etc. All this adds up to is that we adjust our vocabularies, the syntax, the conceptual loading (or un-loading) of our communication. These language adjustments are made on the basis of our concepts of particular persons, groups, situations—in short, the context we find ourselves in.

In any language communication act (as we implied in Chapter 1) several contexts operate simultaneously, and numerous factors are influencing all communication, written or spoken—not to mention how we listen to what is said, or what we think is said. The filtering of all language communication, in all of its modes, is as natural for us as breathing in and out, and as diagnosticians and teachers we have to become especially sensitive to these contexts of communication. Each message we transmit has content, it is formed by phonology and syntax, and colored by semantics; it is also affected by the statistical properties of the language and our shared experiences. If I try to tell you about a personal experience which is totally out of your realm of experience, no matter how effectively I use the words, you will not have the same experience. Even if we went to the same event together, we would obviously come away with somewhat different impressions, reactions, and ways of describing what we experienced—and it would be different not only from the standpoint of the vocabulary. In every communicative act we call up vocabulary with its multilevel meanings and referents; we call up people, places, times, feelings, and attitudes.

This whole area of vocabulary is not attended to enough in most diagnostic or instructional programs. Typically vocabulary development is limited to getting meaning or sometimes several meanings of selected words, usually so-called "hard" words (whatever they are). In teaching vocabulary skills most authors offer two key suggestions:

1. Use of context to figure out the meaning of a word or phrase in that particular context;
2. Use of the dictionary (which really does not help much with varied word usage).

Some authors agree with these limited steps in vocabulary development but add at least one other dimension. Simply, we try to teach students a stock of generative roots (or stems) and some common prefixes. A fairly good list of prefixes, roots, and suffixes will be found in *Concerning Words* by J. E. Norwood. It is good for higher level students who want to polish and expand an already well developed vocabulary.

Earlier I alluded to this structural approach, so I'll just add a little more here. In whatever reading or writing your student is doing in his core concept, pull out some words (or put them in if necessary) which contain generative roots like: path, cred, mort, pend, anim, apt, ept, gen, genit, graph, mut, mutat, vert, vers, thermo, voc, sequ, etc. Pull out words with these roots and show the students the *meaning of that word in that context*, and then seek some derivatives from other reading matter, the dictionary, and from either or all of the listening and speaking vocabularies, thus generating a dozen examples for each root. We note that the root is spelled the same in almost every derivative and that it has the same (or almost the same) meaning in all of them. We then pull out prefixes adding some like a, an, ab, ag, ambi, ante, circum, de, dis, en, ex, hyper, in, inter, mono, non, peri, pre, un, etc. (See the Brown list). Then we note how they have changed the meaning of the root, and substitute several prefixes with the root to note how many shades of meaning we can get, i.e., transpose, impose, depose, oppose, transcend, transport, transduce, transient, etc. One shifts the prefixes attached to key roots, and one can then keep prefix steady and move the root. The same can be done with suffixes although their functions are different. They are grammatical cues, e.g., the suffix typically tells (1) Number: singular or plural; (2) Tense: past, present, or future; (3) Part of speech: adjective, adverb, verb, etc. Rarely do suffixes change the meaning of the root.

The students look at words from their reading, writing, and speaking and identify key roots, look at the prefix and get the general meaning of the word; then they add the context in which it appears to sharpen the meaning or shade the meaning. In Chapter 8 we will look at the more literary uses of words, since a vocabulary can be relatively small in number of different words, but it can be very large in terms of the varied meanings those words can call up in particular contexts. Both Hemingway and Frost used fairly small vocabularies to carry so many meanings, feelings, images; Shakespeare, Faulkner, Durrell, and Cheever use many different words, but in all cases numerous meanings and feelings are transmitted.

This simple procedure for helping students increase their vocabularies by learning a stock of key, generative roots and a stock of common prefixes works very well especially if the words are taken from the context they are studying (to add another dimension of meaning) and if they are required to use the newly formed words in all of their vocabularies (reading, speaking, listening, and writing).

The dictionary is really *not* a key source for real vocabulary development; it is a place for base line definition, synonyms and antonyms, pronunciation, part of speech, and etymology.

Unless you use the OED (Oxford English Dictionary) you will not find the specific uses of words and their histories you look up, so you are left with a handful of definitions and uncertainty as to how to use them "correctly." The worst thing students can do is to get a word in the dictionary and take a meaning from it (whichever is most appealing) and then stick that word into a variety of contexts. Development of vocabulary requires several things at once: seeing the word in context; trying to figure the meaning from what is there; then if that does not work, syllabicating the word to further check if it is in his listening vocabulary. If that fails, the student digs for recognizable roots and prefixes; if that works, the combined meanings of root and prefix are put back into this context to see if the meaning can be shaped more to its place; if it does not work, if the root is not known or the prefix is not known, the student resorts to the dictionary (and hopefully he has been taught how to pick the most likely meaning listed).

In dealing with unfamiliar words in reading, first we try to figure out vowel and consonants singly and in combinations in order to say them; then we group these phonic elements into syllables in order to say them correctly, which could clue us to the meaning and use; if that fails we then go after the roots and affixes. These skills, including the general use of context, assist us in dealing with unfamiliar words. In teaching these word skills do *not* teach syllabication and roots and affixes at the same time, because much confusion will result. The prefixes need not be single syllables any more than roots or suffixes are. So, do syllabication first to get the pronunciation; and only after students can handle syllabication well, introduce the affixes and root skills and activities. Later, when both syllabication and roots and affixes are learned and widely applied by the reader, then he can alternate them as needed in specific words.

Anyway back to some of my favorite words: you can play with them, for your own sense of how you do this: *squeg, steatopygous, hermeneutics, recursive, archetype, zetetic, scission.* The problem with lists of unusual and interesting words like these, no matter what they may be, is that they remain lifeless until embedded in a particular context which feeds them and colors them. But just for fun, you should play with many kinds of words; building and rebuilding them with affixes or placing them in novel contexts, which is the true key to a good vocabulary. That's why there's poetry and novels. For great vocabularies, I recommend Steiner, McLuhan, Lawrence Durrell, and James Joyce. Other dimensions of vocabulary in Chapter 8 (Interpretation) will be covered where we will see the effect of shifting contexts as a fundamental means of altering and shading meanings of words. Using common words with apparently common meanings in novel, unexpected (statistically) contexts alters meaning on several levels simultaneously and provokes in the reader or listener a whole host of related feelings, thoughts, ideas, facts, and concepts. That is the heart of imagery.

Spelling

This may be one of the most difficult of all skills to teach or engender in students. It seems that students who do not spell well by fourth grade have a life-long problem improving their skills significantly. We are not sure why. We are not sure why some people spell so well and some so poorly irrespective of intelligence, sensitivity, etc.

A colleague and I once conducted an experiment with spelling, and it was discouraging. I was teaching a group of about twelve 17–20 year-old poor readers. My friend was teaching a similar group comparable in intelligence, educational backgrounds, socio-economic backgrounds, and problems in reading and writing. My students were taught everything possible to improve their spelling; the control group were presented no spelling skills. We ran this experiment for 6 weeks. The results were that both groups performed about the same at the end of the period. Some of my students improved, but not significantly. What I did was to reinforce syllabication skills and where necessary I upgraded phonic skills (this proved to make things worse). Then we did work on affixes and roots both for vocabulary development and for spelling. Words which usually caused them and others problems were practiced, e.g., words ending in *ible* or *able* and *ence* or *ance*. Also they noted which parts of words were causing them trouble and which words or parts of words they had trouble deciding whether to pronounce as *a* or *e* or *i*. Some of them wrote some words ten or twenty times each. They looked at a word, closed their eyes, and tried to write what they saw in their heads. We had spelling bees (which they loved for some reason). We related reading, writing, and listening activities. We tried dictations of words in and out of context. They read a great deal and noted special words; they wrote a great deal every day and self-corrected each other's papers. In short, we did everything conceivable to develop and practice skills which would help them spell better. For the most part the results were the same as my friend's group—not much improvement.

I know what *not* to do in spelling and maybe that's as helpful as what to do. Don't memorize word lists; don't emphasize phonics (since that is how many of the problems were generated in the first place); don't over-emphasize writing the words many times each. I had little success, very little, getting a few of them to begin to visualize words spoken or read. That is, they could almost see the word spoken or written in their head and then could write it correctly. None of these students incidentally had visual or aural problems.

Try several of these activities as contextually as possible; give the student more responsibility for making the comparisons with the printed form and their version. Try to increase their ability to visualize words since most good spellers seem to do that. If all of the things I have just suggested and described don't work, keep at it, but don't blame yourself or the student. It is not clear at all why some cannot spell, especially after fourth grade.

Summary of Teaching Word Recognition Skills

In many ways this growth area is the most basic and as such has probably attracted the most attention from teachers and specialists. It is easy to argue that if students do not learn their word recognition skills they will not be able to read anything. Unfortunately the need for these skills has been overemphasized in many reading programs, and teachers of beginning readers of all ages have felt the pressure to master this group of skills more than any other group of skills. By so doing, there has been a tendency to teach the letters and combinations in isolation through drill and rote memory using workbooks, flash cards, and other devices. This causes the student to try to sound out every letter, which leads to distortions and frustration for many of them.

I have urged you to teach these skills, like all other skills, in context so that meaning is in the forefront. I have urged you to keep the teaching of the language at this level natural and normal and not distorted. Furthermore, if you keep language at all levels in context and meaningful it means that you are also using the student's life and language experiences as the guide to your instruction and not some arbitrary scope and sequence chart or basal reader program.

Using student interests and experiences and remembering that all of the reading skills in word recognition, meanings, and study skills are interrelated and interdependent will improve your results immediately.

Teach all skills inductively as much as possible so that the students must discover what it is that makes a word sound a certain way in a particular context. When students can formulate their own rules or principles, they understand them and remember them much better than if they merely memorize them out of context. Embedding the word recognition skills in a language-experience, core concept plan will make them more interesting and will enliven all of your instruction.

There are adult illiterates with whom I have worked who can't pronounce most of the words they encounter in print and yet, pronouncing perhaps 40 or 50% somewhat correctly, they understand quite fully what is being said and what it means. No one is quite sure why this happens except to say that the more mature people have had a great deal of life and language experience—they have concepts. They see television, and hear conversations about subjects and they use this information to make the most of the few clues they get from printed matter. To a lesser extent children can also use contexts to aid in deciphering specific words.

Here is a summary of some practical general principles for teaching word recognition skills:

1. Use the discovery, inductive approach to presenting most word recognition elements.

2. Teach word recognition skills in an interesting context (as in the language experience, core concept manner mentioned in Chapter 5).

3. Do *not* teach rules (Clymer's study (1963) explains why that is unreliable); invent them.

4. No isolated activities or exercises; let all applications of learned skills be in context and include not only reading the new words, but writing them and talking about the material in which they are included.

5. When a student becomes confused and frustrated by trying to apply a discovered, induced principle and finds exceptions to it, take the time to explain something of the nature of English (as in Chapter 1), so that he can feel as if he is not the cause of failure, but that language is part of the problem for all of us.

6. Play with words and the language so that the student hears many different words in several different contexts, and enjoys puns or humorous twists; also work with imagery and metaphor. Use some of Bill Martin's work.

7. Don't give definitions of words or ideas; probe them together with the kind of questioning illustrated in Chapter 2; each answer generates more questions. *Get to concepts*.

8. Don't teach too many elements (phonic or structural) in any one lesson; make sure the student has some concept for any generalization about phonics or structural elements he develops, e.g., a concept of consonant blends—not just their names.

TEACHING ESL/ESD

ESL means English as a Second language and ESD means English as a Second Dialect. Although bilingual/bicultural programs have recently come to the forefront superseding many ESL programs in the past decade or so, ESL/ESD is still taught. After some discussion of ESL/ESD teaching principles, problems, and practices, we can look at some underlying concepts of bilingual/bicultural programs. There is some confusion in these fields, and as reading specialists, special needs teachers, or classroom teachers it is essential that we try to clear it up.

All of these program emphases seem to have grown out of the poverty programs and the concomitant educational legislation of the mid-sixties. Additionally, as urban school districts underwent court-ordered desegregation orders, the need to accommodate the special language needs of non-English speaking and nonstandard English speakers became critical. Actually, it was not too long ago that Mexican-American school children were forced to sit in classes conducted entirely in English and were even forbidden to speak their native language in the playground or anywhere in the school. Also, as the Black movement gained momentum and impinged upon the national consciousness, it became evident that the Black English dialect required attention and response.

Approaches to Teaching ESL/ESD

Several approaches to teaching ESL/ESD exist, including a structural/grammatical approach, a saturation approach, a linguistic approach, and the Audio-Lingual Method (ALM) approach, or a combination of some of these. In the bibliography at the end of this chapter you will find a current and fairly representative sample of various viewpoints and approaches. Here we shall confine ourselves to a brief summary of the types so that we can have some basis for choosing which may best serve us and our students.

The structural / grammatical approach

This approach was common in the teaching of English to all of us and in the teaching of foreign languages to many of us. The approach had its heyday in the 1930s, 1940s, and early 1950s. The structural/grammatical approach emphasizes grammar, rules, sentence patterning, and conjugating verbs and other structural elements. Learning to read and translate from Spanish to English and back again are common exercises. Minimal activity in normal, natural dialogues and conversations occurred in this approach.

The linguistic approach

Technically there is no specific linguistic approach to ESL/ESD any more than there is such an approach in teaching reading to native speakers, but we tend to refer to that approach emphasizing linguistic principles as linguistic. Fries (1945, p. 9), a leading authority in linguistics, helped to the lay the foundation for this approach to teaching ESL when he said "The most effective materials are those that are based upon a scientific description of the language to be learned, carefully compared with a parallel description of the native language of the learner." A more recent proponent of this linguistic approach, which compares two languages in terms of their sound systems, grammatical structures, vocabulary systems, and writing systems, is Lado (1957). He agreed with Fries and has developed his own tests and instructional materials to implement this comparative approach to teaching ESL. Some have applied these concepts to teaching ESD as well. At least two recent reading texts have included considerable material for teaching ESL/ESD and bilingual students (Lapp and Flood, 1978 and Harris and Sipay, 1979).

This type of comparative linguistic information is both interesting and informative, but I have not found it to be especially helpful in practical teaching situations. There is a tendency to overemphasize these linguistic facts.

The ALM approach

To a large extent the Audio-Lingual Method supplanted the structural/grammatical approach to teaching ESL and even foreign languages to English-speaking students. This approach seems to be alive and fairly well even today. It emphasizes dialogues and conversational use of the language to be learned, and de-emphasizes heavy doses of grammar and syntax. It also places reading and writing in a secondary position. This approach is rooted in more modern concepts of normal language acquisition, which underscore the primacy of spoken and heard language.

One of the problems encountered with this oral-aural approach is that many students did learn to speak and understand the language being taught but were often engaged in relatively dull dialogues in order to practice minimal vocabulary and general sentence patterning. Also, many students did not learn to read and write the language very well and were thus deprived of significant dimensions of knowing and enjoying the language in depth.

The saturation approach

In this approach to ESL, students are totally immersed in the new language almost all of the time. Berlitz schools of language tend to use this approach since many of their clients just want to be able to survive in a foreign land. They want to know how to ask for directions, order meals, find the bathroom, and the like. The stated strength of this approach is that it presumably prevents the learner from engaging in constant translations from the new language to his own language. It supposedly forces the learner to begin to think in the new language. But its weaknesses derive from just some of these advantages. Such students do not learn how to read and write the language and learn relatively little about the structure of the language they are mouthing. A fair amount of imitation, drill, and repetition are required in such an approach, and since the goals are often very limited, the results are also limited. During World War II many Army language schools apparently used this approach with some success.

Using only this approach for classroom or clinical work is too narrow in its focus. Language is cultural and biological; therefore the teacher should not be limited to any one approach. It is too much like exercising your biceps until they become enormous and out of proportion and function with the rest of your body. Again, balance is needed in this endeavor as in all others.

Clearly, because none of these or other approaches to ESL or ESD teaching is comprehensive enough to achieve all of the desired goals in language learning, many practitioners combine some of these approaches to meet the needs of their students.

Chapter 5 presented several specific examples which dealt directly and in detail with the problems of teaching ESL to non-English speakers, many of whom were illiterate in both English and Spanish. The best of these examples was the "Rainy Day" program, which applied all of the principles and practices offered in this book. A quick review of some of these principles as applied to teaching ESL/ESD is in order.

General Principles of Teaching ESL/ESD

1. Develop and expand speaking/listening vocabularies first.
2. All conversations, dialogues, introductions, and naming activities are contextualized and directly related to the lives, experiences, and needs of the students.

3. Shortly after a speaking/listening vocabulary has been developed, a language-experience story can be dictated, read, written, and re-read by each student.
4. These stories should contain *generative* words, phrases, and ideas so that learning them provides a solid base for generalizations in word recognition and meaning.
5. Cultural values, beliefs, and sensitivities must be kept in the forefront of all discussions, planning, teaching, and expectations.
6. Concrete objects and tangible, live situations provide a context within which most of the talking, listening, reading, and writing occurs.
7. These dialogues, conversations, and discussions can easily be focused, like a mini-core concept plan, on categories of things, feelings, activities, for example, time, places, health, jobs, family, food, holidays, and so on. This would intelligently limit the range of vocabulary, sentence structures, phonic and structural analysis, elements, and concepts which need to be taught and learned.

Summary

Each approach to teaching ESL/ESD has weaknesses and strengths that the teacher has to weigh before he commits himself and his students to one of them. A combination of approaches is probably required, and which approaches you will combine depends on your diagnostic data and knowledge of your own students and the world they inhabit socially, intellectually, emotionally, and culturally.

The language-experience approach embedded in a core concept offers a great deal to these approaches since it can easily draw from any one or any combination functionally. There is always a clear-cut, well-defined context in which to teach meaningful vocabulary, sentence structures, and the necessary reading and writing skills. This approach, as has been said so often before, integrates all dimensions of language learning and usage in sensible and pertinent settings.

The reading and related language skills are the same for all students of any language, that is, they all have to learn word recognition, meanings, study skills, vocabulary, and writing. The principles and most of the practices can follow many of the same paths successfully. The essentiality of limiting the range of language used without becoming dull and boring must be recognized. To avoid the dullness of repetition and practices, one must focus on some emotional and significant content, and that has been the message of this entire work.

BILINGUAL PROGRAMS

There exists a close relationship between ESL/ESD types of instruction and bilingual programs. (I refer you to the bibliography for sources which devote much more time and space to these issues than we can afford here.) Some bilingual programs operate on the basis of teaching the regular school curriculum in the morning in the native tongue of the students, and teaching the same content in English in the afternoon. This is the *least effective* means of achieving true bilingualism for several reasons. First, the curriculum may be a collection of content fragments, which is difficult enough for native speakers. Second, repeating the same collection of bits and pieces of information only encourages translation from the native tongue to English and back again. Most authorities agree this is not desirable. There is simply no way to ensure perfect translations from one language to another in any circumstance. Integrating curricular content would certainly reduce the negative and dulling effects of this type of repetition, but it might not do the whole job.

What then is the alternative to the split-day curriculum? Transition groups for bilingual/bicultural students seem to offer some positive hope. Also, using foreign language students as teachers or tutors of native speakers is promising. Obviously, core concept plans for integrating content would also reduce the vast amount of apparently different information to be learned.

Transition groups work well when the diagnosis of language skills is made with an IDA, and when groupings are built *homogeneously* on the basis of these findings. In the transition groups, students' skills in English would be bolstered to the point at which they could more easily fit into ongoing classes. The value of relatively small, homogeneous groups for intensive upgrading of language skills in the least possible time has been alluded to in the numerous illustrations in Chapter 5, particularly in the examples of the Mexican-American, Indian, and laboratory school projects. Our clinical experience also attests to the value of such an approach. The bulk of the school day would be spent in these small, homogeneous groups utilizing a **language-experience approach** (especially for the beginners) and a core concept curriculum. The remainder of the school day would be spent by these ESL or bilingual students in *heterogeneous* groupings for physical education, art, music, and the like. The saturation approach with modifications incorporating the ALM emphasis on conversation would be my suggestion.

Using foreign language speakers as tutors or teachers of their language and culture to those who wish to learn it, would have all of the positive benefits of any peer tutoring program. This type of mini-course or enrichment program would serve to uphold and enhance the self-image of the non-English speaker, and it would sensitize the native English speaker to another language system and its culture. Mutual respect might be the most conspicuous achievement of such a program, rather than its language learning, and that is a most worthy goal for any school. If a class were doing a core concept on language or communication or some aspect of cultural study, it would be an ideal setting for such language exchanges within a context of general interest and need. Students as well as the curriculum would be integrated in such a manner.

Bicultural Concepts

As to bicultural education, the problems may be more similar to those discussed above than one might think at first glance. Teaching students about other cultures as well as their own is an excellent curricular goal. But too often cultural study and exchanges are limited to teaching a short unit (a week or two) on the Greek culture, the Spanish culture, the Black culture, etc. This is a minimal conception of bicultural or multicultural education. Such practices are often afterthoughts, appendages tacked on to a fragmented curriculum. Bicultural, or *multicultural concerns should be woven into the fabric of the entire curriculum*. Information about various cultures must become an integral part of all curriculum in all schools, for without it the polyglot American culture is diminished and misunderstood.

If one were doing a core concept on migration, for example, it would not be difficult to incorporate information on the contributions of all of America's immigrants in perspective. The history, politics, economics, religions, and art of the numerous cultures which have made America are easily included in such core concept plans. Nothing as important as bicultural/multicultural influences on our lives and society should be tacked onto the curriculum as if they were somehow secondary.

ESD

Many of the problems related to ESD have been discussed especially in Chapter 1. What is not clear from the literature and from empirical evidence of practitioners, is the nature of the differences between ESL and ESD. Do people speaking and hearing Black English, for example, differ greatly from those whose ears and mouths are tuned to the frequency and sound patterns of another language? If so, to what degree? How are the differences to be assessed? What is similar about ESL and ESD? Research in this area would be most welcome.

In both ESL and ESD we find cultural differences playing a significant role in the language acquisition and usage. Along with these differences we find such specific variations as altered perceptions, altered expectations and variant value systems. The language forms to express these differences are idiosyncratic just as the cultures which produce them are, so that the Frenchman does not hear certain sound combinations as we do, nor can he produce certain sounds as we do. If you try to speak German you may have great difficulty making the guttural sounds in it, just as you will probably have some difficulty producing the r in Spanish.

Speakers of Black English do not make certain sounds we expect in standard English, and they make some sounds not normally made by standard English speakers. If we overemphasize the differences in pronunciation and syntax, we lose sight of the fact that ESD speakers do understand standard English speakers and vice versa. However, many problems do arise in reading and particularly in writing for ESD speakers as it does for many foreign language speakers, since they often try to write as they speak.

One solution applied with apparently limited success has been writing instructional materials in Black English as a transitional step toward standard English material. This strikes me very much the same way that using the i.t.a (initial teaching alphabet) did when it first appeared. In both instances we force students to learn another code, another layer of language, in order to cope with standard English. Such an approach is subject to the same problems raised by any form of translation from one language system to another. It adds another layer of learning which the student must discard in favor of the standard forms. Why burden such learners with another code when they are already experiencing difficulties with these verbal skills? Why reinforce the nonstandard forms when you will not accept them as valid for school and professional use?

Students in American schools need to learn how to speak, hear, read, and write something we call standard English, so let's teach it directly. Disguising the language and adding unnecessary sugar-coated steps fools no one and tends to complicate an already difficult problem. Teach standard English in your classroom or clinic and if your older students speaking Black English, or any other dialect, question this, tell them they can be bidialectical or bilingual if they wish, but economic, political, and social success requires standard English. Such students will speak their dialect at home and with their friends as do ESL and bilingual students. We cannot prevent that; but we can point out the advantages of being bidialectical and bilingual. It need not be an either/or situation, but in school, and in those situations requiring standard English, they should feel comfortable using it. They can have the best of both worlds, which is more than many of us have being monolingual and monodialectical.

In your classroom or clinical setting speak in complete, correct English and insist that everyone else do the same. You can use standard English without being supercilious. If you point out some of the problems with using a language or a dialect not widely known and used (such as reducing their ability to communicate their thoughts, feelings, and ideas) it may help. Also some of the information contained in chapter 1 on language, variants, and statistical properties of language may help you explain some of the problems educationally rather than politically.

Many ESD students have difficulty discriminating spoken sounds of standard English or difficulty in speaking them. One useful practice for such students would involve you, the student, a tape recorder, and a list of difficult words or phrases. The student has the list in his hand and you recite into the tape recorder the first word or phrase on the list. You let the tape run blank for a few seconds after you read the first word. Then you read the second word and again pause a few seconds. You continue this alternation until you have completed reading the list. Then the student turns the tape on and hears you pronounce the word or phrase while he reads the word, and then in the blank space he reads his version of the word or phrase just heard. This process continues until the list is completed so that you have on tape your reading of the word and the student's reading of the same word. The student compares and contrasts what you have said and what he has said, while observing each word in print. This helps many students improve both auditory and visual discrimination as well as more standard pronunciation. It is not enough, but it is a start. If this is combined with the usage of standard English in every classroom, and if the students can be convinced that they are not losing a language, but rather gaining one, success is much more likely. Obviously, it would be very helpful if parents, particularly of younger students, could be enlisted in this effort and could improve their own usage while helping their children do the same.

In sum, ESL/ESD teaching shares many common problems and solutions. No single approach to ESL can claim preeminence but carefully selected combinations that incorporate some language-experience and core concept planning and teaching seem to offer the best solution to many of the problems discussed. In the matter of bicultural programs, it was suggested that they become multicultural programs imbedded in an integrated curriculum, rather than tacked on as another fragment. Illustrations in Chapter 5 were cited as specific examples of how to achieve these goals. Suggestions for making typical bilingual programs shorter in duration and more intensive in smaller, homogeneous transitional groups were presented as alternatives to some current practices.

Chapters 7–9 will offer other specific suggestions for teaching essential language skills which are also applicable to these problems.

REFERENCES

Bettleheim, Bruno. Learning to read: a primer for literacy. In *Harper's Magazine*, April 1978, p. 58.

Brown, James I. A master-word approach to vocabulary. In *Efficient reading* (Rev. ed.). Boston: D. C. Heath, 1962.

Clymer, Theodore. The utility of phonic generalizations in the primary grades. In *The Reading Teacher*, Jan. 1963, pp. 252–258.

cummings, e.e. "somewhere i have never travelled." In *A Selection of poems*. New York: Harcourt, Brace & World, 1965.

Dallman, Martha; Rouch, R. L.; Char, L. & De Boer, J. J. A sequence for phonics instruction. In *The teaching of reading* (5th ed.). New York: Holt, Rinehart & Winston, 1978.

Fries, Charles. *Teaching and learning English as a foreign language*. Ann Arbor: University of Michigan Press, 1945.

Full house. A game in Phonics we use—learning games kit, Text from *Manual*. Des Moines: Lyons & Carnahan, 1968.

Harris, Albert & Sipay, Edward. *How to increase reading ability* (6th ed.). New York: David McKay, 1975.

Harris, Albert & Sipay, Edward. *How to teach reading: a competency-based program*. New York: Longmans, 1979.

Lado, Robert. *Linguistics across cultures*. Ann Arbor: University of Michigan Press, 1957.

Lapp, Diane & Flood, James. *Teaching reading to every child*. New York: Macmillan, 1978.

Norwood, J. E. *Concerning words*. Englewood Cliffs, NJ: Prentice-Hall, 1960.

Thomas, Dylan. Alterwise by owl-light. In *The collected works of Dylan Thomas*. Philadelphia: New Directions, 1953.

BIBLIOGRAPHY

Allen, Virginia. A second dialect is not a foreign language. In James Alatis (Ed.), *Monography series on languages and linguistics*. 20th Annual Roundtable: Linguistics and the teaching of standard English to speakers of other languages, No. 22, pp. 189–202. Washington, DC: Georgetown University Press, 1969.

Bond, Guy; Tinker, Miles; & Wasson, Barbara. *Reading difficulties: their diagnosis and correction* (4th ed.). Englewood Cliffs, NJ: Prentice-Hall, 1979.

Burns, Paul & Roe, Betty. *Reading activities for today's elementary schools*. Chicago: Rand McNally, 1979.

Chomsky, Noam. *Language and mind*. New York: Harcourt, Brace & World, 1968.

Dillard, J. E. *Black English: its history and usage in the U.S.* New York: Random House, 1972.

Dixson, Robert. *Everyday dialogues in English* (rev. ed.). New York: Regents, 1971.

Dixson, Robert. *Practical guide to the teaching of English* (rev. ed.). New York: Regents, 1975.

Ekwall, Eldon. *Diagnosis and remediation of the disabled reader*. Boston: Allyn and Bacon, 1976.

Finocchiaro, Mary. *English as a second language: from theory to practice*. New York: Regents, 1964.

Finocchiaro, Mary & Bonomo, Michael. *The foreign language learner*. New York: Regents, 1973.

Fox, Robert (Ed.). *Essays on teaching English as a second language and second dialect*. NCTE, 1973.

Hafner, Lawrence & Jolly, Hayden. *Patterns of teaching reading in the elementary school*. New York: Macmillan, 1972.

Harrison, Brian. *English as a second and foreign language*. English language Services, Edward Arnold Publishers, 1973.

Imhoof, Maurice (Guest Editor). View point: social and educational insights into teaching standard English to speakers of other dialects. In *School of Education Bulletin*, Indiana University, March, 1971.

Kozol, Jonathan. A new look at the literacy campaign in Cuba. In *Harvard Educational Review*, August 1978, pp. 341–377.

Ritchie, William (Ed.). *Second language acquisition research: issues and implications*. New York: Academic Press, 1978.

Russell, David & Karp, Etta. *Reading aids through the grades*. New York: Teachers College Bureau of Publications, 1938 & 1975.

Russell, David & Karp, Etta. *Writing aids through the grades*. New York: Teachers College Bureau of Publications, 1938 & 1978.

Schell, Leo M. *Fundamentals of decoding for teachers*. New York: Rand McNally, 1975.

Smith, Nila. *Reading instruction for today's children*. Englewood Cliffs, NJ: Prentice-Hall, 1963.

Smith, R. B.; Otto, W.; & Hansen, L. *The school reading program: a handbook for teachers, supervisors and specialists*. New York: Houghton, Mifflin, 1978.

Spache, Evelyn. *Reading activities for child involvement*. Boston: Allyn & Bacon, 1976.

Wright, Audrey. Initial techniques in teaching English as a second language. In Kenneth Croft (Ed.), *Readings on English as a second language*. Cambridge, MA: Winthrop, 1972, pp. 7–15.

ADDITIONAL SOURCES FOR ESL/ESD, BILINGUAL PROGRAMS FROM ERIC

Arnow, Beth, *Bilingual/ESL programs for migrant children*. University Park, New Mexico: New Mexico State University, ERIC Clearinghouse on Rural Education and Small Schools, March, 1977. 56 p. ED 134351.

Banks, James A. *Multiethnic education: practices and promises. Fastback 87*. Bloomington, Indiana: Phi Delta Kappa Educational Foundation, 1977. 35 pp. ED 139 700.

Hornburger, Jane M., et al. *Teaching multicultural children*. Boston, MA: Boston University, School of Education, 1977. 63 pp. ED 139 045.

National Council for the Social Studies, Washington, D.C. *Curriculum guidelines for multiethnic education: position statement*. 1976. 47 pp. ED 130 931.

Passow, Harry A. *Urban education: the new challenge*. April 6, 1977. 18 pp. ED 139 850.

Soles, Stanley. *James Monroe High School bilingual program, school year 1975–76*. Brooklyn, N.Y.: New York City Board of Education. Office of Educational Evaluation. 1976. 50 pp. ED 138 694.

Trueba, Henry T. et al. (Comps.). *Bilingual bicultural education for the Spanish speaking in the United States: a preliminary bibliography*. 1977. 174 pp. ED 141 449.

Winkeljohann, Rosemary (Comp.). *A selective bibliography of ERIC abstracts for the teacher of reading, 1966–1974; IV. Reading difficulties*. Urbana, Illinois: ERIC Clearinghouse on Reading and Communication Skills, September, 1976. 66 pp. ED 127 600.

Chapter seven

THE STUDY SKILLS AND HOW THEY WORK

Some of the most useful study skills include previewing, finding main ideas and details, outlining and summarizing, classifying, using guide words, detecting paragraph patterns (question-answer, cause and effect, sequence, and fact and opinion), and following directions. There are more, but these are the most common and most useful. They are all interdependent and interrelated and can be grouped according to their function. For example, study skills, generally, are used as tools by good readers to select the most important ideas in paragraphs, articles, and chapters in history, geography, the sciences—the *nonfictional* materials commonly used in schools. Finding the most important ideas requires some knowledge of the overall structure of textbook material—that is, social studies materials follow certain writing patterns that are not exactly like those in science books. In addition to a knowledge of overall patterns of writing in various subject areas, it is very useful to know how to find the information you need in an orderly fashion so that you will be more likely to remember it and understand what it means. One must learn the basic study skills in much the same way one must learn what certain tools are for; for example, using a hammer as a screw driver won't work, or if you try to find minor details in a math problem or in a novel, you will be frustrated. We look for minor details within the structure of a chapter with its headings and subheadings, as they control the content of each paragraph under each heading. There is a pattern, a plan, a structure that carries out the author's purposes of transmitting important information to the reader in some kind of orderly, meaningful way.

We can talk about groupings of these study skills in several ways,

Study skills

but I shall use the simplest form. Basically, the study skills should be taught to help the reader (at any level) *to know what he is looking for, how to find it, and what to do with it after he has found it.* The study skills offer a fairly systematic and logical way to collect, organize, and think about factual information in a history, geography, or other textbook. Used correctly, the study skills provide the reader with a clearcut guide, a road map, which leads him to the useful and important information in an organized way.

One of the most common problems students have at all levels is that they become intimidated by all the details and specific information like dates and names of people and places that are commonly found in history, geography, or science books. There is so much information in one chapter, and no obvious way to figure out what is most important or how the various pieces or details relate to each other or to the topic under discussion. Study skills give each reader a concrete and specific set of tools for finding out what the author said, locating and organizing the most important information in a sensible and orderly fashion, and giving serious thought to recalling and interpreting what was said and why the author said it.

Usually, work in the study skills is not done before fourth grade in most schools, and often they are not taught even then, or if they are, they are not taught as thoroughly and meaningfully as they need to be. High school and college students give evidence of their inability to get through their reading with efficiency and understanding. The high drop-out rate in high schools and the higher drop-out rate in colleges are due in part to failures directly related to the students' inability to read a great deal of material with any real sense of what he is looking for and how to organize it. Lack of knowledge of study skills explains a good deal of failure students experience on tests. One simply must have some kind of plan for reading as well as some purposes for reading particular material, and then one needs the tools and skills to get the important information quickly and accurately.

Previewing a Book

The first of the study skills we teach individually or in groups at all levels is *previewing*. On the surface it sounds insignificant and simple to do, but it must be taught, practiced, and applied correctly. Previewing means literally "to look before." Before you read any nonfictional material, newspaper, magazine article, chapter, or textbook you should preview it before you start any careful reading or take notes on the material. How do you preview a book?

1. Read and think about the title.
2. Check the author, publisher, and date.
3. Read the preface and introduction.
4. Read the table of contents.
5. Notice visual aids.
6. Skim the index and glossary.
7. Skim summaries.

Title of the book

The first previewing step is to look at the title of the book and think of what you may already know about the subject so that you are raising questions about what might appear in the book. If the title is *A Pocketbook History of the United States*, for example, several facts should come to your mind at once: (1) it is a brief, condensed history, not a complete and thorough study of U.S. history; (2) it apparently covers American history from the beginning—about 1600 to the present; (3) the book is probably divided into chapters according to periods of history which were most important to the author—such as chapters on wars, the revolution, depression, and so on. Even with a limited background in history, you would be able to think of a number of outstanding points in our history. All this just from reading the title, but it sets you up as a reader to begin to draw some borders around the material which might be included in a book with such a title. If the title of the book were *A Documentary History of the Civil War*, you could 1860 guess that the period covered is probably the years between 1860 or 1861 and 1865. The word documentary in the title tells you it is not a book of someone's opinion or his facts, but rather it includes actual documents: letters, treaties, and laws written at that time. It is firsthand material—not material someone is interpreting for you with his own biases and opinions.

If you should pick up the book entitled *Rise of the West: A History of the Human Community*, you know that it will not delve too deeply into any one society in history but will cover all of the civilizations from the beginning to the present in terms of human problems and solutions. It will not emphasize science and technology, but will probably focus on the more human problems in society and institutions, political and religious. A book entitled *The History of Technology* would look at scientific and technological developments more than the human, social, political, or religious problems and relations of men. Naturally, there is overlap, but the author chooses his title to cover the subject about which he is writing for several reasons, mainly its ability to summarize the main idea of his work. He does not just flip a coin for a title. He means something by it— it is a clue, and a good reader uses every clue he can find.

Author and publisher and date

After you have read and thought about the title, you move to the title page and copyright page to see who wrote the book, when it was written, and who published it. The latter is not nearly as important as it once was, since most publishers maintain fairly high standards and are fairly ethical. Of course, some publishers favor certain kinds of ideas and subjects and will search out manuscripts on those subjects expressing their own ideas and beliefs, so the publisher could be important. Just as newspapers and magazines represent some editorial viewpoint, so do some book publishers. Some will not publish books on certain subjects or by certain writers who express ideas which they may not approve of. But most publishers seem to be fairly open-minded in terms of publishing books representing several viewpoints. The *Chicago Tribune* and *New York Daily News* certainly do not believe and publish the same things about a given event, as would the *Des Moines Register* or the *Christian Science Monitor*. So it is worth some time, depending on your purpose and need, to know something about the publisher.

The publication date can be very important, especially in science areas. Since so much happens so rapidly in medicine, genetics, space flight, conquest of diseases, etc. it is necessary to have books that are as up to date as possible. A science book a year or two old (add at least a year to the date for the process of editing the manuscript and publishing it) could be quite inaccurate or at least incomplete. In 1967 most medical books certainly did not have much to say about heart transplants, for example. At the end of 1968 about 100 heart transplants had been done. Certainly the findings of those transplant operations need to be included in any complete, up-to-date study of the problem. The date of a history book can be important, too. If your purpose in reading a certain book is to get first-hand information, written at the time (e.g., the Depression), then you definitely want a book written during the period itself (1929-1939). A more recent book would have to add some biases and judgments about the period and why it happened, which you might not want for your purposes. If you want to know what it was like coming over on the Mayflower, or to be on Iwo Jima in World War II, or in Vietnam, then find the book written in the period by someone who was there, or who uses first-hand documents. If, however, your purpose is to get an overview of a period, and you want a perspective on the material, then read something written recently.

Checking the author out is also of value, once again depending on your purpose for reading this particular book. Authors are people and they have certain ideas, beliefs, and views about the world. They cannot help but include some of their thoughts, feelings, and biases in what they write, whatever the subject might be. A good reader wants to know this before reading the whole book, chapter, or article. A good reader wants to be able to separate fact from opinion so that he can get the information he wants. Of course you might be reading a book just to find out what the author's bias is.

A good example of this relates to Charles Beard, the well-known American historian who wrote many books used all over the country in the public schools. It is a fact that Mr. Beard was a supporter of Franklin D. Roosevelt and the New Deal for several years until 1940. Then Mr. Beard broke with FDR and turned against the New Deal policies. Well, that certainly had to (and did) affect his coverage of certain material and facts in that period of history. If an author does not approve of a person or his programs and policies, you can be sure it will come out in the author's writing. It will affect what facts he includes and leaves out. This is very important to know if you are reading a book critically. If you don't know about these things, then you are much more likely to believe what is in print and to be persuaded by it. You might also pick up a lot of inaccurate information.

A good reader knows when he is picking up facts that can be verified, and when he is picking up someone's opinion or bias. You must know this or you will be misled and misinformed; if you are, then you will not be able to make the most intelligent choices for yourself. You can see that everyone needs to learn such skills for the full development of one's intelligence and perception.

Have you noticed how a simple act like these first steps in previewing a book or chapter or article can open up many other doors into closely related reading areas? Just reading a title, and checking the author, date, and publisher get the good reader set for discriminating, selective reading. It lays the foundation for the meanings skills, particularly interpretational and critical reading. That's the way it should be done, but rarely is in the schools. Reading is so much more than merely learning how to pronounce words and run one's eyes down the page.

Let's see where we've been in previewing: we've read and thought about the title of the book (article, or chapter); we've checked the author's background (who he is, what he knows about the subject, what his biases are); and we've noted the date of publication and the publisher. Now we need to get more deeply into it.

Preface and introduction

What is a preface and an introduction? A preface is, simply, something presented before the regular text of the book. It is important to read the preface over quickly because it usually does several things for the author and for the observant, alert reader:

1. Tells why the author wrote the book.
2. Tells for whom he has written it—professionals, laymen, etc.
3. Tells what the special handling is of the subject in his book, as opposed to all the other books that may have been written on the same subject.

The introduction, often appearing right after the preface, is also very important to preview; it gives a brief of what is contained in the book—the general topics to be covered.

The author often gives himself away in his preface or introduction. He tells his bias or his view of the subject about which he is writing. This is good. The author should have some special reason for writing any book, and the reader should know this reason and use it as a guide when he reads the material. Here is an example of a preface from a science book (*A Field Guide to Rocks and Minerals* by Frederick H. Pough).

> This Field Guide differs from the others in the Field Guide series in two important respects: Its subject is inanimate, and it can be used anywhere in the world . . . In the preparation of this book an attempt has been made to simplify the identification of minerals for the collector and to give as much information as possible to help the beginner form the habit of observing and testing . . . the book is not intended as a textbook of mineralogy. It is perhaps the failure of the professional to think in terms of blowpiping, together with a lack of initiative among the amateurs, that has reduced the chemical testing and identification of minerals to a secondary status. Some suggestions for new tests will be found in the testing section of the mineral descriptions . . . Since this is a practical work, intended to be of the greatest possible value to the amateur, the writer will appreciate additional observations on tests and mineral occurrences . . .

I chose this preface because it is probably not familiar to most of us. What do we know about this book from these few excerpts from a very long preface?

1. The book is for beginners, so it is not highly technical and beyond their reach and understanding.

2. It is not a textbook of mineralogy he says, but a field guide—a practical book you take with you when you are digging around outdoors.
3. He thinks it very important for beginners in this field to learn and practice the habit of careful observation and testing.
4. He seems to be angry with some of the professionals for being so limited in their outlook on ways to test minerals quickly and efficiently. He has a solution and it is included in his work.

I wouldn't read this book if I were a professional mineralogist, or if I were interested in learning to polish rocks. I would read it and look carefully for his new ways of testing minerals if I wanted to go on field trips. Notice that we do get in this preface an overview of the purpose for which the book is written, the author's bias, the way the subject is covered, why this book is different from others, and for whom it is useful. You could save lots of time reading the preface or introduction to books. You would discover whether it had what you wanted or not or whether it was written for people with your interest and background.

Table of contents

After you read and think about the preface or introduction, the next step in previewing a book is to look at and think about the table of contents—which is really the author's outline or road map for his book. The table of contents usually tells which topics the author has chosen to talk about, since he considers them most important. He divides his book into chapters and each chapter deals with one of these important topics.

We have said that one of the key purposes of using study skills in reading various types of nonfictional material—textbooks especially—is to be able to locate quickly and accurately the most important information. All that we have spoken about in previewing so far does just that for you. If the author divides his book into chapters on the basis of what he considers to be the most important, then as a reader you must try to follow his thinking. When an author, in his table of contents, spells out the subjects of key topics of each chapter he is saying that if you (as reader) want to understand this subject you must think about and have information on these topics. You may not agree with him, but that comes *later*. First, find out what he says, how he organizes it, what he emphasizes, and the other information about his biases and reasons for writing the book you picked up in the review. A lot of readers, at all levels, do not do this, do not follow these skills and the process we've been describing, and they end up with the same information and biases they started with.

Let's look at an example. The Table of Contents from the book *A Short History of the United States* by Alan Nevins and Henry Steele Commager will serve the purpose. Incidentally, this is an old version of the book that has since gone through some revisions and new editions. It therefore has been brought up to date (through the Eisenhower years) and some material has been changed, some added, and some taken out. This is sometimes useful information in itself.

Here is the Table of Contents in the 1945 version:

Contents
Preface

1. The Planting of the Colonies
2. The Colonial Heritage
3. The Conquest of New France and the Movement for Independence
4. The Revolution and Confederation
5. Making the Constitution
6. The Republic Finds Itself
7. The Rise of National Unity
8. Jacksonian Democracy Sweeps In
9. The West and Democracy
10. The Sectional Struggle
11. The Brother's War
12. The Emergence of Modern America
13. The Rise of Big Business
14. Labor and Immigration
15. The West Comes of Age
16. The Farmer and His Problems
17. The Age of Reform
18. The Rise to World Power
19. Woodrow Wilson and the World War
20. From War to War
21. The Second World War

That's all there is in this edition of the book. Many textbooks have much more complete and detailed tables of contents. This is simply a listing of the main topics of each chapter with no specifics under each one. Some tables of contents have complete outlines, with much detail about what will be discussed in each chapter. I chose this one because it is general. If you can get the meat out of this one, it should be quite easy to get it from more elaborate and thorough contents in other books.

First, let's look over the topics quickly to try to get a good general idea of what period of time is covered and some of the key topics to be discussed. Also, let's be thinking about what we know about each topic. First, we notice that this history book is not written in a straight chronological form, that is, the authors do not have a specific period of time in each chapter. The first chapter is not stated as 1600-1699 and the second chapter is not listed as 1700-1799, and so on. It is chronological in the sense that it starts with early events and comes up almost to the present, but the authors obviously want to emphasize something other than the periods of time—the dates. What are they emphasizing with this type of outline? Look closely at the chapter titles. They seem to have chosen what they consider to be the most important force or event of a period of time, such as The Planting of the Colonies, The Revolution, Rise of Big Business, Labor and Immigration. These titles suggest that the authors are focusing mainly on key social, political, and economic forces they consider critical to the growth and development of America as a great world power. They are not emphasizing heroes or battles in wars. Nor is this a strictly economic or religious history of America. It seems to be a study of the key movements and forces they think shaped us as we are. This means to the reader that he must be thinking about social institutions and conflicts, about major movements like labor, the effects of immigration and big business, about politics, and economics as well. This is quite different from a strictly chronological account of U.S. history, or a study of the culture of America which would emphasize the arts and religion and philosophy.

At a glance we can tell from this table of contents that the authors will cover roughly from 1620-1945 (in this edition). It is not hard to notice that the Planting of the Colonies is the first chapter and the Second World War is the last one. We bring to bear our previous knowledge to set the borders for the period of time covered. It gives us, as readers, the general limits so we do not waste time thinking about things and periods of time the authors are not concerned with.

If you look more closely at the specific chapter titles in this table of contents you can begin to think about what might be discussed. Chapter 8 is entitled *Jacksonian Democracy Sweeps In*. Maybe you know when Andrew Jackson was President, maybe not. Probably you have some idea that it was fairly early in the nineteenth century, about 1820 or so; that helps you to place it and relate it to other events in America and elsewhere at the same time. You actually make a context for it. Also, notice the word "Sweeps" in the title. That suggests something more than merely a president or presidential election. Why sweeps? Why not just Jackson is elected President, or the Jackson administration wins? Obviously these authors have some special feelings and facts and ideas about Jackson as a person and president and what he did. It does suggest that Jackson came steam-rolling in, that maybe he was different in many ways from previous presidents. Maybe he was tough and earthy, not so polished and refined. Well, in fact, that is all true. You *can* use what you know if you use this skill effectively. This is active reading and thinking, not passive.

The table of contents then gives several important pieces of information to the good reader:

1. The subject of the book.
2. Key and important topics to be discussed.
3. The structure of organization, e.g., chronological, political, cultural, dealing with institutions, or forces, etc.

4. The author's idea of the logical development of the subject.
5. Some biases or attitudes of the author.
6. Some specific facts or information about the way topics will be dealt with.

In short, looking at the table of contents is a very good, quick way to get an accurate overview of what is in the book and what you can expect to find there. Also, you get some idea, by the length of each chapter, how important the author may think it is. He wouldn't spend fifty pages on a chapter of no importance to him and only ten pages on one which was important.

Index

After looking over the table of contents, it is wise to glance at the index in the back of the book. The Index is in alphabetic order and includes specific subjects, persons, or events discussed somewhere in the book. It lists a man's name, for example, and gives page numbers on which you will find some mention of him. If there are many page numbers after any entry, you can be fairly sure that the author finds it important. If he lists an individual's name and gives numbers like this, 3-7, 19, 22-23, 57, 69-70, 111, 193, 245, I would guess the person is very important to this author. In addition to finding out how important a particular subject may be to the author, you will also find where to locate specifically some comments about one man or one event. A glance over the whole index gives you a more specific idea of what the book contains and discusses in a more detailed manner than does the table of contents.

Glossary

The glossary, if there is one (technical books frequently have glossaries), lists in alphabetical order unusual or difficult words or terms. It's like a dictionary. It can be helpful before you read to check over some of these technical or unusual terms. By looking at the glossary you get more of an idea of the content of the book and which terms are important—you don't have to guess. Reading them over quickly before you encounter them in the text could help you to read more smoothly than if you just run into these words without any preparation. It could seriously slow you down or cause unnecessary confusion. If the author puts up signs, as on a highway, use them. If he says "Stop" or "40 mph" or "Curve" or "Hill," watch it. He has a reason for using these various signs. A good reader, like a good driver, follows them carefully so as not to get lost or in trouble.

But most readers don't do these things—or, if they do, they are not too systematic about it. What a waste! A good preview really sets the reader up for getting the most important information quickly, with the fewest mistakes and missteps possible. It tunes you into the writer's frequency. It gives you a road map.

Visual aids

Included in the preview is looking quickly through the book at visual aids: charts, graphs, other illustrative material, and the table of maps or charts appearing in the front of many texts. Some books have summaries or questions at the end chapters—glance at them. All of this will add to your information about what is in the book and what seems most important, and gets you thinking about the subject.

Although it takes a long time to describe each step in previewing a book or chapter or article, it actually only takes a few minutes to do it when you have practiced and know how. You could preview the front page of your newspaper in less than one minute and come up with many facts, names, numbers, and key events of the day. All you have to do is use the skill of previewing.

The Chapter preview

As has been shown, the chapters in a textbook represent to the author, and therefore to the reader, key topics. These chapters are important in the sense that the writer, who knows a great deal about his subject, thinks that you need to know these topics in order to understand the whole subject. As in previewing a whole book, previewing a chapter in a book or an article, we want to get as much information as possible before we do our careful reading. We want to spot the author's key points, his organization, and some overall notion of what we are in for. We want to start thinking about his points, so that we may most effectively bring to bear what we already know about the topic. We want to question his chapter title, his headings, and subheadings. We want to try to understand the relationship between and among his headings, subheadings, and the topic of the whole chapter.

What do we do, step by step, to preview a chapter or an article?

1. Read and think about the title.
2. Read and think about the bold-face headings and subheadings.
3. Look over the visual aids: charts, graphs, other illustrations and think about them, use them as summaries.
4. Read the questions or summary at the end of the chapter.
5. As you do this, try to keep in mind the total context of the book—how the other chapters build up to this particular chapter, and what might follow in the next chapters. We also think about how this chapter develops his ideas. This particular chapter can be thought of as another segment of a total puzzle. Without it, the puzzle would be incomplete and unclear.

Let's look at a chapter from the book *A Cultural History of Education: Reassessing our Educational Traditions*, by R. Freeman Butts. Chapter 21 in this book is entitled:

America in the Twentieth Century (Title)
The Institutions Men Lived By (Sub-title)

Now let's sweep through the chapter picking out headings and sub-headings and immediately put them into some pattern or organization—essentially an outline form just as the author did when he wrote this material:

1. Domestic Political Trends
2. Reform Movements
3. Republican Normalcy
4. New Deal
5. International Relations
6. Contradictions in the American Economy
7. Social Trends
8. Intergroup Relations
9. Nationality Groups
10. Racial Groups

That is not the end of this chapter. The author switches to another broad heading for the remainder of the chapter. His new division of the material is entitled The Ideas Men Lived By. The author has made this a very long chapter in order to include as much as possible about America in the twentieth century. There is almost too much material, and perhaps you can think of some other ways of organizing all this information.

Let's work on the first heading listed above (Domestic Political Trends) in this mammoth chapter. Since previewing is the starting point for a whole series of closely related skills, we start an outline form while we preview. I have listed the headings given in this first half of the chapter. Look them over carefully. Can we condense the number of headings in some logical, reasonable way? If we are to take notes on this material, we don't want to copy everything down, and we do want the information in brief but understandable form.

For example, we might condense the first four headings into a broader heading and use the other headings as subpoints under it. We could easily use the first heading as the hook on which to hang the others:

I. Domestic Political Trends
   A. Reform Movements
   B. Republican Normalcy
   C. New Deal

These are all domestic political trends. In the careful reading, you would be looking for details, facts, and information to fill in the spaces left. But the main heading, Domestic Political Trends, logically connects the facts and information in the other headings. Apples and pears are not the same fruits, but they are fruits, so that if we use that broader heading, fruits, we could logically and sensibly include different kinds of fruit.

That is what we are suggesting in this stage of the preview. The rest of these subheadings pose a special problem, depending on how you think. Most of what is stated in these headings relates directly to American domestic events, conditions, and forces, but the author has a heading on International Relations, which I would leave separate. I would then have a separate heading on Contradictions in the American Economy, since it is not politics or social activity. The others I would group under Social Trends. My version, condensed, would look like this right after my preview of this portion of the chapter:

I. Domestic Political Trends
   A. Reform Movements
   B. Republican Normalcy
   C. New Deal
II. International Relations
III. Contradictions in the American Economy
IV. Social Trends
   A. Intergroup Relations
   B. Nationality Groups
   C. Racial Groups

Under each heading or subheading I leave space so that when I do the careful reading, it is already organized for me, and I will put in the major and minor details appropriate to each item. I have combined previewing with outlining or notetaking, and that makes sense since you cannot outline, summarize, or take any kind of notes on material you have not previewed and organized somewhat.

Another key purpose of these related skills of previewing and outlining is to direct the reader's reading and thinking. When reading history, geography, or science books many readers are confused by all the facts and information, and quickly lose interest in the material. If they could see clearly how the whole chapter or article or book was put together and why it is that way, and if they use the skills we are discussing, they will easily find their way through the morass of information.

We always work on several levels at once in good reading; the schools do not usually do enough of this. Often teachers downgrade students in work of this type, without ever going through it step by step, explaining and discovering with the child, just how books and chapters are put together, and how to take them apart systematically. Many students believe, as I did as a youngster, that somehow books were born that way. I had no real sense of order or planning or relationship. Like most others, I grabbed at what seemed obviously important and tried to remember it. Readers are entitled to a better deal than that. They do not have to guess their way through their textbooks; the skills we are discussing now will give each reader concrete tools for really understanding what's important and how parts relate to each other in the whole of a chapter, article, or book. There is no magic. These skills are easy to teach, because they are so concrete, and because they can be applied to so many types of reading material, every day.

Finding Main Ideas and Details

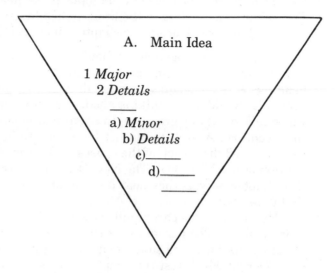

This familiar diagram illustrates quite simply that a paragraph, the basic unit of all nonfictional writing, is patterned as is the book or chapter. We go from a broad statement of topic or subject to the specific details and parts relating directly to it, and which further explain, clarify, or illustrate it. But one topic or one idea is developed at a time. In the chapters in most textbooks, at all levels, a conscious plan is evident. We see an idea or topic broken down into its parts; we get a sense of wholeness— of the relatedness of parts to a whole. When we previewed the chapter in *Cultural History of Education* we focused our attention on the headings, thought about them, then rearranged a few, while condensing some others in accord with what we understood to be a logical development of the author's ideas. Everything in that particular chapter related directly to the broad subject of the chapter: American Education in the Twentieth Century. Certainly that's broad enough to cover quite a wide range of information. When we thought about it, we rearranged parts so that we would not have so many individual pieces but rather we would have clusters of meaningful parts tied together.

When we break a chapter down we find headings and subheadings, which give more particular attention to the parts of the chapter topic. Under each heading or subheading, we find groups of paragraphs that are supposed to fill in the outline the headings represent. Each paragraph is supposed to deal with one idea only, and to contain some pertinent details to support, illustrate, and clarify that one idea. All the paragraphs in a given heading or subheading should relate to each other in developing the broad, general topic stated in it. Logical development would lead to this breakdown:

Groups of paragraphs discuss the topic of the heading or subheading;
The subheadings relate to the broader headings;
The headings break down the chapter title into subdivisions.

All parts hang together, or should. If the topic is American Education in the Twentieth Century, as it is in the text mentioned earlier, then the headings and subheadings should all relate to some important aspect of that. We should not be talking about the nineteenth century; nor should we be talking at any great length about European education in the twentieth century. Also, it would not be logical to have in such a chapter a very detailed discussion of the causes of the Depression, or the exact legislation of the New Deal. The New Deal or the Depression can appear in this chapter only as they bear directly on American Education, because that's the topic.

Now back to the paragraph, which is a basic unit in good reading and writing skills. The paragraph is the basement, the foundation on which headings are built and supported; the headings and subheadings are the first floor on which rest the chapter, the second floor.

A paragraph usually consists of several sentences relating to a particular idea or point. Somewhere in the paragraph is a key idea, the footing on which the rest of the paragraph rests. Also most of what appears in a paragraph is detail, facts. Look back at the diagram: We see a main idea which is fairly broad, general, and inclusive, then we see one or two major details usually restating or paraphrasing the main idea, and then minor details. Notice the details are all related to each other, that is, minor details relate to the major detail or details, and they all talk only about the main idea statement. If this is not true, you are reading a poorly written paragraph, or you are writing one.

In most textbook paragraphs, the main idea is stated in one sentence; in some it may not be stated in one sentence, but may be a combination of two sentences; in others (relatively few) the main idea is not really stated at all, it has to be inferred. So do not teach your students to read the first sentence of each paragraph or the first and last sentence to find the main idea. Frequently that is all right, but it cheats in the sense that the reader does not really know why that statement is or is not the main idea. It also deprives the student of the opportunity to understand how details relate to each other and to the main idea. There are no shortcuts to this kind of solid understanding. Remember what we have said again and again; all of these *study skills are useful because the student can follow clear-cut steps to breaking a chapter or a paragraph apart and getting at its essential meaning.* This is a critical step in the development of mastery over much that appears in textbooks. It provides a system for making sense of enormous amounts of information—a system that works and which the student controls. This is very important to his development.

How to find the main idea

To find the main idea and its related details in the paragraphs the student meets in various textbooks he must learn to ask two basic questions while reading each paragraph:

1. *Who* or *What* is the paragraph talking about? Who could be a person or a group. What could be an event, a force, a condition, a war, etc.
2. *What happens* to the who or what? What did the person do, or what was done to him? Was there a change? What action occurs?

These two questions are almost always answered in one sentence in well-written paragraphs in textbooks. Don't encourage guessing. The idea is there. For example, here's a paragraph from the book *Education for All* by William M. French (p. 310).

> Freedom for a teacher is a two-fold concern. The first aspect is freedom in his professional life and its related activities. This includes freedom to teach what and how one chooses, in the light of his knowledge, his professional conscience, and in the particular personality characteristics he may have. The second aspect is his freedom to lead his own private and civic life as a self-respecting member of the community without undue interference by persons who may hold different standards. Neither is an absolute freedom, for each is conditioned by the environment in which the teacher lives and moves and has his being. We shall first discuss the concept of the teacher's freedom in all his professional relationships, for this is of the greater importance to the advancement of ideas, and then we shall discuss the freedom of the teacher to lead a normal personal life.

The first sentence is the main idea. When you work with your students in this skill, be sure to accept anything they say as the main idea—then, make them prove it by going through the paragraph sentence by sentence, just as I shall do for you:

The key words in the first sentence are *freedom, teacher, two-fold.* Now, if this is really the main idea, the key point the author wants to make, then all the other sentences must relate directly to this; they must further explain, clarify, and illustrate it. If they do not, we're wrong. Let's list the other sentences:

1. The first aspect is freedom in his professional life and related activities.

This seems to be breaking down the two-fold statement made in the first sentence. If it is two-fold, what is number one and what is number two? Well, he says right off that number one has to do with the freedom of a teacher in his professional life, etc. That sentence talks about teacher, freedom, and one-fold of that freedom: In his professional life.

2.   This includes freedom to teach, etc.

This sentence just develops in more specific detail what was just stated in the sentence above. He is developing with details what he means by freedom in professional life and related activities. He lists in his third sentence these specifics: Teaching what and how one chooses; in the light of his professional conscience; and the particular personality characteristics he may have.

These three details all relate to the teacher's freedom in his professional life—that is, as a teacher—so that this sentence also supports the main idea, explains it further. The next sentence talks about the second aspect of a teacher's freedom, which is to lead his own private life, etc. This is a logical development. He started the paragraph by saying he was going to talk about the two-fold nature of teacher freedom. He has mentioned one aspect and given some details, and now he introduces the second aspect of a teacher's freedom. The next sentence points out that neither of the two freedoms, professional and personal, is absolute. This is a detail, which only qualifies the statements about the two-fold freedom of teachers. Then in the last sentence the author tells us how he plans to deal with these two freedoms in much greater detail in the remainder of this subheading, in this chapter. The chapter is entitled *Freedom and Responsibility*. The subheading from which the paragraph comes is entitled *Two Aspects of Freedom*.

So we have a very good example of a fairly well organized paragraph. The main idea gives us the context: Two-fold teacher freedom. Then all the other sentences divide this up into (a) professional freedom; (b) personal freedom. This paragraph is the first in the subheading and serves a key purpose for the author in setting us up for the remainder of the paragraphs in this subheading. We know, in other words, where we are going and what we can expect to find. We shall find much more detail on teacher's professional freedom, as well as some discussion of his personal freedom. The author could develop this several ways, but will probably include some history of teacher professional freedom and personal freedom. He could talk about problems which have arisen and how they were met—something about teacher organizations to protect these freedoms, perhaps the laws aimed in these directions.

Once we detect the writer's plan, we can quite accurately anticipate where he might go with his facts and information.

Let's outline that paragraph as another way to see how it was put together, and how the details relate to each other and to the main idea:

A. Freedom for a teacher is two-fold
    1. freedom in professional life
        (a) to teach what and how he chooses
        (b) in terms of his conscience and personality
    2. personal freedom for teachers
        (a) right to lead own private life
        (b) right to lead his own civic life as a member of his community
        (c) neither freedom is absolute

Depending on your purpose for outlining this material, this outline might do just fine; it shows the basic details as they support other statements quite clearly.

Back up a bit. Who or what was the paragraph talking about?

> *About teacher's freedom.*
> What about it?
> *It is a two-fold concern.*

Then, as we have shown, every other sentence in that paragraph talks directly about the two-fold concern; professional and personal.

Not all paragraphs in all textbooks are as neat and well organized, but the principle is the same whether it is in a third grade social studies book, or a sixth grade science book, or a college sociology text.

The next paragraph in this subheading from the same book (page 310) follows. The subheading under which the next paragraph comes is *Origins of Academic Freedom*.

> The freedom in relation to professional activities is commonly called "academic freedom." There is no more widely misunderstood or more controversial issue in education. It is the product of long centuries of effort. Like a table, academic freedom rests upon four legs. These legs are Socrates, Jesus Christ, the medieval university, and the German university of the nineteenth century.

Notice at once that the author is launching, as he promised, into a more detailed discussion of the two-fold freedom of teachers. The first is professional freedom in the name of academic freedom. What is the main idea of this paragraph? Once again the first sentence looks good. He merely defines what he means by professional freedom: Academic freedom is what we are talking about, but he does not say what happens to it in that sentence. That comes out in the other sentences. The next sentence is merely a major detail because it just restates the issue, it does not give details to explain it. He just says academic freedom is controversial but he doesn't say how or why or for whom. The following sentence points out that academic freedom has not always existed in education. It is a detail relating to the first sentence, but it still is not too specific. The next sentence in this paragraph merely adds that "it" (academic freedom) took a long time and much effort to get. Then he concludes with his statement about academic freedom resting on four legs. This is another introductory paragraph. But he does set us up, again, for what will follow. Obviously, what will follow is to show how Socrates had anything to do with teachers' academic freedom, then how Christ affected it, then the contribution of the medieval university, and finally the German university. It is clear, but he has given us two paragraphs which generally introduce us to something, and he does not develop them yet. However, in the following paragraphs he does, indeed, go into detail on each of these items: professional freedom of teachers; personal freedom of teachers.

Make sure in teaching this skill that your student can go back through any paragraph and prove to you why he has chosen the main idea and how the major and minor details are related to it.

Outlining and Summarizing

Outlining and summarizing are both ways of condensing important information briefly, systematically, and logically. Neither can be done correctly unless the student knows how to use previewing to its fullest extent, and also how to pick out main ideas and details in all kinds of paragraphs. Previewing gives us the overview of the structure and some of the content and its relative importance; finding main ideas and details pinpoints in each paragraph the key idea and the details related to it. Outlining and summarizing build on these skills to record selected information from a given textbook. An outline or a summary represents judgment as well as skill in locating certain information. When a child outlines a chapter in a history, geography, or science book, he uses all the skills we have just mentioned, and adds his own purpose for taking notes.

Basically the two techniques of outlining and summarizing differ in form. Outlining uses a rather formal structure, while summarizing is usually written in a narrative or paragraph form. What is contained in these means of highlighting key information and all the pertinent relationships within it can be identical. The purpose for making notes either way could also be the same. In essence, an outline is a summary; a summary is a condensation of material down to a bare minimum of needed facts, details, and information. Outlining can be helpful to most students when they are taking notes from which they will study for tests. Also the outline process, form and content and selection, requires some special thinking that can be most helpful for reviewing a body of content, and can also serve as a writing guide. Summarizing is useful in all kinds of subjects, particularly when one is writing essay type questions or dealing with literature or history. But the choice is available. What we need to get across to our students is the *process of selecting the most important information and organizing it for better retention and understanding.* Don't worry about the precision of the form of the outline, to the exclusion of the process of thinking about the material in a logical way.

We have already laid the basic foundation for outlining when we were working with main ideas and details. You may recall that after a student has previewed a given chapter or article, he has many kinds of information and an overall idea of the context. This gives him a head start toward understanding and remembering what he has read. The preview gives him a sense of the organization of the material in the chapter, just what he needs to do an adequate outline of his own. He does not need to plow through a plethora of specific facts without any sense of direction, purpose, or use of the information.

Outlining can be done in several ways, and the specific choice of ways is not as critical to the reader as the understanding of the relationships the outline marks with numbers and letters as a guide. The form looks like this:

I. Heading or subheading in the chapter
    A. Main idea of the pararagraph
        1. Major detail
            a. Minor detail explaining the major detail
            b. Same as a
                (1) A very specific detail related to the above minor detail
                (2) Same as (1)

    B. Main idea of the paragraph
        1. Major detail
            a. Minor detail
            b. Minor detail
            c. Minor detail

II. Next subheading in the chapter

This is a usable form, at least most of my students have found it so. Now, the question of how you fill in these divisions and subdivisions, depends on the student's knowledge of the subject and his purpose for these notes (studying for a test, for instance). With practice in making outlines, students usually end up using just a few key words for each division. At the beginning, it might be best to encourage the student to use a sentence type outline or at least a phrase outline. Do this until you are sure he really knows what he means by these statements. Notes are no good if you forget what you meant by your own abbreviations and condensations. Also encourage consistency. To illustrate what a good outline should look like, here is an outline of the growth areas in reading—topics covered in this and the previous chapter:

The Growth Areas in Reading: Outline

I. *Word Recognition*
  A. Readiness Skills
    1. Sight words
    2. Auditory and visual discrimination
    3. Picture and other Context clues
  B. Phonic Analysis
    1. Single consonants in the initial, final, and medial positions
    2. Single vowels (short then long sounds) in the initial, final and medial positions
    3. Blends (two letters, two sounds)
      (a) consonant - st, br, gr, dr, tr, bl, cl, gl, sl, etc.
      (b) vowel - oi, ai, ou, ew, au, etc.
    4. Digraphs (two letters, one sound or a new sound)
      (a) consonant - sh, wh, ch, th, ph, ng, etc.
      (b) vowel - ee, ie, ei, ea, ae, oo, etc.
    5. vowels followed by l, r and w producing neither a long nor short sound.
  C. Structural Analysis
    1. Compound Words - break fast, some thing, base ball, no where, etc.
    2. Syllabication - hop/ing, de/light/ ful, hap/py, etc.
    3. Affixes
      (a) prefixes - in, un, de, pre, im, a, anti, etc.
      (b) suffixes - ly, ic, ate, ed, ion, etc.
    4. Root words - path, ced, mort, anim, port, path, cred, etc.
  D. Using the dictionary as an aid in learning:
    1. syllabication
    2. etymology
    3. accent
    4. pronunciation
    5. common meanings
    6. synonyms and antonyms
II. Meanings
  A. Comprehension
    1. Literal recall *who, what, where, when, how many
      (a) facts, names, places, etc.
  B. Interpretation and Critical Reading
    1. Drawing conclusions
    2. Making inferences
    3. Making generalizations
    4. Detecting propaganda techniques
      (a) glad names

    (b) bad names
    (c) testimonial
    (d) transfer
    (e) plain folks
    (f) card stacking
    (g) bandwagon
  5. Interpreting imagery and figures of speech - simile, meta-phor, symbols
  6. Interpreting satire, allegory, etc.
III. Study Skills
  A. Previewing
  B. Finding Main ideas and Details
  C. Outlining and Summarizing
  D. Classification
  E. Using Guide Words
  F. Patterns
    1. Question - Answer
    2. Cause and Effect
    3. Sequence
    4. Fact-opinion
  G. Following Directions

A quick glance down each page of the outline gives the reader a good summary of the specific subjects discussed, and some of the important details relating to them. By using previous skills, the reader is thinking his way through the morass of information and is carefully *selecting* the meat of the chapter or article, and recording it in very useful forms.

Look at any one of the sections that has been outlined. The Roman numeral I indicates a major division of the material; it was used to mark the *heading* or subheading which is a broad topic within a chapter, and which has several paragraphs within it. The letter A. was used to mark the *main idea* of the paragraph, and the numeral 1. to represent major details. The small letters a., b., c., represent minor details and (1), (2), or (i), (ii) would represent very minute details.

This outline form is clear and direct. We could put the same information into a group of paragraphs in summary form. We could try to summarize the whole thing in a single paragraph, but that would not serve the same purposes for the reader, and wouldn't be as easy to use for locating the basic information. Look at this type of condensed summary of what was just outlined:

> Reading is divided into three growth areas: Word Recognition, Study Skills, and Meaning. Each area is subdivided into specific skills and subskills. Under word recognition we have two broad divisions: Phonic Analysis and Structural Analysis. Study Skills

include previewing, main ideas, details, outlining and summarizing, classification, sequence, etc. Meanings is divided into Comprehension skills and Interpretation skills. All of the skills in each area are interrelated, one to another, and to skills in other areas. Each area depends on the other areas for greater meaning and usefulness to the readers.

This is not a bad summary of the overall content but the reader would not have all the detail so neatly laid out as in the outline form. Use outlining or summarizing as it best fits the needs and purposes of the reader, and don't be too concerned about form. Outlining gives the reader a clear picture of the key information in its basic relationships; summarizing condenses a large body of information into a very short statement which covers mainly the broad outlines or highlights. Summaries do not usually contain a great deal of specific fact and detail. Use the outline for that. This means that for most note taking out of textbooks, at any level, outlining will probably serve the need best.

Classification Skills

To classify is to *group* various kinds of facts or other information according to a *particular system of relationships*. For example, we can classify persons, places, ideas, events and conditions in the following ways:

1. *Alphabetical* as in the telephone book, dictionary, or encyclopedia.
2. *Numerical* as books are classified by the Dewey Decimal system, or postal zones by zip codes, telephone area codes, social security numbers, house numbers (odd one side of the street, even on the other side).
3. By *subject* as seen in the Yellow Pages or a Sear's catalogue or a thesaurus.

In most instances there is considerable overlap of these groupings so that the Yellow pages, for example, lists services alphabetically under a particular subject classification. You might look under Auto Repair and find listed alphabetically all of the companies offering auto repairs. The Dewey Decimal System will place all philosophy and religion books in the category of 100-199. Each book on that subject, with that numbering will be placed on the shelf by the author's last name alphabetically. Some numerical systems are arbitrary, such as armed services service numbers. My own Navy serial number was 765242 only because the man in front of me was given 765241. Zip codes and telephone area code numbers fall into a pattern and indicate geographic location quite specifically.

The concept of classification is much more inclusive than these simple groupings we have just discussed. At the core of all classification and grouping is a sense of order, system, pattern, and above all else a special set of relationships. In developing core concept plans we noted how important and useful classification is for establishing the overall integrated plan of instruction. The skill calls for students to note similarities and differences in time and space; for comparing and contrasting sensory data, and for always seeking a common strand to tie together related events, persons, ideas, etc. Without the ability to classify or group information we would be unable to do any significant reasoning. At the center of thinking is the ability to note relationships of many types and on several levels simultaneously, and classification is an essential skill for doing this.

In this book I have classified, as have many other authors, the reading process into three broad categories:

I. Word Recognition
II. Meanings
III. Study Skills

Under each of these categories I have included subdivisions which are then divided into even smaller related parts. A glance at the outline of each growth area reveals to the reader or listener the system of thought and logic which produced it, and that makes it easier for the receiver to follow and to understand. If we classify holidays we can do it several ways, one of which would look like this:

I. Holidays
   A. Religious
      1. Christmas
      2. Easter
      3. Saints days
      4. Hanukah
   B. National
      1. Independence Day
      2. Memorial Day
      3. Armistice Day
      4. Washington's Birthday

Another way to categorize this last group, National holidays, is to call the first three *political* holidays since they are related to the interactions of governments in wars and revolutions. Washington's birthday could be part of another category including Martin Luther King, Jr.'s birthday, Lincoln's birthday, etc.

In pursuing this concept of holidays we could subdivide the first grouping of Religious holidays in terms of the West and the East, Africa, Asia, Scandinavia, etc. Specific religious holidays would be studied in terms of what they celebrate and why, and then one could compare and contrast the differences and similarities. Another way of dividing religious holidays would be to group them according to the major religious groups in the world, i.e., Buddhist, Christian, Jewish, Mohammedan, Taoist, and so on. Then the next step would be to further classify, under each of these groupings, types of Buddhists, types of Christians, types of Jews, and so on.

All of this dividing and subdividing in the process of classifying reveals the many relationships which exist, and places them into sensible groupings deriving from the concepts to which they are related.

Classification skills are useful throughout reading and writing instruction, as well as in curriculum planning and development. Students are easily introduced to these thought processes called classification through their texts in social sciences, science, mathematics—in short, everything they will ever read. All of the study skills are generic in that they are all applicable to all non-fictional material, but none is more generic and more generative than classification.

Using Guide Words

Another of the useful study skills is the ability to pick out and use guide words in one's reading material. Guide words do just that: they guide the reader to the author's development of ideas or to his conclusions, or signal the reader that there is a change of idea or direction in the writing. Used correctly, guide words are good highway signs or obvious clues to what's happening in the text. You have already learned some of them, perhaps without noticing. For example, when we speak of the cause and effect pattern, we use words like *as a result of*, or *because*, or *the effect* because these indicate a causal relationship, and this clues the alert reader to the pattern and gets him thinking and looking for the causes of a given effect.

Words like *and*, *or*, *more*, *moreover*, *in addition*, *also*, and *furthermore* normally suggest to the reader that what follows them is very much the same as what came before. However, words like *however*, *but*, *yet*, *still*, *on the contrary*, *on the other hand*, and *despite* usually suggest that the author is changing his original statement or clause, that he is changing the direction of this thought.

When you encounter words and phrases like *in summary*, *in conclusion*, and *finally* it is clear that they signal the reader to slow down and get the summary or the final conclusion or statement.

There are many other words, phrases, or grammatical devices that warn the reader, that signal him that something is happening to the line of thought being developed. Children and adults can become quite sensitive to some of these signals and clues, and it can indeed be helpful. Think of the tests you have taken, especially multiple choice and true-false, in which words like *never*, *always*, *generally*, *in all cases*, *every*, or *all* are used to trick the unwary student. This is not a highly intellectual skill, but it clearly can help an unsure reader avoid some obvious and not so obvious pitfalls. We need to take full advantage of every skill, every clue, every signal we can to assure the most accurate and intelligent reading.

In a sense, punctuation of all types serves as a guide to the author's meaning and intent. For example, the colon (:) precedes a series or list of items while a semicolon (;) separates clauses, and is usually a substitute for the word *and*. The exclamation point certainly indicates something being emphasized. Italicized words or phrases also indicate some special importance. The question mark (?) tells the alert reader that he must look for some answers to the questions being posed. Commas surrounding a group of words (a phrase) usually indicate something additionally explanatory or something tangential included within the commas. All of the punctuation can affect meanings and intent of the writer. If the words "What now my love?" were written with different punctuation, like this: "What, now, my love?" the meaning and intent of that sentence is altered. Instead of teaching children the definition, from a dry old textbook, of each type of punctuation, illustrate its effect on the meaning and intent of what is written. Let the child discover this. It can be humorous as well as serious.

Whenever I teach the skill of using guide words, I always include grammar and punctuation, and then return to the Meanings area, because interpretation is involved.

Obviously, we have not discussed all of the possible study skills. I have selected those I have found most useful and general in application in many subject areas and at all levels. We have not talked at all about specific reference skills such as those involved in using a dictionary or an encyclopedia. Nor have we talked at any length about how to use a library to locate information. Since most of these reference skills depend upon the skills already mentioned, I shall pass by them here.

Writing Patterns

Another cue to the reader or listener as to what is coming and how it is organized is the author's writing pattern.

Question-answer pattern

A very common pattern for writing is the question-answer pattern. The paragraph might start with the question or end with it. It might start with the answer and then pose the question to stimulate the reader to go on. But more often than not, the question appears first to make the reader curious as to what the answers might be. It's a good writing device to maintain interest and to vary the writing style. If all paragraphs were written in the same pattern, it would become dull, and communication would be most difficult.

Here is an example of a question that would introduce a paragraph written in a question-answer pattern:

How would you like to be frozen in your present state?

This question does not give all the information and leaves quite a bit of doubt. That's good, if your purpose in writing it is to arouse the reader's interest. After you read that, what comes to mind? How do they freeze you? What happens? Do you remain the same for a long period of time? Are there any dangers? If I were frozen how would it be when I was thawed out? How would my family be? The world? The question in the paragraph stimulates questions for the reader. The reader starts thinking about what the author might include in this paragraph or group of paragraphs: the temperature needed to freeze you; how long it could last; possible effects on you and your organs. Probably the author will answer these questions. You as a reader anticipate this. You are bringing your previous knowledge and experience to bear on his statement or question, and that is the heart of good reading.

Cause and effect pattern

Another common pattern is the cause and effect pattern we have already mentioned briefly. The author might state the effect first, and you, as reader would start thinking of possible causes, or the effect of given causes. Usually he gives the effect: The Great Depression represented a complete breakdown of the American economy. Then he must offer some of your own information from past reading and other experience, so that you stay right with him as you read. This is active reading.

Cause and effect relationships are commonly found in a great deal of science writing, and also quite often appear in history or sociology, and other social sciences. Not only is it a pattern of thinking about what one reads or hears, but it is a pattern of writing, just as classification and sequence are patterns of writing. As we have said before, all of these study skills are writing as well as reading skills. The good reader is aware of these patterns, and can spot them very quickly and thus finds it much easier to follow the author's thinking and conclusions. He can even anticipate the author if he is aware that a particular pattern, like cause and effect, is being used to arrange the information.

If you read "The Great Depression was the result of the complete breakdown in the economy" the good reader looks for a clue, a key word, some sign. He finds it in the word "result" which means the same as effect. Something made it happen. Those would be causes. So you are immediately alert to seeking specific causes for the breakdown of the economy.

Children can be sensitive to this very fundamental relationship—cause and effect—very early in their thinking careers. After all, cause and effect relationships are a form of logical thinking, drawing conclusions, and of discovering special relationships among events, people and conditions. Logic is a systematic and well-organized framework—content—within which reasoning, drawing conclusions, and even drawing inferences can occur.

In reading science and social science materials, the cause and effect pattern will appear frequently and should provoke thought about the exact relationship being expressed. When you hear or read something that says: *because, as a result of, the effect of,* etc., it should clue you in immediately to seek the effects or the causes, one, two, three and four.

Sequence pattern

This is a pattern frequently used for material that gives directions or traces some major event or development. For instance, recipe directions clearly consist of a sequence of steps to follow: First put in two tablespoons of flour, then mix salt and a beaten egg, stir until mixed completely, then put in melted butter, etc. If you do not follow this sequence of steps, you will not get what you wanted from the mixture. In a newspaper story, you can note sequence very often. Either it is chronological, in time, or it deals with spatial relationships: the storm is moving from the Rockies to the Mississippi Valley and into the Carolinas. It is a sequence, because weather moves, generally in a west to east direction. In novels and short stories, sequence is evident. Sequence is a relationship that very significantly alters what occurs—the result. One, two, three, four is a sequence; so is A, B, C, D; or a history of the world.

Science experiments employ a combination of sequence and following directions and cause and effect: *First get the test tube; place 3cm of gob in it; heat over the burner for three minutes; observe color change; cool for five minutes; and add H_2SO_4.* Stand back. Experiments must follow a very careful sequence or they go askew and could be dangerous.

Developing a sensitivity to sequence, following directions, and cause and effect is also useful in reading literature. After certain events have occurred in a story or play, you ask, what do you think he'll do next? Why? These questions force the reader or listener to use the skills just described.

Fact-opinion pattern

Another pattern, usually quite obvious to detect, is the fact-opinion pattern. An opinion is given and is followed by some facts to support it. Or the facts are given, and then the opinion is stated, which may be a more effective way of drawing the reader along with the author. To read material in this fact-opinion approach requires good critical reading and interpretation skills.

Newspaper, news magazine, television, and radio reporting frequently uses this pattern. Quite often it is not obvious whether the facts are really facts and can be verified by objective means; often facts are given as facts, but are not verifiable. Facts change, and people's views and attitudes toward facts often make them opinions. When we delve into critical reading, we will elaborate on this aspect of reading.

These are some of the common patterns in writing, and should be helpful to the reader at any level. Perceiving paragraph patterns are *reading, writing, and thinking skills*, as are the other basic study skills we have been discussing. The skills and the patterns of writing all serve as powerful magnets to the reader, in that they attract the information and emotion one encounters on the printed page. No more random haphazard groping through the pages of textbooks.

Following Directions

Directions for building a model, making a cake, sewing a dress, repairing the transmission in our cars, and programming a computer are given in sequential steps. These steps are important; things must be done at a given time and in a particular way. Many people of all ages have a great deal of difficulty reading and following directions. The reader must be trained to *look for sequence* or some other *classification scheme* as a guide, and even more important, to look for *key words*. In most directions, as in most language, nouns and verbs are key words. The noun names the object and the verb tells what it does. Adjectives are also useful in that they may qualify color or size. Adverbs must be watched because they tell how much to do or where or when, and that relates to the awareness of sequence. Many problems youngsters have in mathematics are caused by not following directions on homework or on tests; they often end up doing something not asked for, and being downgraded for it. The student may know the process or the information, but cannot get through the written material with any clear understanding of what he is to do. So he guesses. The skills just mentioned can reduce that significantly.

Summary

Obviously, we have not discussed all of the possible study skills. I have selected those which are most useful and general in applications in many subject areas and at all levels. We have not talked at all about specific reference skills such as those involved in using a dictionary or an encyclopedia. Nor have we talked at any length about how to use a library to find information. Since most of these reference skills depend on the skills already mentioned, I shall bypass them here.

HOW TO TEACH THE STUDY SKILLS

The basic study skills have been presented *as if* you were going to learn and apply them in your own reading. Now we need to incorporate methods for teaching the skills and ideas for application and reinforcement for your students.

Previewing

To teach a class how to preview a book, article, or chapter in a text-book I usually choose reading material from their own textbooks or the material on Immigration in *Read Your Way Up* (Howards, 1968), or material from Nila B. Smith's series called *Be a Better Reader* (books A, B, C, I-VI), or from *Tactics* by Olive Niles, et. al. Whatever the material you choose, start the lesson this way:

> "I'm going to show you how to get much more information faster and more accurately than you do now. Open *Read Your Way Up* to page 29. There is a short chapter from which I want you to get as much information as you can in one minute. Then I'll ask you lots of questions. OK? Begin."

The following material (pages 315-319) comes from Howards (1968, pp. 29-31).

IMMIGRATION

Introduction

Immigration means moving into a new country to live. It played a vital part in early American history. Without immigration our country would still belong to the Indians. In fact, everyone in the United States who is not pure Indian must have had some immigrant in the family at some time. Immigration has contributed many valuable customs, ideas, and traditions to the American way of life.

Reasons for Immigration

There are two basic reasons why a man and his family wanted to establish a home in a new country. First, some wanted to live free from persecution. Second, some were looking for a better chance to get ahead. A few people came to America for family or other reasons. But the main stream of immigrants came so that they could live free from the danger of persecution and could improve their living condition.

Persecution of minority groups has had a long and sad history in the world. Men have been persecuted because of their political beliefs, their racial ancestry, their religious beliefs, and even because they refused to persecute others. One of the main reasons for immigration to America in the early years of our history was religious persecution in Europe. Many people came to this country hoping to find freedom to worship as they pleased. Today the desire to escape religious persecution is no longer an important cause of immigration. But in many parts of the world persecution continues, sometimes for religious beliefs and sometimes for political or social views.

After 1800 the most important reason for immigrating to America was probably the desire for personal betterment. Two types of immigrants came for this reason. One was very poor, and the other was not. The poor had little hope for a decent living in Europe. The social and economic system there was rigid. The land had all been claimed, and it was difficult to buy. The skilled trades were controlled by guild or craft organization. It was difficult to learn a skilled trade unless one's family worked in it. To enter a business took money, or capital, and the poor had no capital.

So these Europeans came to America to escape from this social and economic dead end. They hoped to build a new life, to acquire land or other property, and to raise a family with some hope for the future. We usually think that life in early nineteenth century America was crude and rough. But we must remember that life for the poor in European cities and villages was even more rigorous.

The desire for personal betterment was not limited to the poor. Many middle class people moved to America, too. Some wanted to make their own fortunes. But many of them wanted prestige, respect, and a feeling of importance even more than they wanted money. They felt that they had a much better opportunity to achieve these things in America than in Europe.

Colonial Immigration

Most of the early colonies were settled by Englishmen. But there were some Dutch, Swedish, and German settlers before 1700. After 1700 the Scotch, the Irish, and the Germans arrived in large numbers. The early settlers had claimed most of the land on the east coast, and so these new arrivals settled further inland, closer to the Appalachian Mountains. A few even crossed the mountains and settled in the interior.

Pre-Civil War Immigration

Beginning about 1830, there was a very heavy wave of immigration from Ireland and Germany. A potato shortage in Ireland in 1845 caused a serious famine. Many died of hunger, and thousands left Ireland for other countries.

The earlier settlers did not care for the Irish. The Irish were Roman Catholics, and the earlier settlers in most areas were usually Protestant. This caused some antagonism, or dislike. But certainly no one persecuted the newcomers. The United States has never used its power to try to force religious views on immigrants. Most of the Irish immigrants settled in the East. But the greatest number of the Germans who came here between 1830 and the Civil War settled in the Midwest.

The New Immigration

The Civil War slowed immigration down for a few years. Then people began pouring across the Atlantic Ocean again. Immigrants from Germany, Britain, and Scandinavia continued to arrive in large numbers. But in the 1890s and after, thousands and hundreds of thousands poured in from Southern and Eastern Europe. They were Poles, Hungarians, Russians, Italians, and people of many other nations. They began a new type of immigration to America. Figure 8 shows the countries from which the greatest number of immigrants came between 1820 and 1957.

It was quite easy to move to America after the Civil War. No passports were needed. The steamship had made travel fast and cheap. Railroad travel was quick. A ticket from Central Europe to the United States cost only about twenty-five dollars. The railroads and large industries wanted people to come to America to work for them. Often they would pay the fare for whole villages to immigrate. The European people wanted very badly to come to the United States. Many were suffering from wars and from a shortage of farm land. In the new country they could hope to own their own land and give their children a better start in life.

Most of the people who came from Eastern and Southern Europe were peasants. They had not been trained to work in skilled trades. Many of them settled in the cities along the east coast of America and worked at unskilled labor. Thousands of Eastern Europeans worked in the heavy industries. The Slavs and Italians, in particular, went into mining and steelmaking. Some immigrants went further west, stopping in cities or settling on farm lands. Many midwestern cities, like Cleveland and Chicago, had very large immigrant populations.

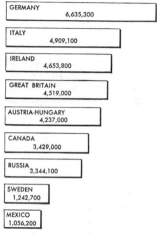

FIGURE 8. Sources of Immigration to the United States, 1820-1957.

Number of Immigrants

The number of people who came to this country before 1924 is really amazing. From 1830 to 1840 only about a half million arrived. From 1840 to 1850, the immigration numbered one and one-half million. For each ten-year period from 1850 to 1880, the figure stood at two and one-half million. Most of these people came from Northern Europe.

After 1880 a regular flood started. In the next ten years we took in over five million people. Ten more years brought almost another four million. Over eight and one-half million immigrants came here between 1901 and 1910. A few returned to Europe, but the vast majority stayed in America. Almost three-fourths of this latest group came from Southern and Eastern Europe.

Immigration continued high until it was slowed down by World War I. Over five and one-half million came between 1911 and 1920. Only about four million came during the 1920s, since by that time immigration was slowed down by the Immigration Act of 1924 (which will be explained later in this text). For the last thirty years or so, usually less than 150,000 immigrants have arrived each year. Competition to come to the United States is very strong, and most countries want us to increase their quotas.

Figure 9 shows the number of immigrants that came to the United States from 1790 to 1950.

Where the Immigrants Settled

Where did all of these people settle? Most of them went to the newer states in the West. The older states, like Massachusetts, Vermont, and Virginia, did not increase in population very much between 1860 and 1890. Land was scarce and expensive in these states. It was not good farmland anyway.

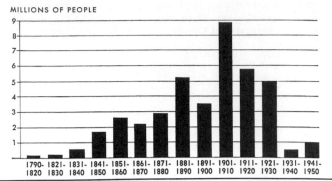

FIGURE 9.   Immigration to the United States, 1790-1950.

Most of the immigrants settled in the Midwest and the Great Plains. Between 1860 and 1890 Iowa increased its population from about 675,000 to almost two million. At the same time, the population in Kansas rose from about 100,000 to one and one-half million; Nebraska from 29,000 to over a million; Minnesota from 200,000 to over two million. These and other Western states took most of the immigrants during these years.

The remainder of the immigrants settled in the large cities. New York City gained more than one million people in the twenty years from 1870 to 1890. Philadelphia increased a half million, Boston a quarter of a million. Cities in the Midwest expanded even more. Chicago, Cleveland, and Detroit tripled their population during this same period, while Denver's population rose from about five thousand to about 100,000.

The total population of the United States has increased steadily. In 1820 about ten million people lived here. In 1860 there were thirty million. By 1900 the population of the United States was about seventy-five million. In 1930 it was up to nearly 123 million. Today we have a population of 200 million spread across the country. The graph in figure 10 shows how our population grew from 1790 to 1950.

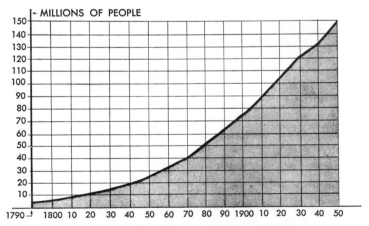

FIGURE 10.   Growth of Population in the United States, 1790-1950.

The Immigration Act of 1924

By 1918 Americans had begun to worry about this steady stream of new people coming to our country. A law was passed requiring that all immigrants know how to read and write. But this didn't stop the flood; so a new law was passed in 1924. This law set a quota of 150,000 immigrants a year to the United States. It limited any one country to a few thousand immigrants a year. Since the act was passed in 1924, immigration is no longer important in increasing our population.

Assimilation of Immigrants

The new immigrants soon became Americans. Most of the older folks knew no English. But their children learned quickly and usually spoke without an accent. Their grandchildren were complete Americans. They knew little or nothing of their grandparents' language. The old customs and languages gradually died out. Today, wherever you go in America, you will find people whose parents and grandparents came from different places all over the world. It is impossible to tell them apart. They are all Americans. No one knows or cares very much where their ancestors came from.

In about a minute (I tend to cheat the first time and give less than a minute), I stop them and start firing questions on the material.

1. What period of time was covered by this article? (I expect the answer: from the Colonial period—1620 to the present or 1950).
2. From which country did most immigrants come? And how many? (Germany, 6.6 million)
3. From which country did the fewest come? How many? (Mexico, 1 million)
4. During which period of time did most immigrants come to the United States? (1900-1910)
5. What else will this chapter discuss? (Reasons for immigration, where immigrants settled, the Immigration Act of 1924, assimilation)

Naturally, most readers unfamiliar with previewing will miss several of these questions. So we go back to the chapter together and compare the right way to preview it with the way they did it. We look at the title, table of contents, preface, etc.

By using this type of pressured approach, I see how the student goes about the skill; I see if he knows how to do it at all; I see how he works under a time pressure; I find out how well the student has done the preview; I find out how well he thinks about a title like *Immigration*; and I learn what he knows factually about the topic. After we have gone through the chapter from title to headings, visual aids, questions, etc., I have the students make a list of the steps to be followed. Then, I have them apply the skill in different material—textbook chapter, newspaper, magazine, etc. If their previewing is still not well done, I'll try other applications and go back over each chapter to make sure the students really know what they are looking for and how to find it and to think about the material quickly. It is critical to time them the first time or two; it is critical to question them fast and hard; it is critical to go back over the material heading by heading, visual aid by visual aid slowly. *As with all reading skills, they must be continually applied in a variety of contexts*; a little review in the next couple of lessons is wise. Take four or five minutes to have the students preview the next chapter, and then question them and verify their ability to do it quickly and thoroughly.

Main Ideas and Details

The ability to find main ideas and details may be the most important of all the study skills, so the way you teach, review, reinforce, and apply it is absolutely critical. I never define the skill for students; I'd rather throw them into doing something they do not fully understand, so that they can see for themselves, first hand, what they do, how they do it, and how to improve it.

For main ideas and details, I will use some of the source material already mentioned under previewing. I start by asking the students to read the first paragraph and tell me the one sentence they think is the most important one in the paragraph—the main idea. I tell them to read it. They read it and often try to give their own version of a sentence. I stop them right there and insist that they give me a sentence printed in the paragraph. I want the class to know the answer is usually right there and I want them to get used to using whole sentences. So a student picks a sentence. No matter whether it is right or wrong, I put it on the board and require him to go through the paragraph sentence by sentence proving to me and himself that each sentence is or is not a detail related to the main idea.

> A. Too old to get a job at 40? A new law says that people between 40 and 65 will be protected against discrimination by employers. A person between 40 and 65 cannot be fired because of age. He cannot be paid different wages or get fewer benefits because of his age. Not only employers, but unions cannot refuse to accept a person because of age.

If the student chooses the first sentence, sometimes I just point out that it is a question (as in the question-answer pattern) and is the technique the writer uses to get you interested in his material, but that it usually is not a main idea. Sometimes, though, (depending on the student's background, maturity, level of functioning, etc.) I will let it go and prove it wrong. With this particular paragraph most people (from fifth grade level on) get it right by choosing the second sentence. So I put it on the board and ask him to prove it to me by giving me the facts and details supporting it and relating to it, because if it is the main idea, everything in the paragraph will talk about it. The rest of the sentences in the paragraph will define, explain, amplify, and illustrate the one idea.

I write on the board:

A. A new law says . . . etc.
 1. A person between 40 . . . etc.

Then I ask what the detail has to do with the main idea. Usually students say that this sentence is one part of the law that forbids discrimination on the basis of age. I almost always ask to clarify the concept of discrimination, not just the definition of the word. Many youngsters think of discrimination in terms of race. I want them to know that it is more inclusive than that and that it really refers to segregating any person or group on the basis of one or two characteristics including color, race, religion, age, sex, ect. I will take a few moments to talk about it in this context. We look at the sentence and I probe for what it means to fire someone because of age; I give an example of my working, doing the same job as another person for the same number of hours, producing the same amount and quality of work but being fired because I am 40 and he is 18. We talk about it a little to enrich the context and to highlight the logic of good nonfictional writing.

I write the next sentence:

 2. He cannot be paid . . .

What does getting different pay or benefits (I give examples of benefits or elicit some from the students) have to do with the main idea? I'll return to the example above and try to illustrate and dramatize the situation in which an individual and I are working at the same job, and I (at 40) get $150 per week and he gets $175 plus Blue Cross/Blue Shield. We discuss how that relates directly to the main idea.

I put the next statement on the board:

 3. Not only employers, but . . .

We talk about unions so that I am certain the students understand what it means and how unions control certain trades and crafts, and how some people who do not belong to a union cannot work at all. Then we tie it into the whole sense of discrimination of another kind, related to the main idea. Then we go over the whole paragraph and review how the details develop and explain the general statement in the main idea sentence.

Note that the illustrations I use, are always in an outline form. I do not mention this to the class because the next skill I teach is outlining and I want the students to have a bridge to understanding what it is.

It is very important at the beginning of teaching main ideas and details to be sure you get well-written paragraphs, like this one, and that you use several different kinds of content (social science, science, sports, etc.) so the student can see that this skill is applicable in *all* nonfictional material. Be sure you have ready five or six paragraphs composed of one main idea and three or four related details. Give good examples first then you can deal with some of the badly written textbooks they will encounter. First give the rule then the exceptions, not the reverse. Go through enough good paragraphs, sentence by sentence, to be certain the student knows what a main idea is and what it is not, and the critical relationship of details and facts to it.

How does this differ from the typical way of presenting this skill? Usually what happens in classrooms and clinics is that the teacher will say, Today we will learn how to find the main idea and details in some paragraphs. She gives a definition of main ideas and then says, Here is an example, choose the main idea. The students do it, some choosing a or b or c or d. The teacher then says, Jane what is the answer; she says b. The teacher says right. Often Jane does not know why b is right; Joe got c and has no idea why it is wrong and why b is right; and so on around the room, with probably half the students not knowing what they are doing. Teacher says, let's do another one. Same procedure. Then she says, do the next ten in the workbook. So off they go, half of them not at all clear on what they are looking for or why; so they guess. When the exercise is over, they give the answers to 1-10, in a, b, c, d format as before and when it is completed, about half or so still do not know what it is they have done. *Don't do it this way*. Don't do it for any of these useful study skills; in all instances put the students through the skills as I have suggested; it works much better because the class knows what they are doing and why, and they grasp a deeper and more confident sense of what a main idea is and what it is not. They get the key relationship between general and specific, part and whole. And this is critical to all the other study skills, not to mention logic and general thinking.

As with all of these skills, main ideas and details will not usually be taught, learned, and made automatic in one lesson; it needs review, reinforcement, and wider application to many nonfictional texts and sources. They must see that these skills work on all nonfiction.

Outlining and Summarizing

The way in which we have presented main ideas and details has already started our work on outlining. Usually I tell students that I never understood outlining because I was convinced that the important thing about it was knowing what letters and numbers followed each other. Does 1 follow A and then under 1 do we put (a) or (1) and under that do we put (i)? I tell my students that we can simplify the whole process of outlining (especially as a note-taking technique) by using this form:

Title of the textbook chapter on top of the page
I, II, III, etc. for headings in the chapter

A, B, C, etc., for the main idea of each paragraph

1, 2, 3, etc. for details

(a), (b), etc. for the smaller details explaining the 1, 2, or 3 they are under

If more minute detail appears in the paragraph, use (i), (ii), etc. for even more minute details under the (a), (b), etc.

We talk about the uses of outlining not only for note taking on text books, but as a guide for writing papers, giving oral presentations, and for writing essay questions on tests, and I illustrate.

Presenting it this way, by using the outline form while presenting main ideas and details, does seem to make it much easier for most students to make the transition from main ideas and details to the written schema. I work hard on making the interdependence and interrelatedness of these skills as clear as possible. The students make an outline and we go over it, just as we went over each detail for each main idea in the paragraphs we used for teaching that skill. Make them prove their every choice when these skills are introduced. We want them to know what they know, and we want them to use these skills in their regular school and other nonfictional reading. I sometimes give wrong main ideas or make an error in an outline to see if they can prove their point. To know something with confidence means knowing what is right and why and what is wrong and why.

Then we move into summarizing. The simplest way I have found to present summarizing (following this sequence of skills) is to have them look at a subheading in a chapter in a textbook, and to find the main idea of each paragraph and put them together. Let's say we use the heading in the Immigration chapter (which we used for previewing) called *Reasons for Immigration*. There are five paragraphs under this heading. Here are the main ideas of these paragraphs:

Paragraph 1   The two basic reasons people came to America were (1) to be free from persecution; (2) for a better chance to get ahead.

Paragraph 2   Persecution of minority groups has had a long and sad history in the world.

Paragraph 3   After 1800 the most important reason for immigrating to America was probably the desire for personal betterment.

Paragraph 4   So Europeans came to America to escape from a social and economic dead end.

Paragraph 5   The desire for personal betterment was not limited to the poor.

After the students have chosen each main idea, challenge them to make sure they are correct and that they know why these are the main ideas. Ask them to read over these main ideas and to decide how to condense these five sentences (which is a good, but long summary) to three sentences. Then state your challenges, going through several of their versions of the summary and question why they included the three sentences they did, and why they left some information out. We argue and we settle on what the three most important sentences are and why the other two are not as important. If they decide to use the first three main ideas for their summary after our discussion, we note that #5 really restates #2, and that #1 really says the gist of what is in #4. We can then agree on these three sentences for the first stage of the summary. Then I ask them to reduce these three to two sentences and go through the same process as before. Finally, I ask them to write a one-sentence summary of the heading. Some might choose the first sentence and could make a good argument for it, but however they decide to boil down these sentences into one, we go through the process of challenging and proving, and putting the summary sentence into their own words.

The ability to condense material is an essential skill and it is one of the most difficult things for most of us to do. It is easier to ramble on redundantly and divergently than to focus in on a few critical and significant points and say them succinctly. I have my students look at TV, movies, and book reviews, and chapter summaries in their texts, and compare them with their own versions of the same material. We note how much this skill is dependent upon knowledge of main ideas and details and how we can use summarizing in reading, writing, and speaking activities and lessons. Again application of the skills in many contexts is essential. I point out as we go through working on summaries that good literature, especially poetry, reflects an artist's ability to condense feeling, thought, sound, and sight in very few words.

All of these skills just discussed teach students about how nonfictional material is organized, what goes with what, and what is most important, and provides structure for recall and summation (which does require some judgment and selectivity).

Classification

This is one of the most generic skills of all, since forms of classification are at the core of human thinking and reasoning. We discuss common classifications in everyday life like those mentioned in the earlier part of this chapter. Try to probe as deeply as possible into the way classes or groupings are set up, what is the logic behind some of the systems, like phone numbers with their three digit prefix, or area codes, or zip codes. I try to get them to see what is being grouped, and how and why.

With younger children, I'll often just put a list of words on the board:

man	rich	largest	blue	seven
do	otherwise	the	drain	never
car	love	fly	but	bank

(I will usually simplify this for young children by using some animals, plants, people, and inanimate objects in the list so that they have to note which are plants, animals, people objects, etc.)

As soon as possible have the students use this skill in their everyday reading, noting what grouping would accommodate certain characters in a story on certain historical events or certain scientific facts.

Sometimes I will give students three or four items, such as government, vote, laws, representatives, and ask for possible one-word categories to accommodate all of these, such as Political. In the social sciences at any level it is critical to know how to group facts and events into the following categories: political, social, economic, religious, and cultural. You can use the sports section of the paper (itself a form of classification) to work out some activities with specific sports like basketball, baseball, and hockey.

Classification is one of the most pervasive of skills and one of the most useful thinking tools; reinforce it as much as possible in all content fields (themselves a form of classification, e.g., history, geography, science, etc.). If we could convince classroom teachers of content to reinforce these study skills in their subjects, most students would learn the skills very quickly, and their speed, comprehension, and sense of order would be marvellously improved.

USING STUDY SKILLS TO IMPROVE WRITING

Study skills can be used as guides to better nonfictional writing. After I teach main ideas and details, and before outlining and summarizing, I give the students a main idea and ask them to write three details for this main idea. Then we go over their details one at a time just as we did when we read the paragraphs and picked out the main idea and proved each detail. A number of main ideas will be given this way and the details are written by the students and then gone over as before. Then I reverse the procedure and give them three details and ask them to write the main idea, and we go through those the same way.

In order to improve narrative, nonfictional writing, I lead the students from single paragraphs just described to using their previously learned skills of previewing. For example, I'll have them write a subheading with four paragraphs, each with its own main idea and details, and then link the four paragraphs to the heading—from one heading to a group of headings, until we have written a rather long, coherent, and logically structured group of paragraphs. When they write their papers or exams or make oral presentations, all of the skills will be reinforced and challenged to insure real mastery of these skills both in reading and in writing.

Classification, guide words, following directions, and patterns are reinforced similarly. If they can practice these skills in their reading activity, there is no reason why they cannot be led to see how to use them as guides to good writing.

Teaching guide words, patterns, following directions, and sequencing follows the same principles illustrated above: Make the student does something he is not sure about, challenge and question him, go back over the material and identify the skills' components and functions, then apply it as widely as possible in all the student's nonfictional reading matter. *Do not define the skills; do them and discover their nature and functions and applications.*

These foundations of structure, relationship, and selectivity build a base for students to work in interpretation, the subject for the next chapter.

REFERENCES

Butts, R. Freeman. *A cultural history of education: reassessing our educational traditions.* New York: McGraw-Hill, 1947, chapter 21, pp. 579-617.

French, William. *Education for all.* New York: Odyssey Press, 1955.

Howards, Melvin. *Read your way up.* New York: Manpower Education Institute, 1968.

Nevins, Alan & Commager, Henry Steele. *A short history of the United States.* New York: Random House (Modern Library), 1945.

Niles, Olive; Bracken, Dorothy; Daugherty, Mildred; & Kinder, Robert. *Tactics in reading.* Chicago: Scott, Foresman, 1961.

Pough, Frederick. *A field guide to rocks and minerals.* Boston: Houghton Mifflin, 1960.

Smith, Nila. *Be a better reader (I-VI).* Englewood Cliffs, NJ: Prentice-Hall, 1968.

BIBLIOGRAPHY

McNeil. W. H. *Rise of the west: a history of the human community.* New York: Mentor Books, New American Library, 1963.

Chapter eight

INTRODUCTION AND OVERVIEW

The skills and sensitivities required for any reader, viewer, or listener to make interpretations are *qualitatively different* from those needed in word recognition and in study skills. They are qualitatively different because they require detecting, analyzing, and synthesizing several types of relationships. Certainly there are relationships in word recognition and study skills, but these tend to be one-dimensional relationships among letters which produce a speakable word, or which identify a main idea as different from a detail. Interpretation requires that pronouncing words in print or received in speech become part of a whole phrase or sentence which then generates meaning dependent upon that context. The qualitative difference between word recognition and study skills and interpretation is also that between means and ends, individual facts and generalizations and abstractions from them.

Interpretation skills such as drawing conclusions, making inferences, generalizing, and understanding symbolic usage and imagery require the ability to relate information on several levels simultaneously, and to draw on previous learning and experience to enrich the context within which the information can be compared, contrasted, and conceptualized. As we have seen in Part 1, the whole, the context does shape, alter, and reconstruct its component parts. The meaning of a word, phrase, idea, or group of facts is dependent upon the syntax of each sentence and the structure of each paragraph. Where words appear in a sentence determines the part of speech and the meaning. Earlier we illustrated the part-whole relationships in language when we applied them to core concept planning and when we spoke of paintings, poems, and music.

Teaching interpretation skills

The figure in a painting is only large or small, foreground or background in terms of what else is in the picture. The same holds true for a musical piece—no single note or even small group of notes expresses the theme or the melody of the whole piece. One must pick the whole theme, the tempo, the key. In reading and listening one does not hear one letter or sound at a time, or speak one letter or sound at a time. One hears words as units and one speaks words, and these words must appear in some acceptable syntactic form in order to be understood by another.

Thus interpretation skills require relational thinking embedded in a definable structure of language or communication. We have offered the core concept approach to planning integrated lessons as a means of providing the structure and context within which letters, words, ideas, and information derive meaning. Without this meaning there can be no interpretation; there can be recitation of letters sounds, words, and facts, but no generalizing or real thought.

Another significant qualitative difference between word recognition and study skills and interpretation is that one is *literal*, the other *figurative*. Interpretation of an editorial, poem, play, painting, novel, or movie depends upon the receiver's ability to go beyond the literal, stated information into the figurative dimension. A major problem for teachers and specialists is how to move students from literal appraisals of material to figurative ones. Many reading programs tend to emphasize in the first four years in school the word recognition skills and literal recall skills often in fragmented and isolated activities. Later, it is fairly common to continue emphasizing literal recall skills. Thus many high school and college students are inept at interpreting literature and social, political, and economic forces. Often such students can tell you what happened, where it happened, and when it happened, but not why it happened. And they cannot tell why a certain array of forces and events produced a particular reaction.

Unquestionably it is very difficult to lead some students from such literal activity into figurative perspectives, but we must try. It is especially difficult if these students have not encountered interpretation skills and sensitivities prior to your instruction, and that is why I have emphasized the need for developing a sense of the whole learner, the whole language, and the wholeness of the learning process. If we were building interpretational skills and awareness into the entire reading/ language program from kindergarten onward, fewer students would be bored, and it would become natural for them to seek relationships in everything they might read or hear. The foundation for these interpretation skills is making students aware at all stages of the reading processes of context and its direct affect on pronunciation of words, their meanings, and their figurative aspects. Interpretation is a frame of mind, a perspective on how things go together, of what goes with what and why, and in what circumstances.

Why is so little done in this area of reading and language learning? What do some of the leading authorities have to say about teaching interpretation skills? Harris and Sipay (1975) have surprisingly little to say about how we should teach these critical skills. Mainly what they do is to quote individual studies of individual parts of what they call comprehension. Neither they nor the studies investigate and probe the processes necessary for good interpretation. Harris and Sipay include vocabulary as a part of interpretation and merely list the following under that heading: "study word lists; roots and affixes; vocabulary notebooks kept by students; the dictionary; work on synonyms, antonyms, and homonyms; use of context; discussion of connotative and denotative meanings; idioms, multiple meaning words, etymology." (Harris and Sipay, 1975, p. 446) They also cite the fact that most of the research on vocabulary methodology is "inclusive." When they talk about learning to recognize implied meanings they remain very general, essentially saying that students who can deal with analogies, metaphors, and circumlocutions will do fine and those who can't will do poorly. They say that getting implied meanings requires a high level of verbal intelligence, but what of those who do not seem to have such a high level? What do we do for them? How do we do it? They state (p. 456): "The person who lacks facility in understanding verbal relationships is likely to grasp only the obvious stated meaning." They go on (p. 456): "Probably the best way to develop a real understanding of figurative or indirect language is through practice in paraphrasing . . . Erroneous interpretations can be discovered and the correct interpretation can be explained." How will it be explained? How does the student who thinks literally going to become figurative in thought? Just vocabulary development? Just paraphrasing? Both of these have some place in the scheme of teaching interpretation, but how and in what context?

Steiner offers us a little help in understanding some aspects of interpretation if we can paraphrase and interpret his remarks. In essence Steiner (1975, chapter 1) tells us that "reading is an act of translation, and that every act of translation is a multiplex act of interpretation." He goes on to point out that "translation occurs between and among languages, as well as within each language." Not only is he referring to variants such as we have discussed, but he is emphasizing the personal quality of any language. He points out that "any language can just as easily hide meaning as transmit it, and that any language can transmit many messages at the same time." "Language informs and misinforms equally easily," he adds (p. 17). In his difficult book *After Babel*, Steiner is seeking the meaning of translation especially as it relates to the interpretation of any translation. The key to translating and interpreting any piece of writing is possible only "When using a word we wake into resonance, as it were, its entire previous history. A text is embedded in specific historical time . . . to read fully is to restore all that one can of the immediacies of value and intent in which speech actually occurs" (p. 24). Later (p. 28) he says "Words rarely show any outward mark of altered meaning, they body forth their history only in a fully established context."

I agree with him fully on the essentiality of context as the key to translation and interpretation. The ability to re-create the time, place, feelings, and senses in what we read is the gist of good interpretive reading (and writing), since it tells us what an author really meant by what he said. We have an expanded context within which to analyze relationships on many levels.

One of the major problems in teaching interpretation skills is that we must take all of the sub-skills as a whole in order to develop the new perspectives, attitudes, and approaches to reading which are quite different from what word recognition and study skills have given us. If we teach each of the interpretation sub-skills separately and as if they were complete, we miss the layers of meaning, innuendo, and bias so prevalent in all types of writing. To grasp meanings, innuendo, and bias as well as the author's purpose and style, we have to get our students to put all of their previously learned skills to work in a new and broader setting. We have to change their basic attitude toward the purpose of reading and writing or any other medium (movies, TV, film). Also we have to help them move from their relatively literal approach to reading to a more figurative and critical approach. How shall we help them across that chasm of strewn facts and information into the more literary, imagistic, and figurative realm? In Chapter 1 I alluded to such interpretive work when I briefly mentioned the problem of helping students realize that *Alice in Wonderland, Gulliver's Travels, Don Quixote, The Old Man and*

The Sea, and *Animal Farm* are not unusual tales of peculiar people in strange places, but rather that these, and so many others, are very serious, if oblique, interpretations of the political, social, economic, and religious conditions and behaviors of man in various contexts and societies. Some teachers take their students on this intellectual journey by telling them that *Alice in Wonderland*, for example, is indeed a satire, with allegorical overtones, which attacks the institutions of Victorian England because the little girl, the rabbit, Tweedle-dee and Tweedle-dum and the Queen represent so and so in the real world. Often however, they do not give the student the opportunity to dig out of the book itself the relevant contexts of that time and place, why Lewis Carroll used a pseudonym in the first place and then wrote this diatribe on his country's (and others') institutions. We want to make sure our students understand why the images and symbols used in any piece of writing, especially literary writing, mean what we say they do. We can help them discover the pertinent sources to amplify and clarify the allusions in the work itself.

DETECTING PROPAGANDA

Overview

I have had the most success with moving students from the literal to the figurative in reading and writing by introducing them to propaganda techniques as a first step in critical reading and to the related interpretive skills, such as drawing conclusions, making inferences, and dealing with imagery and symbolism. Students of various ages, from second grade level to adults with limited reading skills and limited educational backgrounds easily learn propaganda techniques. The students have fun working with the techniques to learn how they are used in ads in magazines, newspapers, radio, and television, and so develop a kind of global sensitivity to word usage, multiple meanings, allusions, and unstated purposes. When students have learned the propaganda techniques, have critiqued them fully, and have written their own ads or other propagandistic material, or have given short biased speeches, their attitude changes; they become more suspicious of what they read, see, and hear. Once the shift has occurred in their thinking about what they are reading, it is much easier to move them into the more literary and subtle usages of language. The techniques of propaganda, properly taught, can move the reader from literal to figurative thinking, opening the whole realm of enjoyable reading on many levels in all kinds of materials.

All of the interpretive skills may be taught at several levels of abstractness and complexity. When working with the propaganda techniques with second grade students, I develop the idea that some things we read and hear are not true. We look at ads and make fun of some of them. We talk about them in terms of what the advertiser wants us to buy or do. How do we know that? What is there in the language, the picture, the place we find the ad, that gives us any clues to what is really intended?

My students wrote their own ad copy for toothpaste, cars or candy. Most of them grasped the purpose of advertisements. Some of their ads were really funny and revealed their understanding of how to say things so that others believe you or are willing to buy something you want to sell.

In going over the ads the students brought into class for the initial discussion of the propaganda techniques, and the ads they wrote, we uncovered much about word usage, synonyms, antonyms, and logic. Could it be true that this toothpaste will get you more boyfriends; do cats and dogs really like one food better than the others? Why? They read, wrote, and discussed, sharpening their perception of what is written or spoken. They learned to ask questions and began to notice whether the answers were indeed answers to their questions or to another question. One of my techniques is to provoke the class with contrary views in order to force them into proving whatever they say, using the text and their own reasoning.

I have not yet worked with any group of any age or background that did not respond well to this approach and to these skills. Whatever the age group, it is easy to make them aware of the amount and type of propaganda in their everyday lives, including their own use of it as they deal with parents, girlfriends and boyfriends, teachers, or police. After the students have brought in their ads and we have gone through them discussing what is being sold and said, we note how it is achieved through language usage: Why those words? What do they conjure up in your head? What do you associate with such words and pictures? Next we learn the names of the techniques and how to label the ads. Clearly, the techniques overlap each other and not all propaganda is bad or good. The goodness or badness of propaganda must be determined in the context of the purpose of the ad, the sponsor of the ad, and his ulterior motives and potential gains.

The Techniques

The labels for propaganda techniques come from the National Institute for Propaganda in the early 1940s and are widely accepted:

1. Bad Names
2. Glad Names
3. Testimonial
4. Transfer
5. Bandwagon
6. Plain Folks
7. Card Stacking

Teaching these techniques will follow the basic principles spelled out throughout this book; teach them *inductively*. The students themselves discover how they work and then must prove their conclusions and analyses. *Nothing is told or defined at the outset*. First, do the task and then let's see how you did it, what was right about it, what was wrong about it and why? How can you get more information from the use of these skills? Such an approach engenders a certain immediacy for the students; it ceases being theoretical or "right" just because someone said it is. Give your students opportunities to catch you in some bias, overgeneralization, faulty reasoning, or poor definition and inconsistency. Keep them on their toes and alert to every propagandistic statement or gesture—stated or implied.

Introducing Propaganda Techniques

You can begin with an example from a film, a TV show, some written matter, or your own deliberately biased statements on some current issue, then have them work with you to determine whether what was said or seen or heard is true; how do they know it is true or false? Does the writer or speaker provide you with enough information to draw some conclusion or make some inference? What's missing?

Another way to introduce these propaganda techniques is to start a general discussion of propaganda—what they think it is and what they think it is not—and then move into examples from magazine advertisements, newspapers, TV, radio, and the like. Discuss the ads and decide in general how they feel about them and why they feel that way. Have them bring in their favorite, or least favorite, ads from magazines and newspapers, and tell them you are going to explore *how people convince each other to think or act in a different way*. Some students may offer as examples the way people dress, make themselves up, their manner of speech, the way they carry themselves, or some movie or TV show and so on. The key to these critical reading skills is that students become sensitive to language usage, body language, and pictures so that they can easily uncover attempts to change their thinking and behavior. When they bring in ads, go through them and have the class identify which of the seven techniques the ad uses.

Bad Names

A few years back this technique was probably the easiest to identify since various propagandists and advertisers were very blunt in their use of this technique. Simply, Bad Names is characterized by the use of negative words or pictures, or both. Words like *inflation, fat, bulges, pimply, inadequate, deficits,* and so on trigger negative or unpleasant images and feelings in most of us. As is true of all of these propaganda techniques bad names is usually mixed with other techniques, frequently with Glad

Names to produce a sharper contrast. If you look through women's magazines like *Vogue* or *Cosmopolitan* you will find numerous ads which talk about weak hair, or limp hair, or cracked fingernails, or overweight in one or two paragraphs in the ad, and then offer their product to fix the problem. A good place to lead your students to bad names, after you've done some ads, is the newspapers and news magazines where feature and editorial writers have a fairly free hand to make their case.

Exhibit 8-1 shows examples of Bad Names taken from a magazine ad.

The headline shrieks the warning that America is being "trapped" by foreign steel just as it is by foreign oil. We all know what grief we have had in 1974 with the Arab oil embargo and again the problems of the summer of 1979 with long gas lines and fear of limited fuel oil supplies. This raises many ominous specters for all all of us. The corporation has tied in new concerns about foreign steel, which they hope we will associate with our misery over the oil from foreign countries. The word foreign is being used negatively here and is almost synonymous with intruder or enemy or the others—them.

The copy under the picture is very much like an editorial sprinkled with facts and figures as we see in card stacking ads. Notice the expression "shipped an all-time record" which makes a bad thing worse. The next sentence speaks of a massive "deficit," always a bad word because it means that we spend more then we take in. "But the worst is yet to come." Then we get their data which we have no way of verifying, but which sound terrible.

This is followed by strong, cold language which is urging us to reduce our trade deficit and by implication urging us to let our government know that we support their view that we must reduce foreign steel imports at once. They have shifted their own production problems to the government for solution and they want us all involved. The picture excellently summarizes their message: American ships carry money abroad and foreign ships bring in steel which competes with Bethlehem Steel Company.

We are moved by their argument and may even feel inclined to support their position; it does not take too much for many of us to be riled up by the negative use of words like foreign, deficit, and the like.

Have your students deal with ads like this and take special note of the use of words in negative or positive fashion in the particular context of the ad. Have them rewrite the ad from the standpoint of someone else: a consumer, a construction company, the foreign exporter. Find antonyms and synoynms for some of the charged words. Have the ads or other propaganda written from the standpoint of a conservative republican and a liberal democrat, and carefully compare and contrast the language they use to convey their message and the feelings they wish to evoke. Discuss the logic of this steel ad deciding what other information is needed to determine if they are telling the truth. Also, probe to discover why this

Is America getting trapped by foreign steel as it is by foreign oil?

Last year foreign steelmakers shipped an all-time record of 21.1 million tons of steel to our shores. And our nation's trade deficit in steel was more than $5½ *billion!*

But the worst is yet to come. By 1985, unless we soon start expanding our domestic steelmaking capacity, 25 to 30 million tons of steel imports could be entering the U.S. market annually. That would mean an outflow of $12 to $15 *billion* a year—and a huge increase in our steel trade deficit.

What's needed to *reduce* America's trade deficit in steel? Governmental policies that will allow the American steel industry to generate the additional funds needed to modernize and expand.

Bethlehem Steel Corporation, Bethlehem, PA 18016

Exhibit 8-1.   Advertisement using the Bad Names technique. (Courtesy of Bethlehem Steel Corporation)

company might be placing this expensive ad in so many national magazines.

Exhibit 8-2 shows another Bad Names ad from a woman's magazine. First a beautiful face, then, "Are you bothered by brown spots

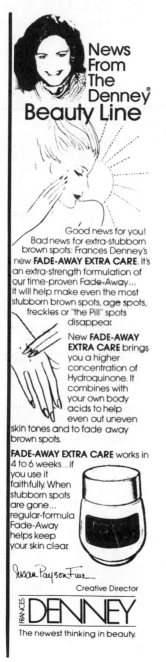

News From The Denney® Beauty Line

Good news for you! Bad news for extra-stubborn brown spots: Frances Denney's new **FADE-AWAY EXTRA CARE**. It's an extra-strength formulation of our time-proven Fade-Away... It will help make even the most stubborn brown spots, age spots, freckles or "the Pill" spots disappear.

New **FADE-AWAY EXTRA CARE** brings you a higher concentration of Hydroquinone. It combines with your own body acids to help even out uneven skin tones and to fade away brown spots.

FADE-AWAY EXTRA CARE works in 4 to 6 weeks... if you use it faithfully. When stubborn spots are gone... regular-formula Fade-Away helps keep your skin clear.

Susan Payson Fine
Creative Director

FRANCES **DENNEY**
The newest thinking in beauty.

Exhibit 8-2.   Advertisement using the Bad Names technique. (Courtesy of Frances Denney Beauty Line, 437 Madison Ave., New York, N.Y.)

. . ." No one wants to have brown spots, age spots, "pill spots" or un-even "skin tones" or "freckles in all the wrong places." They make it sound like a disfiguring disease. Freckles aren't bad and as far as I know are not permanently removable. The ambiguity in this ad is deliberate, and it makes nervous people more nervous to think they have these brown spots or pill spots for everyone to see and smirk about.

Then of course they offer their solution to these ugly, disfiguring spots. Now the glad words, the solution to your problems. Not only does their cream work but it does so in "as little as" 6 weeks "if you use it faithfully." It is not clear what they mean by "faithfully" nor is it clear which "Thousands of women—*and* men have used it." This type of ad-vertising and propaganda is fairly straightforward because the compari-sons and contrasts as well as the specific language used give it away. This is the kind of ad I like to have students rewrite with a humorous twist, e.g., "Fade-Away will remove you if you inhale for sixteen minutes while spreading its marvelous balm over your gaping pores." If the students can turn and twist some of these ads, this way or more humorously, they will develop a better insight into how words and phrases can alter mean-ing and evoke particular responses in others.

On a more serious note, take ads like these and dig for the logic, the reasoning—can we really obliterate freckles? Safely? By what medical research is this idea supported, or not supported? Additionally, have your students pursue such questions as who is advertising, where is the adver-tisement placed, why is it placed there and how valid is the presentation. By keeping your focus on the use of the language and on the logic of the presentations you will develop some essential interpretational skills and sensitivities. Using the ads as a starter is more fun than going directly to editorials or feature stories or textbooks, but the principles are the same in both instances.

As you have the students analyze such ads noting positive and neg-ative uses of words and pictures, note the denotative and connotative uses of words. Moving from a particular ad or group of ads, you can then detect denotative and connotative usage in other sources of propaganda. In elec-tion years this activity is easily carried into political speeches and plat-forms. Wherever possible add some humor or satire to your analyses in order to open that avenue of interpretation to your students.

In ads or other propaganda take another step into what kinds of ap-peals are being made, ie., sex, fear, status, etc. Have the students, who are ready for this level of work, identify the language, the source, and the possible motives of the propagandists for appealing to certain emotions as part of their presentation. Why do we react in certain ways to sexual appeals or status appeals? Obviously, this sort of inquiry is not for younger students, but for bright junior high school students it is possible to begin this type of investigation.

Glad Names

This technique is easy to identify since it uses benign words like beauty, slim, "most advanced therapy," long lasting, unique, roomy. Exhibit 8-3 shows a Datsun ad illustrating the point well. "New Economy", "Makes You Feel Rich", "Amazing", "Lowest-priced", and in every line of copy in this ad are positive words plus the lovely picture of the wagon and its spaciousness parked in front of a very substantial home. It is easy to get students' reactions to words like graceful, roomy, inspired. Ask them to offer antonyms and synonyms for these words. Also, with more mature students, you can expand their awareness of how the language used in such ads does or does not appeal to our fears, needs, desires. One could easily pursue that aspect of the techniques of propaganda into sociological and psychological paths.

As in all of the propaganda techniques students need to notice that most ads, and other propaganda, include more than one technique. This Datsun ad has Glad Words and some Bad Words: "doesn't scrimp", "lock out rattles and road noise", "Finicky?" Also this ad has a touch of transfer in it with its suggestion that such a car owned by such a tasteful person would fit easily in front of such a lovely home. Dreadful logic of course, but good appeal.

Testimonial

Testimonial is the oldest and most obvious of the propaganda techniques. A well known person, sports figure, or Hollywood star claims in his or her own words (with the aid of the ad agency) that such and such a product is good, or that he or she uses this toothpaste, soap, or golf club. The idea is quite simple: a respected or at least a public figure whom you know and probably admire uses this product so it must be good. After all would Joe DiMaggio or Dr. J mislead you? This type of ad appeals to our insecurity and lack of faith in ourselves. This famous person's life and judgment are better; his or her money and fame make him an expert.

Exhibit 8-4 illustrates an effective use of the testimonial technique. Most people would recognize Wilt Chamberlain at a glance towering over the VW. Wilt does not say anything about the car in this ad, but he has made several TV ads in which he speaks of the reasons for owning this car. He mentions the fact that the VW Rabbit has more headroom than his Rolls Royce, and since that ad has been seen widely by almost everyone with a TV, this ad requires no quotes from him. But the ad is striking and gets our attention, as all good propaganda must. The logic is simple: if a giant like Chamberlain who is 7 feet 2 inches tall can comfortably fit into the Rabbit, everyone else can.

Again this testimonial technique is combined with Glad Names, and a hint of Bad Names (look at the first sentence). You can have the stu-

Exhibit 8-3.   Advertisement using the Glad Names technique. (Reproduced with permission)

dents rewrite this type, or any type of ad for humorous purposes or for serious ones. The key throughout this work with the techniques is to sensitize the students to the power of well chosen words and pictures to create needs, to feed desires, and to cause people to draw conclusions. The power of language (and pictures) to convince people to think or act differently is the point of these lessons on propaganda techniques.

Exhibit 8-4. Advertisement using the Testimonial technique. (Courtesy of Volkswagen, Englewood Cliffs, N.J.)

GOOD NEWS FOR PEOPLE 7'2" AND UNDER.

If you've always thought a little car meant a lot of crowding, you've obviously never looked into a Volkswagen Rabbit.

There happens to be so much room in a Rabbit that all 7'2" of Wilt Chamberlain can fit comfortably into the driver's seat.

With space left over.

Because the Rabbit has even more headroom than a Rolls-Royce.

As well as more room for people and things than practically every other imported car in its class. Including every Datsun. Every Toyota. Every Honda, Mazda, and Renault.

Not to mention every small Ford and Chevy.

And, of course, what's all the more impressive about the room you get in a Rabbit is that it comes surrounded by the Rabbit itself. The car that, according to Car and Driver Magazine, "...does more useful and rewarding things than any other small car in the world..."

So how can you go wrong?

With the Rabbit you not only get the comfort of driving the most copied car in America.

You also get the comfort of driving a very comfortable car.

Because it may look like a Rabbit on the outside.

But it's a Rabbit on the inside.

VOLKSWAGEN DOES IT AGAIN

*The Bronx's finest blend of whiskey. 2 weeks old.
One hundred seventy-two proof. Bronx Distillers,
Inc. New York, New York.*

Exhibit 8-5.   Advertisement using the Transfer technique.

Transfer

Transfer is a somewhat more sophisticated and subtle technique for persuading people to change their behavior. It involves an ancient and primitive belief that was common among many tribes, namely, that if one killed a ferocious beast like a lion, he should eat a piece of the meat so that he could develop the lion's ferocity. In transfer, we find the same notion. The common political practice of Republicans in which they frequently call up the name, work, and image of Lincoln is an example of this. The idea is that the aura and charisma of a great and powerful figure will somehow rub off on them.

Ads which show beautiful Hollywood stars with a bar of soap are intended to serve the purposes of Glad Names, Testimonial, and above all of Transfer. Simply, if you use this soap, etc., you will take on some of the same characteristics as the star.

Exhibit 8-5 shows an ad employing the technique of transfer. This ad for Tiara Whiskey would have glistening gold letters and a diamond-studded tiara to attract our attention—to let us know how special it is. It has very little copy and might be on a red or purple background to enhance its royal qualities. The ad seems to be appealing *only* to the rich, elite, and special people, *but* if you purchase this royal brew, you would absorb these characteristics. The royal qualities of the liquor and of the people who are supposed to purchase it are transferred to you. Thus do you steal their status and set yourself above the ordinary people who buy other whiskies, beer, or wine.

Again, the logic of these ads lends itself to humorous attacks on the reasoning employed by the propagandists. Students of all ages enjoy taking ads like these apart and then rewriting them in several different ways. The point is to illustrate to them how to be critical of the techniques and the language used to convince so many people to buy the products so expensively advertised.

Bandwagon

The Bandwagon technique of propaganda is at least as old as Testimonial. This technique says that everyone else is doing it, or buying it, or voting for Joe Blow, so join them. Be like your peers and go along. If all your neighbors are buying such and such a snow blower, or car you should because they can't all be wrong. Bandwagon does appeal to our insecurity and need to belong. Most of us cannot bear the weight of being a loner; we need the approbation of our fellows. Also, getting on any bandwagon reduces our need to think and to decide for ourselves what we want or need.

Exhibit 8-6 shows a good example of the Bandwagon technique with a touch of the Plain Folks technique. Here are nine totally unknown, ordinary persons who give a brief testimonial about how they like Campari. But it also adds a hint of snobbery when it says: "9 out of every 10,000 Americans prefer Campari." This is not yet everyman's drink, but should be. Join the bandwagon and drink this stuff and you will be both distinctive and one of the guys. This ad is more appealing and a little less obvious than the older bandwagon type ads.

Plain Folks

The plain folks technique, like the bandwagon technique, is rampant during political campaigns. Plain Folks says "I am like you, you can trust me." The ad in Exhibit 8-6 for the bandwagon technique contains this lement in it: ordinary folks like yourself drink this drink so you'll like it

Exhibit 8-6. Advertisement using a combination of the Bandwagon technique and the Plain Folks technique. (Courtesy of Liggett Group, Inc., 100 Paragon Drive, Montvale, N.J. 07645)

9 OUT OF EVERY 10,000 AMERICANS PREFER CAMPARI

Compared with Europeans, Americans are meager consumers of Campari & Soda.
But a few new converts are won every day by its unique bittersweet taste.

"I used to drink Campari on the rocks. Now, I drink it everywhere."
—G. Knight, Redwood City, CA

"I've learned to savor life's contrasts—setbacks with success, the bitter with the sweet. That's why I drink my Campari with orange juice."
—S. Wolff, Baltimore, MD

"Whenever my man asks for something different, I give him Campari in bed."
—M. Zapoleon, San Francisco, CA

"The first time I tried Campari and Tonic, it was the beginning of a tasteful relationship."
—N. Bovino, Manteca, CA

"I used to order what everyone else did. But that was before I found myself—and Campari."
—C. Ledbetter, Dunedin, FL

"At a New York art gallery, I was served Campari while contemplating a purchase. I decided to buy two bottles."
—K. Wall, Los Angeles, CA

"One night, I had to try it twice to like it, and now I like it twice a night!"
—O. Rosenstadt, Bethesda, MD

"After shooting pictures on safari, my best shot is of Campari."
—J. Jividen, Stow, OH

"When I order a Campari, it doesn't just say what I like to drink—it tells the world how I like to live."
—H. Millam, St. Louis, MO

CAMPARI & SODA

Pour a jigger (1½ oz.) of Campari over ice in a tall glass. Add 4 ounces of club soda. Squeeze in a wedge of lemon or lime to taste, if desired.

©1979—Imported, prepared and bottled by Austin, Nichols & Co., Lawrenceburg, Ky. 48 proof bitter liqueur.

<u>You too can be in a Campari ad!</u>
Just send your "Campari Quip," snapshot, and phone number to P.O. Box 2782, SR, Grand Central Station, New York, N.Y. 10017. If selected, your photo, name and witticism will appear in a future Campari ad—and you'll receive $100. (Sorry, nothing can be returned.)

too. Compare this with the whisky ad discussed which made a snob appeal to the chosen few in the know. In a sense, both of these ads are very much alike, they just define *special* or *chosen* a little differently, but the purpose is the same.

Look at this example in Exhibit 8-7 of Plain Folks from the Charlestown Savings Bank. Their slogan, "That's my bank," suggests everyone

Exhibit 8-7. Advertisement using the Plain Folks technique. (Courtesy of Charlestown Savings Bank, Boston, Mass.)

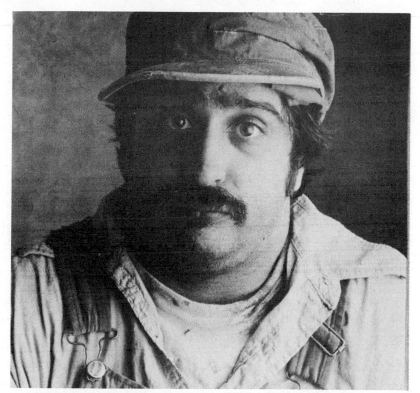

DON'T LET ANYBODY TELL YOU THERE'S ONLY ONE WAY TO GET A MORTGAGE.

The mortgage that's right for everyone hasn't been invented yet. So finding one that's right for you is important.

Charlestown Savings offers you a choice of two kinds of residential mortgages. FIRM. And FLOAT.

FIRM is a traditional mortgage. And like all traditional mortgages, has a fixed rate of interest. So if you're on a fixed income, it's ideal. It's also right for you if you feel more comfortable with an interest rate that's guaranteed.

FLOAT has an interest rate ½% below the FIRM. That rate is guaranteed for one year, then reviewed semi-annually. So if you're not planning to stay in your home for long, or if you think interest rates will drop, FLOAT is your best bet.

Two ways to get a mortgage is another way Charlestown Savings helps you look out for number one. And why more people say, "That's my bank."

that's my bank™
CHARLESTOWN SAVINGS
Member FDIC/DIF

CHARLESTOWN HELPS ME LOOK OUT FOR NUMBER ONE. THAT'S WHY THAT'S MY BANK.

BOS/8

can claim possession. The picture of the worker is appealing and clearly plays on our need to join a bandwagon of ordinary folks like ourselves. He is a good, hard-working man who puts his money into this dependable bank which serves his (your) needs.

During the political campaign for the presidency in 1968 Nixon, Agnew, Humphrey, and Muskie all played up their rags-to-riches odyssey in life. They revealed their humble beginnings in poverty and how, through hard work, they made it to the top. It is hard to resist the Horatio Alger type story; it appeals to our general sense that in America you can make such changes in your life.

Card Stacking

Card stacking is somewhat more difficult to detect and criticize than the other techniques because it usually involves the use of figures and facts in various kinds of comparisons and contrasts. Most of us are not always aware of the validity of the facts and statistical data presented so that it is very difficulty to decide if what is said is true. Card stacking literally means to arrange the deck of cards so that you get the hand you want. When you apply this technique you present the facts and figures supporting your case or viewpoint, and you omit those that seem to contradict it. In short, you load the dice in your own favor. Editorials, feature columns, politicians, and salesmen all use this technique to impress their listeners. Somehow many of us believe that if you state "facts," give numbers and percentages, that you are telling the truth. Don't let your students believe this. Identifying this card stacking technique and then taking it apart will reduce the chances of their being hoodwinked.

For example, if they read that three out of four people surveyed agreed that Grimy soap flakes clean best do they believe that 75% of a large number of persons agreed? Could it be that only 4 persons were asked and three said they liked Grimy soap flakes? Students must be directed to ask such questions whenever such data are presented. Three out of four sounds very impressive, but until you know the total number polled, it is meaningless. Years ago a survey of cigarette smokers was carried on by a certain large cigarette company. They reported three of four doctors surveyed smoked their cigarette. It seemed impressive that doctors, who know about health and what is good for you, smoked this cigarette. Some time later it came out that the company went to some towns and gave out free cartons of this cigarette to doctors. A day or two later they returned to ask which cigarettes the doctors were smoking. Many were smoking the free cigarettes they had just received, but did not regularly smoke them.

Exhibit 8-8 is an effective and common use of the card stacking technique. Facts are presented about each brand in terms of its tar content, and Puff cigarettes wins with fewest milligrams of tar. Superficially, this ad appears to be a comparison of many well-known, popular brands of

Exhibit 8-8. **Advertisement using the Card Stacking technique.**

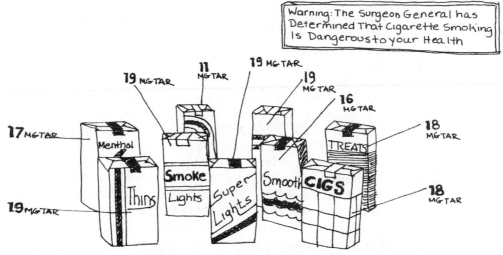

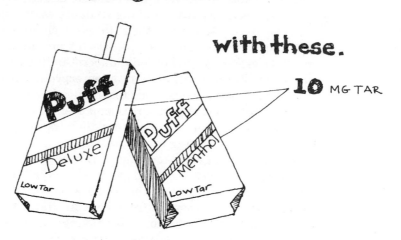

cigarettes, but this comparison is limited since those brands that contain fewer milligrams of tar than Puff are omitted from the comparison. Good critical readers suspect that and read such ads with questions like: what other brands are there and what is their tar content? The cards are stacked in favor of the advertisers' product even though objective facts are presented to lend authority and truth to the claims being made. Also, note the use of bad names in the copy: "reduce tar", and "without skimping on taste." This implies that other low tar cigarettes, especially those that may be lower in tar than Puff cigarettes, cannot offer the good taste Puff cigarettes can.

In all card stacking propaganda it is easy to be mislead by the factual, statistical data presented in favor of a certain product, or a certain candidate for office, or soaps, or a car. Remember who is doing the advertising and why. Also, expand the context of any comparisons and contrasts offered by the propagandist as we suggested above for Puff cigarettes. What facts and information have been omitted; what facts have been rearranged in a particular order to create a particular impression, and what are these related to economically, politically, socially? Of all the propaganda techniques, card stacking may be the most effective in persuading people to think or act differently since it seems to be rooted in solid logic and hard data. Beware.

Summary

These seven propaganda techniques are usually combined in several ways and appeal to sex, status, fear, and other psychological needs; they impinge on our lives everyday and affect our choices and behavior. Teaching these techniques and having students write their own propaganda of different types sensitizes them to word choice and usage, to multiple meanings, and to logic. They can learn from these how to draw valid and invalid conclusions. All of these understandings help students bridge the gap from literal recall activity to interpretation. If you have your students detect these propaganda techniques in newspapers, TV, radio, movies, textbooks, and other sources, and then have them write various types of propaganda, you will maintain their interest and prepare them for later work interpreting literature.

These propaganda techniques can be and have been introduced to youngsters as early as second grade with excellent results. Starting with advertisements from all of the media with which the students are familiar smooths the transition from work in literal recall to critical reading and thence to interpretation. Also having students write and rewrite various types of ads or other propaganda such as editorials or book reviews reinforces the student's ability to use the language to create attitudes, change established views, and to draw word pictures. These skills and sensitivities are also part of much good literary work.

DRAWING CONCLUSIONS AND MAKING INFERENCES AND GENERALIZATIONS

Drawing conclusions, and making inferences and generalizations are closely related skills of reasoning which are an integral part of all interpretation. When you try to draw a conclusion about a student's reading performance you attempt to collect as much information as possible on his word recognition, meanings, study skills, vocabulary, writing, intelligence, and his behavior in general. When you have this information, these facts and observations, you try to summarize them so that you can say succinctly that this student is functioning two years below his grade placement and exhibits weaknesses in structural analysis, interpretation, and vocabulary requiring remedial work of a particular type.

If you were to make some inferences about the student, you would look at the data collected and try to note if they reveal patterns of errors made, and strengths exhibited, and the way in which the student reacted to the testing emotionally and intellectually. Then you would attempt to go beyond the stated information and infer what these patterns of errors, for example, suggest about why the student may be making some of these errors while getting other similar items correct. Inference goes a step beyond the stated information; it requires analyzing and synthesizing the data in a broader context, one which may not be stated directly. Simply, when you draw a conclusion on the basis of stated facts or information you stay close to the data; when you make inferences about the data you use the data as a basis for hypothesizing what the results you have on this student may mean.

Generalizing usually means the process of making sweeping statements (conclusions and inferences among them) based on one or a small, unrepresentative sample of facts or behaviors. Many illustrations of generalizing were discussed in Chapter 2 when we noted that when we test a student's knowledge of initial consonant blends, for example, and use only three test items to do this we may be generalizing too readily that he will make the same type of error with all consonant blends.

Your students can easily be shown how to draw conclusions and make inferences and generalizations more rationally through some of the work in detecting propaganda techniques. The logic and reasoning of many ads reveal some of the fallacies we want our students to avoid. Our own ability to draw accurate conclusions and to make valid inferences as well as to generalize logically are absolutely essential to all of our own diagnostic and corrective work.

IMAGERY, SYMBOLISM, AND OTHER LITERARY DEVICES

Introduction

It is difficult to know where to begin with this massive topic representing some of the more significant but abstract dimensions of reading artfully and interpretively. Certainly we want our students to learn or re-learn some of the common devices such as similes, metaphors, and personifications. We also want them to know how to recognize satires and allegories, and we want them to know how to deal with symbolism. Some of these are extremely oblique and obsure. We must teach them not only to think more figuratively, but *we must teach them how to derive from several sources and related contexts that which is ignited by the text*. Some teachers of literature insist on providing their students with gossipy accounts of author's lives as a titillater and as a guide to their potential hidden meanings. I'm not sure about this practice when it used that way because it really does not often matter. For example, it adds very little to my knowledge, understanding, or appreciation of Vidal's writing to know that he is homosexual; or that Coleridge was on dope. The masculinity of *Streetcar Named Desire* with all of its symbolism of death and despair does not seem to jibe, on the surface, with its author's homosexuality. That Poe might have been syphylitic or that he was an alcoholic is not the most pertinent information in terms of enjoying his work and his creativity. That Ken Kesey spent time in a mental hospital may have helped him in his writing of *One Flew Over the Cuckoo's Nest*, but the book is valid without that piece of information. I could go on and on, but the point is made.

Emphasize the work itself, its temporal, spatial, and cultural boundaries. Occasionally, personal information about authors might throw some light on interpretation of the work, but only if that information is about his experiences. Save that other information for later. Good students may be able to figure out what kind of experience the writer had or imagined in order to create his characters and plot.

Where possible, use the students' experience and language as a take-off point for teaching literary devices. Cite examples of similes, metaphors, personifications, and other literary devices from their normal usage. Using slang and colloquial expressions, graffiti, lyrics of current songs, and the current "in" words such as *laid back* and *cool*, *dig* and *dive*. People are saying things like "I can't relate to that", and so on. One interesting exercise is to trace colloquial and slang phrases to their source. For instance my class discovered that "pressed vines" was an elaboration of "vines," which was used in the 1940s. We noted what it is that vines do, how they look, and how they could be compared to good clothes. After imaging with it for a while it was clear that there was an implicit comparison being made between the vines that grow snugly against a building, shining and decorative, with clothes that fit just right and improve one's appearance.

When the students see that some of their own everyday language are examples of literary devices it surprises them and they do not feel so alien to literary devices used by other writers and speakers. Play around with these expressions, thinking of synonyms, antonyms, and other variations of each one. Get the class to tell what they visualize, what sounds they hear, what colors they see, what textures they feel. Introduce onomatopoetic words like *buzz*, *roar*, and *whirl* particularly with younger students and get them to offer some. Write a few on the board, pronouncing them, and ask them what they hear and see. Encourage sensory descriptions of the environment. Things are simply not beautiful or skinny or ugly—the class thinks of similes or metaphors to emphasize what things look like, how they feel, how they sound. Try to sharpen the imagery and the comparisons. Read to the class good poetry (Frost, Eliot, Thomas, Cummings, Eberhart) which provides unusual word usage, music, and imagery of a sensory nature. Read any good writing to them from any source as a kind of counterpoint to main theme.

Example: Eliot

T.S. Eliot used vivid sensory imagery in much of his work even though he is known as an intellectual poet. For instance, in "The Love Song of J. Alfred Prufrock" (Eliot, 1971, p. 4) the second stanza begins: "The yellow fog that rubs its back upon the window panes . . ." and ends with "Curled once about the house, and fell asleep." This whole stanza is an extended metaphor, comparing a cat to the smokey, listless night. The "fog" is seen as a cat rubbing against the windows of the houses of the evening. If you have watched cats nuzzling against people, furniture, etc., you will see that the image is perfect. The first two stanzas of the poem set the tone for the entire poem, which emphasizes middle class hollowness, mistiness, and ennui. Also, the stealthiness of cats is likened to the stealthiness of time passing for Prufrock and his group.

Although much of Eliot and certainly of Prufrock is well beyond the knowledge and abilities of most elementary school children, choice images and metaphors like the cat are so vivid, so recognizable that children can and do respond to them. With older students in high school, you certainly could go through Prufrock and identify the figures of speech and literary devices, but try to get beyond that activity into evoking from students what they see, hear, and feel and why. How is the cat like the fog? In what ways? How does this affect your own attitudes and feelings?

Using carefully selected passages such as the one from Prufrock and others from Frost, Sandburg and others you can easily stimulate elementary school age children to respond and appreciate well-shaped meta-

phors, similes, and other figures of speech. You might even select cat
images from several authors and illustrate how many different ways one
can see, hear, and feel catness.

If students would like to paraphrase imagery of this type, it might
help them to feel why there was only one Eliot or Frost or Sandburg. But
get them all to write their own images and make sure they imbue them
with this kind of concreteness, vividness, and life.

Perhaps you would prefer to start with some basic examples of simile
and metaphors, but they should come from good literature even if the
students cannot fully understand the meaning. For example, Dylan
Thomas's "Altarwise by Owl-light" is abstruse for youngsters and
many adults, but the music of the poem is so striking one senses it beyond
meaning. One cannot find words for such art, one feels it and reacts deep
in a place where words do not go. Make comparisons of similes and metaphors in order to get the students into the feeling of comparison. They
can attempt to fit it into their own experience and perceptions. Frost is a
good place to start with this. The literary devices can easily be picked out
of good literature, and then can be written by the students. Try to get
them to use the fewest possible words to do it.

Example: Walk

An interesting yet simple lead into poetry involves using one word,
walk. Other words could do just as well, but I used this particular word
with the class in the Indian project discussed in Chapter 5. The teacher
had left the room to speak with a parent and there I was with twenty-
three Indian children sitting around. I put the word WALK on the board
and asked anyone to tell me what it was and what it meant. Someone
finally cracked the shell of silence and said, "To move from one place to
another." I said right, show me how you walk. With great courage, he
did so. I said, when you walk, how do you feel, what's in your head? Are
you happy, sad, in a hurry? We talked about it and decided when you
walk you generally want to go from one place to another and therefore
have a purpose, so you move right along. Then I asked for other words
that meant the same as walk. They offered *meander, stroll, march, strut*.
For each word, I asked the person to get up and show us how one would
meander or stroll or march. Then we talked about who might meander,
stroll. When? Where? How would that person feel? If one marched into a
room would he be happy, angry, in a hurry? Why? Who would do that?
Have you done it, when, under what circumstances? We thought about
the feelings for each word and tried to create the scene in which it might
occur, including the attitude and physical posture to go with it.

After the class had done a number of such words with accompanying dramatics, we made images and metaphors out of them and they wrote a short paragraph. We spoke of mood and purpose and how the language carried that meaning, imagery, and sensory matter. This lesson turned out to be a concrete way of illustrating the concept of imagery (both physical and emotional) and how to use words to transmit feelings, attitudes, and physical characteristics. It also emphasized the power of descriptive verbs like walk, strut, meander, and march and relegated the usual accretion of adjectives to a place of much less significance.

In teaching these common literary devices I try to get the students to become aware of how they use these devices every day and how they can sharpen their comparisons and observations consciously. In using this example the students not only dramatize and fully image the action and feeling and the sense and meaning of the word or phrase, but they make new images using the same process. You touch upon the definitions of simile, metaphor, and personification in the context of making and analyzing these devices. Try to choose vivid poems, narrative selections, and even pieces from newspapers and magazines—wherever you find good language usage of an imagistic nature. We also make comparisons with nonliterary language usage as in some propaganda and especially in textbooks and factual reporting. We note the similarities of the vocabulary used and precision of meaning and intent in such materials. Encourage your class to talk and write much more sensitively. This is also very effective with younger children, grades K-3.

With preadolescents, adolescents, and young adults I have often used the lyrics of popular songs. These days that is not as easy as it was during the 1960s when political, social, and economic criticism was embedded in many songs by Bob Dylan, Simon and Garfunkel, Judy Collins, Joan Baez, and that host of social critics. They wove into their lyrics social criticism reminiscent of the novels of the early twentieth century by Howells, Sinclair Lewis, Dreiser, and others. In the 1960s the criticism took a lyric, poetic, and popular form and hence was communicated to incredibly large audiences: Literacy was not prerequisite to catching the spirit of discontent with our institutions and government. The pied pipers played their irresistible siren songs and a generation became a cacophonous choir of dissent. (I might ask my group to restate what was said in three or four other ways for both literary form and for content, because what was said was opinion and propagandistic, but somewhat literary.) As student do things like that, they get a much better feel for the power of words. Draw out their emotional reaction to such expressions and to other forms so that they get a sharper perception of purpose, mood, and intent in writing.

By making metaphors and similes we can see how different they really are in their ability to evoke certain kinds of intellectual and emotional responses in others, and why that is so.

Example: Proverbs

Another activity for teaching interpretation skills is analyzing proverbs. Proverbs have become somewhat obsolete, but still linger as cliches.
I sometimes use three or four of them as a writing sample during the
IDA, and sometimes as an introduction (after propaganda) to figurative
thinking. Take the saying "One swallow does not a summer make." Responses vary with age, maturity, and intelligence as well as experience;
country children do much better at interpreting proverbs than do city
children. You might get a response such as, "It does not make sense";
here the reader interprets swallow to mean eating. That's rare and certainly worth noting diagnostically. Usually you will get answers such as,
"It takes more than one bird, or swallow to make a summer." This is
essentially a literal restatement, not an interpretation, so probe with
questions like; What do you mean? Well one bird does not make a summer because other things are in the summer. What else? Well, its warm.
What else? You go swimming. What else? Flowers and trees are out. Anything else? No. Next get the student to try to generalize about the swallow and summer, to see if he can grasp the essential relationship between
a part (the swallow, or any single component of summer) with the whole
(summer). In teaching students who have trouble at this relatively low
level of interpretation, guide them into doing this kind of thinking and
analyzing: What is the relationship being stated? How is a swallow related to summer? What is a summer? It is many things: temperature,
trees, flowers, no school, certain activities, etc. How does it differ from
other seasons? How are the appearance of a swallow, green trees, and 90-
degree weather part of this thing we call summer? Have them to detect
the part-whole relationship and offer other sayings containing it, such as
"Can't see the forest for the trees," or "A journey of a thousand miles
begins with one step." This kind of activity helps students move from
literal interpretations into the connotative and figurative uses and meanings of words and phrases so essential to all work in interpretation. These
activities and the propaganda techniques combine to get students off the
literal track and into the realms of meaning and feeling derived from
imagery and figurative language.

Example: Pictures

Another technique for teaching the awareness of literary devices is
having the students write or talk descriptively about what they see in
selected pictures. Good books on this approach are *Stop, Look and Write*
(Leavitt and Sohn, 1964); the *John Day Urban Education Series*; and;
Read Your Way Up (Howards, 1968). I frequently have all the students
write about the same picture and then we read their descriptions and
discuss the differences in perceptions and expressions.

For example, students of various ages have said that the old man in Exhibit 8-9 is waiting at the market to sell his cabbage; he is waiting for the bus or train because he is leaving; he's tired, depressed, poor. Some catch the resolution in the man's face and build stories about his life as a hopeless minority person; others have taken an almost opposite view. Whichever they choose, we discuss in detail what clues in the picture led them to their conclusions about the man and his life. This kind of activity can be fruitful for generating descriptive language and more probing sensitivity. It works well with young students as well as older ones.

To start you might have students just focus on the man's face, his clothes, his location, generating descriptions of these and then explaining why their description is true or accurate. Hence we combine figurative language usage with propaganda and opinion. Have the students think of synonyms and antonyms for each description of the man, and build similes and metaphors, which they compare with the picture and with each other.

In all such activities we reemphasize how well the literary devices are being used, we generate others, and discuss them fully. In the background of a group of such lessons on interpretation I read my favorite poems, excerpts from good literary writing by, for example, Thomas Wolfe, Lawrence Durrell, and John Cheever and, as needed for adolescents and young adults, by more popular writers like Vonnegut and Barth and the poet Allan Ginsburg.

Example: Modern Songs and Lyrics

Interpreting the lyrics of modern songs is an interesting activity, done without the music and then with the music so that the students can sense the differences and the impact of the music on the lyric. One of my classroom activities is to put familiar lyrics to another melody and to note on all levels the dissonances the students feel. The discussion of why they feel that way, and whether one type of melody is more appropriate than another for a particular set of lyrics is also fruitful. Use many types of music and sensitize them to the differences between what I call electric rubber band music, 1940s swing with it's tight harmony, clearly defined melody and snug lyrics, and Bartok and Copeland, or Cage's aleatory music. For more mature groups we'll look at some aspects of the base of music historically and now. I'll play in a darkened room without introduction a symphonic excerpt, a '40s or '50s piece, Stan Kenton, or a vocal piece. Listening to the music is followed by a discussion of their emotional reactions to the different types of music they heard and who they think wrote them and when. We discuss how these changes in musical form correspond to a fair degree with poetic and literary changes. Stan Kenton represents a variation of the standard, almost rhyming musical patterns by his insertion of dissonance and big brass emphasis; that can be related

Exhibit 8-9.

to blank verse in poetry which can be dissonant and not rigidly rhymed and structured. But these must be heard and then you can dig in. It helps to emphasize the relationships among the languages, music, math, and literature, and the means for evoking meaning and feeling. Music helps to enrich the sense of emotive expression for those not yet into literature, and sometimes helps them bridge that gap. Emphasize the language of all these modes and forms so it adds up to a deeper awareness and broader concept of language and communication.

POETRY

Introduction

The best way to tie these parts together is in poetry, which most children think they hate. If you move from propaganda techniques to proverbs to pictures, to reading to them, and using varied language in your every day conversation, the next step is poetry, which is the most complete and artistic form of language usage. This is not say that there is not high quality prose; there certainly is, and much of it is filled with poetic gestures. Here is a fine example from the introduction to Thomas Wolfe's *Look Homeward, Angel* (p. 1):

> ". . . a stone, a leaf, an unfound door; of a stone, a leaf, a door. And of all the forgotten faces. Naked and alone we came into exile. In her dark womb we did not know our mother's face; from the prison of her flesh have we come into the unspeakable and incommunicable prison of this earth. Which of us has known his brother? Which of us has looked into his father's heart? Which of us has not remained forever prison-pent? Which of us is not forever a stranger and alone? O waste of loss, in the hot mazes, lost, among the bright stars on this most weary unbright cinder, lost! Remembering speechlessly we seek the great forgotten language, the lost lane-end into heaven, a stone, a leaf, an unfound door. Where? When? O lost, and by the wind grieved, ghost, come back again."

I don't know what that does for you, but it has always captured my heart and soul, and all the in-between. Not only do I find the language perfect, and evocative on nine levels, but I feel the melody in head and heart; for, indeed, which of us is not a stranger, unknown and unknowing of mother, father, the world? The marvelous, unexpected phrases like ". . . Naked and alone we came into exile," when we would have expected "Naked and alone we came into life." Born into exile, when all our associations with exile are people being put out of their own country, never to return. And the womb is not the home he seeks since that was ". . . the prison of her womb." We know neither mother, father, brother (in family and in the world). And how about ". . . this most weary unbright cinder . . ." How to characterize our planet!

This piece is a statement of despair, but a poetic, shared despair; it is an attempt at universality of man's nakedness and frailty—his inability to love, to know. We came out of the prison of flesh and remain imprisoned in it, on this unbright cinder. He didn't believe that literally and neither do you or I, but we know somewhere that is *the* question for all man: who are you, what are you, why? Quo vadis? It is poetry in prose format. The meter is not strictly poetic, but when you read it out loud you will feel its melody. And the last, painfully poignant line. What shall come back? The silence of nonexistence? Another kind of life? The love we never had, and cannot seem to find; the togetherness of friends? And what is the "great forgotten language, the lost lane-end into heaven"? Is it nature, is it God or has he failed us, or we him? I won't belabor this because if you feel the power of this mournful poetry, nothing *need* be added; if you don't then nothing *can* be added, except to point some of it out. We don't know how to develop the appreciation for that kind of language in older youth and adults without a major excision of their past educational experiences. I have found that by reading such poetic pieces dramatically to certain groups of people of various ages and backgrounds I could get some of them to feel the music and its meaning. We could then ask ourselves why poetry is so different from other modes of language. Archibald MacLeish wrote a poem saying that a poem must *be*, not be interpreted, or be a certain form or shape or content, but just *be*, like a painting or a spring day or a summer storm. For if the students do not catch this feeling for poetic language, they will be, "lost and by the wind grieved." Consider the kinds of thinking and feeling that went into making that statement: grieved by the wind. How could it be? What is the sound of grieving wind? When do people grieve; what are its components and manifestations? How is that likened to the wind—that apparently indifferent force in the universe? Why does it grieve man's nakedness and frailty? Your best bet in all work on interpretation is choosing profoundly moving examples like that, or whichever you happen to like. Use Shakespeare, the Bible, whatever. Have your students try their hand at it and care about it; they will, usually, if you do. *Emotions are contagious*, much more so than mere intellectual prattle.

Reading Good Poetry

In order to take full advantage of what our students, especially our minority students, bring with them as part of their culture use poetry to draw out of them their own special insights, values and perceptions. Good poetry, good literature tends be universal in its appeal so that it can help bridge the cultural gaps in your own classes. The Blacks bring a long oral tradition in verse and song; the Hispanics can trace their literary and artistic roots back at least 400 years; the American Indian groups hold poetry and story telling in high esteem. If students can share with each other the outstanding poetry of their own culture, then compare and contrast that with the best of the American culture, then we have not only broken down barriers between them, but we have learned a more universal tongue. Good poetry and literature unleash our thoughts and emotions on human concerns. Many believe that it is out of pain, suffering, and persecution that many peoples on this unbright cinder have fashioned art.

Especially good poems for me include Yeats' *Second Coming* and *Sailing to Byzantium*; Eliot's *The Love Song of J. Alfred Prufrock*, (and other of Yeat's poetry); Frost, especially *Two Roads* and *Acquainted with the Night*; e.e. cummings, especially *somewhere i have never travelled* and *my father moved through dooms of love*; Eberhart's *Groundhog*; Wallace Stevens' *Thirteen Ways of Looking at a Blackbird*; Shelley's *Ozymandias*; Vachel Lindsay's *Congo* for music and his *Leaden-Eyed* for serious purpose; Shakespeare's plays and sonnets; some biblical poetry like the *Songs of Solomon*.

It is important that you have your own special list so that when you are ready to teach poetry and literature (as an English teacher or classroom teacher or reading/language specialist) you wrench from your soul those things most dear to it. That will enrich and enliven your presentation and its contagion will spread to many students. All students need to be exposed to reading material that someone feels very deeply about and which can touch their own lives. So little emotion occurs in schools and teaching, except negative reactions of anger, hostility, and icy indifference, that this will come as a pleasant (if unclear) surprise. Be sure in working with these interpretational skills and sensitivies that the students get into the act and write a lot. They must make simile and metaphors, and build images.

Most of the poems and authors mentioned above have been used with various age groups in many parts of the country with good success. Disadvantaged youth, illiterate adults, little children, and ambivalent adolescents have generally responded well to dramatic and emotionally presented poetry and literature, and even written their own. The Indian project mentioned in Chapter 5 produced not only the two books on Montana, and Rivers and Cities, but a book of poetry; in an adult program (WIN) a book of poetry was written; Appalachian children, Mexican-American, Black urban children have all written poetry for me and my students, even those who most hated poetry and English and reading. You have to believe in it and love it; because *you can't spread what you haven't caught.*

Teaching Poetry

I'll interpret several poems now and point out the use of the literary devices, as well as word usage and meanings, and allusions, imagery, and symbolism.

Example: "The Second Coming"

This poem, by William Butler Yeats (1951, pp. 184-185), I have used with junior high and high school students and with adults of varying levels of reading ability.

The Second Coming

Turning and Turning in the widening gyre
The falcon cannot hear the falconer;
Things fall apart; the centre cannot hold;
Mere anarchy is loosed upon the world,
The blood-dimmed tide is loosed, and everywhere
The ceremony of innocence is drowned;
The best lack all conviction, while the worst
Are full of passionate intensity.
Surely some revelation is at hand;
Surely the Second Coming is at hand.
The Second Coming! Hardly are those words out
When a vast image out of Spiritus Mundi
Troubles my sight: somewhere in the sands of the desert
A shape with lion body and the head of a man,
A gaze blank and pitiless as the sun,
Is moving its slow thighs, while all about it
Reel shadows of the indignant desert birds.
The darkness drops again; but now I know
That twenty centuries of stony sleep
Were vexed to nightmare by a rocking cradle,
And what rough beast, its hour come round at last,
Slouches towards Bethlehem to be born?

First try to get the students' general impression of what the poem is about. After some discussion, go back through the poem almost line by line noting good imagery and allusions, and then try to get the total impact of the symbolism of the Second Coming, the rough beast, and Bethlehem. Many students have difficulty with words like "gyre" in the first line, so we work that through, finally noting that it is the root of *gyroscope* and *gyration*. We try to figure who the falcon and falconer are. We agree it is man and God respectively, because the context of the poem and its title, point to a religious theme and one of Christianity. The remainder of the first stanza is clear to most: the world is anarchic and brutal.

We talk about that and why it might be so, and where and when Yeats might have written the poem and how that may have influenced Yeats to write these harsh and despairing statements. (It was written after World War I.) We talk about such phrases as "the best lack all conviction, while the worst are full of passionate intensity," and try to find correlates in their lives and world. Is this such a time? Why? Why not? Give examples.

The second stanza is heavier. We note the relationship between "revelation" and "Second Coming." We speak of the first coming and its promise and failures, and talk about what the expression "Second Coming" means to Christians. We define "Spiritus Mundi," the world spirit, and the troubling image in the desert—the desert, which is the birthplace of Christianity. Then we note in the next lines the image of the sphinx staring eternally and blankly indifferent to man and his rise and fall. The shadows of the "indignant desert birds" (personification) and the clouds of darkness fall on this cruel scene—this womb of darkness. What cradle I ask and the twenty centuries? We come up with Christ, the first coming filled with hope, and then, the last two lines recall the beast slouching toward Bethlehem. It is not difficult now to get the students to tell what Yeats thinks of us and of our abuse of Christianity, and what he foresees as our reward: more brutality and beastly religion, or how religion has failed.

Images abound: falcon and falconer; the widening gyre; blood-dimmed tide is loosed, ceremony of innocence is drowned. Some of it is intellectual imagery, not of nature, but still powerful. The second stanza requires a knowledge of allusions, especially the Christian myth, the Sphinx, the "indignant desert birds" (as vultures), and the coup in the choice of the word "slouches."

Try to bring the poem up to date and into the current world situation. Ask if this could have been written now, or ten years ago? Do you think it will be pertinent and accurate in ten or twenty years? Why? Why not? This discussion emphasizes how much is needed in order to really interpret poetry or other literary writing.

Do writers really always say exactly what they mean? Why not? How do you present certain information to certain people; how does your language reflect the differences of those social contexts within which you speak?

Example: "Footprints"

For younger children one can always find collections of children's literature, especially in Arbuthnot's classic *Children's Books* (1976), but I personally find most children's literature, especially the poetry, to be of low quality and basically written for other adults. Here is a poem I wrote (Howards, 1971) some years ago for my youngest child, Jason:

Footprints

I walk upon the wet, soft sand
and feel my cool feet
sink into the beach.
I sink in just a little
and see the marks
my feet have made,
and I wonder if some of me
is still there, in the sand,
or whether I just touched
the sand with my feet
so we'd both know
WE ARE REAL!

I love the beach, the sand, the waves
that slide over each other
and onto the sand, and under it,
back and forth, in and out,
    out and in.

I love to see where I have been,
    my feet and I,
    my footprints—two by two—
up and down the beach
like writing in a book.
But soon the waves come in
and wash my footprints away.
When I return to see the places
where I felt the sand, and the sand felt me,
it is as if no one ever was there before.

Perhaps the sand does not remember me
or, perhaps, the water doesn't want me
to mark the beach with my footprints.
Maybe the water and the sand
    forget very quickly.
I wonder how many other feet
have stepped into my footprints
    on the beach,
and I wonder where all the feet have gone.

It is simple and concrete, yet suggestive with imagery familiar to a young child. Clearly, footprints and their washing away could have numerous other connotations and associations. The poem is a little sad and full of wonder. Younger children will not wonder as deeply as older ones will about the issue of change and of our being able to make an impression or a mark on the world; or about man's relative impotence in the face of nature. But it's a soft summer day on a warm beach, a place mainly for play and just a bit of wonder.

With very young children one must get them to re-create the specifics of such a day in such a place, and then get them to add to it by making other comparisons and contrasts, using other words to describe thoughts and feelings about specific things like sand, water, sky, feet. Get to the sensory matter by asking, Cold as what? Warm as what, or When? Rough as? Big as? Start with simple similes and sensory images. Speculations on the last few lines of "Footprints," particularly how many other feet have stepped into my footprints, who they might have been, when, how they felt, why, and so on could follow. This generates a great deal of language and makes the vocabulary more precise and descriptive, and all of this is rooted in a simple, real, common experience of walking on a beach. One could have elementary level students describe the boy or girl in the poem and give reasons why they think he or she looks or feels that way. From each such probe, many exercises and activities will flow especially in vocabulary and writing. Making images and visualizing scenes with all the sensory impressions possible directs the language production, and it makes it much clearer what these devices such as simile, metaphor, and personification really are and how they are made. *This cannot be done very well by defining the terms and giving examples alone.* When students undergo these experiences and activities their appreciation of well written prose or poetry is enormously enhanced.

Example: "Groundhog"

I am still startled and almost in awe when I read Eberhart's (1944, p. 464) "Groundhog":

> . . ."And bones bleaching in the sunlight
> Beautiful as architecture;
> I watched them like a geometer,
> And cut a walking stick from a birch."

He describes his final return to the spot where he had first encountered a dead groundhog, and notes what was left after three years of exposure to the elements. In a preceding group of lines he spoke of the "bony sodden hulk," so that the contrast is extremely vivid and arresting. How often have we seen dead animals and been able to feel our own mortality, our fear, and our fascination as well as to observe the striking contrast between its ugliness and its absolute beauty? Does that not truly characterize our ambivalence about death and about life? He concludes the poem with these deeply moving lines:

> There is no sign of the groundhog.
> I stood there in the whirling summer,

My hand capped a withered heart,
And thought of China and of Greece,
Of Alexander in his tent;
Of Montaigne in his tower,
Of Saint Theresa in her wild lament.

Now we see the connection between his viewing this apparently insignificant groundhog (not even a lion) and how it brought him to his own mortality, and then he historicizes about outstanding humans like Alexander, Montaigne, and Saint Theresa, and of China and Greece, all of these filled with earthly or mystical glory, and he comes to the perspective that all living things die no matter how mighty or exalted: people and civilizations as well as the groundhog—in short, all of nature's prodigy.

Example: "Ozymandias"

Shelley's poem "Ozymandias" (p. 99-100) strikes the same chord:

I met a traveler from a distant land
Who said: Two vast and trunkless legs of stone
Stand in the desert. Near them, on the sand,
Half sunk a shattered visage lies, whose frown,
And wrinkled lip, and sneer of cold command,
Tell that its sculptor well those passions read
Which yet survive, stamped on these lifeless things,
The hand that mocked them and the heart that fed;
And on the pedestal these words appear:
"My name is Ozymandias, king of kings:
Look on my works, ye Mighty, and despair!"
Nothing beside remains. Round the decay
Of that colossal wreck boundless and bare
The lone and level sands stretch far away.

The poem uncovers even that imperial boast, since none escape, and all are bound by nature. It does jolt one into humility. Clearly, in dealing with poetry like this, one does need to know history, other literary sources, and even mythology and anthropology in order to imbibe the bulk of meanings embedded in all these related sources. All poetry and literature is part of a particular cultural heritage, so that it follows some basic rules for imaging and symbolizing, for if it didn't, like language itself, we would not understand its referents. There must be a common core of experiences, language, and history to make poetry, literature, and art possible as a medium of communication.

Poems like "Groundhog" and "Ozymandias" and poems of Eliot, Frost, and e.e. cummings touch our sense of human mortality, frailty, and tragedy while reminding us of our place in nature and in the scheme of the universe. Kenneth Burke, the brilliant scholar of language and man, said that we stand (all of us) hand in hand at the edge of the precipice. I agree to that much mortality, but with the same hope that we can do it hand in hand. Life, the world, Man, are in danger, but some do stand with dignity, pride, and unselfishness. Shelley's "Ozymandias" (Ramses II of Egypt, reigning about 3300 years ago) is proud and imperial, but mortal, and like Alexander, and that host of conquerors, has come and gone . . . *sic transit gloria mundi.*

It is so easy to lose perspective on Man, Nature, and the world filled with anger, greed, and violence, but also filled with love, hope, and creativity. We have art, music, theatre, poetry. We are small and great; wise and foolish; beautiful and ugly. Nothing says it like poetry or good literature.

A good technique used when I was a college freshman for developing sensory imagery was blindfolding a student who comes up to a table full of various objects of various sizes, shapes, textures and having him pick one up without seeing it. Then the student returns to his seat and writes a description of the object. After a number of students have done this, they look at the objects and match them with the descriptions. This leads to great discussions and revisions of the language, as well as focusing observational skills and sensory reactions. *Do it with all the senses*, noting which are most accurate. Also the language generated in these activities heightens the student's consciousness of what is sensed and how to transmit it, to recreate it for another. If this type of activity is tied in with the activity in which we used a word like "walk" (described previously) we clearly improve the student's visualization and imaging. Attaching language to it is relatively easy after that is achieved. Most of us do not observe carefully at all.

Examples: Observing

Ask your students questions that concern typical activities taking place in the morning. For instance: What was your mother wearing this morning? Describe the smell of bacon, or the way you looked in the mirror brushing your teeth. One could do this with numerous other everyday activities. In some VISTA training programs at Northeastern University and at the University of Colorado in Boulder under the incomparable and ingenious Howard Higman, volunteers were sent to low-income neighborhoods, downtown hotels, bars, street corners, and hang-outs of various types, and were instructed to make notes (as unobtrusively as possible) about the conversations they could overhear—a businessman's conversation in a fancy hotel lobby, or one at a bar next to four guys playing pool in a sleazy pool hall, or a conversation between two women looking at clothes in a store, or conversations over lunch or between lovers on the grass. The eavesdroppers then made comparisons and contrasts with content and style, language usage, mood, and tone.

These activities sharpen one's observational skills and lead into deeper interpretations of who these people are and why they dress, speak, and behave as they do in those contexts and what that might tell you about dealing with them.

Vocabulary and sentence analyses can also be made of this material. With such guided observational activities, in school or out of it, it is easy to sensitize students to so many aspects of human language and behavior. This is excellent raw material for writing activities in either poetic or prose forms. This type of activity broadens the base and enlarges the context within which sensory impressions link to cognitive assessments, and, all in all, make the student a much more sensitive instrument.

In classrooms it is easy enough to do similar activities describing the room's size, color, shape, and feel. Getting youngsters to respond to music of different types and from different cultures is easy. Adding to their affective responses to such music the dimension of trying to talk about how it makes them feel, what they see, what they hear, etc., produces more language and vocabulary and imaging. If you use Bill Martin's (1967) materials, most of it is right there for you for elementary age students, and once again I urge you to read or re-read Warner's *Teacher*, and Cullum's *Push Back the Desks*.

Let young children hear and feel the music, beat and rhythm of poetry without too much concern at the outset about their understanding of the words or allusions.

Example: "Bells"

Every child responds affectively to Poe's "Bells":

> Hear the sledges with the bells—
>   Silver bells!
> What a world of merriment their melody foretells!
> How they tinkle, tinkle, tinkle,
> In the icy air of night!
> While the stars that oversprinkle
> All the heavens, seem to twinkle
> With a crystalline delight;
> Keeping time, time, time
> In a sort of Runic rhyme,
> To the tintinnabulation that so
>   musically wells
> From the bells, bells, bells, bells,
>   Bells, bells, bells—
> From the jingling and the tinkling
>   of the bells.

It almost sings itself! The meaning is quite secondary here, but the auditory imagery is superb. How about the word "tintinnabulation" itself said slowly, then faster and faster? "Jingling and the tinkling" make

the sounds and find others like it and different from them. What else
tinkles, what else jingles? Then note synonyms, antonymns, make different images, visual, and tactile. In working with poetry start with sensory,
concrete feelings, and then move to the more abstract, but not too far.
The worst poetry has always been the abstract, moralistic, or political, or
abstractly philosophical. Morals, politics, and philosophy are certainly
worth literary effort, but the way it is done is critical, because the topics
lend themselves to pomposity, ambiguity, and abstraction. Stay with Nature and the immediate environment; use concrete words and descriptive
verbs before qualifying adjectives and adverbs. Starting this way makes
it possible for the students to participate at once.

Example: "Somewhere i have never travelled"

Before we leave poetry I must share with you e.e. cummings' poem
"somewhere i have never travelled" (cummings, 1963, p. 88). I have
seen his poetry, and this poem in particular, turn on the most unlikely
youngsters. There is something about his unorthodoxy in capitalization
and syntax which calls to them. Perhaps they feel a kindred spirit rebel-
ling. Whatever does it, it works. I think this is the best love poem in the
English language and because e.e. cummings has so mastered English
syntax, and his imagery is so vivid and real, one always feels it and understands:

> somewhere i have never travelled, gladly beyond
> any experience, your eyes have their silence:
> in your most frail gesture are things which enclose me,
> or which i cannot touch because they are too near
> your slightest look easily will unclose me
> though i have closed myself as fingers,
> you open always petal by petal myself as Spring opens
> (touching, skillfully, mysteriously) her first rose
> or if your wish be to close me, i and
> my life will shut very beautifully, suddenly,
> as when the heart of this flower imagines
> the snow carefully everywhere descending;
> nothing which we are to perceive in this world equals
> the power of your intense fragility: whose texture
> compels me with the color of its countries,
> rendering death and forever with each breathing
> (i do not know what it is about you that closes
> and opens; only something in me understands
> the voice of your eyes is deeper than all roses)
> nobody, not even the rain, has such small hands

Love is such an impossible subject to write about or talk about at all,
and uniquely difficult to do so originally. Try to say something original,
creative, and artistic about love. Read it through once with feeling and
then the students are normally dazed and ready for more. Then read it

again, looking at it much more closely. Take the first two lines and try to get from them what it means to them, what is the poet saying. After one or two dead literal transliterations, we usually get closer to cummings' intent. This is an experience, this love, like no other he has ever had. Ask students to try to say the same thing in other ways. Compare. They tend to say too much too literally, in too many words, or too abstractly. Older poetry of the eighteeneth and nineteenth centuries can be brought in for contrast. The contrasts are so clear that little has to be said usually. As we continue through the poem we pick out phrases like "your most frail gesture" and the line after that at the end of the first stanza and we talk about it as an unusual way to say it. The class tries other ways, which we discuss. Constantly we work on condensing their work so that it becomes poetic; nothing is more condensed than good poetry. It is easy to illustrate how few words and good imagery can tell so much. Concrete sensory images and brevity are accented.

The imagery in the next stanza of cummings is elegantly simple, so tangible, so compelling a metaphor: . . . "you open always petal by petal myself", and simile, ". . . as Spring opens (touching skilfully, mysteriously) her first rose." Or one of the truly inspired images: ". . . my life will shut very beautifully, as when the heart of this flower imagines the snow carefully everywhere descending." Unspeakable. When students try to say the same things their own way they begin to fully appreciate and admire this mastery. When we have done this with the whole poem, we try to sum up both our feelings evoked by this imagery, unusual syntax, and choice of words, and we try to sum up our overall impression, comparing it with our initial reaction to its music. Let them try to imitate him, modify him, not because we want them to be copiers, but because we want them to try to feel through his use of language. Then they must find their own tongues. They must rediscover their own senses. If some of these ideas were implemented in the early elementary school years, more students would enjoy poetry and good language usage. It would not remain in the domain of the boring.

In teaching students of all ages and backgrounds, it is my habit to drop unusual words—not just weird ones, but words with special meanings and live images. A couple of students will come in with unusual words of that they like and we are off and running. We put words on the board like: *hermeneutics, squeg, ideogram, indefatigably, chromatopore, ire, ilk.* You can use a wide variety of words and expressions in conversation and discussion with them so as to provide them with enough context to figure them out. Try to keep the air they breathe filled with the scent of new words, new perspectives, new images.

Beyond Wishes, Lies and Dreams

After some work with reading, writing, and enjoying good poetry and literature as already described briefly, and after the word-play, it is time for the class to do more of their own writing. A good idea, which went astray mainly because it did not go far enough, is found in Koch's *Wishes, Lies and Dreams*. He had urban students write various kinds of images, metaphors, similes, etc., but he did not develop the skills in the book itself.

I applaud Koch for trying it in that setting, P.S. 61 in New York, and what he did is more in the right direction, but so much more could be developed. Maybe he did more in his classes and just did not include it in his book. The idea of having children write their own poetry of course is good, just as having them write their own textbook as the Blackfeet Indian children did (Chapter 5), but that does not free you as teacher from the responsibility to get their best.

Koch (1970, p. 147) explains how he got his students to deal with metaphors:

> I told the children to think about a thing being like something else (the cloud is like a pillow) and to pretend that it really was the other thing; thus, to say IS instead of IS LIKE (the cloud is a pillow). Then, if they liked, they could elaborate on this one metaphor (I rest my head on the cloud) for the entire poem . . . or start a new metaphor in each line. Metaphors are a good, enjoyable experience for children, though they are a little difficult. They are harder than comparisons, and I'd suggest giving them after rather than before the Comparison Poem.

Compare this with the suggestions I have made and you will find the contrasts. He misleads children if he does not encourage them to understand that similes and metaphors are both forms of comparison, and if he does not work much harder on helping them to note the differences. Reading the poems the children wrote in this section of his collection supports my contention that these children do not really understand or fully appreciate the power of these devices; particularly the metaphor. Here is an example of what I mean (Koch, p. 149):

> Someday I hope to see a face with roses
> A hat of kisses
> A stripe of hair
> A kiss of babies
> An eraser of kittens
> A baby of mittens
> A lady of decks. . .

Clearly these do not relate to each other as they do in real poetry. Each metaphor is separate and distinct, violating the essence of metaphor, which should direct the flow of thought and feeling in its own context and related contexts. This is almost a listing of fragmented expressions. In this example and in the ones to follow you will notice that none of these expressions and utterances masquerading as metaphors really comes from the lives and experiences of these city students. Why didn't he use that rich resource for making images? As these stand, they are not much better than what might appear in a workbook where one is required to fill in blanks calling for a metaphor. There is no sensory impression in these; they are strangely abstract without being either abstract or perceptive—just statements resembling a metaphor's form but not its content. These kids can make real images and some poetry; this is a poor model since it misleads them about the nature of imagery and denies them their own senses and experiences, the heart of all good writing, especially poetry. These are so bad I don't know that they can be salvaged, except by questioning the children as to whether they can indeed see, hear, feel, the metaphor they just wrote; is it real; could it be? How can we fix it to say what you want to say? This activity as he has done it seems to be a game without rules, or rules one makes up as one goes, ad hoc, and irrespective of meaning. These have no meaning.

Here are a couple more examples (Koch, pp. 150, 151):

> A blackboard of moons
> A window of kisses
> A flag of boxes
> A swimming pool of doorknobs
> A shirt made of tulips. . . . .
>
> A shirt of beads
> A flag of water
> A door of windows
> A person made of toys
> A flower made of a person. . . .

The first problem he had was that he did these metaphors at random. Since metaphor, like any imagery, is comparable to a concept, it is essential that relationships are clearly explored and explained. This obviously did not happen. If nothing else, Koch could have limited the metaphor-making to those related to flowers, city noises, or smells, or to something taken directly from their immediate environment, including their room. Then whatever imagery would be generated could be sharpened much more easily. Also these kids need some direction and some boundaries for such work; they are not used to it and have little experience handling language in this figurative manner. Just saying this is a metaphor or personification or image does not make it so. The students must have a concept of imagery which they can only derive from the kinds of activities I have been suggesting. What he has done is so artificial and unpoetic.

With the Blackfeet Indian children who put together the two books

Montana and *Rivers and Cities* (see Chapter 3) we added some work in poetry derived from the "walk" activity. The decision by teacher and students in that instance was to write poetry about a general topic. They chose "What disturbs me." At least that limited them. And although the poetry they wrote was not very good, it was at least coherent and the images and metaphors were related to each other on that topic. I would heartily recommend such limitation in the early stages of writing poetry or descriptive narration by students. When they have heard and discussed the kind of poetry included earlier in this chapter they have a much better concept of what poetry is and how it creates the moods, feelings, and ideas that it does. Good models are important. Also, *make the imagery sensory and derived from their immediate environment and lives*, before you wander off into abstractness. Frost would have helped these P.S. 61 students get a much more concrete idea of how to describe thoughts and feelings very simply using what is at hand.

My experience with students like these has been that they can write decent poetry and make good images, but they want to know that what they have written is real, is good, is like other poetry, and not some pale image of it. By using this material produced by Koch's students, not too much could be done to sharpen their ears, eyes, or other senses, nor their choice of words. It is so much like a game of Scrabble before you start to play.

I don't want to belabor Mr. Koch's well-intentioned idea, but I cannot let it go by without these critical remarks, because I know kids can do so much better. If you **have** attended to the language usage of young children, especially preschoolers, you have noted that they often come up with unusual, literary remarks. Some of this is due to their immaturity in life and in language usage. It is also attributable to their lack of experience and concepts, and it is attributable to their childish wonder. A three-year-old I know once reported to his mother that he had a "noise in his pocket"—something in it was living and communicating with him. The logic of this statement is traceable but like poetic expression it goes beyond logic and pure reason. It fits into the category of early man's descriptions and explanations of the events, the objects of their lives. Causation does not operate the same way for them.

Why not take advantage of this kind of language usage so common to most youngsters and build on it? We keep trying (and succeeding most often) in inserting foreign objects, notions, relationships into these zetetic minds, full of wonder and curiosity. If it is so common for youngsters to wander into metaphor and simile, why can't we use the process already there, and then hone it to a finer edge?

When you move into poetry read your favorite poems to them, have them read their favorite poems (silently and aloud, dramatically), and have them write poetry or good imagery as soon as possible and as often as possible. If you focus their attention on some theme it may be easier for them to decide what to write about.

Do a group of poems, stories, plays about love, hate, war, family, animals, friends. In reading and discussing their various views on any one of these themes or topics, they will gain an enriched sense of the multiple ways one can express these powerful emotions and deep thoughts. You could easily tie this type of writing activity into your core concept which already provides a clear focus. Students cannot learn to make all kinds of similes, metaphors, and images in all kinds of contexts at once, so limit the context thematically and that will make it easier for them to overcome their hesitancy about writing, and especially about writing poetry.

There are many levels of poetic and literary activity one can present as a means of developing sensitivity to language, sharpening observational skills, and developing some appreciation for this form of art. You will have to determine how much, how fast, and how far you can proceed with any given student or group. *Expect more than you have in the past and make them all produce much more, but make it matter what they say or write, and how they say or write it.* Start with less than good images and work into better ones focusing on their feelings as well as their thoughts, and stay close to Nature for your source of imagery. Keep reading good poetry and literature to them; let that be a counterpoint to the theme.

What I have done with poetry and with Koch is relatively easy to do; what is much more complicated to do and even more complicated to explain is how to make metaphor or imagery. I have tried to work backwards in order to offer you some further suggestions on how to guide students in making their imagery. I have picked a few images from my own poetry and other writing and followed the completed image to as many of its sources as I could uncover. For example, throughout this book I have used certain images and metaphors which control and direct the flow of my thought, feeling, and reason. I have used *tidal* as an image of learning anything in the world, with its obvious ebb and flow in *circadic* fashion—in every six hours and out every six hours, twice each day. Bruner and others use the image of spiral curriculum, spiral learning, but I find that less accurate than tidal, because spiral evokes in me the sense of circles, going round and round, and tides do not. You will decide for yourself which of these two metaphors most aptly summarizes your understanding of learning. I have also spoken of *wholes*, and the relationship of parts to wholes, and have amplified this with discussions of music, painting, and other arts to clarify my image and metaphor. Others, like the behaviorists, could not use such metaphor or imagery, since their view is one of sequential steps, repetition and machine-like operations in teaching and learning. There is no flow in their concept; it is linear, alphabetic; mine is ideographic.

Making Images

Here is some of my poetic imagery (Howards, 1952) and how it was constructed:

> Down what forgotten paths have I not travelled
> Only to be undone at the sight
> Of a throbbing in her throat
> Like birds expecting flight. . . .

Notice, of course, the touch of e.e. cummings in the first two lines. Then the image in the last line. The image is real and common, birds in flight, taking off, landing, but the word "expecting" really alters the mood and action drastically. Now the reader must dig into his life experience of being in love and seeing if he can re-create such a feeling of certain uncertainty. The birds mumbling, gurgling, moving about uneasily, almost fretfully, will take off if you come too close, but you do not know when. What is it in the moment which urges them into the air away from you or any imagined danger? One could have said, prosaicly: I do not know how you feel about me, or me about you. I am not certain if you will stay with me or leave; you are as restless as birds. But that would have overstated the case and buried the feeling of doubt—expectancy in verbiage. *Poetry is very lean; very succinct.* I tried to mesh our common experience with birds with a common feeling of doubt about a lover. I don't know if it works for you as it did for me, but however it moved you is fine. I would prefer that it would re-create for you the same deep but uncertain feelings it did in me when I wrote it.

You can guide students into this kind of awareness and analysis as they write poetry or literary material of any kind. We have to help them get into the heart of their feelings, thoughts, and experiences so that their imagery will make the feelings common to us. Making, unmaking, and remaking images like this is a critical step in having them really express what they want to, and to give the reader the same experience. The context of the writer's experience is best reconstructed by a reader when the imagery is like this, or like the examples given earlier in the chapter. One knows love and feels it again reading e.e. cummings "somewhere i have never travelled," and one is sobered by one's own middle-class conventionality by Eliot's "Prufrock."

Here's another image from a poem by Howards (1969):

> eyes inhale you
> dissolving gray and
> blushing boldly into bloom
> cells and sense
> coalesce
> you are present as pulse.

This is the last stanza of a poem so that it is a bit unfair to isolate it for scrutiny, but perhaps it will serve our purposes. I juxtaposed sensory functions in the first line, "eyes inhale," for impact and for its striking image; and somewhat similarly the use of the phrase "blushing boldly into bloom" is an oxymoron since blushing is not done boldly under normal circumstances, and blooming is not normally associated with either, yet it describes the kind of paradoxical behavior we all experience in love. At least I hoped it would engender such emotions and thoughts. The last line is the result of the cells and sense coalescing, and I cannot think of a better way to put it. What is more present than pulse, after all?

As we shall see when we discuss Gordon's (1961) *Synectics*, the use of such metaphors requires in the writer or thinker the ability to turn the world upside down and inside out. It requires the suspension of some natural law, while drawing on the rest of it. One must work toward new perspectives of animate and inanimate behavior. Work with paradox (oxymoron) to crystallize for your students the *allness of every*. Do not be afraid to violate established concepts, laws, principles, and observations, but do not fall into the trap that Koch did when he tried this. Students can easily be sensitized to the paradox in their own life, in school, and at home: how cheaters escape the law or get uneven treatment, and how institutions seem to veer off their original course and purpose and become what they were established to eliminate. Examples abound in all our lives. The sense of wonder and the awareness of paradox are absolutely essential to literary work.

Perhaps a more concrete way to achieve some of these literary ends particularly for students with less aptitude for this kind of imaging would be to do some rewriting or paraphrasing. Have students rewrite news stories in a more literary fashion, and then go over them and critique each other and then rewrite. Talk about mood, tone, and the images themselves. I try to emphasize the need for the metaphors and similes to bear directly (and logically) on the information in the story. If they turn in material burdened by clichés, we discuss what a cliché is and why it so blunts the point of the story and dulls the reader's senses since the nature of cliché is a novel expression gone stale with overuse. I have even conspired with students (of various ages) to insert new words into their vocabularies and to see how long it takes for others to pick them up. We'll choose one word or expression and all the children use it, and then they observe how fast it spreads, if it does. We discuss why it did or didn't. This gives insight into how all language changes, and what it is about certain expressions which seem to catch on and those that do not. We try to notice if it matters who says it, children or teacher. In fact good research could be done along this line to give some inkling as to what does make language change. Anyway, the weight of cliché is heavy because it is so automatic; it requires no thinking; it is reflexive and that is easier and more convenient for most people. So you might start with a cliché-laden piece from a paper or magazine and then clean it up; or go the other way. Another dimension of cliché, incidentally, is to probe the source of these in their original form and usage. The OED* is one good source for this as is the Bible and Shakespeare, since so many of our current expressions can be traced to those sources students think they hate. When you compare prosy writing filled with clichés (and sports stories may be the worst offenders), with the poetry and other literature we have discussed here, it will become obvious to the students what the differences are. This sort of thing is really great fun even with younger students in the elementary grades. In fact, in some ways it may be more fun with them because they do so naturally play with words and allow the world and nature much more latitude than we do. Novelty, surprise, and paradox are generally accepted by youngsters.

Be sure to consult Leavitt's (1964) book *Stop, Look and Write* for more ideas on this kind of writing. Newspapers, magazines, textbooks can all be used for this kind of activity.

We have noted numerous examples of some of the widely used literary devices and techniques, expecially metaphor, simile, and personification. I hope you have derived from my illustrations and discussions, and your own experience, knowledge of what a metaphor *does*. Just as a concept is a cluster of related facts, ideas, and feelings which is generalizable to many contexts, so metaphor and imagery borrows from many sources and then is applicable to many other contexts. Metaphor, like concepts, directs the flow of thought and feeling within and among contexts.

If you want to delve into imagery and symbolism much more thoroughly read some of the reviewers of literature, such as Williamson (1953), and once again realize why so many college students feel inundated by abstruse verbiage. Not that Williamson's interpretations are not accurate or perceptive but the allusions (which abound in Eliot) require so much academic background in history, sociology, psychology, religion, philosophy, and anthropology that most students feel totally inept and ill-prepared to deal with so many additional texts to make a complete interpretation of his work possible. The interpreters try hard to recapture the "resonances of the word" referred to by Steiner, and in so doing they take us into many times and places. The text is simply not nearly enough. All literature and much other communication is laden with similar allusions and referents to other contexts.

Synectics

Synectics tries to apply many of the principles of imagery and metaphoric thinking to the solution of problems and to invention. Gordon's *Synectics* (1961) applies these literary devices and behavior to solving

---

* *OED-Oxford English Dictionary*, which gives definitions, etymology, and historical uses of words by leading authors like Shakespeare, Johnson, Byron, and others.

industrial problems which may result in the invention of new machinery or processes. The book gives numerous illustrations (actual transcripts of synectic sessions) of how this kind of metaphoric imaging works in this context. The word synectics means joining together different and apparently irrelevant elements. *Apparently* is the key word here, for as in literature and symbolic matter of all types, things, ideas, feelings, and concepts fit together surprisingly. Novelty is found in all creative activity, especially problem solving, and as we have already noted, novelty does frighten many people because it is not as predictable as normal activity or communication. Poetry is novel in that it does not lend itself as readily to prediction as most prose. This statistical property of language was mentioned in Chapter 1.

Gordon describes four types of analogy, metaphorical in character, which are used in this creative problem solving approach:

1. Personal Analogy   3. Symbolic Analogy
2. Direct Analogy   4. Fantasy Analogy

Personal analogy

In personal analogy Gordon leads the participants into personal identification with the elements of the problem which frees the person from the bonds of the past as he approaches the problem at hand. Gordon quotes Faraday and Einstein describing briefly how they personalize and become one of the elements in the problem. Gordon (1961, p. 38) says: "The creative technical person can think himself to be a dancing molecule, discarding the detachment of the expert and throwing himself into the activity of the elements involved." This same activity can be done with children particularly in the process of learning how to make and understand imagery and ways of interpreting problems. More of this kind of presentation might really enliven science work for youngsters. Can you see second graders dancing about like molecules, or atoms, moving like the tide? Certainly this would provide more opportunity to build the kind of imagery we have been discussing. Some of the dynamics of this kind of imaging is similar to role playing and can be equally overdone and misleading, but it has some potential for uncoiling children.

Direct analogy

Direct analogy "describes the actual comparison of parallel facts, knowledge or technology" (Gordon, p. 42). He gives the fascinating example of Brunel who figured out how to do underwater construction by watching a ship worm tunnel into the timber. The worm constructed a tube for itself as it moved forward, and the classical notion of caissons came to the inventor. Of course, we have all heard of people watching birds and trying to emulate their action in some kind of flying machine.

Remember poor Icarus who made a very literal analogy with birds when he supposedly made a pair of very large wings for his shoulders. He fastened them with wax and down he went. Direct analogy and too literal. Even jet aircraft these days do appear as similes of birds in flight in some ways and we say helicopters hover, like gulls. For a class activity, students could take any modern product of technology, such as guns, cars, or planes, and first be them, and then compare them with the thing in nature which suggested it. Great possibilities for individual activities and for core concepts.

Symbolic analogy

Symbolic analogy is more abstract, as you might expect, and uses imagery more poetically than the other more literal forms of analogy. Gordon (p. 46) points out something cogent here when he says, "The cultural bifurcation of art and science in our society, and the prevalence of advanced trade schools where limited experts are ground out of the curriculum, tend to make it difficult for technical graduates to understand or use the esthetic qualitative mechanisms." This is the price we pay for our over-specialization of work and of people to do that work. Remember Charlie Chaplin's classic film *Modern Times*? Exactly on target more than forty years ago, Chaplin saw the dangers to persons who do monotonous, repetitive mechanical tasks all day, every day. No sense of self or of the product being made. That is bad enough in industry and on assembly lines, but what about schools, art, feeling? If Tom Wolfe is right and the 1970s were the decade of the *me*, then Chaplin's fears have been realized. People have become separate pieces, highly specialized for self-concern. But just as words or images cannot be taken out of context to study alone, people cannot be taken out of the context of others or they, like words, become meaningless or distorted in meaning.

Gordon gives the example of symbolic analogy in a group discussion dealing with the problem of how to invent a jacking mechanism that would fit into a box four by four inches, capable of extending out three feet and supporting four tons. Two key images came up in the discussion: the penis and the old Indian rope trick in which a limp rope in a basket comes out to music, rigid and able to support a man. Also brought in was the way a steel measuring tape works. Note how they think in similes and metaphors, in order to see the problem altogether differently from the usual trial and error approach or by dealing directly with mechanical apparatus. This metaphorical/analogic thinking with some emotion and personal involvement, alters the entire context and usually produces a fine product which works. Part of what happens, according to Gordon, is that looking at problems this almost literary way releases scientists and inventors from being caught up entirely in what has been done before. They get a fresh look at a problem in totally new ways. They get more directly to the core of the problem and see it *whole*.

Fantasy analogy

The last analogy he describes is the fantasy analogy. He derives some of this from Freud's work on wish fulfillment (Gordon, p. 49): "Success depends upon his ability to defer consummation of the wish in fantasy and to make real the wish by embodying it in a work of art." Perhaps this is a bit over-simplified, but the idea is generally acceptable. The key to this approach to problem solving is for the participants to feel free to *imagine the world as they wish*. In dealing with a problem of how to make a vapor proof closure for space suits the inventors ask, "How do we in our wildest fantasies desire the closure to operate?" They start by saying they could *will* the suit closed perfectly. Then they talk about magical insects which would run up and down closing the space; then they move to a mechanical application of this including how to stitch with steel, then the insect becomes a wire. Finally they work it out (see pages 49–51). The point of it is to free the head and feelings from established modes of solving problems and getting yourself, your fears, fantasies, and crazy ideas into a group interaction. Analogies abound in the process of working out how to make a thing loose, raise, pull, and lift. In other words, the process frees people to imagine, to use metaphor, and to approach problems altogether differently. Slowly they narrow the possibilities in the real world based on their own scientific knowledge. We have all heard how so many inventions were accidental, but I suspect what really happened was the inventor got off the track of careful, scientific pursuit and let his head wander into *metaphoric musings*, playing with words, ideas, and physical laws, juggling them, turning them upside down and inside out to get a new perspective on them. All of this can be applied to developing interpretation and problem-solving skills in the classroom or clinic. It ties in very well with what we have already said about teaching interpretation. Try it, especially with younger children, so they can physically and intellectually move around. With older students one does most of the movement intellectually guided by these sensory and metaphoric imaginings. Gordon sums it up very well (p. 53): "Thus one may view a problem pretending that the laws of physics are not valid. The immutable laws usually do hold, but by pushing them out of phase for a moment one can peek in between." An approach not too different from creative writing or reading. In writing a poem, play, novel, etc., one does need a new perspective in order to create the mood, feeling, and sense of another time, place, and person. The writer and the reader have to travel through time, space, and feeling to meet each other; it is murky; it is the crossing of a deep, wide abyss; it is learning to wear another's moccasin for a day. How indeed does language and art bring us together? Imagery and good metaphor.

REFERENCES

cummings, e. e. "somewhere i have never travelled." In *A selection of poems*. New York: Harcourt, Brace & World, 1963.

Eberhart, Richard. "The groundhog." In Conrad Aiken (Ed.), *A comprehensive anthology of American poetry*. New York: Modern Library, 1944.

Eliot, T. S. "The love-song of J. Alfred Prufrock." In *The complete poems and plays, 1909–1950*. New York: Harcourt, Brace & World, 1971.

Gordon, William. *Synectics: the development of creative capacity*. New York: Collier Books, 1961.

Harris, Albert & Sipay, Edward. *How to increase reading ability* (6th ed.). New York: David McKay, 1975.

Howards, Melvin. "Forgotten paths." (Unpublished), 1952.

Howards, Melvin. "Present as pulse." (Unpublished), 1969.

Howards, Melvin. "Footprints." (Unpublished), 1971.

Koch, Kenneth. *Wishes, lies and dreams*. New York: Vintage, 1970.

Leavitt, Hart & Sohn, David. *Stop, look and write*. New York: Bantam, 1964.

Poe, Edgar Allan. "Bells." In *The complete poems and stories of Edgar Allan Poe*. New York: Alfred Knopf, 1946.

Shelley, Percy Bysshe. "Ozymandias." In Robert Hollander (Ed.), *A poetry reader*. New York: American Book, 1963.

Steiner, George. *After Babel: aspects of language and translation*. London: Oxford University Press, 1975.

Wolfe, Thomas. *Look homeward angel*. New York: Charles Scribner's Sons, 1929.

Yeats, William Butler. "The second coming." In *The collected poems of W. B. Yeats*. New York: Macmillan, 1951.

BIBLIOGRAPHY

Cullum, Albert. *Push back the desks*. New York: Citation Press, 1967.

Dallman, Martha; Rouch, Roger; Char, Lynette; & De Boer, John. *The teaching of reading* (5th ed.). New York: Holt, Rinehart & Winston, 1978.

Ekwall, Eldon. *Diagnosis and remediation of the disabled reader*. Boston: Allyn & Bacon, 1976.

Harris, Albert & Sipay, Edward. *How to increase reading ability* (6th ed.). New York: David McKay, 1975.

Howards, Melvin. *Read your way up*. New York: Manpower Education Institute, 1968.

Lapp, Diane & Flood, James. *Teaching reading to every child*. New York: Macmillan, 1978.

Martin, Bill, Jr. *The sounds of language*. New York: Holt, Rinehart & Winston, 1967.

Ogden, C. K. & Richards, I. A. *The meaning of meaning*. London: Routledge & Kegan Paul, 1923.

Spache, George. *Diagnosing and correcting reading disabilities*. Boston: Allyn & Bacon, 1976.

Warner, Sylvia. *Teacher*. New York: Simon & Schuster, 1963.

Williamson, George. *A reader's guide to T. S. Eliot*. New York: Farrar, Strauss, 1953.

Chapter nine

INTRODUCTION AND OVERVIEW

Several levels and types of interpretation are discussed and illustrated in this chapter which will improve the quality of your teaching and the quality of student understanding and thinking. Almost all students including those just below average in ability and intelligence to those who are above average in ability and intelligence respond very well to the skills and activities already suggested. The bright and gifted students will benefit from this work but we can do more for them if we take this next step in interpretation.

When we discussed core concept plans of instruction we saw that many disciplines were logically integrated and sharply focused on a broad concept which increased the meaning of each aspect under study. The subconcepts, the facts and ideas, which comprise a particular core concept are essential parts of that special cluster of relationships we call context. Meaning then flows in both directions: from the whole, core concept to its components and back again. The core concept *Migration*, illustrated in Chapter 5, may help to clarify my point. The germinal (or core) concept in *Migration* is movement: people, animals, plants, ideas all move from place to place. Subconcepts within this include Why do they move? How do they move? Where do they move? When do they move? What happens when they arrive at their destination? The answers to these questions draw in data from history, science, geography, sociology, anthropology, mathematics, and even literature. Hence we have a comprehensive context, incorporating clusters of relationships controlled by the concept of migration (the whole) and modified by the data collected from these closely related disciplines. Everything we study in this context re-

Advanced interpretation skills: major schemata

lates directly to migration and the interrelatedness of the information exposes many types of relationships; that is how we can interpret and understand this concept multidimensionally.

Core concept planning then is a medium of curriculum (the organization of learning experiences) which directly affects the message it transmits. This is comparable to McLuhan's discussion of the special generative and interactive relationship between the technology a people create and what it does *for* them as well as what it does *to* them. The curriculum is indeed a medium of learning experiences, and the core concept curriculum I have been espousing to you is the most wholistic and comprehensive, and hence, the most meaningful and the most conducive to interpretational skill. Contrast it with the typical behaviorist curriculum of fragments, which tend to be composed of unrelated parts and which is unfocused. If your goal is to develop understanding and the ability to interpret whatever students may read, hear, and see, and to use that information as a base for making choices and solving problems, then the decision should be evident.

Therefore we already have a successful approach to interpretational skills and now we need only to know how we might increase its potential. What is the next step in interpretation? The answer is what I am calling major schema.

A major schema in interpretation means *a comprehensive system of thought which integrates information and concepts from many sources generating inferences, generalizations, and conclusions applicable to other systems of thought and action*. The schema serves as a base for comparisons and contrasts, multidimensional analysis, and the context for concept development and refinement. Some of the pervasive major schemata include *psychoanalysis, evolution, relativity, Marxism/capitalism, Gestalist/behaviorist*, among others. Each of these major schemata encompasses many related concepts, so that each is like the tip of an iceberg intellectually.

These major schemata easily encompass core concepts. For example, if we were studying *war* as our core concept we would want to investigate the political, social, economic, and religious reasons for a particular war. We could also investigate the psychological environments in the countries at odds so that we could get to the root of what is causing this war; we would note the psychology not only of the leaders and military men, but we would try to assess the fears, anxieties, superstitions, guilts, or old grudges which may be operating within the total society. Evidences of this could come from newspapers and other media, personal letters, previous history and animosities (as in the Hundred Years War, the War of the Roses, the German-French antagonism of the past couple of centuries, etc.). All of this data, plus the actual events and specific conflicts, would become part of the context of our study, which would incorporate geographic factors in addition to the rest. The whole would be *war* whose root concept is conflict and violence, which include competition in several realms, especially economic.

All of this information and interrelated concepts bring us to a fuller, multidimensional understanding of what really happens in the etiology (a medical-psychological metaphor) of war so that we don't settle for mere names, places, dates, and superficial causes to explain how so complex a human social act could get under way. Leaders try to simplify the reasons for going to war and they repeat them emotionally as they appeal to human fears and anxieties (as in good propaganda) but rarely are those reasons enough to understand why a war begins.

. What I am now suggesting as a way to increase the quality of interpretation is to imbed all of this into an even more inclusive context. Since the major schemata are really Man's attempts to *explain* how the world works and why things happen as they do and what may happen in the future, we must know more about them. We also must learn to identify the kind of language, imagery, and metaphor which is used to express these germinating concepts and explanations. If words are windows as I have suggested earlier, then what can we see through them? What can metaphor and symbol tell us about the true thoughts and feelings of those expressing them?

One of Hitler's key metaphors was *lebensraum*—living space, a concept that appealed to a defeated country. He also used the most ancient of metaphors, scapegoating one group of people—placing upon their backs many of the social, economic, and political problems of Germany. As in primitive tribes and groups, he then drove them out—in fact, killed them as one kills the evil in the world.

Let me start by illustrating from something familiar to you: professional reading books and other educational books. What does the language, the metaphor of such writing reveal to us about the basic principles and true beliefs of the writers? First, most professional books are written in an almost indistinguishable style; they contain a type of professional cliché with appropriate jargon and vocabulary. Some of that vocabulary is essential to characterize and name certain facts, events, principles, and concepts, some of the language, the key metaphors controlling the presentation, can become transparent to the well taught reader, or they can remain opaque and literally interpreted in a one or two dimensional fashion. Look at this sampling of language and metaphor from the indexes of some recently published reading texts and assorted educational books: teaching strategies, tactics, behavioral objectives, competencies, early intervention, information processing, checklists, inventories, self-concept, taxonomy, scope and sequence, assessment, evaluation, reinforcement, models and modeling, diagnostic-prescriptive, formula, standardized, criterion-referenced, basal reading, reliability, validity, operational, decoding/encoding, expectancy, contracts, high frequency, psycholinguistic, programmed instruction, aphasia/alexia, neurological, brain damage (or minimal brain damage), output, input, feedback, store, retrieve, etc., etc.

The best way to begin this analysis is to classify these terms: *military* (strategy, tactics, intervention); *psychological* (reinforcement, self-concept, psycholinguistic); *linguistics* (decoding/encoding, psycholinguistic, high frequency); *reading* (basal reading, programmed instruction, scope and sequence, decoding/encoding, criterion-referenced, standardized); *medicine* (aphasia/alexia, brain damage, diagnostic-prescriptive, neurological, etiology); *business* (inventories, checklists, contracts, product, input, output).

This is a small sampling, but it should be evident that the field of reading includes vocabulary and metaphors from numerous other fields. That is true of most disciplines; that is, we do use the vocabulary and metaphors from numerous disciplines to help us clarify, augment, and amplify our meanings in our own field. The good interpretive reader knows this and takes the next step. That step is to analyze this mixing of vocabulary (mainly multiple-meaning words) and metaphors in an effort to get to the root or core of the true meaning. Frequently we notice that someone's use of the language obfuscates or blurs the meaning intended. In many cases the metaphoric usage and vocabulary can reveal the true thoughts, beliefs, and attitudes of the writer/speaker. In short we must teach our students to understand the words they read in a particular context, and we must teach them to follow these meanings to related contexts as they do in the core concept, and then to place all of this into the broader interpretive schema, noting especially the metaphors used.

THE PSYCHOANALYTIC SCHEMA OF INTERPRETATION

The psychoanalytic interpretation and explanation of human behavior is one of the most pervasive of all in current thinking. This does not mean that many people are Freudians or Jungians or Adlerians, but that this system of thought and interpretation, with several mixtures, is evident in history, literature, politics and propaganda, sociology, anthropology, and even economics, among others.

A most pertinent example of the psychoanalytic schema of interpretation can be found in Norman O. Brown's classic monument to interpretive scholarship, *Life Against Death* (1959, pp. ix–x). In his introduction he tells us,

> "In 1953 I turned to a deep study of Freud, feeling the need to reappraise the nature and destiny of man. Inheriting from the Protestant tradition a conscience which insisted that intellectual work should be directed toward the relief of man's estate . . . But why Freud? . . . It is humiliating to be compelled to admit the grossly seamy side of so many grand ideals. It is criminal to violate the civilized taboos which have kept the seamy side concealed . . . Freud was right: our real desires are unconscious. It also begins to be apparent that mankind, unconscious of its real desires and therefore unable to obtain satisfaction, is hostile to life and ready to destroy itself."

He apologizes for his Protestant ethic of work and doing good and in fact for being a bit negative and a bit anal, and proposes to assist us to undo our repressions and other deadly neurotic symptoms. He wants more love (eros), more openness and honesty; he wants us to be "polymorphous perverse" rather than conforming, anal, and unable to give and accept love. In essence, this psychoanalytic interpretation of history requires major changes in all our attitudes toward life and love, as well as to our attitudes toward death and hate, and it requires a shift in our child-rearing and educating activities. All of this is part of classic Freudian psychoanalysis, which tries to dredge up the past and to place it in perspective; it tries to define the shadows and echoes which frighten and haunt us throughout our lives; it tries to free us from neurotic repressions of feelings so that we will stop hoarding our true feelings and thoughts as one hoards (in capitalism) privately.

Tawney's *Religion and the Rise of Capitalism* (1926) reveals, among other things, the key relationship between the Protestant ethic and the capitalist system and thereby offers an explanation of how those two sets of thinking and feeling (economic and religious) influenced each other and how they supported each other. It also points out some of the economic roots of capitalist economy as a result of the psychology which guided the Protestant ethic. It was deeply rooted in guilt feelings engendered by particular child-rearing practices and values.

If we take a psychoanalytic perspective, consciously or unconsciously it obviously draws the boundaries of our thinking and interpreting, which in turn selects our vocabulary and metaphors, so that one is detectable from the other.

The best way to understand Freud or Jung is to read them, and specific sources will be included in the bibliography at the end of the chapter, but be sure to read Freud's *Psychopathology of Everyday Life* and the *Interpretation of Dreams* as a minimum. If you want a better sense of how this system of thought and interpretation developed read his *History of Psychoanalysis*. Jung's *Man and His Symbols* is pertinent to my point and will also be of interest to you because of its universality. The entire field of psychoanalysis concerns itself with the most basic and universal topics such as why we are what we are; how we symbolize and metaphorize throughout our lives, what is hidden in our unconscious minds. Nothing is more basic except, perhaps, for medicine and its counterparts in physics and chemistry of the body particularly.

Psychoanalytic interpretations of history, politics, and literature are fairly common in high level materials and therefore should be presented to your best students who are mature enough to handle it. They need to become familiar with the key concepts, symbols, and metaphors in order to enhance their interpretive skills and perceptions.

In the last ten years there has been a spate of do-it-yourself books based on what the authors understand to be psychoanalytic concepts. Books on how to read other people through their clothing, their body movements, and gestures; books on how you can improve yourself sexually and socially; books on interpreting your dreams, your astrological signs, your latent, unconscious need to win, to succeed, to outdo. All of these are derived from various interpretations of the psychoanalytic explanation of human behavior and motives. Some are haphazard, slipshod, and illogical, but all sell many copies, suggesting that we may be more interested in ourselves and why we are as we are than we used to be.

Sociologists and social psychologists, even many large corporations, spend much time and money trying to assess and plan their activities for maximal effect psychologically. The sociologists depend very heavily on psychological and psychoanalytic concepts to interpret social activity and behavior; school administration courses, once they get through their budgeting and scheduling analities, concern themselves with these same behavioral phenomena. Management, in business or in schools, or in any institutional setting, must concern itself with the dynamics of human behavior and interaction; they must know, like good propagandists, what appeals to which people: is it sex, money, power (or any one which might metaphorically call up the other); fear, guilt, anxiety, etc.

Students who are ready for this higher level of interpretation will enjoy applying these concepts and perspectives to numerous fields of human endeavor and then comparing and contrasting them with other schemata. Or they might note in some writings how several schemata may be intertwined and how that effects the interpretation.

The metaphors and symbols used in psychology or psychoanalytic modes can easily be selected and analyzed with your students as a means of sensitizing them to the hidden messages of metaphor and symbol, which is critical to this kind of advanced interpretation.

This is a good place to look at a concrete example of psychoanalytic interpretation taken from a newsletter published by a noted mental institution. Two things must be noted in these excerpts, besides the metaphors and symbolism, and those are the emphasis on group therapy as opposed to the one-to-one therapy of the early psychoanalysts and the elements of classical psychoanalytic interpretation. Behavior, in short, is taken both symbolically and as a metaphor. The group leader explains two key areas of concern, transference and resistance: "transference is the experience of thoughts and feelings for a person which do not befit the person, i.e., essentially a person in the present is reacted to as though he/she were a person from the past . . . resistance means opposition, and the first function refers to the forces of resistance which oppose affective understanding . . . Resistance takes a variety of forms: Silence, Absence of Affect, Inappropriateness of Affect, Rigidity, Trivia, Posture, Avoidance of Topics, Secrets, and Lateness, to name but a few." (From the Charles River Hospital Newsletter, Spring 1978.)

At the heart of the metaphor of persons "as though" from the past, or as a different person, refers to the concept of shifting characteristics from one time and place, one person, to another. Certain similar attributes or characteristics in time, place, and person are shifted from one to another. It is comparable to the transfer propaganda technique we described in Chapter 8. The behavior is symbolic and its metaphor derives from the original source in time and place.

The therapist writing in this newsletter describes a patient who tries to avoid the pain of listening to or talking about her feelings about her mother by curling up next to the therapist in a fetal position and sucking her thumb. The therapist interprets this to mean, psychoanalytically, that she is using her psychosis to protect herself from her feelings of longing for her mother, and that she is expressing her desire to sleep with him in a pregenital fashion, *as if* he were her mother. This is not uncommon psychoanalytic interpretation based largely on early Freud. Can we see through this metaphoric and symbolic behavior of the patient? An implicit analogy (as in metaphor) is that we sucked our thumbs when we were babies and a bit insecure. The fetal position easily recalls the *in utero* position of the fetus when comfort and safety and nutrition were all provided. It is a totally dependent state.

Psychoanalytic interpretations like this abound in case studies and psychiatric literature, as well as in psychosomatic medicine which was mentioned earlier in our discussion of causes of reading/language failure (see Chapter 4). Symbolically one can see failure to read and communicate as a form of resistance or an attempt to punish significant others like the parents; it is also a dependency condition requiring special attention and affection of an unloved person. When psychologists speak of "acting out" behavior they mean that the observed behavior is both symbolic and metaphoric in that it spells out in action certain repressed, even unconscious, needs, desires, frustrations, guilt, and anxiety. The child who breaks the doll of a mother or father figure is acting out his repressed feelings of powerlessness and anger. The guilt which accompanies such behavior masks it to the conscious mind according to psychoanalytic interpretations.

The therapist in our newsletter concludes his article with the nature and value of group therapy: "In a more specific sense, the group becomes "the family," and on a more basic level, "the mother." The way the individual uses time and space in the group repeats the way he has used time and space historically. This fact enables the therapist to use the individual patient's behavior in the group to reconstruct the history of the individual . . ." (From the Charles River Hospital Newsletter, Spring 1978.)

"Group as family" is the key metaphor and the behavior of individuals in such a group therapeutic setting is symbolically playing or acting out their roles as children in a family. Many people who would extend the interpretation apply it to any group situation at work or play or in meetings. What can we make of this report?

We must ask in all such interpretational sorties, how does the present stir and evoke the past? Is it the unconscious? Does talking about the past dredge up the feelings and thoughts you had at that time in those circumstances? How does the time between your childhood and the present filter your feelings, memories, and ability to express them? How does one react to a group of strangers, often in a mental hospital? Is it really comparable to a family? Is any group a family metaphor? How is the world of feeling, daily interactions, or special relationships of family congruent with that of temporary and forced relations with sick persons? And what of the process of talking about one's feelings, anxieties, and fears? Isn't oral communication a somewhat conscious act requiring sentence structure, syntax and vocabulary? And doesn't that kind of consciousness in the presence of these strangers alter what is said? Isn't the anticipated reaction also part of this behavior?

The language of the therapist (from the Charles River Hospital Newsletter, Spring 1978): "Buried feelings are like a wound that is infected and unhealed . . ." is hyperbolic as is most metaphor. But it does highlight the potential for the spread of sickness if one does not purify one's mind of repressed fears, angers, and guilts. Some people do not buy this kind of interpretive schema; some prefer the more tangible, more measurable dimensions of behavior. They cannot cope with so much affect and such complex interactions among thoughts, feelings, and experiences. They want human behavior to be more orderly and more predictable so they use some form of science to view human behavior. That is the gist of the behaviorist theories.

Much of the imagery, metaphor, and symbolizing involved in any psychoanalytic schema derives from the child in all of us who yearns for love, attention, and security from our parents first and then from others. The key image is that child.

There is no way I can include all that belongs here, but this may be enough to ignite your interest and further study. It is important, no matter what you or your students believe, to know about this powerful and pervasive mode of thinking and interpreting human behavior in all fields.

THE MARXIST SCHEMA OF INTERPRETATION

Any major interpretive schema rarely operates apart from others, like the propaganda techniques; there are combinations. For example, the Marxist interpretive schema has major bearing on how to look at and understand economic and political behavior, but it too is imbued with psychological matter. The Marxist perspective and interpretation should be read in the original sources. In essence, the Marxist schema sees the world economically in the sense that it is very much concerned with the production and distribution of goods and services, and even more concerned with how the wealth and power from these are distributed. Marx hated capitalism because the power economically and politically was in the hands of the few at the expense of the many. The workers who produce the goods do not share proportionately in the profits from their labors, he said. Marx wanted the state to own, operate, and distribute the economic goods and services more equitably—almost evenly among the workers and producers of this wealth. Where this kind of equal distribution does not exist, Marx and his followers called for revolution by the workers (peasants in the earlier age) to overthrow their government and to institute communism (Marxist variety). This kind of revolution would, in their version of the world, give the power economically and politically to those who produce and to those who have been oppressed. The early slogan of Leninist communism was "To each according to his needs; from each according to his ability." Man is viewed as a political pawn of economic forces. Remember *Animal Farm*?

Think now of how many ways these basic concepts have influenced thinking and behavior in other fields. Theoretically, in a communist society (Marxist, Leninist, and Maoist versions) all contribute to the state, and the state, controlled by one party, sees to it that all are treated and rewarded even-handedly. Competition for wealth and goods is presumably eliminated in favor of cooperation to make more for all. Its social pressures are such that the individual seems to get lost in the shuffle. Also Marxist theory calls for planning to insure evenness of production and consumption; the Soviets, Chinese, and the Cubans have had 5-year economic plans spelling out just how much of everything will be produced, and where and how it will be distributed. Contrast that with capitalism, which has been the predominant mode in the West for the past two hundred years or so, and which calls for a "free market" and for individual enterprise and for market dynamics to handle supply and demand interactions. Planning in a capitalist system does not occur in the same way that it does in a communist system, so that we do indeed make more than we need, and we make much that many cannot afford to purchase. But it is left, theoretically, to *individual initiative* to create the tensions in the market and to make it possible for some to make millions and to control much material wealth of all kinds, and for others to be unemployed.

The communist system provides work for all, and the ability to purchase at least the minimum of goods and services in order to survive. The state, of course, provides from the collective wealth services like health, housing, pensions, and work. Here such things are earned according to one's ambition, skill, and push or pull. But our state, like other capitalist states, has modified its attitude toward welfare services, so that many are supported by the state from tax monies. The inequities are not considered a problem since the opportunity, theoretically, is provided to all equally. Well, obviously no system can insure that kind of economic equality even when it controls the political machinery as completely as do such totalitarian states as communism and fascism. *Communists emphasize group; capitalists the individual*; one stresses cooperation and the other competition.

Without getting any deeper into this budding dissertation on communism and capitalism, the point here is that if you see the world as described by either group, your data collection, organization, and interpretation will be predictable. Evidence of communist thought has appeared everywhere in the world in literature, the arts, politics, economics, and social life. Communist movies do indeed carry a message of the worth of the system; communist plays, novels, poetry, art all extol (almost like editorials) the greatness of the state and its benefits to its citizens—the value of the labor of the ordinary person. In capitalist countries the propaganda keeps trying to convince us that we are free to choose our representatives who make our laws, and that economically we are also free to try anything in the market place. *Communism is not about persons or feelings, but about functions*. However, we all know realistically that major corporations and multinational corporations do indeed control much more of our lives than we want to admit. They get into international politics as well as into economic control over parts of the market place so that it is not nearly as free and open as we would like others to believe. Try to dig an oil well somewhere and see what happens.

Marxist metaphors are found in every discipline; a good example in education is found in Paolo Freire's *Pedagogy of the Oppressed* (1968). He does not actually admit to being a Marxist, but his whole theme is educating the peasantry to overcome their oppressors by collectively gaining economic and political control of their lives. He uses a kind of core concept approach to educating these illiterate, oppressed persons, and I find myself agreeing with his curricular concepts, but the undercurrent to all of it is Marxism, revolution, and radical solutions to Man's problems and I do not have the stomach for such unsubtle political radicalism, because as I have said repeatedly, learning is tidal, not like lightning, and *politics and education do not mix well.*

Framing educational principles and practices in a political world view, or an economic one, concerns me very much since the symbols and metaphors we use (and that use us) define to a large extent our beliefs and those we transmit to others. If the metaphors of business or the military or médicine or Marxism seep into our language, they enter our thoughts, reason, and psyche. This alters our perceptions and interpretations. Man is neither a product, nor a coin, nor a pawn in a nationalistic movement, nor a lonely, greedy consumer nor, a machine. He is a creature of nature and one of many animals which fit incredibly into a patterned universe. He is an organism—whole. The invidious comparisons (metaphors) which derive from those other schemata alter our view and behavior toward each other.

THE EVOLUTION SCHEMA OF INTERPRETATION

Darwin's theory of evolution has been widely used as a model, a metaphor to comprehend genesis, growth, development, decline, and death, as well as the natural selection of species (or societies) and survival of the fittest. The controlling metaphor in evolution is slow, progressive change and survival of living species of all types (plant and animal) as a result of the interaction of genetics and environment and adaptability or lack of it. This metaphor is applied to human societies and their growth and decline, and differs greatly from earlier interpretations and metaphors describing Man and his culture. When Man was imbued with religious fervor and filled with magical assumptions about how the world works, their explanations of what happened and why it happened were considerably different from those interpretations based on the evolution concept. In short, the evolutionary metaphor says that each individual in a species will grow biologically in certain predetermined ways according to the laws of nature, including progressive growth, development, and decline of cells, organs, and intellect. Individuals or societies which do not adapt to their environment tend to be destroyed by stronger, more aggressive species and societies, the fittest tending to survive. Toynbee's *A Study of History* (1972) is rooted in his application of the theory of evolution to the history of whole civilizations. It is his key metaphor. He notes the quality and quantity of the challenge, the magnitude of the stimulus, and the quality of the response by different groups with some prospering in the wake of major challenge, a major stimulus, while others wilt in that heat. The life of a civilization is comparable to the life of a species in this metaphor.

Reading Toynbee then, noting this major metaphor, helps the reader fully understand what his bias may be, and more fully grasp his perspective. It clues us to what he will include and where and what he may not include. We may not agree with that metaphor as the way to comprehend how civilizations rose and fell and why, but it gives us some means of sorting out the almost unmanageable data available. We must find some order, or we cannot as historians, natural scientists, social scientists, or just plain people comprehend what is happening and why it is happening, and hence what to do with it. Even if our ordering is wrong in some way, whether for lack of data, or lack of the ability to see the key relationships and concepts, it seems better than no ordering at all. That would leave us, as it did many primitive groups, without any systematic, verifiable way of dealing with our world and its dynamic forces.

Whether we use Freudian, evolutionary, Marxist, or relativity, metaphors to interpret ourselves and our world shape our personalities and the perceptions filtered through it. The continual interaction of what we are and what we think and perceive is thus guided and bounded by the particular interpretive schema we have learned, adopted, and adapted throughout our lives. My own Pragmatist/Gestaltist schema makes me think, feel, and perceive wholes which integrate and hence give meaning and form to everything in my world. I am uncomfortable dealing with pieces, parts, and fragments of information or skills, and could not teach from a basal reading series, or from a linguistically oriented program, or from workbooks or flashcards. I would be uncomfortable both intellectually and emotionally, and each of us is similarly bound and guided by the major interpretive schema of our lives and times. The behaviorist notions of human learning and development irritate me and produce a sense of incompleteness—of disorder. So my world, like your own, is shaped and inhabited by these perspectives on what the world means and how its parts do or do not relate to each other, and they control much of our behavior.

If you will recall my critiques of standardized and criterion-referenced testing and the case studies (all in Chapter 2) you will understand what I mean. A Pragmatist/Gestaltist mode of interpretation generates metaphors of wholes, like a Beethoven symphony, a Renoir painting, a poem by Eliot, hence I have urged that we diagnose and correct reading and language problems in this organismic, poetic—wholistic fashion, rather than in parts and pieces like the behaviorists who control education. The essence of my interpretation of learning, growth, language, etc., is that *the whole so integrates related parts that it infuses each with its essence. Meaning and form are altered by the fact that any given part is in a particular whole.* The dots of painted color in a Seurat painting achieve meaning and feeling because of the whole impression they create within the total painting. It is not the summing of individual dots of color, but the whole impression.

THE MILITARY SCHEMA OF INTERPRETATION

We have all noticed the continual invasion of military metaphor into business and industry and of course into education, where, like Marxism, it has no place. I stumbled upon a writer whose feelings I share about the military metaphor in education. Anabel P. Newman (1977, pp. 5–9), writing in a journal called "Integrating Language and Reading," a collection of papers presented at the Ninth Annual Reading Conference in April, 1977 at the University of Northern Colorado in Greely, said:

> Strategy is a word which has crept into the educator's vocabulary in the past ten years. One didn't hear much about strategies when I was in graduate school. "Methods" was quite good enough a term to describe the different ways of teaching something. As the media folks talked about the strategies used by militarists to handle large-scale combat operations, and perhaps as educators began to realize that on some fronts they had a combat on their hands, the use of the word strategies began to appear commonly in the educator's bagful of new and useful terms. Today, if you don't have strategies for meeting this and that educational problem there is little hope that it will be met. . . .

She goes on to give a dictionary definition of the word strategy and compares it with tactics (also widely used now by educators). At the core of the word strategy or strategem she quotes: "A military maneuver designed to deceive or surprise an enemy; a deception." She says she hopes we will change the meaning and intent of the word very soon, implying her (and my) distaste for deception, for maneuvering against an enemy. Look at that metaphor: we must combat students as we combat enemies in a war through maneuvers and deceptive acts so that we can overcome them and impose our will on theirs. You see why it is important what language, what metaphors we use to guide and shape our thinking? If you think in this metaphor you cannot help but get caught in its web of meanings and attitudes such as described.

METAPHOR

Susan Sontag's *Illness as Metaphor* (1978) succinctly states the power of metaphoric thinking and behavior as it affects illness. She vividly portrays historically how we have viewed both TB and cancer, with the latter replacing the former in our fears and metaphors. The romance of TB in the nineteenth and early twentieth centuries has given way to the mystified dread and shame of cancer in the past few decades, and she shows how these metaphoric descriptions and attitudes affect each of us, with or without the disease. The power of these metaphors is well documented throughout, and is perhaps best summarized by her statement at the end of the book (pp. 87–88):

> "Concepts have started to shift in certain medical circles, where doctors are concentrating on the steep buildup of the body's immunological responses to cancer. As the language of treatment evolves from military metaphors of aggressive warfare to metaphors featuring the body's "natural defenses" (what is called the "immuno defensive system" can also—to break entirely with the military metaphor—be called the body's "immune competence"), cancer will be partly de-mythicized; and it may then be possible to compare something to a cancer without implying either a fatalistic diagnosis or a rousing call to fight by any means whatever a lethal, insidious enemy. Then perhaps it will be morally permissible, as it is not now, to use cancer as a metaphor . . . Since the interest of the metaphor is precisely that it refers to a disease so overlaid with mystification, so charged with the fantasy of inescapable fatality."

She concludes by attributing these misuses of metaphor and the mystification of the disease to our society's social, political, and economic failures all of which are rooted in violence.

The sources suggested in Chapter 4 on psychosomatic medicine give other insights into how metaphor and symbol act as both cause and effect in many illnesses, including school failure. The behaviorists have steered away from such study and analysis because it does not appear to them to be scientific, measurable, and quantifiable, and we have lost a great deal of significant insight into human behavior as a result.

We need more sensitivity to the dynamics of metaphor as it characterizes, creates, and alters our perceptions of self and others. Metaphor is an integral part of the organism's symbolizing; it is, in fact, the essential element. Hence, we must take as part of our job in teaching people to read and write and communicate more effectively helping them understand metaphor. Some religions, especially the more fundamentalist types, tend to see Man as God's metaphor; other groups see God as Man's metaphor. Among primitive groups symbols and metaphors clearly express

Man's yearning for order and the understanding which can come from it. They personify a great deal. Ruth Benedict, in her *Patterns of Culture* (1961), brilliantly describes three cultures using the Greek metaphors of Apollonian, Dionysian, etc., and in which she says: "The three cultures . . . are not merely heterogeneous assortments of acts and beliefs. They have each certain goals toward which their behavior is directed and which their institutions further. They differ from one another not only because another trait is found in two regions in two different forms. They differ still more because they are oriented as wholes in different directions." Not only does she emphasize the wholeness, the Gestalt of societies, but her approach is metaphoric. The study of anthropology is itself a beautiful metaphor and simile in that it says here's how others live, think, act, feel, symbolize, solve problems, and how does that compare with the way we do in our culture? Are there universalities, common elements in all societies?

Her sense of the organismic nature of any culture, including its own contradictions, is critical to this whole book. Nothing that people do is done out of context; genes and culture are so closely interwoven one cannot pull out one thread and call it the whole. Benedict also shows us how to apply the *theory of relativity* to social anthropology so that when we look at other cultures we do not fall into the trap of saying one is better than another because of certain characteristics, but rather she wants us to see cultures as we see organic individuals. In all cases man must pool his uniqueness for certain social and cultural needs and goals or he would be roaming the fields alone. See Benedict's assessments of biological interpretations of culture, as well as environmental and cultural interpretations where she emphasizes relativity of cultures rather than their absolute qualities.

Others you should read include Susan K. Langer *Philosophy in a New Key*. Her subtitle tells why I strongly recommend it to you in this context: "A study in the symbolism of reason, rite and art."

These are excellent works which will certainly clarify and elaborate some of the ideas I have been trying to transmit particularly in this chapter on interpretation. Much of anthropological, psychological, educational, even medical thinking is rooted in metaphoric interpretations and explanations of human behavior. If one is to reach the higher levels of interpretation in communication, this must be understood: Man is a symbol maker and user, and he is made and used by the symbols he makes. Also Man, wherever he is and has been, does face some of the same problems of self, others, order, the crying out for art, for improved communication so that it is not surprising to find "archetypal" symbols used by men around the world whether in art, literature, history, or social organization. The gist of understanding Man and his behavior is that we must take him whole, organismically, not in parts. This has been my main message in diagnosing and teaching reading and related language skills to persons of all ages. Just as Beethoven's Fifth Symphony is so much more than so many specific notes in certain tempos and keys, so man is ever so much more than 206 bones, billions of cells, many muscles, and tissues.

Clearly this is so vast an area of inquiry it is not at all possible for me to lay bare most of what I would like to see teachers develop with students at higher levels of abstraction involving such symbolizing and metaphoric analysis. But if I can whet your appetite along these lines and get you and your students into this I will be satisfied. Marxism, capitalism, evolution, psychoanalysis, and Einstein's Theory of Relativity, which saturate all of our thinking about almost everything psychologically, educationally, medically, politically, economically, and scientifically are all illustrations of the power of metaphor as a shaper of human thought and behavior. It is not just for poetry and good literature. *Metaphor, wherever it appears, is a major instrument of human intellect and feeling; it provides a richer context for comparing the known with the unknown, hence making the unfamiliar much more familiar and related to our experience.* It is the artist's language all of us use and need for coping; what it touches springs to life multidimensionally.

SUMMARY

We have come a long way from our simple introduction of the propaganda techniques as a step toward teaching interpretation skills. If you keep this type of advanced interpretation in the back of your head when you start with the propaganda techniques and as you glide into poetry and other literary forms, you will be leading your students to the goal of all good reading: in-depth multilevel interpretation. Students must understand that there is order in the universe and in Man's understanding of it; all psychological, scientific, and literary systems of thought are rooted in order that explains what happens, to whom and why. Behavior is seen within the broader context of the author's controlling metaphor, whether it be evolutionary, relativistic, Marxist, psychoanalytic, or militaristic.

Reaching this advanced level will require that all parties in the learning environment read widely and deeply in history, philosophy, psychology, literature, and science. There is no substitute for that. Core concept thinking and metaphorizing brings us all closer to the understanding and interpretation which should be the outcome of all teaching and learning. How far we have come from isolated phonics, syllabication, from study skills and even propaganda techniques! This road will not be covered all at once, but developmentally, tidally over time. Like the circadian rhythms of your body, like the tides, like the seasons, teaching and learning this way will support and supply itself.

REFERENCES

Benedict, Ruth. *Patterns of culture*. Boston: Houghton Mifflin, 1961.

Brown, Norman. *Life against death: the psychoanalytical meaning of history*. Middletown, CT: Wesleyan University Press, 1959.

Charles River Hospital *Newsletter*, Spring, 1978.

Freire, Paulo. *Pedagogy of the oppressed*. Myra Ramos, trans. New York: Herder & Herder, 1971.

Newman, Anabel. Adapting reading to the language of the learner. In D. A. Brown, N. A. Glaser, & E. V. Wolfe (Eds.). *Integrating language and reading: presentations at the Ninth Annual Reading Conference*. Greeley, CO: University of Northern Colorado, 1977.

Sontag, Susan. *Illness as metaphor*. New York: Farrar, Straus & Giraux, 1978.

Tawney, R. H. *Religion and the rise of capitalism*. London: Murray, 1926.

Toynbee, Arnold. *A study of history* (abridged ed.). London: Oxford University Press, 1972.

BIBLIOGRAPHY

Freud, Sigmund. *The basic writings of Sigmung Freud*. A. A. Brill (Transl. & Ed.). New York: Random House, 1938, 1966.

Howards, Melvin. *Interpretations of dyslexia*. In George Spache (Ed.), *Reading disability and perception*, IRA Proceedings of the Thirteenth Annual Convention. Newark, DE: IRA, 1968.

Israel, Lucien. *Conquering cancer*. Joan Pinkham (Transl.). New York: Random House, 1978.

Jung, Carl. *Man and his symbols*. New York: Dell, 1964.

Langer, Susanne. *Philosophy in a new key*. New York: New American Library, 1942.

McLuhan, Marshall, with Wilfred Watson. *From cliche to archetype*. New York: Pocket Books, 1971.

Chapter ten

Where have we been and where are we going? We have looked at the major components of language, the learner and the processes of reading, as seen through the eyes and professional experience of a Pragmatist and Gestaltist.

Part 1 of this book has emphasized foundational concerns and issues in the diagnosis and correction of reading and related language problems for students of all ages and backgrounds. Part 2 has emphasized practical teaching activities and techniques in word recognition, meanings, study skills, as well as in vocabulary and writing.

Practically and theoretically this book reflects the author's deep belief in the wholeness of Man, the wholeness of learning, and the wholeness of reading and related language skills. Integrating skills and content in a core concept imbues both with added meaning, value, and interest to students and teachers. We can break the lock-step linearity of behaviorist curricula and teaching; there is a practical and successful alternative. The IDA and the core concept curriculum planning described here represent significant modifications of past and much present practice.

The critical importance of leading students to discover principles, patterns and concepts has been underscored throughout this work. Such "discovery" is urged within a well structured, clearly defined context rather than in an amorphous, unbounded group of learning activities and experiences. Relationships have been emphasized rather than mere collections of specific information and isolated skills or facts. Interpretation skills have been presented more fully than in almost any other current text. Performance and competencies are identified in the IDA and are monitored in each instructional session. Skills have been viewed as an

Past, present, and future: summary and conclusions

integral part of the content *re-establishing the primacy of context as the meaning base for all teaching/learning*. Diagnosing, planning, and teaching reading and related language skills and concepts have been described as interdependent and interrelated parts of the whole act of reading and writing.

The distinctive viewpoint of this book was supported by similar views derived from numerous fields of study including medicine, psychology, neurology and neuropsychology, biology, and linguistics. *The whole is greater than the sum of its parts defining and nurturing the all of every.*

THE PRESENT

Current trends in criminal justice, counseling, medicine, and mental health are beginning to reflect a shift in emphasis away from the view that the individual is a collection of behaviors and feelings to a more wholistic view of individuals as parts of families and communities—from part to whole. Many states have developed community-based delinquency programs which have moved delinquents out of large institutions into smaller groupings in halfway houses and similar settings. Prisoners receive furloughs on weekends to return to their families and communities. Mental health programs seem to be following the example of delinquency and prison programs in this regard.

In medicine, an embryonic trend seems to be developing in the direction of training General Practitioners who will serve whole patients in whole families living in whole communities. This is a shift away from some of the over-specialization which has burgeoned in the past few de-

401

cades. Although some of the diagnostic work leaves much to be desired, the field of special needs/learning disabilities has moved toward more comprehensive assessment of special students. Teams of specialists in reading, LD, special needs, social work, psychology, and classroom teaching all participate in core evaluations.

What does it all mean? I suggest that these examples reflect a shift in focus from parts of people's problems and needs to a more wholistic view of them. It suggests that more and more professionals are coming to realize the critical importance in any assessment of human behavior of seeking the interrelationships between and among the relevant parts of the whole person.

THE PAST

Look at education in this century and you will find that we have shifted from a heavy emphasis on basics and specific subject matters at the turn of the century until the 1920s roughly. Then in the late 1920s we moved toward a more permissive, open-ended and experiential type of educational experiment. The Progressive Education movement, which was fairly popular in the 1930s, frequently misapplied John Dewey's educational philosophy so that openness, discovery, and problem-solving approaches to teaching earned a bad name. In the 1950s reformers emerged who wanted to shift away from any traces of the Progressive movement and wanted us to re-establish the subject-centered curriculum. They wanted basics in reading as well as in the curriculum. At this same time, however, the usual paradoxes of American education operated so that a movement to reform the school curriculum with "discovery" approaches in biology, physics, chemistry, and mathematics held sway for about 10 years.

In the sixties a kind of synthesis seemed to have been reached so that some open-ended, discovery, and experiential types of curricula coexisted with some lingering emphasis on basics. During that decade more experimentation similar to that of the 1930s occurred in the form of nongraded schools, contract systems, performance contracts, more electives and minicourses, Joplin plans, computer-assisted education, and alternative schools. Cluster systems and house systems also appeared. Even the alphabet was altered as in the case of the i.t.a and several other variations.

The 1970s gradually retrenched on experimentation and innovation and at the end of that exhausted and exhausting decade we heard increasingly louder complaints about children's lack of basic skills. Those complaints have encouraged the development of competency-based assessment and teaching.

Approximately every 20 years or so American education seems to recoil from its current practices and beliefs and reverts to past practices and beliefs especially when the current situation is as unstable and insecure as it is now. But these shifts, this *pendulumitis,* does take hold and become the basis for general practice. It is my contention that we are ready now for such a shift and that the direction of the shift is toward more wholistic assessment and more integrated planning and teaching.

To return to an earlier example, placing delinquents, prisoners, and the mentally ill back into their families and communities even for short periods of time is based on the rational assumption that isolation and *invented environments* cause as much difficulty as they purport to resolve. Placing such persons into the "normal" environment or context serves at least two purposes: (1) it requires that the person face the problems and conflicts at their source rather than in a simulated family or community setting; (2) it provides the person with some natural support in family and community, which is essential to anyone's mental or social health.

This movement towards wholistic perspectives in several fields must now return to education, especially to reading and literacy instruction. The compelling logic of such perspectives has become clear to many other professionals and has been clear to some of us in education for some time. *We do not need to invent the past, nor to relive it; we need to imagine and invent the future.* We need a unified theory of learning and teaching similar to Einstein's theory of relativity.

Can we now begin to see a student as a whole person rather than as a Title I student, or a special needs student, or a student with mathematics problems or writing problems? Can we stop testing specific skills and aptitudes *as if each were all*, rather than integral parts of the whole?

The future will echo the past unless we are willing to change ourselves in classroom and clinic, in universities, and in other closely related institutions. No one changes easily since it requires relinquishing established and habitual modes of thinking and behaving which have become comfortable and secure. Old practices and beliefs do work to some extent, and most people do learn how to read and write the language, so why take a risk on the unknown? Institutional inertia and its bureaucracy weigh heavily on any reformer or innovator. The path of least resistance is what we have usually taken. But communities are becoming more outspoken and much more politically influential and they will not wait indefinitely for change. Budget crunches, inflation, energy problems, and revolutions are not easily resolved and people begin to feel impotent, so they turn their energies to what they think can be changed. The most conspicuous and vulnerable target are the schools and their perceived failures. There is some scapegoating in such a movement, but we all know that it is not totally unfounded. The schools *have* failed many students and teachers and since no other institution requires everyone to participate in it, it is most available for the pent-up frustrations generated by the more massive problems cited above.

This is not intended as the reason for changing what we are doing, but it is the realistic backdrop to some of our current problems. Change for its own sake or as a result of political or social pressure is *not* the answer either. There are some valid alternatives as I have tried to demonstrate throughout this book. We must stop noticing, labeling, weighing, measuring, and participating in the problems and we must turn toward solutions which are indeed *qualitatively different* from what we may be doing.

THE FUTURE

Where are we heading in the remainder of this exhausted century? Is the current push for "back to basics" and its concomitant "competency-based" assessment and teaching the new wave for education, especially for those of us engaged in diagnosing and teaching reading and related language skills? Can we place behaviorism in better perspective? Can we develop a unified and unifying theory of learning and teaching that will integrate rather than fractionate our diagnosis and teaching?

It is risky to make predictions of this type, but let me try with the understanding that I cannot avoid incorporating my own wishes and dreams. I do believe that competency-based assessment and teaching will increase its hold on education and this will undoubtedly reduce our reliance upon standardized testing as we have known it. It means that the arbitrary statistical grade level placement standards will have to change. We will develop IDAs that are more uniform in administration and scoring as a major means of establishing competency-based criteria. It is not too likely that the competency movement will hold sway for the decade of the 1980s at least in its current form. If all goes as it has in the past, some synthesis will be achieved between current mass testing and individual measures of performance.

In the area of curriculum, more teachers and specialists and school systems will attempt integrated curriculum planning similar to what I have presented in Chapter 5. With such changes, college and university curricula will have to change for the preparation of teachers and specialists in order to prepare them to implement such plans skillfully.

More schools will move into experiential programs, expanding current work-study, cooperative, and distributive education types of learning. This will necessitate essential changes in the curriculum so that more and more linkages between these experiences and the academic program occur. Such current ambiguities as career education, multicultural education, and even special education may become integral parts of the total curriculum rather than afterthoughts or appendages as many of them presently are. Career, multicultural, and vocational education are easily woven into the fabric of a core concept curriculum with or without

an experiential dimension. Many schools will recognize this and restruc-
ture their programs in these areas, that is, they will find ways to exploit
the experiences students have in shops, factories, industry, in the community, and elsewhere as a source of curricular materials, activities, and
concepts.

The special needs boom should bust in the 1980s as a result of more
careful diagnosis of the IDA type, which will reveal that a large percentage of those currently labeled LD, dyslexic, or minimally brain damaged
will be found to have been misdiagnosed. A more balanced perspective
will develop in relation to such students and the vast majority of them
will be freed from the stigma of the label; others may have to give up
their dependency on such labeling. Teachers, parents, and students will
be released to raise their expectations of each other, but they will need
our help to do so.

As behaviorism loses its hold over educators, we may see a revival of
some of the humanism of the 1920s and 1930s *with restraints* so as to
avoid the pitfalls of those days.

Society in the 1980s will move away from the "me-ness" of the
1970s and will provide more support for families and will focus much
more on the prevention of such atrocities as child abuse, divorce, drug
addiction, and school failure. The crises in the world related to energy
shortages, inflation, and revolutions will continue to exert significant influence over our lives, but it will result in greater cohesiveness and cooperation. We will begin to pull together much more than we have been
recently. *We will learn how to make more of less*, and our ingenuity will
respond to such a challenge producing some unexpected solutions.

These changes in viewpoint will cause publishers of educational materials to develop more realistic and pertinent materials at all levels and
for all kinds of students. If integrated curricula become more popular
than they are now, this will require different kinds of instructional material to meet our needs and those of our students. It is equally clear that
technology will not lose its fascination for educators and home computers
will certainly run counter to the predictions I have been making, but
there is reason for optimism. Television should take on a greater role in
education than it has so far, and I see it becoming *the* major medium for
the eradication of illiteracy in the world.

The apparent paradox of increased technological activity in education and more wholistic and humanistic education will coexist. Paradox
is inimical to Man and I do not see it changing. The struggle between
these antithetical forces—humanism and technology—will result in a
synthesis which will emphasize the wholeness of Man and Nature.

In short, I see a shifting away from behaviorism in educational practice toward Gestalt concepts and practices. Linear curricular patterns
will be on the wane, while integrated patterns will be waxing. In education we will make technology the tool it is supposed to be rather than the

filter it has been. The 1980s will be the time of establishing a balance in educational thought and practice if for no other reason than to learn how to make the most of diminishing resources. The sooner we can accept the notion that *each one contains the all, and the all infuses each with meaning and form*, the sooner will that balance be reached.

BIBLIOGRAPHY

Anderson, Charles. *An investigation into teacher perceptions of differences in male and female students in selected Massachusetts elementary schools*. (Unpublished doctoral dissertation). Boston: Northeastern University, 1978.

Appendices

APPENDIX A

Definition of Grade Level

The term is inappropriate and misleading when applied to children and is even more misleading when describing adults. Among the key problems of using grade level standards or equivalents are the issues raised in the discussion of standardized tests in Chapter 2 relative to norms, item sampling, and so on. Another problem with using grade level standards even for elementary and secondary students is the assumption that we know what skills and concepts are appropriate for a wide diversity of students of a certain age. This ignores everything we know about human growth and development and about individual differences, including cultural and language differences. Few would say that we can safely indicate exactly which skills, concepts, and understandings third grade or ninth grade students should have. Our curriculum has been devised in such a way that it leads us to believe that because we have identified what we consider essential skills in reading, writing, mathematics, and so on that those who do not achieve them at our estimated level of proficiency are below or above the norm. This leaves out critical factors of differential growth and learning rates and all of the social and cultural and psychological factors which directly influence learning.

For adults, grade level estimates are even more off the mark since grade levels are age-dependent as well as test-score related, but they were never intended for adults in the first place. Our use of grade levels in this chapter is a convenience since most of us have used the term for many years in spite of its inaccuracy. I am using it here in relation to adults in a generic way to indicate roughly that the skills we normally include in the instructional program for third or seventh grade students are being addressed. I am thinking of the level more as a competency in specific skills usually associated with grade levels. We definitely need a new mode of indicating relative performance for both children and adults. Wider use of the IDA could assist here in emphasizing as it does specific performance and competency in all of the skills areas.

APPENDIX B

Two topics which did not receive as much attention as needed are learning disabilities, its diagnostic and corrective assumptions and programs, and boy-girl differences.

Learning Disabilities

The diagnostic measures and their interpretations done by most practitioners in this field are subject to all of the concerns and criticism I expressed in Chapter 2 and in an article in the IRA Proceedings (1968). From the beginning, or the second coming of LD, in about 1960, the quality of the diagnosis, interpretation, instructional planning, and teaching has been dubious. The definitions of the ailments are vague, unclear, and unscientific at best. The diagnostic instruments measure analogously the functions of reading/writing, so that the interpretations of student performance are often misleading. The corrective work for most students so labeled tends to be the same: a lot of isolated phonics, and some physical work, like tracing, creeping, crawling, etc., none of which has any special claim to success. If students do improve in such programs, we never know whether the improvement is due to the instructional approach or to the *special* attention received during the corrective phase. In short, *most students diagnosed as LD or perceptually handicapped really are no such thing; most have been misdiagnosed and are being mistaught.* A minute percentage (perhaps 1% or 2%) has anything like the kind of neurological or brain problem which could produce the symptoms. Alexia and aphasia are real problems, as is limited intelligence and emotional disturbance, but LD as currently defined and measured is a good example of what Sontag called "mystification." Avoid such labeling and the predispositions it leads to diagnostically and correctively. Almost everyone is better than he thinks he is; diagnose as I have suggested and plan your instruction in core concepts and many of these problems will disappear.

Watch out for your own metaphoric usage insofar as both diagnosis and correction go. If you are a behaviorist and hold to a more rigid "germ theory" of reading failure, try to assess that as well as the student. If you believe that there are measurable, physical causes of reading/language problems irrespective of the negative neurological and other physical studies, then reconsider your own logic and observations.

Boys and Girls

Another topic I have neglected to deal with has to do with the boy-girl problem. Research has reported for a long time that boys tend to have reading/language problems in a vastly disproportionate ratio to girls of equal intelligence and background. Estimates range from six boys for each girl requiring reading help to eight or ten to one. Such a disproportion was noted about ten years ago and some school systems hired male teachers for the first three or four grades of elementary school to offset the female dominance of these grades. Some improvement was noted, but not enough, apparently, to convince administrators to continue the practice, but the problem remains the same now: six or eight boys for every girl experience difficulty in learning how to read and write in our schools. Something is wrong somewhere. The research has generally, but not overwhelmingly, supported the notion that this disproportion does exist and that it may be related to the overwhelming influence of female teachers in the early grades; to the kinds of rules, expectations, and measures these teachers make of boys as opposed to girls; to the physical differences in growth and development between boys and girls—in short, boys are different from girls, not only culturally, but physiologically, and that seems to affect their performance. Culture certainly does *not* account for *all* behavior. Simply, why are boys more susceptible to reading/language failures than girls of similar qualities? Why do they predominate in clinics, in special educational programs like Chapter 766 and 91.142, in a ratio of about six or eight to one over girls? What is the impact of so much female control over the lives of boys from infancy through third or fourth grade? A good review of the literature and an interesting study was done by Anderson (see references to Chapter 9) in an unpublished dissertation which attempted to measure teacher perceptions of male-female differences in the elementary grades. Two surveys were given to 171 elementary teachers; one measured the teacher's "held" beliefs about boys and girls and one measured their "espoused" beliefs. Among the conclusions of the study were that teachers stereotype boyish behavior and tend to react negatively to it; they hold contradictory views—one is a set of established, correct notions about treating everyone the same in the class room, and the other is the set of views which clearly discriminates against boys generally in grading, selection for special education programs, remedial work, etc. The teachers responded as they were "supposed to," but behaved in terms of the stereotypes.

A book by Restak (1979) called *The Brain: The Last Frontier* published by Doubleday devotes considerable attention to boy-girl differences. His research findings are that girls are more sensitive to sounds than are boys; girls have increased skin sensitivity, are more attentive to social contexts, they speak sooner than boys, and use larger words, they sing before boys do, they read earlier, and learn foreign languages more easily than do boys. Boys, he continues, have superior visual mastery and they learn best when manipulating objects.

Restak's work is very much in line with the majority of other researchers into boy-girl differences psychobiologically. The point of all of this is that these critical differences between the sexes particularly in the early school years must be recognized and responded to in the classrooms. For example, boys probably would behave better and learn more if given more opportunity to move around and to manipulate things like taking clocks apart. Teachers must recognize that the physical differences between boys and girls in the early years mean boys are less likely to be able to do tasks requiring small muscle control like writing, drawing, and other fine work. To require boys and girls of 5 or 6 or 7 to perform the same tasks in the same way and with the same quality is unreasonable. Such unrealistic expectations punish the boys and help create problems which are easily avoided. Very simply, we *have to admit and accept the fact that boys are not girls*.

APPENDIX C

Ideas For Research

I have been critical of much of the research in reading and language because I have found it to be either impractical, or too technical, making it very difficult if not impossible to implement the findings in a classroom or clinic. At the root of this problem is that *many of the wrong, or unimportant research questions have been asked and answered*. It would be ideal, if somewhat impractical, if classroom teachers, reading specialists, LD specialists, and clinicians could do research more often on actual cases and situations they face. The answers to those live questions would then be applicable to improved instruction or diagnosis. As it is, it is very difficult to make much use of a great deal of the research which is relevant to us whether in linguistics or psycholinguistics or reading itself.

Following is a list of research ideas.

1. Take the original Thorndike word lists (10,000, 20,000 and 30,000 common words) and study them in the '50s, '60s and '70s to see if they remain as common and frequently used as they were in the '20s, '30s and '40s. Note the changes in frequency and also note the semantic variations and try to tie that to the rest of our culture in those periods.

2. Develop a readability measure which accounts for meanings of words, rather than just their physical size and frequency. Try to assess in all this how meanings of words, long or short, are affected by certain contexts.

3. Why do some people have so much trouble learning a language— any language, and why do some have no trouble at all? How do intelligence, sex, age, socioeconomic background, and culture bear on this? Is there, as I have hypothesized, an *l* factor? Is the *l* factor a generic quality like intelligence itself? Is it like Spearman's *g* for generic intelligence, above and beyond the specific components? For it is clear that many perfectly intelligent, well adjusted, middle class persons of varied cultural backgrounds do indeed learn languages with ease, while similar persons with similar backgrounds and teaching do not.

4. Can we find out what it is in teacher education that works with certain kinds of people and what does not? What kinds of personality variables can we identify, and how can we discover how those interact with student variables of personality? How can we change either or both? Or does it not really matter?

5. Can we write good children's poetry and literature which is not adult in interest and substance? What is it that does get youngsters involved in the reading act in this realm? And what kind of student gets involved in which ways? Why? Why not?

6. Trace the key metaphors controlling various approaches to diagnosing and teaching reading and language skills, or other fields, to discover how they affect choice of grouping, materials, evaluation, and methodology. Compare and contrast them.

7. Why do teachers, clinicians, etc., choose a particular approach to teaching reading; why certain materials, methods? This is related to #6, but has some additional aspects.

8. How can we accurately measure progress in learning on the short-term and in the long-term without standard instruments? This of course involves transfer of learnings and who transfers what, when, where, and why. Can IDAs be more uniform?

9. Try my core concept approach and let's see how it works with certain teachers and students, and compare it with other approaches to reading and language skills curriculum.

10. A careful, thorough analysis of the content of professional books for teachers and clinicians in reading and language. A topic by topic analysis; suggestion by suggestion and hint by hint evaluation. How alike are they; how different? What is the impact of this on the field, especially on how teachers react to, use, or discard such information. What really alters their thinking and teaching? Why?

11. Investigate a range of adult readers to determine, among other things, why is it that those functioning at low levels (below fourth grade level) can so often comprehend and interpret what they have labored over with their minimal word recognition skills.

Many other notions for research could be listed, but I am hoping that some of the ideas presented in this book have stimulated some of your own interests and curiosity so that you will generate your own pertinent research questions. One thing is certain about educational research, particularly in reading and language: we need many more *longitudinal* studies in order to truly measure and assess the effectiveness of a particular approach or diagnostic procedure. A little more boldness and imagination in research questions would also be a major contribution.

APPENDIX D

Migration Charts

LITERATURE

These literary activities will occur concomitantly with
the appropriate history activities

READINGS		ACTIVITIES
Required	Extra	
Phase I		
Sandburg, "The People, Yes", "West Side Story" "Blues for Mr. Charlie"		1. Dramatic readings of one of the plays. 2. Drawing either a cover or scene design for either play.
Phase II		
My Antonia Walt Whitman poems Teacher's choice	de Crevlcoeur, Letters of an American Farmer Forbes, Johnny Tremain Sinclair, The Jungle Walden An American Songbag	Write: 1. Interpretation of characters: Was there a change? How did it occur? Why? 2. Write a prose version of a Whitman poem.
Phase III		
The Prairie The Luck of Roaring Camp	Giants in the Earth The Virginia Grapes of Wrath The Sun Also Rises	1. Compare the reasons for migration in The Prairie to that in The Sun Also Rises or the Grapes of Wrath. 2. Write a short story (after reading The Luck of Roaring Camp). It should contain a main character who undergoes change as a result of migration.

MIGRATION I   Phase I: Boston Today

CONCEPT DEVELOPMENT	FACTUAL CONTENT	SKILLS	ACTIVITIES	READINGS & MATERIALS
1. Nationality (a) similarities among people, mores, culture, religion, etc. (b) differences among people, mores, culture, religion, etc. (c) the culture of man	Origins of Bostonians England Ireland Scotland Italy, etc. Why left Why settled here	1. Map skills tracing routes of migrants 2. Geography of their countries compared to where they stay here.	Get names off mailboxes in different parts of Boston--trace to national origin Bring in long-time residents from South End etc. to tell where from originally	1. John F. Kennedy, A Nation of Immigrants, Chap. 1, 2, pp.1-9.
2. Mobility The need for more political, social, economic, religious	What they brought--skills and customs How treated here How affect Boston and vicinity	3. Demography general social statistics 4. Organizational skills	Take poll on streets of Boston--discover who is really from Boston--who elsewhere	
3. Assimilation and nonassimilation--culture contact	Origin of ghetto in immigrant sections of cities Current Boston politics--Kennedy, Lodge, McCormack, Bellotti, Volpe	5. Critical reading--recognizing propaganda	Research on each aspect in the conceptual development phase	

MIGRATION PHASE II   Migration to America, 1600-1800

CONCEPT DEVELOPMENT	FACTUAL CONTENT	SKILLS	ACTIVITIES	READINGS & MATERIALS
The Unknown--and what it presents (then and now)	Who were the early migrants? Trading companies; their economic and social implications. What motivated the early migrants?	Mechanics of English 1. Punctuation 2. Grammar 3. Spelling 4. Vocabulary	Field trip Mayflower, Plymouth Plantation Theme: Speculate on problems in leaving homeland, crossing, settling.	1. Muzzey and Link, Our Country's History, pp. 4-21. 2. Margaret Mead, People and Places, Chaps. 1, 2.
Adaptation-- changing goals and needs	Failure and transformation of trading colonies. Changing trend in migration Changing picture in old and new world	1. Reading: Main ideas, details 2. Writing: Synopsis and summaries of factual material 3. Study Skills: Outlining a chapter--taking notes. 4. Oral Reports: From notes (or individual reading) oral expression and presentation.	Individual reading on colonial period	1. Handlin, The Americans, "The Permanence of Plantations" 2. Muzzey and Link, Our Country's History pp. 4-21
Migration (change) follows a pattern of impetus-- transition-- resolution-- Adaptation has many dimensions, many implications (personal, social, economic) Economics: The law of supply and demand	Unsettling effect of the new environment. Results of the above.	Constructing graphs	Field trip Sturbridge Theme: Typical day in colonial period (relate to trip) (immigration and facts) Statistics--on early settlers (into graphs) illustrations of typical day	1. Oscar Handlin, The Americans, "Civil Society in a Remote Place," "A Nation of Immigrants," Chap. 3 2. Oscar Handlin, The Uprooted

414

Understandings	Content	Skills / Activities	Activities	References
Motivation--role in migration, adaptation Compulsion vs volition--meaning and significance of each	3 waves of migration in 1800s. Compulsory vs voluntary migration--implications. Conditions of migration. Who came and why. The effect of the new immigrant.	1. Reading charts 2. Graphs 3. Cartoons	Individual reading on specific migrations in 1800s	1. Oscar Handlin, Immigration, "Dimensions of the Problem." 2. Kennedy, A Nation of Immigrants Chapter 4
Disruption of economy, labor demand leads to migration Trust vs fear in facing the unknown Injustice (power) and dependency in migration	Migration from Ireland, Germany, E. Europe, Italy	Creative writing 1. Making outline from ideas 2. Writing paragraphs and selections from outlines	Contemporary migrations (See VI)	1. Oscar Handlin, Immigration, "The Old World Background," Chapter 2 2. Kennedy, A Nation of Immigrants Chapter 4
Nature and significance of choice (restriction and expansion)	Basis for Restriction Basis for Expansion Canadian Migration, Alaska, Hawaii, Puerto Rico, Outer Space, Ocean	Writing a book report on individual reading from Phase II	Field trip--Hayden Planetarium Theme: Future Migrations (refer to concepts learned) Research on legislation pertinent to reconstruction	1. Oscar Handlin, Immigration, "Restriction" and "Aftermath" Chaps. 8, 9. 2. Oscar Handlin, The Americans, "Men in Space," 3. Muzzey and Link, Our Country's History, pp. 505-507, 674, 690

MIGRATION PHASE III   Migration within America

CONCEPT DEVELOPMENT	FACTUAL CONTENT	SKILLS	ACTIVITIES	READINGS & MATERIALS
Overview of Unit: East-West, North-South Migration Bring up to present with Alaska, Hawaii Discrimination continues as impetus for migration. Concept of "running."	Why was Eastern seaboard settled first? People arrive and stay where they land. (I) Beginning of Westward Migration: Why they went west. Get fertile land cheap. Desire to escape political, social and religious discrimination of eastern communities. Pressure of economic depression--especially 1890 panic/unemployment.	Map reading: (where movement occurred) 1. How to read legend 2. Latitude and longitude 3. Accounting for map distortion 4. Reading geographical features 5. Estimating distances Time Line	Semester Activity: Time line from 1800 to present, showing: 1. Movement to and within U.S. 2. Conflicts involving U.S. and other countries 3. Immigration and naturalization laws 4. Major contributions in aesthetic and scientific development of the country	1. Hansen, The Immigrants in American History, Chap. 1, 2 2. Seaberg, The Pioneer vs the Wilderness, Part I, II 3. Handlin, Boston's Immigrants, Chap. 1.
Colonists vs immigrants (artificial dichotomy) What does this spirit show?	"Colonists" came before 1776 immigrants--after 1776 prerevolution was established a colony; Postrevolution was established a country.			Same readings as previous lesson
Character of the West	Routes taken West: 1. Wilderness Road 2. Cumberland Road 3. Lancaster Turnpike 4. Genesse Road What were some of the hardships? Physical means of travel.	Map reading; making maps from information Outlining a chapter for main ideas	Film Immigration in America's History Draw map showing major routes and cities	1. Turner, Rise of the New West, Chap. 3. 2. Seaberg, The Pioneer vs the Wilderness Part II, III

What was the Westerner like?

1. hated political parties, financial monopoly
2. social distinction
3. all men equal
4. demanded a government responsive to popular will

MIGRATION PAHSE III   Migration within America continued

CONCEPT DEVELOPMENT	FACTUAL CONTENT	SKILLS	ACTIVITIES	READINGS & MATERIALS
Expansion and National Development The frontier: a safety valve. "West becomes east" end of frontier.	American Revolution War in 1812 with England when America wants to expand to Canada. Civil War--North vs South. Slavery in territories. French Revolution. How did Colonial America differ from contemporary Europe? Land awaits occupation. New frontier established. Frontier prevents land monopoly and distinct industrial class. 1890, end of frontier free land over.	Comparative reading, comparing sources for different viewpoints and validity. Differentiating between fact and opinion.	Theme: If free land accounted for equality and prevented social stratification, what was to happen now that the "frontier" as at and end?	1. Hansen, The Immigrant in American History, Chap. 3 2. Seaberg, The Pioneer vs the Wilderness Part IV, V, VI

MIGRATION PHASE III   Migration within America continued

CONCEPT DEVELOPMENT	FACTUAL CONTENT	SKILLS	ACTIVITIES	READINGS & MATERIALS
Democracy	Were immigrants seeking better political conditions in America? Who were the immigrants? (middleclass) What were conditions like in home country?	Library skills: 1. Card catalogue 2. Reader's guide 3. Make bibliography 4. Find books on shelf 5. Dewey Decimal System	Field trip Boston Wharf (fishing industry) Trace development of political parties; include how formed, types of members, platform, policies (between 1800-1900)	1. Hansen, _The Immigrant_, Chap. 4
What they were seeking	What were they seeking in new country? -- individual freedom, social well-being, free enterprise, no unions, guilds, wanted place in society.			
Feelings toward motherland--shown in new life	Positive feelings toward motherland? Retaining language, customs, newspaper news from abroad.			

MIGRATION PHASE III   Migration within America continued

CONCEPT DEVELOPMENT	FACTUAL CONTENT	SKILLS	ACTIVITIES	READINGS & MATERIALS
The South (southern portion of west)	Importance of cotton production upon: prosperity of South; effect on Southern social system. Social system--close of 18th century. Planters with slaves; small farmers.	Research skills: 1. Using different resource material 2. Organizing material 3. Writing a bibliography 4. Organizational skills	Field trip: U.S. Carrier Wasp Research Paper: How Southern and Western society differed--economics, personality, daily life, government	1. Turner, Rise of the New West Chap. 4 2. Quarles, Negro in the Making of America Chap. 4 3. Turner, Rise of the New West Chap. 7
Results of America's mixed heritage	Results of America's mixed heritage on humanitarian reform: 1. education 2. culture 3. science 4. slavery 5. legislation Improvements that the West brought. Origin of names in Boston area (Copley, etc.)	1. Review of notes 2. Mnemonic devices 3. Charts and graphs 4. Anticipating questions 5. Answering multiple choice questions 6. Organizing to answer questions	Field trips Antique auto museum General Motors	1. Hansen, Immigrant in American History, Chap. 6 2. Turner, Rise of the New West Chap. 13

Index